Developmental Strategies for Helpers

Individual, Family, and Network Interventions

Developmental Strategies for Helpers

Individual, Family, and Network Interventions

Allen E. Ivey

University of Massachusetts

Brooks/Cole Publishing Company
Pacific Grove, California

Brooks/Cole Publishing Company
A Division of Wadsworth, Inc.

Printed in the United States of America

10 9 8 7 6 5 4 3 2 1

Library of Congress Cataloging in Publication Data

Ivey, Allen E.
    Development strategies for helpers: individual, family, and network interventions /
Allen E. Ivey.
        p. cm.
    Includes bibliographical references and indexes.
    ISBN 0-534-13512-9
    1. Counseling. 2. Developmental psychology. 3. Developmental therapy.
4. Psychotherapy.   I. Title.
BF637.C6I94   1990
158' .3--dc20   90-39234
                                                       CIP

Credits continue on p. 333

Sponsoring Editor: *Claire Verduin*
Editorial Associate: *Gay C. Bond*
Production Coordination: *Marlene Thom*
Production: *Julie Kranhold/Ex Libris*
Manuscript Editor: *Evelyn Mercer Ward*
Permissions Editor: *Carline Haga*
Interior and Cover Design: *Lisa Thompson*
Interior Illustration: *Lisa Torri*
Cover Printing: *Lehigh Press Lithographers*
Printing and Binding: *Arcata Graphics/Martinsburg*

Dedication

Developmental Strategies for Helpers is based on a co-constructivist model—that is, *knowledge is constructed in a shared context and in relationship with others.* Four colleagues and co-constructivists have been particularly important in generating the ideas behind this book. Their seminal contributions are warmly acknowledged, appreciated, and respected.

Machiko Fukuhara (Tokiwa University, Tokyo) conducted the first systematic research on the developmental model and first demonstrated the multicultural utility of this model.

Oscar Gonçalves (University of Minho, Portugal) challenged every idea and his cognitive processes intertwine with the conceptual framework presented here.

Sandra Rigazio-DiGilio (Bristol Hospital, Connecticut) showed me the family implications of development and how the treatment of depression could be conceptualized from a positive frame of reference.

Mary Bradford Ivey (Amherst, Massachusetts, schools) constantly asked, "What are the practical implications of the theory? How does it work?" Through her model of clinical excellence and applied practice, the ideas presented here do indeed transform theory into direct practice.

About the Author

Allen E. Ivey is professor in the Counseling Psychology Program at the University of Massachusetts, Amherst. He received his Ed.D. degree in counseling from Harvard University, and has served as a Fulbright Scholar at the University of Copenhagen, Denmark, and Fulbright Lecturer at Flinders University, Adelaide, Australia.

Dr. Ivey is well known for his more than twenty years of writing and research in microcounseling—the video-based skills approach to counselor and therapist training. His current interests are in cognitive-developmental theory and its special applications in multicultural thought and in the generation of systematic treatment plans for specific client diagnoses.

Dr. Ivey has been actively involved in counseling and psychological professional organizations for many years. He is a Diplomate in Counseling Psychology of the American Board of Professional Psychology, past president of the Division of Counseling Psychology of the American Psychological Association (APA), and is a fellow of the APA and a founding member of the American Psychological Society. He is a lifetime member of the American Association for Counseling and Development (AACD).

A prolific author, Dr. Ivey has written seventeen books (translated into nine languages) and more than 170 articles, chapters, and monographs. Among his works are *Intentional Interviewing and Counseling, Essential Interviewing* (with David Evans, Margaret Hearn, and Max Uhlemann), and *Developmental Therapy: Theory into Practice.*

Preface

Developmental Strategies for Helpers: Individual, Family, and Network Interventions shows in concrete terms how developmental theory can be integrated into the counseling and therapy interview and treatment planning. The importance of developmental theory has long been recognized by our profession, but we are only beginning to apply the various developmental approaches in our clinical and counseling practices.

This book shows how five developmental models can be used in the immediacy of counseling and clinical practice: Erikson's life-span theory, Haley's family life-cycle theory, Bowlby's attachment theory, minority identity development theory (MIDT), and my developmental counseling and therapy (DCT) theory. The first three of these theories are widely discussed in psychology, social work, and educational curricula. The last two—MIDT and DCT—are relatively recent.

Life-span development is a personal growth process. If we are to include developmental theory in our interviews and treatment plans, we need to understand our place in the developmental scheme. Thus, exercises that elicit personal involvement permeate the book. These exercises, derived from Piagetian theory, Erikson's life-span theory, Haley's family life-cycle theory, and multicultural development, are designed to help the reader think through his or her own process of development. The first step in integrating developmental theory into practice is to understand our own developmental history.

The most obvious application for this book is in the newly expanding area of developmental theory and its relation to practice. Developmental approaches to therapy and counseling are also increasingly used in social work and psychology departments and in programs accredited by the Council for Accreditation of Counseling and Related Educational Programs (CACREP). Courses that adopt the developmental model stress the relevance and importance of developmental processes to practice.

This book is written on the assumption that most students have had at least one theory course in individual and/or family therapy and have achieved competence in listening skills as presented in my microskills books (such as

Intentional Interviewing and Counseling, 2nd edition, 1988, or *Essential Interviewing*, Third Edition, 1989 (with D. Evans, M. Hearn, and M. Uhlemann), published by Brooks/Cole Publishing Company). Another highly useful approach to listening can be found in Gerard Egan's *The Skilled Helper*, 4th edition (Brooks/Cole, 1990). Students without this prior background do best if they spend more time on the first four chapters of the book before moving to the advanced material in the later chapters.

The concepts presented in *Developmental Strategies for Helpers* have been tested in several courses I have taught at the University of Massachusetts and in numerous workshops in the United States and abroad. The book can be highly useful in the following courses and workshops.

1. *Developmental Counseling and Therapy.* In this course, the focus is primarily on material in this book. My theoretical book *Developmental Therapy* (Jossey-Bass, 1986) can also be used to provide further background and for the exercises it contains.

2. *Theory and Practice in Interviewing, Counseling, and Therapy.* For this course, this book works well, with any of a variety of theory texts used as adjuncts. Students can study different theories (behavioral, humanistic, psychodynamic) and, using this book, can learn to integrate different theories into a coherent eclectic or metatheoretical framework.

3. *Psychodynamic Therapy.* This book works well as a supplement to courses based on psychoanalytic, Jungian, attachment, and object relations theories. *Developmental Strategies for Helpers* provides useful and specific techniques for conducting clinical interviews. The chapter on personality disorder is particularly relevant.

4. *Cognitive Therapy.* The DCT model is a constructivist and cognitive-developmental model. My colleagues Michael Mahoney, Victorio Guidano, and Oscar Gonçalves and I believe that the cognitive-developmental model of therapy is an important direction for the helping field. The DCT model is also compatible with the orientations of John Bowlby (attachment theory) and Aaron Beck (cognitive theory). For treatment planning, a networked, integrated approach (as presented in Chapter 8 of this book) is especially appropriate.

5. *Developmental courses.* This book is a useful text to accompany Erikson's *Childhood and Society* (New York: Norton, 1963) and/or Carter and McGoldrick's *Changing Family Life Cycle* (Boston: Allyn and Bacon, 1989) or another developmentally oriented text. The instructor can combine theory with exercises on the practice of DCT. In this way, it becomes possible to expand individual or family developmental concepts so that they are more practice oriented.

For applications of DCT to moral development, an instructor might design a course to explore the theories of Kohlberg, Gilligan, and other developmental theorists and use the DCT framework as a means to determine new clinical uses of such theories.

6. *Practicum.* A number of instructors have used my *Developmental Therapy* (Jossey-Bass, 1986) as an integrative practicum text. *Developmental*

Strategies for Helpers also seems to be a highly suitable book for students in beginning or advanced practicum. Particularly relevant is the chapter on Carey's model of developmental supervision.

Developmental Strategies for Helpers contains chapters that may be useful as supplementary reading for other courses. Concepts covered include multicultural counseling and therapy, family therapy, and vocational counseling and the workplace considered from a DCT perspective.

Teaching using the DCT model is challenging and exciting and is also a learning experience. Microskills, such as interviewing skills of questioning and reflection, are crucial to the effective application of DCT concepts. The DCT model can enhance an appreciation of traditional behavioral, Rogerian, cognitive, and psychodynamic theories. DCT can help in understanding how theories relate to one another and how they can be used with a consistent developmental rationale.

We are moving toward a paradigm shift in counseling and therapy education and practice. This paradigm shift is oriented toward a more developmental model. The DCT approach builds solidly on past theory, but also integrates developmental theory into clinical practice and research.

Development concepts are a means of integrating traditional theory and practice. We have long known that the basis of counseling and therapy is development, but only recently has research and theory advanced to the point at which we can use these concepts in a practical way.

Major Features and Teaching Aids

The basic teaching philosophy and techniques of DCT are organized in the text in the following manner:

1. Cognitive information focuses on central concepts.

2. Exercises in the reading enable students to think about their own developmental history and how the ideas presented might be used in practice.

3. Theory into Practice sections include group exercises and homework assignments oriented toward making learning experiential. Particularly important are the generalization exercises in which students are encouraged to apply specific ideas in their own interviewing practice. Microtraining techniques of small-group practice sessions are applied to developmental concepts. Isolated aspects of DCT can be practiced in small groups, with feedback sessions following.

4. Supplemental readings in each chapter include specific suggestions for using the more theoretically oriented book *Developmental Therapy* in conjunction with *Developmental Strategies for Helpers*. In addition, key works relating to the chapter concepts are listed.

5. Research suggestions are made based on concepts presented in the chapters, which stimulate questions, many of which are amenable to empirical testing.

The chapter structure outlines a basic instructional philosophy: Cognitive information is presented in a relatively abstract manner, and practical exercises, which are often feelings based and elicit students' sensorimotor or concrete life experiences, follow and help make concepts personally relevant. The Theory into Practice sections focus on concrete practice in analogue counseling situations. The sections on generalizing the concepts focus on taking cognitions and behaviors into the real-life world of the interview and daily living.

Teaching aids include the following:

1. *An instructor's guide* (available from Brooks/Cole on request). This guide is available on Macintosh Word 4.0 and can be obtained from me at 2 Cranberry Lane, Amherst, MA 01002. (Include a self-addressed envelope and a formatted disk). These data can be converted from Macintosh to IBM. Course outlines and homework procedures can also be obtained from me at the same address.

2. *Material for making overhead transparencies* (available from Brooks/Cole on request). This material highlights key concepts in each chapter. Overhead transparencies are particularly useful for lectures and for brief one- to two-day workshops.

3. *Videotape models.* These models illustrate the main ideas of each chapter and are available from Microtraining Associates, Box 641, North Amherst, MA 01059. The videotape series includes a brief Instructor's Guide and useful handouts for students to use as they watch each tape segment.

Acknowledgments

This book really began with a visit to the Yakima Nation Museum in Toppenish, Washington. The Yakima conceptions of human development provided the stimulation that helped me integrate the several approaches to development contained in this book. Brycene Neaman, museum curator, has been very cooperative. My most sincere thanks to the Yakima Nation. I hope this book correctly represents a part of their spirit.

Mary Bradford Ivey; Oscar Gonçalves, University of Minho, Portugal; and Sandra Rigazio-Digilio of Bristol Hospital, Connecticut, have been central in the generation of the developmental ideas presented here. Their clinical work with children, individuals, and families and their scholarly contributions and criticism have done much to shape the concepts in this book. Jay Carey, University of Massachusetts, has been very kind in sharing his evolving understanding of how development plays itself out in the supervision process. Ideas describing his important work conclude this book.

Two Japanese scholars have enhanced the ideas contained in this book: Machiko Fukuhara presented the first research validating the constructs of the model, and Koji Tamase has contributed his ideas of introspective-developmental counseling (Chapter 5). A conversation with John Bowlby in London several years ago was influential, particularly to my understanding of personality disorder. Lois Grady's creative vision of the developmental sphere has been particularly helpful for those of us who seek to develop an integrated visual picture of the helping process.

Other important figures in the development of this book include Derald Sue, California State University, Hayward, and Paul Pedersen, Syracuse Univeristy, who reviewed the chapter on minority identity theory. Teresa LaFromboise, Stanford University, reviewed the network treatment chapter and provided helpful information on her work with Native American clients. Terry Anderson shared his thinking about style-shift theory. Larry Brammer, University of Washington; Theodore Remley, Mississippi State University; and Joe Wittmer, University of Florida shared their models of professional disclosure for clients. Important, among many others, to the history of this developmental approach are Ursula Delworth, University of Iowa; Gracia Alkema, Jossey-Bass Publishers; and George Forman, University of Massachusetts. Maurie and Fran Howe, Swinburne Institute of Melbourne, Australia, and the Palmer Hospital read early drafts of this book and provided important criticism that helped clarify many key ideas. Bruce Oldershaw and Betty Koss have been important in holding this project together in some sense of order and coherence.

Reviewers who offered helpful suggestions for improvement and criticisms of the manuscript are Gerald Corey, California State University, Fullerton; Richard Percy, Vanderbilt University; Gary Miller, University of South Carolina, and David Towers, Heidelberg College.

It has been delightful to work once again with Brooks/Cole. This time, it has been wonderful to work with Claire Verduin, Gay Bond, Lisa Thompson, Lisa Torri, Carline Haga, and Marlene Thom. Julie Kranhold of Ex Libris produced the book, and Evelyn Mercer Ward has now edited two books for me. I have appreciated the gracious and constructive suggestions. Indeed, writing is a co-constructivist process.

A book is only a moment in time. It may look solid and permanent, but in actuality it is a developmental process that changes every moment and with every reading. *Developmental Strategies for Helpers* at this point is perhaps best considered a beginning. Clearly, it is time for us to focus on how development plays itself out in the helping process.

Allen E. Ivey

Contents

Before You Start

6 Using DCT with Personality Disorders
A Positive Developmental View   157

7 Multicultural Development   197

Before You Start

The Yakima Nation Museum in Toppenish, Washington, presents the proud heritage of the Yakima Nation. One way in which the Yakima shared tradition and knowledge was through proverbs.

One proverb especially caught my eye and helped me understand at a new level the importance of the unity of our development. A Yakima woman used a hemp string to "tie her history or diary throughout her life. To do this, she would mark her first courtship with a bead or knot as well as her marriage and any other event in her life. After each year, the story was tied onto her ball of hemp" (Yakima Nation Museum, 1984, p. 2).

> Time is a relationship between events,
> Kept fresh in memory by selected objects on knotted hemp.
> Connection is as vital as separation.
> By the time she is a grandmother,
> The unity of life is wrapped
> and remembered
> in a Time Ball.

Development is indeed a unity. We are connected with one another, and it can be difficult to separate ourselves in a comfortable fashion. We can divide development and describe it from different perspectives, but each part of our development affects our total being and each contact with another person provides us with another opportunity for connection and further development.

In terms of your own personal development as a professional helper, through your work in this book, you may be able to accomplish the following objectives:

1. Identify key levels of development among clients and match your interventions to their special needs and abilities.

2. Use specific questioning and intervention techniques to facilitate individual and family growth and development.

3. Recognize client reactions to your interventions in the immediacy of the interview and change your style as the client either accepts or rejects your ideas.

4. Integrate individual and life-span developmental theory into the helping interview and treatment plan.

5. Examine your patterns of development and how your own developmental history may appear in your interactions with clients in the interview.

6. Learn how to apply developmental theory in understanding and working with difficult cases such as clients with personality disorders or depression or cases involving child abuse.

7. Generate your own integrated eclectic developmental view of the helping process.

8. Recognize differing levels of development among culturally different populations and begin the process of generating culturally relevant helping theory.

9. Develop treatment plans for a wide variety of clients and families that focus on a network of interventions.

10. Use developmental theory in practicum, your own supervision of others, and in case conferences.

The Importance of Supervision, Consultation, and Ethics in Developmental Counseling and Therapy

Some of the questioning and intervention techniques in this book are quite powerful and should be used with caution and sensitivity. You will find that skilled use of questions at the sensorimotor level can easily produce tears and other strong emotions. Similarly, the self-exploration encouraged by Tamase's introspective-developmental counseling in Chapter 5 can be upsetting to some individuals. You will also find that Chapter 6, which focuses on personality styles or disorders, may cause you to look at your ability to help in some challenging ways. This, too, can be unsettling.

Thus, I strongly recommend that you use the techniques and strategies described in this book in supervised practice sessions first. Ideally, you will work with someone who is in the same workshop or course with you and who has some sensitivity and empathy to your needs. You will want to offer them the same support and understanding. Learn to provide a secure base from which your clients and others can explore new ways of thinking and being.

Supervision and consultation should be available when you practice the techniques described or use them for the first time in actual interviewing practice. Videotape and audiotape can help the process, but even more important is your own willingness to be open in looking at yourself.

An awareness of ethics is important in any course in professional helping. The basic rule of "do nothing to harm the client" holds here. Although you are not bound by legal confidentiality in role-playing, do maintain your client's trust and don't share what you have heard unnecessarily.

In any experiential practice, there is always the possibility of self-disclosure in a role-play that goes too far. A participant may develop a new awareness that is painful. Role-playing clients should share only as much as they feel comfortable. Inform your clients ahead of time of these issues and obtain their consent before moving on.

Similarly, participants playing the role of clients have the ethical responsibility of informing their "counselors" of the context of the issue they are sharing. Otherwise, counselors in the role-playing may feel betrayed when they find that their "client" was only acting. Acting is fine as long as both parties are aware of the context.

Desired Attitudes, Skills, and Knowledge

Empathy, caring, and the ability to listen well are assumed in this book. If you have had a course in basic helping skills, you will find your ability to use questions, paraphrasing, reflection of feeling, and summarization even more important as you work developmentally. Clients grow when people listen to them. If you haven't had a basic course in listening and the empathic dimensions, you will want to obtain a basic book on this subject and work through it with a friendly and experienced peer or supervisor.

Knowledge of individual and family counseling and therapy theory (family, humanistic, behavioral, cognitive) is helpful. At times, I will refer to certain theories as if you should know them. Frankly, very few professionals (including myself) know them all equally well. But, you will find that the developmental concepts here are more useful if you have some background in traditional approaches to theory. In the future, it may be anticipated that counseling theory will be increasingly integrated with the developmental approach.

Helping, Interviewing, Counseling, and Psychotherapy

This is a book for the helping professions. The developmental concepts are useful in nursing and medical studies, education, psychology, human services, and social work. For this reason, we use the broad term *helping professions*.

All the helping professions do interviewing. Whether with an individual or a family, the interview is basic to obtaining information and planning. Furthermore, a counseling session or a psychotherapeutic meeting is based on the interview. Thus, interviewing is described here as a generic process common to all helping professions. In addition, interviewing has special meaning in some social work and nursing settings and can be seen as a form of treatment in itself.

The distinctions between *counseling* and *psychotherapy* are complex, partly because they overlap considerably and partly because some professionals work hard to make them as distinct as possible. You will find that each professional you work with interprets the two terms, as well as interviewing, slightly differently. Common practice, however, is to consider counseling as the more developmental process and psychotherapy as remedial. In short, professional helpers often see counseling as designed for "normal" individuals, and psychotherapy is for those with "pathological symptoms." Also, counseling is often thought to involve fewer sessions, whereas psychotherapy is seen as a more long-term treatment.

However, these traditional distinctions are currently breaking down. For example, brief psychotherapy with a positive developmental orientation seems to be gaining ground. Family therapy tries to conclude treatment within six to ten sessions. On the other hand, extended developmental counseling sessions, particularly with a psychoeducational focus, can last many sessions. An elementary counselor, for example, may work with a child who has experienced abuse for several years.

Nevertheless, in this book psychotherapy refers primarily to more serious and long-term issues, whereas counseling is thought of as shorter-term and more oriented to client strengths. For the most part, the two terms will be used interchangeably. The theme of this book is developmental counseling and therapy (DCT), which focuses on both short- and long-term treatment with a positive developmental orientation.

Audiotapes, Video Recordings, and Practice

This book is based on a practical approach to counseling and interviewing. Each concept must be practiced to be truly useful. My first recommendation is that you purchase an inexpensive audiocassette recorder. This is one of the necessary tools of the trade. You'll need frequent practice and audiotape feedback to master the skills discussed.

Videotape is an even better tool. It is increasingly available in many homes, colleges, schools, and community settings. Try to see yourself as others see you at least once during the time you work with this book.

Also, many of your clients will benefit from taking audiotapes of sessions home with them to review their interviews. This practice helps clients internalize what they've learned. It is also a way of encouraging mutuality and equality in the interview.

Using the Taped Sessions for Research and Accountability

You may find that the concepts in this book are quite measurable, especially once you have mastered the ability to classify clients at varying cognitive-developmental levels. Each chapter ends with a short segment suggesting alternatives for research.

Developmental counseling and therapy (DCT) and the related concepts in this book seem to be sufficiently precise that you can classify your own behaviors and your client's behaviors in the interview by listening to tapes of the sessions. You will be able to check how well you match your client's way of thinking about the problem. Furthermore, through use of the Confrontation Impact Scale (Chapter 5), you will be able to obtain data on how clients respond to your interventions—not just confrontations, but any intervention.

The research section in Chapter 4 is longer than the others. The work of the eminent Japanese psychologist, Machiko Fukuhara, is presented. Note that Fukuhara used DCT measures as a way of examining client progress through the interview series. You will be able to examine and assess your client's developmental progress in the same way and ask whether clients actually expand their developmental potential and ability to experience life at multiple levels through the process of therapy.

Another research possibility closely allied with issues of accountability in helping is the client–helper contract mentioned at several points in the text. Here you and your client actually set up specific objectives for change at each of the several developmental levels. The accountability objective is determined by whether clients actually achieve what was agreed to in the contract. Research relating to your client's or clients' change patterns can be developed in this way.

In our professional helping practice we often do not do enough to show that we are indeed effective in our work. Perhaps some of the ideas in this book will help bring research more in concert with effective practice.

Focus on Your Own Development

Counseling is about development, and both the client and the professional helper are developing, growing human beings. This book provides many specific ideas that you can use to help clients solve problems from a positive frame of reference. But, at the same time, it encourages you to look at yourself, your own developmental history, your family relationships, and yourself as a cultural human being.

You will find many exercises and suggestions that enable you to examine your own life images, situations, and patterns. This book encourages you to look at yourself and your professional practice from a multiperspective developmental frame of reference. If you wish to understand and help others, understanding yourself can be especially beneficial.

Helping, be it counseling or therapy, is a process of development. I hope you will find this book useful in your own growth process both as a person and a professional. I know that the process of writing, teaching, and working with the exercises here has greatly helped me understand myself and the profession of helping. I hope the ideas in this book are valuable to you as well.

Allen E. Ivey

1 Our Developmental Nature

Progression from childhood to maturity
   is the work of the young,
But it requires the guidance and support
   of the family and society.
Education of each boy and girl is the
   gradual revelation of a culture.
When thoughts and actions become one with
   culture,
Maturity is the result, and
Respect is the reward.

Yakima Nation Proverb

Our task as professional therapists and counselors is to facilitate client progression over the life span - to help individuals and families learn from the culture, learn how to act within that culture, and when necessary, change that culture. Becoming one with the culture requires that we as professionals and those who seek our assistance develop maturity and mutual respect.

Our relationships with others help us navigate the passages of life. Enjoying the protection and warmth of a good parent, spending quiet time with a close friend, coming home from college, participating in weddings, having a satisfying sexual relationship, and holding a child are times of connection and attachment. We really cannot become separate and autonomous unless we have a solid developmental foundation, which is built through our connections and attachments.

Changes and life transitions can present difficulties for individuals and their families. A small boy entering kindergarten may cry the first week of school, afraid of leaving his mother. His teenage sister may find the task of establishing her own unique personal identity too much and turn to alcohol and drugs. At the same time, the parents may be facing the challenges of middle marriage and be contemplating divorce.

Life changes represent our developmental movement over the life span and can also be times of celebration—a mark of achievement, of growing up. These are also times of separation, which brings sadness for past relationships that are changing. As our children mature, we mourn the loss of the child as we celebrate the birth of an adult. If attachment and trust have not solidly developed, life transitions become especially difficult.

Twin developmental tasks—separation and attachment, autonomy and connection—guide the developmental process. Family theory is concerned with issues of enmeshment/involvement and disengagement/individuation. Again, as helping professionals we seek to assist individuals and families to develop and find a balance between these tasks. In this effort, we need to acknowledge that each client has widely varying patterns of coping with these issues. Some families and cultures stress individuality and autonomy, whereas others seek a more relational, connected orientation.

Throughout this book, a variety of exercises are provided to help make the abstract concepts more immediately meaningful and concrete. You can make each concept more personally useful to you by "interacting with the book"—by writing in the spaces provided or in the margins. Gaining an awareness of your own development may help you better understand and facilitate the development of others.

Take a moment to try the following exercise. Focus on one specific developmental transition, one that signified for you a major separation or connection in your life. This could be entering school, starting a new job, enduring a difficult breakup of a relationship, getting married, having a child, or surviving the death of a loved one.

Relax, take a deep breath, and gradually move your attention to a single *image* (visual, auditory, and/or bodily feeling) that occurs to you connected with that transition. Single images, usually visual, often provide summaries of key events in our lives. Some find that sounds, internal feelings, tastes, and key scents are helpful ways of generating images.

Then allow yourself to get in touch with your thoughts and feelings surrounding your image.

What did that time of transition mean to you? Was it a time primarily of connection, or one of separation, or perhaps some balance of both?

Who are the key people who helped you work through that time of developmental progression?

Summarize your thoughts and feelings below:

_____

_____

_____

_____

_____

_____

_____

_____

In reviewing this beginning exercise, are you personally more comfortable with connections or separations? How might your orientation affect your work with clients facing similar developmental progressions?

Virtually all clients seeking help are going through one or more developmental transitions. They may be trying to cope with losing a job in midlife, a child on drugs, or divorce. They may have failed to work through developmental issues from the past, such as a parent's alcoholism or having had a deprived childhood. If we are to help others, we must be aware of our own developmental issues and what they mean to us personally. You provide your clients the opportunity to learn how to connect and attach to you as a person and, then to learn how to separate and become more autonomous.

Four Main Strands of Developmental Theory

Clearly, much of counseling and therapy are about human development. Yet developmental theory tends to be separated from interviewing practice. This book shows how to integrate developmental theory in practice—during the immediacy of the session, in treatment planning, in case conferences, and in the supervisory process. Four main strands of developmental theory run through this book:

Developmental theory. Developmental relationships are the caring relationships we have with one another. Traditional counseling theory, which discusses empathy and relationship, is concerned with the importance of relationships. The separation and attachment theories of the developmentalist John Bowlby (1969, 1973) are particularly useful in understanding the nature of relationship.

Life-span developmental theory. We move through a life span of individual and family development. The individual developmental theories of Erik Erikson (1963) and the family life-cycle theories of Jay Haley (1973) provide informative, practical frames of reference. Gilligan (1982) and Schlossberg (1989) challenge Erikson's developmental theory as being insufficiently oriented to women. This book will suggest ways in which life-span theory can be broadened to include gender and multicultural issues.

Developmental counseling and therapy (DCT) theory. DCT is a new interpretation that illustrates how cognitive and affective development are manifested in the clinical and counseling interview (Ivey, 1986).

Minority identity development theory. As the Yakima proverb states, "Education of each boy and girl is the gradual revelation of a culture." Sue's (1981) theories of minority development provide clear examples of how individuals of minority groups view the world.

The discussion in the first pages of this chapter includes the exercise in which you examined your own developmental connections and separations, relates to the first developmental approach. Unless we can connect with another human being, change is virtually impossible. The centrality of the developmental relationship is emphasized throughout this book. Specifically, Chapter 6 gives attention to what form separation and attachment issues take in difficult counseling and clinical cases. Specific suggestions are offered on relating with client types as varied as the dependent, borderline, or narcissistic.

Life-span development is discussed in several places in this book. In this first chapter, the theories of Erikson and Haley are described and critiqued. These theories and their adaptations are basic to any developmentally oriented practice. You will want to become familiar with them and reflect on how you can use their concepts in your own work.

Developmental counseling and therapy integrates counseling theory and practice. As noted previously, DCT is a new interpretation of Piaget that illustrates how cognitive and affective development are manifested in the counseling and therapy session. The emphasis is on joining theory and practice in individual and family work.

DCT will aid you in learning how to assess client development and how to help clients expand and change their view of the world. DCT will also help you to understand both normal and severe psychological difficulties (such as personality disorders and depression) and generate treatment plans.

Yet, we must recall that development is a cultural phenomenon, and minority identity theory provides a frame of reference that will give you additional flexibility for developmental counseling and therapy.

Life-Span Development

Life-span development is presented here through two orientations. The first view is that of Erik Erikson, who focuses on the movement of the individual through the lifespan. We do not develop alone but rather we grow toward autonomy in the context of some form of relationship with the family. Jay Haley's family life-cycle theory provides a perspective on the constant interactions the individual has with others throughout the life span.

As we move from birth through to death, we share common life sequences and experiences. Usually we think of life-span periods such as childhood, school age (or latency), adolescence, young adulthood, middle adulthood, and old age. Each age has different developmental tasks associated with it.

Erik Erikson (1963) lists eight key stages of development, with accompanying developmental tasks at each age. If these developmental tasks are not completed, achieving maturity at the next stage will be difficult, perhaps impossible. As you review the following stages, think about what stage you are at currently and some of your own key developmental tasks.

Infancy (ages 0 through 2)—the developmental issue is generating a sense of trust versus mistrust. If the child does not develop a sense of trust at this stage, it will impact the form of attachments with others throughout life.

Early childhood (ages 2 through 4)—the developmental issue is autonomy versus shame and doubt, or in Eriksonion terms, "letting go" versus "holding on." In this critical separation task, can the child find a unique personal space among many demands made by family and culture?

Preschool/kindergarten (ages 4 through 7)—the issue is initiative versus guilt. Can the child start to direct his or her own life or will he or she be determined by others?

Elementary school (ages 7 through 12)—the issue is industry versus inferiority. Can the child develop a sense of competence and capability?

Adolescence (ages 12 through 19)—the issue is identity versus role confusion. Can the adolescent define a separate and distinct role identity as an individual? If earlier developmental tasks are incomplete, accomplishing this task may be impossible.

Young adulthood (ages 19 through 30)—the issue is intimacy versus isolation. Building on the past foundation, can the young adult find a sense of closeness with others?

Middle adulthood (ages 30 through 60)—the issue is generativity versus stagnation. This task is similar to the elementary school child's need for competence and industry, but this time it takes an adult form.

Later adulthood (ages 60 +)—the issue is ego integrity versus despair. The fully mature adult accepts both failures and successes and is able to integrate them into a meaningful life pattern.

Erikson's life-span theory maintains that the major developmental tasks of early childhood are to develop a sense of trust, autonomy, and initiative. To master these tasks requires a supportive family and cultural environment. If early life stages are not negotiated successfully, difficulties will develop later for the child, adolescent, or adult and may take the form of problems in developing a sense of autonomy, identity, or generativity. Each life stage requires a varying balance of separation and attachment.

Although all individuals work through similar issues in the life cycle, each culture has different ideas of what comprises a healthy personality and family. Some families and cultures stress autonomy and separation (as do, for example, some New Englanders or some middle and upper class British), whereas other cultures emphasize relationship and attachment (as do some Italians, Asians, and Blacks). Although no culture can be stereotyped, Erikson's framework can help explain some of the differences in individuals and families seen in counseling and therapy settings.

Just as individuals grow and develop through stages, so also do families move through a predictable set of developmental sequences. Haley (1986) has defined the family life cycle as consisting of six stages (see Table 1-1). Again, cultural differences and affectional orientation modify the family life cycle. Table 1-1 outlines some key developmental issues as well as the separation and attachment tasks of each stage of the family life cycle.[1]

Furthermore, gender issues are particularly important to consider throughout the life cycle. Boys and girls are treated differently in infancy and early childhood, the demands of adolescence vary for the two sexes, and many women simply do not easily fit the later patterns defined by Erikson. Again, recall Gilligan's (1982) and Schlossberg's (1989) critique of Erikson as being too male centered.

In the course of the family life cycle, issues arise that make Erikson's life-span theory more complex. For example, a teenager still struggling with issues of identity may find herself pregnant and confronted with the choice of marrying early or becoming a single parent. For the young married couple, separation from parents may be compromised as the in-law family demands new attachments and the stresses of establishing an independent home and finding career direction take their toll on the couple. The difficulty of coordinating the family life cycle with individual development is apparent. Thus two developmental frameworks seem essential for understanding any client: individual development and family life-cycle theory.

Individual development occurs in a family context. The impact of the death of a parent will be different on a five-year-old child than on a teenager in the same family. Middle marriage will have a different effect on a 40-year-

---

[1] A difficulty in any book that focuses on development and the family life cycle is that it gives insufficient attention to individuals and families whose experience is unique. As appropriate, adapt the concepts so that families with alternative styles (single parent, gay or lesbian relationship, blended family) receive adequate consideration. When looking at family history, the issue of adoption often looms important in the adoptive child's development. As you work through this book and its exercises, give some special attention to the unique developmental issues associated with adoption. Adoption and alternative family styles open the door to individual developmental differences.

Table 1-1. The Family Life-Cycle Model and Issues of Separation and Attachment

Developmental stage	Developmental tasks and issues of separation and attachment
Young adulthood	Increasing attachment with peers; separation from parents; courtship and selection of mate; choice of career or job initiated.
Early marriage	Attachment to mate and new friends; further separation from parents as a "child" and reattachment to parents as an adult; attachment to in-laws; establishing home, career, or job initiated.
Childbirth and childrearing	Separation from dyadic spousal relationship and attachment to infant; establishment of new relations with parents, in-laws, peers; beginning separation from child as school starts; establishment of career—balancing sex role and work and establishing economic sufficiency.
Middle marriage	Progressive separation from children; reattachment with spouse or further separation or disengagement. Mid-life crises—success or failure of career or other endeavors.
Leaving home	Separation of children from parents; reattachment of couple as dyad or separation of couple; new attachment to child, spouse, or lover; deeper attachment to parents as couple becomes caregiver. Mid-fifties crises—reassesment of work and of relationship with spouse and parents; awareness of one's own vulnerability and approaching old age.
Old age and retirement	Separation from careers, more attachment as dyad; reattachment of adult children as caregivers. Crises—use of leisure; concerns about health, finances; review of one's life.

SOURCE: Fleming, 1986, p. 1. Used by permission.

old woman than on her 55-year-old husband. She may be moving into the working world and finding her "own space," whereas the man may be having a mid-life crisis concerning job stagnation. Both may have to cope with teenagers leaving home and older parents who need increasing assistance.

One of the most critical life-span developmental tasks is finding a personal identity. We usually negotiate this task during our teenage years. Teenagers tend to be very much focused on themselves and their peer group, but they still operate in a family context that affects their identity development. How were things between you and your family during this crucial developmental period? What life tasks and crises did your family face? How did their issues affect your own personal identity, then and now?

_____

_____

_____

_____

_____

_____

_____

_____

_____

_____

After you complete the exercise, think about the different experiences men and women may have in this critical period and how sociocultural issues affect the concept of personal identity. Gilligan, Ward, and Taylor (1988) provide compelling evidence that gender development is very different. Also, many of us are raised in families that do not fit the Haley norm. Carter and McGoldrick (1989) remind us clearly that the family life cycle varies with single parents, divorce, and other alternative family structures. Did any of these factors change the way you viewed yourself during the critical adolescent period?

_____

_____

_____

_____

_____

A Developmental Approach to Helping: Integrating Theory and Practice

"There is nothing so practical as a good theory," Kurt Lewin once said. Developmental counseling and therapy (DCT) began with the observation that Piagetian theories of child development and cognition also apply to adolescent and adult development. Children go through identifiable processes of growth, and so do adolescents and adults. When we face a new developmental transition (for example, the birth of a child, a divorce, the loss of a loved one), we often "lose" our adult selves and return to cognitions and feelings similar to those of a child. There is no definable end to development except death. DCT offers specific methods for facilitating change and developmental transition for clients. (For a complete theoretical exposition, see Ivey, 1986, which illustrates how DCT theoretical constructs may be implemented in practice.)

Our first task as professional helpers is to understand how the client makes sense of the world.

By understanding the client's frame of reference, we can better plan interventions to facilitate change and life-span development within the appropriate cultural framework. *Empathy* is a word we use when we talk about understanding the world as others experience it. DCT offers techniques that can facilitate a more complete sense of empathy with the client.

Our understanding of the client's world is shaped by our theoretical orientation (Rogerian, behavioral, psychodynamic, family systems). If you work effectively within your theoretical framework, you will find that your client begins thinking, speaking, and acting within your theoretical system. Research shows that over time, clients tend to take on the language of their counselors (Meara, Pepinsky, Shannon, & Murray, 1981). Rogerian clients tend to talk about the self, behavioral clients speak of action, and psychodynamic clients focus on interpretations of past life history.

Imposing our theoretical orientation on the client may be helpful, since it can provide the client with a new or expanded frame of reference for viewing the world. The drawback is that we start with our theory rather than with the client's world view. Furthermore, even the most humanistic theory might limit the client's expression of self. Fortunately, it is not that easy to impose our ideas on clients, particularly those of subcultures. Research shows that 50% of Third World or minority students do not return for a second counseling interview (Sue, 1981). We need to understand the client's way of making the world meaningful.

Counseling and therapy can be rooted in philosophy.

Until the turn of the century, psychology was considered part of philosophy. Perhaps it is time to bring the two together again. The philosophic and practical framework from which developmental counseling and therapy is derived is based on an alternative reading of the Swiss psychologist/epistemologist Jean Piaget. Perhaps Piaget's main contribution was his concept of the four cognitive stages children move through: sensorimotor, preoperational, concrete, and formal. Parallels can be found in Plato's and Piaget's conceptions of human consciousness. Specifically, Piaget's four stages can been related to the four levels of consciousness described by Plato (see Table 1-2).

Piaget and Plato define some critical underlying dimensions of how we think. DCT is based on a four-level interpretation[2] of Piagetian and Platonic constructs. This interpretation, however, is different in many ways from that which Piaget or Plato intended. For example, DCT is less hierarchical, arguing

Table 1-2. Platonic and Piagetian Views of Cognitive Development

World view	Piaget	Plato
Appearances (Concrete world)	Sensorimotor Preoperational	Imagining
	Concrete operations	Belief
------------------ (The line between the concrete and the abstract worlds)------------------		
Intelligible (Abstract world)	Formal operations Postformal	Thinking Dialectic

Source: Ivey, 1986, p. 12.

---

[2]DCT has actually identified eight specific levels of functioning: early and late stages of sensorimotor, concrete operational, formal operational, and dialectic/systemic thinking. For the most part, we will focus on the four basic dimensions, but we will sometimes talk about these early and late concepts. For a fuller explanation of early and late definitions, see Appendixes 1 and 2.

against Piaget's and Plato's ideas of best or more perfect forms of knowledge. So-called higher forms of cognition and affect are not necessarily better. The intellectualizing client often can benefit by returning to the more direct realm of sensorimotor and concrete experience. All cognitive styles are useful.

There are two key concepts shown in Table 1-2: the concrete world and the abstract world. The concrete world is composed of what we can see, hear, and feel—a world of events, situations, and action. The abstract world is concerned with ideas—things that cannot easily be defined in clear-cut, concrete language.

A client sitting in front of you is a concrete, specific person, and his or her behavior is observable and measurable. As you look at that client and hear what he or she is saying, you are focusing on concrete things. The client, in turn, may describe concrete, specific events and situations, providing considerable detail about what has been seen, heard, and felt.

At the abstract level, and equally important, are the ideas you have about this client. Note that the word *idea* is an abstraction; an idea cannot be seen, heard, or felt. Much of counseling and therapy language concerns abstractions. Words and phrases such as *self-concept, empathy, congruence, Oedipus complex, defense mechanism* and *personal meaning* are abstractions.

Through a complex form of reasoning, Plato points out that we could not recognize a table as a table unless we had an idea about a table. To stretch the point, the table does not exist; only an idea of the table exists. Plato argued that the abstract world of the idea is the more critical dimension for human experience. Thus he termed the concrete world of behavior and action as "imaginary," as made up of mere "appearances." In a similar way, Piaget tends to talk about higher forms of knowledge as being "best."

Much of counseling and therapy theory (client-centered, psychoanalytic) focuses on the abstract world of self-development and self-understanding. Behavioral theory emphasizes the concrete world of action.

Which is more significant, the concrete world of sensory experience and action or the abstract world of ideas, thoughts, and contemplation? Not everyone agrees with Plato on the primacy of abstractions and ideas. This question has inspired a debate that runs throughout the history of Western philosophy. Philosophers such as Locke, Bentham, and Mill argue for the primacy of the empirical, data-based, concrete, scientific world. In contrast, Kant, Fichte, and Hegel, the German idealist philosophers, and others argue for the primacy of ideas and abstractions.

Cognitive-behavioral theory attempts to resolve this dilemma by facilitating both client thought and action. In a similar way, the philosophical position of DCT is integrative. Cognition becomes grounded when tied to behavior. In turn, behavior is guided by cognitive frameworks.

However, it is useful at times to treat the concrete and the abstract as separable. With some clients, a therapist may, for awhile, focus on abstract ideas about the self but may later emphasize concrete action. With other clients, it may be better to focus on concrete specifics, since subtle, abstract understanding often follows from behavioral change. At issue is matching one's interviewing style to the cognitive-affective style of the client. Higher cognition is not necessarily better.

It is possible to make philosophy part of the "here and now" of the interview.

Abstract and concrete thought patterns are also revealed by the client's language patterns. Concrete clients will talk to you in seemingly endless detail about the facts of their life situation. For example, a teenager may say:

Yesterday, I skipped school. I went to a movie with Bill.
(Describes the movie and an important scene for five minutes.)
Anyway, after we got out, we went to get something to eat—at the diner. We had fish and chips and a soda. It was good. I don't like school much.

This type of client may describe every event in lengthy, linear detail. You will find that concrete clients often do not respond well to a Rogerian reflection of feeling or a complex Freudian interpretation. Such clients seem to understand and appreciate concrete behavioral interventions.

Counselors and therapists generally are abstract, formal-operational thinkers and can become impatient with ongoing concrete description. Many professional helpers prefer clients who observe patterns in their lives and discuss abstract ideas underlying the concretes of daily experience. For example:

Yesterday, I skipped again. School is so boring and I generally have a great time with Bill. This time, however, it was different. Usually my pattern is to ignore that empty feeling in my stomach. But this time it got me. Even during the film, I found myself thinking about what's going on. I didn't used to do this. I think I need your help to understand myself.

Note that this client's language has few concretes, specifics, or observables. The client talks about repeating behavioral patterns and is able to examine his own behavior. The concrete client's perspective is limited to a single situation and focused on simple description. Clients in this abstract mode will often respond best when an abstract theory is presented. The point is to match the language of the therapist to the language of the client. This point cannot be emphasized strongly enough, and thus is repeated succinctly as follows:

It is possible to identify the cognitive-developmental level of a client by listening to and observing language used in the interview. Once you have observed the cognitive-developmental level of the client, match your counseling or therapeutic intervention so that the client can understand and act on what you have said.

Mismatching your interventions may be equally helpful. If you have an overly abstract client, he or she may benefit from an approach that focuses on concrete specifics. Similarly, as the concrete client develops, you may help him or her toward an understanding of self and of situations by facilitating more abstract conversation.

The concrete and abstract clients described above could both profit from examining the specific situation and what happened to them during the day they skipped school. Each also would benefit from examining the pattern of missing school and their ideas about themselves. The abstract client may need to become aware of more concretes as well as underlying abstract patterns. We are all familiar with the individual who analyzes the situation very well but does nothing to change it. Ideas and analysis are not enough. The concrete client needs to learn that he or she is repeating the same actions again and again. Clearly, both individuals need different styles of counseling and therapy.

While some clients will present themselves as totally concrete and others as totally abstract, most clients are mixtures of several cognitive-developmental levels. On certain topics, they will be concrete, whereas at other times they may be abstract. Be flexible and ready to change your language as the client changes. Failure to be where the client is results in miscommunication, misunderstanding, and, all too often, labeling the client as resistant when it is the therapist who has failed to understand the client's way of making sense of a confusing world.

Following are examples of client statements. Classify each statement as primarily concrete or primarily abstract. You will gain considerably more practice and thus have more suggestions for interventions in later chapters. (Answers to this exercise may be found at the conclusion of this chapter.) Circle C (concrete) or A (abstract) below:

C A   1. I cry all day long. I didn't sleep last night. I can't eat.
C A   2. I feel rotten about myself lately.
C A   3. I feel very guilty about being late so much.
C A   4. Sorry I'm late for the session. Traffic was very heavy.
C A   5. I feel really awkward on dates. I'm a social dud.
C A   6. Last night my date said that I wasn't much fun. Then I started to cry.
C A   7. My father is tall, has red hair, and yells a lot.
C A   8. My father is very hard to get along with. He's difficult.
C A   9. My family is very loving. We have a pattern of sharing.
C A 10. My Mom just sent me a box of cookies.

You will find that the distinctions between abstract and concrete concepts become more complex as we progress through this book. We have thus far discussed only two levels of client cognition. The major emphasis in this book is on four levels of cognition, two of which are concrete (sensorimotor operations and concrete operations) and two of which are abstract (formal operations and dialectic/systemic operations). Each of these four levels can be divided into at least eight specific, identifiable types of cognition (see Appendix 1). As you become more experienced with the model, you will find that increasingly specific aspects of these levels can be identified.

DCT rests on the assumption that types of consciousness identified by Plato and Piaget are repeated again and again throughout the life span, not just in children but also in adolescents and adults.

Differences in cognitive processes appear repeatedly in daily conversation and also in the helping interview. Failure to understand these differences often results when one person views the world from a concrete standpoint and the other takes an abstract point of view. An example of ineffective therapy with an abstract therapist and a concrete client follows:

Client: Last night I had a fight with Meg. I wanted to have sex, but she refused to cooperate.

Therapist: That seems to be a pattern. You talk about your needs and desires but fail to take her frame of reference and how she feels into account.

Client: But, it's me that isn't satisfied. Like last night we went to a sexy movie. (Describes the movie plot in some detail while counselor listens politely, with a bored expression.) Well, anyway, when we got home, I kissed her and she actually kissed me back. Then I reached for her breast, and she pulled away. "If you're going to be that way," I said, and I started rubbing her. She really got mad. Damn woman is frigid.

Therapist: Bill, that's a pattern with you. You want sex very much. Last night is another situation where you didn't think of her feelings. How do you feel about yourself when you think of it from her point of view?

Client: Really ticked! I don't see why she is that way. We used to get along fine. All she needs to do is relax and go along.

Concrete clients tend to talk about their issues linearly and in highly specific detail. Most counselors and therapists tend to be somewhat abstract and analytical. The client here is looking for an answer to a concrete problem, but the therapist is asking the client to look at repeating patterns and to see his wife's point of view. The therapist's objectives may be correct, but the client isn't ready to think abstractly. A more solid foundation in concrete thought is needed.

The following example illustrates a counseling approach that matches the client's cognitive-developmental level:

Client: Last night I had a fight with Meg. I wanted to have sex, but she refused to cooperate.

Counselor: Could you tell me more specifically what happened? (The counselor is searching for concretes and specific sequences of action and thought.)

Client: We went to a sexy movie. (Describes the movie plot in some detail while counselor listens intently and paraphrases and reflects feelings, accepting that it is necessary to listen to details as part of work with concrete clients.) Well, anyway, when we got home, I kissed her and she actually kissed me back. Then I reached for her breast, and she pulled away. "If you're going to be that way," I said, and I started rubbing her. She really got mad. Damn woman is frigid.

Counselor: So, Bill, I hear that the two of you were feeling good about each other—your wife had held your hand and put her head on your shoulder in the movie. The two of you felt close for awhile.

Client:	Yeah.
Counselor:	And when you got home she even responded to a kiss for the first time in almost a month. Right?
Client:	Yeah.
Counselor:	Now let's see, after just one kiss you reached for her breast, she pulled away, and then you got angry and reached for her again, and then the two of you were off and running with the yelling again. (The counselor has summarized the lengthy description briefly.)
Client:	Yeah, that's what happened. I get tired of that. It just makes me mad as hell.
Counselor:	I can see that. Even right now you're mad as hell.
Client:	Yeah. (He calms down a bit).
Counselor:	Bill, let me feed that back to you. You start off feeling good about your wife. *If* you move faster sexually than she wants, *then* an argument starts. (The counselor's lead here is intended to help Bill move toward more advanced concrete thinking through the introduction of if/then causal reasoning.)
Client:	Yeah, she calls me "fast Bill" and says I never stop for her to catch up.
Counselor:	So, *if* you move fast and don't stop for her, *then* the two of you have an argument, and certainly there isn't any sex.
Client:	I guess so.

In this example, the counselor has chosen to work in a more deliberate fashion and talks about the problem at a more concrete level. Interviews with concrete clients can be agonizingly slow for the formal-operational, abstract counselor or therapist unless he or she becomes aware of necessary cognitive progressions in development.

DCT maintains that with clients such as Bill, it may be necessary to listen to several concrete examples of repeating behavior while paraphrasing and summarizing what has been said. It does little good at this point to ask Bill, "Is that a pattern?" Once the client has been listened to thoroughly, the therapist can help the client understand the situation by using late concrete, causal (if/then) reasoning. *If* Bill moves too fast, *then* Meg will reject him. Bill must first understand the ineffectiveness of his present behavior before he can look at his self-defeating, repeating patterns.

Seeing the world as someone else sees it (empathy) requires Bill to engage in formal-operational, abstract thinking. At this point, Bill simply is not able to make this cognitive leap. DCT provides a framework for systematic cognitive progressions that will help you first identify the cognitive level of the client and later either explore on that level or help the client move to new modes of thinking.

Piagetian Stages and DCT Levels Compared and Contrasted

A distinction should be made between the concepts of stage, as used by Piaget, and of level, as used here. Piaget's stage concepts are related to age and cognitive competence. For example, a child must develop sufficient horizontal development (competence) in sensorimotor cognitive tasks if he or she is to move to the next stage. In the DCT model, the Piagetian concepts of sensorimotor, concrete, and formal operations are used more metaphorically.

Children, adolescents, and adults move through varying cognitive levels again and again as they learn and develop.

Bill worked as a manager of a computer firm. He was clearly formal-operational and abstract as he dealt with complex problems at work. Yet, as is true for many men, he was highly concrete and insensitive in his relationships. Most therapy and counseling clients will talk about their lives and issues at more than one cognitive developmental level.

Our clients are mixtures of many developmental tasks.

The central developmental task of adolescents is identity versus role diffusion, according to Erikson. A developmental task may be described as a set of abstract thought patterns and concrete behaviors necessary to negotiate a particular life stage. Erikson's developmental tasks are primarily abstract in nature and can benefit by more concrete definition.

A sense of identity is an abstraction that relates to how we feel about ourselves. Male and female adolescents will negotiate this developmental period differently. Males tend to focus on themselves and their particular needs for self-definition that relate more to issues of separation. Women's development is more complex, according to Gilligan (1982). Women tend to give more attention to interpersonal relationships as part of their identity and thus perhaps attachments are more important to them. Furthermore, males and females have varying developmental histories and will have worked through tasks of trust, autonomy, and industry in different ways. Again, Erikson's formulations were derived primarily from observations of male development; and his life stages, while still valuable, need modification for gender differences.

An adolescent has many developmental tasks that must be accomplished to achieve a full sense of self-identity. But to achieve abstract identity takes concrete action. One teenager may have concrete developmental tasks of learning to relax, dance, ask for a date, type, or describe an event clearly in writing. The same teenager may also have abstract developmental tasks that include learning to analyze a poem or a social studies assignment, understanding math, discovering how others see the same situation differently (gaining perspective), and becoming a team member. A variety of abstract and concrete developmental tasks must be completed if one is to achieve a sense of personal identity.

Mastering the developmental tasks of identity will be difficult, perhaps impossible, if the teenager has not previously mastered earlier abstract tasks of trust, autonomy, and industry as well as the associated concrete skills that enable a feeling of self-worth. The generation of trust requires attachments and connections, whereas autonomy and industry require separation. The first step to helping a client find a sense of identity may be to establish a trusting relationship so that the client can establish connections and attachments to you as a person.

The abstract idea of intimacy with another is something we all strive for in one way or another. If you have difficulty with intimacy in your past or present relationships, this may appear as a road block in your interviewing process. Similarly, it will be hard for you to help clients find a sense of identity if your own identity is in doubt. A particular challenge of intimate relationships is how an individual can maintain a separate identity while simultaneously becoming intimately attached.

Bill, the client who came for marriage counseling, is facing the developmental task of generating a sense of intimacy and caring with Meg. Bill has other developmental tasks on which he may be further along. He may be a good manager and able to listen to his staff; he may be able to plan a complex budget having a variety of economic contingencies; he may be able to analyze a baseball game in infinite abstract and concrete detail. But despite his effectiveness on these developmental tasks, he may still fail in the relationship domain.

List below some specific abstract and concrete developmental tasks that are part of the larger developmental task of attaining a sense of intimacy required by a client such as Bill. Or you may prefer to think about yourself and your own developmental tasks as you seek to achieve a sense of intimacy and caring with others.

_____

_____

_____

_____

_____

_____

_____

_____

In terms of family life-cycle theory, Bill and Meg are in the middle marriage phase of life. Their family faces key concrete and abstract developmental tasks as well. They have two children, a 12-year-old son and an 18-year-old daughter. List below the key family developmental tasks. (Again, you may prefer to generate your own list from your own life experiences.)

_____

_____

_____

_____

_____

_____

_____

_____

What Is Your Own Cognitive-Developmental Level?

As you read this chapter, most likely you have thought about your own style of conversation. Do you give many details and illustrations when you talk? Do you tend to get bored by abstract theorizing and seek practical solutions? This may be an indication that you are concrete in your interactions. Or do you find theory fascinating, like to talk about generalizations, and engage in self-analysis? Do you find yourself impatient with details? This may suggest that you prefer abstractions.

Reflect for a moment. What are you personally most comfortable with—concretes or abstractions?

_____

Although few of us are solely concrete or abstract, most of us are more comfortable with one mode of conversation than with the other. Those from one cognitive-developmental level sometimes find people from the other level difficult to listen to and talk with. Can you identify a specific time when you felt bored or disinterested in a helping interview or personal conversation? A time when you found yourself especially involved, interested, and stimulated by the interaction? List the two below.

_____

Were the situations abstract, concrete, or a mix of the two?

_____

In any helping interview, you will work with both concrete and abstract clients. A developmental task for you as you read this book may be to broaden your perspective and learn to understand another way of thinking about the world and acting in the world.

Empathy is often defined as seeing the world as the other person sees it. Being empathetic requires you to take a different perspective, to anticipate and understand how the client thinks and feels. But abstract understanding is not enough. Warmth and empathy are communicated through concrete action. Although you may be especially good at understanding how others think, this is not enough. Thought and cognition must be translated into concrete action if empathy is to be communicated to clients. Some of the most direct, warm, patient, and caring counselors will operate primarily from a concrete perspective.

Each of us as helping professionals needs to engage in self-examination. Self-examination is most often an abstract, formal-operational task. An important part of DCT theory and practice is your ability to consider your own developmental history and how it affects the counseling and therapy interview. Each of us is a unique person with unique skills and understandings. If you are to help others grow and develop, it will be useful if you examine your own developmental processes throughout this book by participating in the suggested exercises of self-examination.

 CAUTION!   Your own personal identity and ability to be intimate with others is of central importance if you are to help others develop. Some of the exercises and questioning interventions suggested in this book are surprisingly powerful. Particularly as you explore the sensorimotor area, you will find your clients being moved rather quickly and easily to tears. How comfortable and experienced are you with a client's emotion? In the early stages of such exploration, you will need adequate supervision from a certified counselor, psychologist, social worker, or medical professional.

As you enter the world of developmental counseling and therapy, you will need to develop caring and listening skills. Your caring and listening abilities should be focused both on your clients and on yourself. At the same time, share your experience of the helping relationship with your peers and supervisor.

Chapter Summary

The purpose of counseling, therapy, and all helping interventions is the facilitation of human development over the life span. When we integrate counseling with development, we find ourselves focusing on the client's unique way of knowing the world. Our task is to help individuals, families, groups, and organizations reach their developmental potential. We hope that they will expand their cognitive and behavioral repertoires and develop new alternatives for thought and action, since flexibility and resilience are required for living in a changing world.

Four main developmental theories undergird this book:

Developmental theory, which focuses on the attachments and separations that repeat throughout the life span.

Life-span developmental theory, which includes both individual and family development.

Developmental counseling and therapy theory, which provides specific guidelines for the helping interview and for implementing treatment plans.

Minority identity development theory, which explores how members of minority groups view the world.

Developmental counseling and therapy, then, is a complex framework that can be approached from several different vantage points. If you wish to facilitate your client's growth, you may want to think through your own development and your integration of developmental theory into the interview. What do your life experiences and theoretical commitments bring to your clients?

DCT theory and practice maintains that our clients provide us with varying understandings of the world. In this chapter, we explored an example of a concrete client, for whom concrete behavioral strategies may be most appropriate. We have also considered the abstract client, who may prefer more abstract, reflective theories such as those of Rogers, Frankl, Jung, and Freud. Later chapters will enlarge on these examples and offer specific suggestions for action.

In helping, counseling, and therapy, it is not a simple matter of matching client and helper styles. There are times when the concrete client needs to be challenged by abstractions, when more abstract theories may be required. Similarly, there are clients who are too formal and abstract, who have lost touch with the "real" world. These clients may need to act concretely—to sing or play—rather than intellectualize. They may need behavioral counseling rather than an abstract cognitive approach.

The ability to listen and care for yourself and your clients is essential. The skills and intervention techniques presented in this book can be very powerful, and therefore awareness of professional ethics and responsibilities is required.

This book is about learning intentional and purposeful helping interventions while remaining in control of yourself as helper. This book also stresses how to recognize the variations in clients, how to change your interviewing style as clients grow. The concepts presented here will help you understand people in a new and a freeing way. Equipped with that knowledge, you will be better able to integrate your thoughts and actions in a caring manner with each individual, family, or group you encounter.

> When thoughts and actions become one with the culture,
> Maturity is the result, and
> Respect is the reward.

The Self as Helper

Think back on this chapter. It should be clear that individuals change, develop, and grow in relationship to others. What skills, attitudes, and knowledge do you personally bring to the counseling and therapy relationship? As you start work with *Developmental Strategies for Helpers*, it would be helpful if you reviewed your own developmental history and how it may impact your work in the interview and treatment process.

Following is a brief outline of things you may wish to consider and write about as you develop as a professional helper:

1. How have issues of separation and attachment manifested themselves in your own life? In what situations is it easy for you to become close to others? When do you prefer to be separate? Identify some specific events from your own life relating to these issues. Do you see patterns in your lifestyle? How might all these issues affect your relationships with clients?

2. What strengths and positives do you bring from your developmental history? First, survey your developmental resources, both within yourself and from others. How does your life-span history affect the counseling relationship? For example, if you are the child of alcoholic or abusive parents, how does this affect the interview? If your parents have been too easy on you, will you be able to confront clients directly? Are there developmental issues you need to explore further? Our own personal developmental history inevitably affects relationships made in individual and family therapy.

3. Do you see yourself more as a concrete or an abstract person? Will you be able to be patient with the concrete client who needs specifics and behavioral action? Will you be able to challenge and work with the abstract, intellectualizing client? In terms of therapy theory, do you tend to favor more concrete, behaviorally oriented approaches or more abstract, self-reflective approaches? Will you be able to shift your helping style as client needs vary?

4. Development is a cultural expression. The theologian Paul Tillich, points out that we are literally thrown into the world. By the act of being born, we become part of a cultural script that directs many of our actions. Individual and family development do not occur in a vacuum. A middle-class White person develops certain frames of reference from his or her culture. In the United States, this represents a highly individualistic frame of reference. Black and Hispanic cultures often stress relationship and communal development. What is appropriate development in one culture may be inappropriate in another.

The following are some key areas over which we have little control, yet these cultural dimensions have immense impact on our personal development. First, fill in the left column, which itemizes the givens of your life experience. Second, imagine and note how your life might have been different if your path of development had occurred with different givens in a different cultural or societal setting.

Societal/cultural category	How would your life be changed if your social and cultural conditions were different?
Gender _____	_____
Race _____	_____
Religion _____	_____
Economic status _____	_____
Ethnicity _____	_____
Nationality _____	_____
Physical capacity _____	_____
Affectional orientation _____	_____

You may notice that these societal and cultural variables at times may affect human development even as much as or more so than individual or family interactions. How might these cultural issues affect your counseling and therapy practice?

Suggested Supplementary Reading and Activities

Additional Reading

Ivey, A. 1986. *Developmental therapy: Theory into practice.* San Francisco: Jossey-Bass.

Chapter 1 explores the philosophic foundations of developmental counseling and therapy. Useful supplementary exercises may be found on pages 26–33. The Epilogue of the book includes Plato's Allegory of the Cave from *The Republic.* The cave can be likened to life's journey and to our relations with one another. What particular special meaning does the Allegory of the Cave have for you?

Erikson, E. 1963. *Childhood and society.* 2nd ed. New York: Norton. Originally published 1950.

A particularly useful and interesting supplement to the developmental concepts of this book is Erikson's pioneering work in life-span psychology. This book contains some sexism and perhaps devotes insufficient attention to family development. However, Erikson was one of the first prominent theoreticians to emphasize the culture as central to individual development.

A useful exercise is to start your own life review based on Erikson's concepts. Where are you personally on issues of trust, autonomy, industry, identity, and intimacy? How will your own personal issues affect your work as a counselor or therapist?

Haley, J. 1973. *Uncommon therapy.* New York: Norton.

Haley's family life-cycle theory of development consists of six stages: young adulthood, early marriage, childbirth and childrearing, middle marriage, leaving home, and old age and retirement. This is a useful model for the intact, traditional family. But the traditional family is not the only family structure. You will want to adapt Haley's framework for various types of families, including single-parent families, gay and lesbian families, divorced and blended families, and families of different cultures.

Where are you in the family life cycle? How do these family issues affect your own personal development and attitudes toward individuals and families?

Carter, B., and McGoldrick, M. 1989. *The changing family life cycle: A framework for family therapy.* 2nd ed. Needham Heights, Mass.: Allyn and Bacon.

This book updates family life-cycle theory and takes into account issues that Haley failed to consider in 1973. Useful chapters on family issues such as culture and ethnicity, divorce, remarriage, death, alcoholism, and economic deprivation are included as are expanded discussions of the family life-cycle stages.

Ivey, A. 1988. *Intentional interviewing and counseling: Facilitating client development.* 2nd ed. Pacific Grove, Calif.: Brooks/Cole.

Ivey, A., Ivey, M., and Simek-Downing, L. 1987. *Counseling and psychotherapy: Integrating skills, theory, and practice.* Englewood Cliffs, N.J.: Prentice-Hall.

These two books summarize key concepts and provide practice opportunities in the listening skills of questioning, paraphrasing, reflection of feeling, and summarization. The second book provides an overview of theories of individual and family counseling and therapy plus a discussion of key cultural issues in therapy.

Rogers, C. 1951. *Becoming a person*. Boston: Houghton Mifflin.

> This is the classic book on the caring helper. It may be necessary to have competence in interviewing skills as one enters the helping relationship, but it is not sufficient. An attitude of caring and respect for others is essential.

Schlossberg, N. 1989. *Overwhelmed*. Lexington, Mass.: D.C. Heath.

> This small book provides a concrete and stimulating challenge to the life-span conceptions of Erik Erikson. Schlossberg points out clearly that Erikson's framework was generated primarily from a male perspective. She also points out the importance of the "non-event" or non-transition and other unexpected happenings. Some things we expect to happen as part of life simply don't happen—someone is sterile and the baby doesn't come, you are passed over for an expected promotion, or you are suddenly forced into early retirement.

Research Suggestion

Developmental counseling and therapy has been designed not just as an abstract theory, but also as a concrete set of observations and techniques that are subject to empirical testing. Each chapter closes with a brief suggestion for research on the concepts presented. In this chapter, one possible research alternative is to test how well counselor and therapist trainees are able to identify abstractions and concretes in client statements. Assemble a list of client statements representing each category and present them to trainees. How reliably are they able to classify these statements?

This exercise may be extended to include interview transcripts of practicing therapists. Do the clients of behavioral counselors use concrete or abstract language? Do clients of more formal-operational therapists (client-centered, psychodynamic) use abstract language?

Answers to Chapter Exercise

1.	C	6.	C
2.	A	7.	C
3.	A	8.	A
4.	C	9.	A
5.	A	10.	C

2 Assessing Developmental Level

In the Interview and Daily Life

The smooth surface of the water does
not reveal the depths.

The lesson is—see the problem from more
than one point of view.

Yakima Nation Proverb

One important goal of the helping interview is to aid clients in examining their personal issues from a different frame of reference. As described in the preceding chapter, some clients tend to view the world from a concrete perspective; others, in a more abstract fashion. Both perspectives have value. Helping professionals can identify concrete and abstract points of view and match or mismatch interventions to facilitate client development.

This chapter extends developmental assessment to four perspectives: two that represent the concrete world (sensorimotor and concrete operations) and two that represent abstractions (formal operations and dialectic/systemic thinking). All four perspectives offer us additional understandings of the world. No one perspective is necessarily "better" or "higher" than another. DCT stresses expansion and enrichment of cognition and emotion at all levels.

Most of the chapters of this book are divided into four sections.

Presentation of key ideas of the chapter—the major concepts of the chapter are presented, often with exercises to illuminate the ideas.

Chapter summary —a summary of key concepts and their potential value in the interview and treatment process.

Theory into practice—practice exercises that provide experience in using the concepts in actual practice.

Generalization: Taking the concepts home—specific suggestions for using developmental assessment concepts in your own life and work.

With this brief introduction, let us turn to the most important and basic dimension of this developmental framework: assessing the cognitive-developmental level of a client.

Developmental Assessment: An Overview

Developmental assessment procedures have been tested with many different counseling and clinical populations. Children and families with normal problems, agoraphobics, and hospitalized inpatients are three populations that have received extensive analysis (Ivey & Ivey, 1990; Gonçalves, 1988, 1989; Rigazio-DiGilio, 1989). This research shows that counselors and clinicians can identify the cognitive-developmental level (CDL) of clients and use this information to facilitate interaction in the interview.

It is possible to assess the cognitive-developmental level of clients from what they say in the interview, often from only 50 to 100 words. In this type of assessment, the clinician or researcher listens carefully to a selected segment of the interview and classifies the information into one of four to eight cognitive-developmental levels. In one study, 20 hospitalized, depressed patients were the object of investigation (Rigazio-DiGilio, 1989; Rigazio-DiGilio & Ivey, in press). It was found that independent raters could classify with satisfactory agreement (0.90) the presenting cognitive-developmental level of a client from the first 100 words spoken. The research also showed that specific therapeutic interventions tied to such assessment affected clients' ability to talk about their problems at eight distinct concrete and abstract levels.

DCT stresses that learning how to recognize cognitive-developmental level is an important part of any interview or treatment plan. Most experienced therapists and counselors learn, over time, that they must use concrete approaches with some clients and abstract approaches with others. The transcripts of prominent therapists reveal that they use developmental sequences in their sessions. DCT makes the learning sequences underlying much of counseling and therapy more specific and observable and provides a rationale for changing counseling interventions in an eclectic fashion as clients change, grow, and develop.

The first step toward integrating a developmental approach is the ability to recognize client cognitive responses during the interview. This takes practice, but with experience and supervision, you will be able to access and assess a client's level during the initial phases of the interview. Then, with further practice and experience, you will find that it is possible to assess general family and group cognitive levels as well as the general tone or culture of an organization.

Four sample transcripts of the first 50 to 100 words of an interview are presented to give you practice in sharpening your developmental assessment skills. Refer to Box 2-1 for guidance in making your assessment or to Appendixes 1, 2, and 3, which provide further specifics. Box 2-1 presents the central dimensions for classifying the four developmental levels and the basic ways to determine the late stage of each level. Do not worry about distinctions between early and late categories until you feel comfortable with the four basic dimensions. If you have difficulty with the four levels, move back to two levels of observable concretes (behavior, action) and abstractions (ideas, concepts). As you make your assessment, recall that your assessment is based on only one question in one area. Remember that clients will tend to talk about their issues at different levels at different times.

Box 2-1 presents the central dimensions for classifying the four developmental levels and the basic ways to determine the late stage of each level. Do not worry about distinctions between early and late categories until you feel comfortable with the four basic dimensions. If you have difficulty with the four levels, move back to two levels of observable concretes (behavior, action) and abstractions (ideas, concepts).

Example 1. A 45-Year-Old Hospitalized, Depressed Client

Therapist: I would like you to say as much as you can about what happens for you when you focus on your family.[1]

---

[1] This question was selected by Rigazio-DiGilio (1989) for two reasons. First, it provides the client with an open question that allows for many possible interpretations. Second, it is useful, as clients' issues are often tied to their families. The examples of depressed cognitive-developmental clients in this book are based partially on Rigazio-DiGilio's work, but the content of the conversations has been markedly changed for reasons of confidentiality.

Box 2-1. Four Cognitive Levels (CDL) of Developmental Assessment

---

Sensorimotor: Focusing on the Elements of Immediate Experience

The client presents concerns in a random, disorganized fashion, and frequently jumps around on topics. Behavior will tend to follow the same pattern—namely, short attention span and frequent body movement. There may be intense concentration on here-and-now experience. At the late sensorimotor level, client exhibits some magical or irrational thinking and some beginning ability to be concrete.

Concrete-Operational: Searching for Situational Descriptions

The client gives concrete, linear descriptions of individuals, often with a fair amount of detail. However, nonverbal clients may give short yes or no responses. Emotions will be described but not reflected upon. At the late concrete level, the client will display some causal reasoning, which is exemplified by *if/then* thinking.

Formal-Operational: Discerning Patterns of Thought, Emotion, and Action

These clients can talk about themselves and their feelings—sometimes even from the perspectives of others. Their conversations tend to be abstract. At the late formal level, these clients can recognize commonalities in repeating behaviors or thoughts.

Dialectic/Systemic: Integrating Patterns of Emotion and Thought into a System

Most people do not ordinarily make sense of their worlds from a dialectic/systemic frame of reference. A woman who recognizes that sexism may be responsible for some of her difficulties is displaying this level of thinking. In this case, the client is aware of systems of knowledge and is learning how she is affected by the environment. A client who reviews the interview and examines it from several perspectives with varying emotional responses is also operating at the dialectic/systemic level. At the late dialectic/systemic level, the client will be able to challenge his or her integration of systems of operations. Technically, the client is able to reflect on systems of systems of operations. Highly abstract, this form of thinking can lead to complex forms of multiperspective thought.

Client:	I feel such love.
Therapist:	Can you say more about that?
Client:	My wife is wonderful. We have a loving and caring relationship. She has always hung in there with me throughout my hospitalizations. I feel very dependent on her. When I visit home I tend to rely on her a lot. She gets angry sometimes when I'm depressed, but for the most part, we get along fine. I sometimes feel that I never satisfy her.

Is the client primarily sensorimotor, concrete, formal, or dialectic/systemic?

Example 2. A 22-Year-Old Hospitalized, Depressed Client

Therapist: Could you tell me what occurs for you when you think about your family?

Client: What do you mean?

Therapist: Well, as you sit here, focus on any aspect of your family at all, any part of your family, and tell me what kind of things just happen right here and now for you.

Client: What do you mean by family? Like my husband, my daughter, my husband's mother? I don't know what you mean.

Therapist: Who seems most in your mind today?

Client: Well, I guess my mother.

Therapist: Tell me more about what's on your mind.

Client: Well, she lives with us now to help take care of my daughter while I'm here. She came in yesterday for a visit and she got mad at me. It really hurt my feelings. (tears) I can't help it if I'm in here. She said that I was just faking and didn't want to take care of Jamie. Then I started to cry, and I said to her . . . (continues)

Is the client primarily sensorimotor, concrete, formal, or dialectic/systemic?

Client number 1 is formal. His comments are all abstract, with little in the way of concretes. He is able to identify some of his and his wife's patterns, although he may well be unaware of other patterns (such as his wife's seldom being satisfied with him) or unable to do anything about them. DCT would view this depressed patient as having several cognitive-developmental tasks. One of these is to think about the meaning of the patterns he and his wife share and how these affect his depression. This is a formal-operational, dialectic/systemic therapeutic task that may involve family therapy as well as individual work.

On the other hand, if this client is distanced from his emotions, he may need work at the sensorimotor level in terms of Gestalt exercises, relaxation training, and body work. If he becomes seriously depressed, sensorimotor treatment using drugs may be useful. If he is too abstract, the therapist may need to focus on the specific concretes of his conflict. Long-term depressives sometimes learn the jargon of therapy, talk very well at the abstract level, and, with the therapist's collusion, fail to examine themselves at more basic levels.

The second client is concrete. This type of client is often difficult for therapists to work with, as most of us are formal-operational, dialectic/systemic thinkers. Two key developmental tasks face this concrete client. This brief interview segment suggests that the client is so mired in concrete description and experience that sensorimotor experiencing may be lost. Thus she may need the same type of body and experiential work required by the formal client above. In addition, this client needs to be able to reflect more on the self and recognize patterns. At the concrete level, the client may benefit from skills training and problem-solving counseling, all aimed at resolving situational specifics.

Concrete clients typically do not move easily and readily to formal pattern thinking. (The next chapter provides specific guidance to facilitate this process.) Thus, the therapist working with this type of client may need to operate for a period of time at the concrete level and listen to the detailed stories of the client.

If you are a primarily formal-operational person, you may find yourself bored, impatient, and "spacing out" (thinking about lunch or your last client) when you talk with a highly concrete client. Needless to say, this can jeopardize the relationship. If you are first willing to be with the client wherever he or she is at the moment and listen to the concrete details, you can later use the techniques and strategies of DCT to help broaden his or her understanding. The concrete client, for example, may have real trouble in seeing repeating patterns. Don't move to discuss patterns until the client has first described several specific situations (early or middle concrete levels) and has shown some ability to engage in late concrete-operational reasoning (if/then causal thinking).

Example 3. A 35-Year-Old Client Just Arrived at a Women's Shelter

Counselor: Could you tell me what's been happening?

Client: (tears) I couldn't take it anymore. He just reminds me of the devil. I don't know what to do. Where are my children ? Are they OK? He hit me and hit me. I ran out of the house. Look at my arm. (breaks down sobbing)

Is the client primarily sensorimotor, concrete, formal, or dialectic/ systemic?

Example 4. The Same Client Three Days Later

Counselor: How is it for you right now?

Client: Better, but I'm still confused as hell. I find myself wanting to go back to him. When he's not drinking, he's fine. But he's beat me so many times, and this last time he started for the kids. I'm not sure where I should go.

Counselor: You're confused right now, wondering what to do?

Client: Yeah. I've been thinking about it all week. The counseling sessions have helped me put it together more, but I'm still not sure. If I go back, I can see a lot of trouble ahead. I know he won't go for family counseling. And I can visualize a lot of pain and more beating for me if I do. In that context, it makes no sense to go back at all. But when I think about it a bit more, I know he had an abused childhood himself and relationships are difficult for him. He needs my caring, and when things are good for us, they are really good. Then I think about how difficult it will be for me and the children on our own. Even though I'm a college graduate, I haven't worked for five years. I'm not sure I could support myself. Its very scary. And weirdly enough, a piece of me really wants to get back to him. I know I play into his abuse by being so dependent on him. I wish I didn't think so much. It just mixes me up.

Is the client primarily sensorimotor, concrete, formal, or dialectic/systemic?

The first interview represents a sensorimotor presentation of self. People in crisis or experiencing trauma are often embedded in the emotional experience. The therapeutic task here is not to ask this woman concrete questions or to engage in formal analysis but simply to be with her and protect her in her moment of need. Housing and a safe relationship are what is needed. With some clients in crisis (for example, a rape victim), it may be helpful to encourage them to talk about what happened from a formal-operational point of view, as this provides some cognitive distance from the trauma. Later, as appropriate, the counselor can move toward helping the client re-experience the event in both sensorimotor and concrete detail.

The second session with the same client is more analytical. The client touches on several topics, each one of which seems to represent a pattern. When a client analyzes his or her situation in this manner, the distinctions between pattern and dialectic/systemic thinking often seem minimal. This client can be considered dialectic/systemic, since she looks at systems of operations. She is able to look at her situation from several perspectives and can recognize that her staying in an abusive relationship at times supports her husband's pathology. This ability to see a problem from several perspectives at once characterizes dialectic/systemic thought.

But the dialectic/systemic approach can also have drawbacks. In this interview, the client's self-analysis has safely distanced her from her deeper feelings; she can avoid the concrete specifics of what is likely to happen if she returns to her husband. The client would benefit from examining specific patterns of her behavior rather than considering multiple perspectives. She also could be helped to consider the sexism in the system in which she lives—that bears on her husband's abusive behavior—and to look at the system of interaction in her family that may aggravate the difficulties in their relationship.

With each of these three clients, it is wise to start at the client's developmental level. But staying at the same level throughout the session may not be enough. A more comprehensive interview and treatment plan may involve helping the client examine her or his difficulties from multiple developmental perspectives.

Preoperational: Defining the Problem

Piaget's second stage of cognition is termed *preoperational* and roughly covers ages 2 through 7. The child learns to represent the world through language and to use some abstract symbols. Characteristic of this stage is egocentric, magical thinking, which denies external reality but functions well for the child. What Piaget terms preoperational, DCT calls late sensorimotor.

The word *preoperational* is another way of describing client problems. DCT points out that most, perhaps even all, clients are preoperational. If they were operating effectively with others and in their environment, they would not be clients and would not need the help of counselors and therapists. Thus, in this book clients and their problems are considered preoperational.

Our task as helpers is to aid clients in addressing their problems using sensorimotor, concrete, formal, and dialectic/systemic modes of thinking and action. The first part of this task is to learn how to recognize the four levels in individual clients. Later, this assessment may be extended to families and groups.

Sensorimotor: Focusing on the Elements of Experience

The first Piagetian stage is the sensorimotor period (0 through 2 years of age); in this stage the child has little sense of self. A particularly striking example of this lack of separation of self is the young child who cries when seeing another child hurt. This child is unable to separate the self from others. Another example might be a child having an angry tantrum during which the child loses the self in total emotion. Typical of the sensorimotor period is a reliance on what is seen, heard, and felt—that is, immediate sensory and perceptual experience.

Sensorimotor functioning has many positives. When people can enjoy the closeness of a sexual relationship, sing and dance, experience the sun's warmth, swim and play baseball and are conscious only of the moment, they are experiencing the best of what life has to offer. For example, to work through the grieving associated with serious loss requires the client to experience emotions at the deeper, sensorimotor level. One may say that there is more satisfaction in tasting an apple than in analyzing its chemical composition. Much of the helping endeavor focuses on getting clients in touch with this part of themselves.

People frequently handle an experience in their lives in an ineffective, embedded, sensorimotor fashion. Examples are an individual suffering the agonies of divorce or an adolescent out of control in an outburst of temper. Illogical and/or magical thinking may be common at such times. Such individuals may have difficulty separating themselves from others and display boundary problems. An example is, as family therapists term it, the overly enmeshed family. Clients can be so deeply affected by a traumatic experience, such as rape or an automobile accident, that they become, for a time, totally absorbed in their emotions.

A key to identifying clients who think and operate at the sensorimotor level is their immersion in the elemental.[2] Clients who present at this level often talk randomly in disorganized fragments. This type of client usually has a short attention span. As interviewers, we can bring out this level of cognition by asking these clients to focus on the here and now and to note what is seen, heard, and felt in terms of direct experiencing.

---

[2] Weinstein and Alschuler (1985) describe four levels of self-knowledge, which can be defined as the way an individual describes and thinks about self. The first level is elemental, which corresponds roughly to DCT's late sensorimotor period. The second level is situational and is similar to the detailed concrete descriptions one often finds with children and adults. The third stage is termed pattern and is similar to formal operations. The fourth is transformational, which is close to dialectic/systemic. Weinstein and Alschuler have valuable scoring systems for rating self-knowledge that can be used profitably in conjunction with DCT.

However, if a client has just experienced a major trauma, such sensorimotor focusing might be totally inappropriate. At such times, some clients need to be more formal and analytical to provide some distance from the event. Later the therapist can return to the basics of the experience and begin the process of working through the feelings.

Illogical and magical thinking can be considered sensorimotor in nature. For example, irrational ideas such as "She made me hit her"; "It's my fault—he wouldn't have abused me if I had been a better wife"; "I don't have a drug problem—I only take drugs when I need them"; and "It's important to be perfect" are common for those at the sensorimotor level.

Nonverbal behavior of sensorimotor clients tends to be random as well. Movement is frequent with a certain jerkiness characteristic of this level. However, severely depressed clients who move very little are also classified at the sensorimotor level in that they are overwhelmed by their feelings.

Examples

Child. An example of a child at the sensorimotor level is the 7-year-old who has a fight on the playground, is crying, and talks about the situation in fragments. It is difficult to get a concrete, linear explanation of what occurred. The child *is* her or his feelings.

Adult. An example of an adult at this level is the otherwise well-functioning adult who is going through a divorce and is currently so overwhelmed that he or she has difficulty staying on a single topic. More complex sensorimotor behavior is found in the emotionally cold sociopath who has split feeling from thought. Similar patterns of separating thought and feelings may be found in the acting-out child or adolescent or those with other personality disorders.

Family. Families predominantly operating at this level tend to be chaotic in their functioning. The family reacts to the latest and strongest emotional event, and family interaction is thus guided by affect rather than reason. Families who underutilize this level tend to be less connected and less responsive to the feelings of others. Cultural differences particularly affect this dimension. Some Italian-American families tend to exhibit a great deal of sensorimotor affect in their interactions, whereas a British-American family may be more reserved. What is healthy behavior in one family may differ markedly from healthy behavior in another. It is important not to impose your definitions of what is culturally appropriate on individuals and families.

What is desirable for human development is a balance between the ability to enter into a full expression of feelings, as represented by sensorimotor experience, and the ability to become more concrete and analytical as the situation changes. Remaining at one level of cognition can be a problem.

Personal. Think of a time when you were overwhelmed by a situation and by your thoughts and feelings connected with it. Relax and "get into" that experience as much as you can. Summarize your thoughts and feelings below.

Allow yourself to be random and free in developing a visual image of that time. What are you seeing? Hearing? Feeling? Did you engage in some magical thinking at that time?

_____

_____

_____

_____

_____

_____

Concrete-Operational: Searching for Situational Descriptions

The developmental task of the elementary-school-age child is described by Erik Erikson as achieving a sense of industry versus inferiority. Young children achieve industry and capability by being able to operate concretely in the world. In elementary school, children learn to read, do elementary math, engage in basic sports, and participate for the first time in a peer group. The concrete, operational world is concerned with action.

Concreteness is an important counseling construct. We have learned that getting specific, concrete examples from our clients is critical if we are to understand them. We have many concrete approaches to counseling, including assertiveness training, instruction in basic living skills via social skills training, and the Adlerian approach of logical consequences.

Clients at this level tend to talk in very concrete terms about their problems, using many specific details. They may describe situations blow by blow, saying "He said this" and "I said that." Clients at the late concrete level exhibit causal, if/then thinking. As interviewers, we encourage concreteness in our clients by asking "Could you give me an example?" There is little analysis and reflection in concrete thought. It is difficult for the concrete thinker to see patterns of thought, feeling, or behavior.

Concrete clients tend to describe their emotions and feelings, making such statements as "I feel sad" or "That hurts me because. . . ." In skills-training programs on reflection of feeling, counselors and therapists are often instructed to say to their clients, "You feel ____ (insert emotion) because (insert cause of emotion)." This type of statement is representative of a late concrete-operational feeling statement.

Concrete clients are able to name emotions but have difficulty thinking about and reflecting on them. In helping a person work through a deep emotional experience, it is useful to move back and forth between sensorimotor and concrete modes. Alternately naming and experiencing emotions is basic to therapy. Formal-operational and more analytic clients may resist sensorimotor and concrete expression of feelings.

Concreteness is highly desirable for the individual or family constantly "up in the clouds" of abstraction or enmeshed in sensorimotor experience. The description of concrete events can be helpful for both types of clients. However, too much concreteness can also be a problem, particularly for clients who keep repeating the same counterproductive behavior while failing to see the pattern. As with all other cognitive dimensions, achieving a balance is important.

Examples

Child. Most children talk in very concrete terms. They may say very little (early concrete or late sensorimotor), or they may talk endlessly about small details of their experience (middle concrete) or they may describe situations from an if/then perspective (late concrete). Perhaps the best way to identify concreteness is to ask a 10-year-old to tell you about a recent movie or TV show—the concrete description can be endless.

Adult. Adults do not differ much from children when they talk in concretes. Helping professionals need to move clients from the random, magical thinking of the late sensorimotor stage to the specific concretes of the situation. These specifics give us an understanding of the client's world.

Family. The clearest family example is the verbal family in which parents talk in the abstract while the young children, dealing in the concrete, wonder what is going on. Work with such families might focus on helping parents learn to talk and play with children. Some families have a very concrete style; at the dinner table or in the interview they may give detailed linear descriptions of the day's events, with little accompanying analysis and reflection.

Personal. Consider the specific situation you described above (when you felt overwhelmed) and write down the concrete, linear details. Describe the event in specific detail. What happened before the event? What happened afterward? Name the feelings you had. This linear presentation of specifics represents concrete thinking and emotion. If you can attach an if/then set of causal reasons to the specific situation, you will be describing the event in a late concrete-operational mode.

_____

_____

_____

_____

_____

_____

_____

Formal-Operational: Discerning Patterns of Thought, Emotion, and Action

The question "Who am I?" is particularly characteristic of formal thinkers. The search for a personal identity requires the reflection on patterns and consistencies in the self. The formal thinker is well able to generalize and to synthesize several concrete situations into an overall pattern.

Piaget notes that the first abstract stage, the formal-operational period, starts between ages 11 and 17. In formal operations the individual learns to reflect on the self and to recognize patterns in the world. To develop a sense of self or a personal identity, an adolescent must have some formal-operational skills. Success in junior high or high school requires abstract, formal skills. However, most Piagetian scholars estimate that a quarter of the U.S. population never reaches full formal operations. They may be able to see some patterns, but not consistently. This poses an interesting challenge for the professional helper using DCT methods. DCT holds that with careful systematic questions, virtually all clients can see patterns in their thoughts and behaviors and many reach the dialectic/system level as well.

Much of counseling and therapy theory is formal-operational in nature. We are interested in self-actualization, changing patterns of cognition, and discovering how present-day life patterns go back to childhood. If our clients are not ready to engage in formal operations, our formal theories must be adapted. A concrete client may indeed need to have a better self-concept, but using abstract words to emphasize the importance of self-examination will most often be ineffective. It is possible to build a positive self-concept in a more concrete way by focusing on specific things clients can do or have done that make them feel good about themselves.

The ability to be abstract and formal is not always positive. We all know individuals who talk a lot but are very short on action. A family or individual may analyze and talk about issues in a charming and interesting way, thus seducing the helper into thinking there is real self-awareness. Instead, these individuals may have learned to avoid coping with the real world and other people by using abstraction and analysis.

Critical to identifying formal-operational mode is abstraction. One cannot see, hear, or feel abstractions. A self or a pattern is an abstract construct that exists only in the mind. (Recall the discussion in Chapter 1 on concrete versus abstract conversation.) When we talk in counseling and therapy about reflecting clients' feelings, it means we often are operating at the formal level. You may have had the experience of reflecting feelings to a concrete client and having the client, looking somewhat puzzled, reply, "Yes, that is what I just said." The ability to analyze and reflect on one's feelings and thoughts is critical to finding a sense of self and a personal identity. The ability to step outside and look at oneself is very useful. This type of emotional expression is very different from sensorimotor and concrete experience.

As counselors, we often encourage formal thinking when we ask "Is that a pattern?" or "Do you feel that way often?" or "Does that happen in other situations?" If the client, adult or child, is able to recognize underlying patterns of behavior or emotions, he or she is operating in the formal mode. Young children are not usually believed capable of formal thought, but they do go through a form of pattern thinking that is structurally similar to adult formal thinking.

Examples

Child. Children exhibit a form of pattern thinking, as represented by such statements as "Daddy does that all the time," "That's the same as mine," or "I feel good about myself most of the time." These statements are, of course, not fully formal-operational in the Piagetian sense but do illustrate that children are capable of a form of pattern thinking.

Adult. Examples of adult formal statements are: "That seems to be a pattern of mine," "The two situations are very similar in that . . . ," "That's typical of my father," "As I think about my feelings, I find . . . ," "My reflection on that is . . . ," or "Comparing and contrasting the situations, I see . . . "

Family. A professional family who tends to talk in abstractions represents an overly formal approach. The members may be able to analyze their issues but are unable to act on them or to change. They may talk about feelings rather than really experiencing them at the sensorimotor level.

There is also a late formal level in which the client integrates patterns of patterns. Successful therapy often helps the client integrate several patterns of thought and behavior into larger patterns. For example, the client may have come to therapy with a vague sense of anger and discontent, blaming the spouse for difficulties in their marriage (a preoperational problem). The client may be blaming the spouse totally, exhibiting magical thinking characteristic of the late sensorimotor level.

As counseling starts, the therapist typically will ask for concretes about the marital relationship. If all goes well, the client will then discover that there are certain situations that seem to repeat again and again. This is pattern thinking. The client may later discover that problems with a boss follow the same concrete, behavioral sequences and patterns as do problems with the spouse. When the client begins examining interrelated, repeating patterns, he or she is moving into the late formal-operational stage. The therapist might look for patterns in the client's developmental history with his parents that are now repeating with the spouse and boss.

Personal. Consider the situation when you felt overwhelmed. Has this happened in other situations? Is there a pattern? If so, what are some of your feelings about this pattern? What does the pattern imply about your own identity? Can you identify some repetitions of this pattern of thought and feeling in your own daily life now?

_____

_____

_____

_____

_____

_____

Dialectic/Systemic: Integrating Patterns of Emotion and Thought into a System

Piaget also identifies postformal thought, considering it a variation of formal operations. The most critical distinction between the two is the capability of the individual to step back, look at patterns, and reflect on the system of operations. Postformal thinking and emotion require the capability for very abstract formulations. This level is exemplified by the adult who, having developed a sense of self, can step back and see the self and situation from varying perspectives. This ability to see one event from several perspectives is perhaps most indicative of postformal cognition.

Counseling and therapy often seek to help clients take several perspectives on their problems. For example, a client may have a very strong self-concept, but the view of self may be so rigid that the client fails to see how he or she is hurting others in the family. A therapeutic task here, of course, is to help the individual change cognitive style so that he or she can see other points of view. DCT classifies this postformal cognitive-developmental level as dialectic/systemic.

Thinking at the dialectic/systemic level requires one to step back to a third-order perspective and reflect on the systems of operations. Consider the following examples of different levels of thought on the issue of death and dying:

Sensorimotor. There is no perspective taking, no separation of self from others or from the situation. The response to a serious loss would be extensive crying and emotional catharsis—"I am my feelings." This may be the only level on which an individual genuinely works through grief and loss. Thus experiencing feelings at this level is a natural, essential part of grieving. Many clients who have experienced trauma have not yet explored their great sadness at this level.

Concrete-operational. The self is separated from objects or situations, but there is no awareness of self—for example, "I feel sad" (early concrete) and "I feel sad because my mother died" (late concrete).

Formal-operational. The self is now able to look at the self looking at objects or situations—for example, "When I look at myself, I see myself feeling very sad about the loss" or "When my Grandma died, I felt sad, but I wasn't quite as upset as I might have been." Here there is a necessary distancing from the immediate impact of the death and an acceptance of the life process. However, this type of conversation is quite far from the actual feelings.

Dialectic/systemic. The self is able to reflect on the total system. Feelings may change in the context of varying systems—for example, "I felt overwhelmed and I cried a lot. I felt very sad about the loss. It's a pattern with me. I'm lucky now to be able to let some of it go. But I can think about it from another perspective. My mother was so full of pain from the cancer, that I get a feeling of relief about her death. I guess I learned from all this that life goes on. She lives in me. Sometimes I look at it one way and feel really sad, but at other times I know it was for the best." It would be difficult, perhaps impossible, to achieve this type of thought without first having gone through the other levels of grieving.

Another concept closely associated with the dialectic/systemic frame of reference is that of transformation. In the above example, the client was able to look at the situation from several perspectives and to transform the data into a new gestalt. Although such transformational thought is valuable, it is very intellectually abstract. Many clients prefer to stay at the abstract level and may fail to deal with concrete reality or come to grips with the depth of emotional expression found at the sensorimotor level.

As helping professionals, we assist clients to think at the dialectic/systemic level when we help them consider a range of data and ask them such questions as "Can you look at your situation from another perspective?" or "How does all this look to you now that we've talked about it for awhile?" or "How would you integrate all this?" Such questions encourage more complex, integrative thinking. When we ask clients to take another perspective on themselves or a situation, we are moving them toward the dialectic/systemic level.

Personal example. Review your written responses at the sensorimotor, concrete, and formal levels. As you reflect on your various responses, how would you integrate them? What sense do they make to you? Can you now take another perspective, perhaps one different from the one you just arrived at? What stands out from your personal examination?

Chapter Summary

Clients come to us with a unique view of the world. It is our task to enter into their way of understanding the world. Before we intervene, we must learn how they think about themselves, their situations, and their problems. Developmental assessment is one part of developing empathy and helping us join the client where she or he is.

Piagetian terms are used here in new ways. A client who has a problem and some difficulty in operating on the self or situation is described as preoperational. Clients present themselves for counseling at one of four primary cognitive-developmental levels: sensorimotor, concrete-operational, formal-operational, and dialectic/systemic. The four cognitive levels, in turn, can be subdivided into early and late levels. (Specific modes of identifying and classifying the eight levels may be found in Appendix 1).

Most clients will present at multiple levels. Cognitive-developmental assessment is a guide to understanding the client's world. These concepts should not be used to stereotype individuals. In summary:

Sensorimotor clients tend to talk in a random and disorganized fashion and tend not to separate themselves from their experience. A severely depressed client is also illustrative of this cognitive-developmental level. At the late sensorimotor level, there is magical thinking and some beginning ability to be concrete. Key words: elemental, see/hear/feel.

Concrete clients describe their situations and emotions in specific, linear terms, with many details. At the late concrete level, there may be if/then causal reasoning. Key words: situational, specifics.

Formal clients move to abstractions, talking about self and patterns of self or situations. They tend to reflect on feelings rather than experience them directly. At the late formal level, clients consider patterns of patterns. Key words: patterns, patterns of patterns.

Dialectic/systemic clients are able to operate on systems of knowledge and can take a multiperspective view. Complexity of thinking and extensive abstraction mark this level. At the late dialectic/systemic level, look for the ability to work with and reflect on systems of systems of operations. Key words: postformal, integrative, systemic, transformational, multiperspective.

It is possible to identify the client's cognitive-developmental level, whether the client is a child, adolescent, or adult. The same assessment principles can be applied to family, group, and organizational counseling and consulting. Cultural variations, which will be elaborated in Chapter 7, are particularly important to consider when working with an individual from a cultural group different than your own.

CAUTION!   Clients, families, and groups present their issues at multiple levels. Do not allow yourself to become ensnared in assessment to the point that you blind yourself to the complexity of the human being before you. Also recall that the concepts of stage and level presented here are metaphorical. We could divide development into 4, 8, 80, or 800 levels and stages if we wished.

Theory into Practice

As we move from theory and description to direct practice, we can look at specific practice objectives for this chapter. By the end of this section, you may be able to

1. Assess client cognitive- developmental level through written client statements.
2. Identify client cognitive-developmental level when conducting a role-played practice interview or by observing someone else conduct a role-played interview.
3. Identify client and counselor cognitive-developmental level when observing a role-played interview.

These three objectives provide a foundation for later transfer of this knowledge to direct interview practice.

Identifying Written Client Statements

Which cognitive-developmental level do each of the following examples represent? All of the following statements might be the first thing a client says to you. It is possible to reliably identify the cognitive-developmental level of the client just by evaluating a few words or phrases. Also, remember that client cognitive-developmental level often changes throughout a single interview. Relatively few clients present or discuss their problems at only one developmental level.

Each of the cases below involves some mixture of developmental levels, as clients seldom present at just one level. Your therapeutic response affects how these clients talk about their issues, a point elaborated on in the next chapter. Circle the cognitive-developmental level(s) (SM—sensorimotor, CO—concrete-operational, FO—formal-operational, DS—dialectic/systemic). (At the conclusion of this chapter is an interpretation of the cases.)

1. SM CO FO D/S (age 16; ambitious high school student who has just done poorly on an examination, in tears) I just can't do it. I tried hard. I'm so confused. My dad will really get angry. (more tears) And my teachers are on me about it.

2. SM CO FO D/S (age 35; parent talking about a problem with her 13-year-old) Sally and I just had an argument. I wanted her to wash the dishes and help for a change. She said "No," with a very angry and nasty face. Then she ran upstairs. I ran right after her just as mad as she was. But she had locked the door. I just sat there and fumed.

3. SM CO FO D/S (age 40; just working through a divorce) I just had another date. This is only the second person I've dated, but again I'm repeating that pattern. My perfectionism got in the way of my marriage. Even with the

first person I dated, I noted that I started criticizing and making suggestions after the third time we went out. My perfectionism showed itself last night when I told my date that her car could stand some cleaning! How can I get rid of this pattern?

4. SM CO FO D/S (age 63; just entering into a new executive position) As I look back on my years with Carter Finance, I'm seeing so much. In my first years, I simply worked to make a living and didn't worry much about how the company was working either for me or against me. I just wanted the money. Then, when I was promoted to assistant head of the department, I started noticing that a lot of people had a pattern of not caring for the company. As I moved up in administration, I began to see how the company could be reorganized to meet personnel needs more effectively. And in the last few years, I've got a better handle on how the company relates to the external market. Each time I look at it, Carter Finance seems a bit different.

5. SM CO FO D/S (age 24; documented problem of alcohol abuse and absenteeism on the job) I had a really great time last night. I really hung one on. James beer is the best. Just looking at the can makes me feel good. I love the sound of the tab popping open.

6. SM CO FO D/S (same client as above) Yeah, I got drunk last night. Just before I went out, I found out that my wife had left me because I drank so much. I decided to hang one on. I went to my favorite bar and drank perhaps a six-pack of James. Then my friend and I went to another bar across town. (more details) At the end I didn't recall anything.

7. SM CO FO D/S (same client as above) This is typical of me when I get upset. In situations where things don't go the way I want them to, I just have to get away. It's been a pattern for me throughout the marriage, too. Whenever Sue didn't pay enough attention to me, I threatened her by leaving. Then I'd go out and get drunk. I think I'm happier drunk than sober.

8. SM CO FO D/S (same client as above) Drinking has been important in our family for generations. Drinking is a way we express ourselves. My Dad drank a good bit but was able to hold it. I understand Grandpa died of liver disease at 42. I understand people from our ethnic group have a higher probability of alcoholism than most people. As I look back on the pattern in the family over the years, I guess I have reason for concern.

9. SM CO FO D/S (age 12; concerned about peer group pressures) If I don't dress better, others may not like me. I need to look good to keep up with other people. The way I look determines how other people see me. I've tried to talk to my parents, but they said the way I dress is fine. They treat me like a child!

10. SM CO FO D/S (age 4; talking about father) Daddy took me to his office. He said he wanted to show me to his friends. He held me up in front of them. I put my face into Daddy's shoulder. He laughed. I felt good.

11. SM CO FO D/S (age 15; in a dilemma about vocational choice) The career course is a bore. I know what I want to do. I want to be an actress. The tests they gave me suggested I should think about selling things. I don't want to be a salesclerk.

12. SM CO FO D/S (age 45; during a family counseling session.) My husband has a pattern of always telling the children what to do. Right now, look at him—so smug! He always thinks he is right. There is no way you can change him.

Identifying Cognitive-Developmental Level in a Role-Played Situation

Find a volunteer partner with whom to practice identifying cognitive-developmental level (CDL). Each can take turns identifying client CDL. Following is a list of interview openers and questions with space for you to take notes on the client answer. Identify the client's CDL and your evidence for making that assessment. Evidence usually consists of specific verbal behaviors of your partner/client. However, recall that nonverbal cues can be equally useful in your developmental assessment.

An alternative to this exercise is to divide into groups of four. The first individual acts as client; the second, as interviewer; the other two are observers. The interviewer asks the first question and, by using listening skills, draws out data. The session is stopped after about 50 to 100 words are spoken by the client, and the entire group discusses the CDL of the client. Once the discussion is complete, the client becomes the interviewer, and one of the observers asks the second question. Again, the CDL is determined. Continue rotating through the questions until there is some feeling of comfort about being able to identify client CDL on the spot.

Write down key words and thoughts of the client in the space provided. Then identify the cognitive-developmental level, using specific evidence to back up your decision.

1. Tell me about a time when you were late with an assignment.

_____

_____

SM CO FO D/S Cite specific evidence for your decision below.

_____

_____

2. When you hear the words *alcohol* and *drugs*, what comes to your mind?

_____

_____

SM CO FO D/S Cite specific evidence for your decision below.

_____

_____

3. Tell me about an interpersonal conflict you had in the past.

_____

_____

SM CO FO D/S Cite specific evidence for your decision below.

_____

_____

4. What occurs for you when you think about leaving home for the first time?

_____

_____

SM CO FO D/S Cite specific evidence for your decision below.

_____

_____

5. What happens for you when you focus on your family?

_____

_____

SM CO FO D/S Cite specific evidence for your decision below.

_____

_____

6. When you think about your first job, what comes to mind?

_____

_____

SM CO FO D/S Cite specific evidence for your decision below.

_____

_____

7. Formulate your own question.

_____

_____

SM CO FO D/S Cite specific evidence for your decision below.

_____

_____

8. Formulate another question.

_____

_____

SM CO FO D/S Cite specific evidence for your decision below.

_____

_____

Practicing Developmental Assessment for Client and Counselor in a Complete Interview

Appendix 3 contains a full interview for practice in classifying client response. You can also categorize the helping leads of the counselor on the same four-level scale.

Client and Counselor Developmental Level in a Role-Played Session

Given that client cognitive-developmental level can be identified, let us turn to a more complex observation process: the identification of *both* client and counselor CDL in a role-played session. Do not expect to be immediately proficient in this type of rating skill. With practice over time, you will develop increasing skill.

Groups of four are required for this type of practice, which is similar to microcounseling practice sessions (see Ivey & Authier, 1978; Ivey, 1988; Ivey & Gluckstern, 1982).

Step 1: Divide into Practice Groups

Get acquainted with each other informally before beginning.

Step 2: Select a Group Leader

The leader's task is to ensure that the group follows the specific steps of the practice session. It often proves helpful if the least-experienced group member serves as leader first.

Step 3: Assign Roles for the Practice Session

- Role-played client. The role-played client will be cooperative, talk freely about the topic, and not give the interviewer a difficult time. In later practice sessions, it is critical that difficult problems or clients be selected.
- Interviewer. The interviewer will ask one of the questions above (including any question the interviewer and the client agree to beforehand) and practice drawing out the client in conversation about the selected topic. The interviewer should feel free to use his or her natural style and theory of helping.

- Observer 1. The first observer will fill out the feedback form below, summarizing observations on the client's CDL.
- Observer 2. The second observer will fill out the feedback form, summarizing observations on the interviewer's CDL.

Step 4: Plan the Session

- The interviewer and client must first agree on the topic. The interviewer may wish to facilitate client talk with his or her own natural style of interviewing.
- The client may wish to think through how he or she wants to talk about the agreed-on topic through the session.
- The two observers can examine the feedback forms and be ready to classify each client or interviewer statement. You will find that it is possible to list the main words of the client; this will help in reconstructing the interview for the discussion period.

Step 5: Conduct a 5-Minute Interviewing Session

The interviewer and client will discuss the issue for five minutes while the observers keep track of their progress and classify the statements of each. It is helpful to videotape and/or audiotape practice sessions.

Step 6: Provide Immediate Feedback and Complete Notes (5 Minutes)

This is a highly structured session, and there is often immediate need to personally "process" and discuss the session. In particular, it is helpful for the interviewer to ask the client "What stands out for you from this practice session?" Allow yourself some time to provide true personal reactions to the practice.

The interviewer needs the same opportunity to reflect on what happened. The client may ask for these personal reactions to the session. This change of role can be useful to both. At this point, the observers should sit back and let the participants take control. Use this time to complete your classification and notes.

Step 7: Review the Practice Session and Provide Feedback (15 Minutes)

It is important in giving feedback to allow the person receiving the feedback to be in charge. Thus, the interviewer should be the person who asks for feedback rather than getting it without being asked. At this point, the observers can share their observations from the feedback form. Feedback should be specific, concrete, and nonjudgmental (that is, avoid saying "That was terrific" or "That was terrible. You should have . . ."). Pay attention to the strengths of the interview.

You will find that classification of client and counselor CDL is not easy when you focus solely on single comments, because most people talk on multiple levels. Thus, in the first stages of learning, allow yourself time and be satisfied with the ability to note the clearest examples of each level. Later you will be able to recognize cognitive style and shifts in style automatically.

Cognitive-Developmental Level Feedback Sheet
(For Both Client and Interviewer)

Date _____

Interviewer _____

Client _____

Observer _____

Instructions: First, write down the main words of the client or interviewer statement (one statement only). Then classify each client or interviewer statement for cognitive-developmental level. Do not expect your numbering system to exactly match the other observer's. Most important is getting a few main words so the interview can be reconstructed. This also provides evidence and a rationale for your classification.

 1. SM C F D/S _____

 2. SM C F D/S _____

 3. SM C F D/S _____

 4. SM C F D/S _____

 5. SM C F D/S _____

 6. SM C F D/S _____

 7. SM C F D/S _____

 8. SM C F D/S _____

 9. SM C F D/S _____

10. SM C F D/S _____

11. SM C F D/S _____

12. SM C F D/S _____

13. SM C F D/S _____

14. SM C F D/S _____

15. SM C F D/S _____

Informal observations of the session:

Client and Counselor Developmental Level in a Role-Played Family Counseling Practice Session

An extension of the preceding exercise can be done in a role-played family counseling session. Experience reveals that groups of six work best in this situation. Given the complexity of the many personalities, using video- or audiotape is very helpful.

As a first step in family practice, it is useful to do a family demonstration, while the rest of the class or workshop watches the session. Approximately one hour will be required for development and debriefing of the family session.

Step 1: Select Six Willing Participants

Two of these will be co-therapists and the other four will be the family. The remainder of the members of the class or workshop will observe the entire process and later serve as process consultants who reflect on the session.

Step 2: Have the Workshop Leader Assume the Leadership Role

Due to the complexity of the process, the workshop leader or teacher should assume the leader role and ensure that the group follows the specific steps of the practice session.

Step 3: Assign Roles for the Practice Session

- Role-played family. For this first session, a "typical" family should probably be used (that is, a couple having an intact first marriage and family consisting of father, mother, daughter, and son). Later, other common family patterns—such as blended, single-parent, and gay-lesbian—can be used.

- Interviewer. The family will be cooperative, talk freely about the topic, and not give the interviewer a difficult time. In later practice sessions, however, it is critical that difficult problems and families be selected. A useful first topic is family fighting or a teenager who is acting out.

- Therapists. Two therapists/counselors can work together in this session.

- Workshop/class observers. All remaining individuals in the session will sit in a circle around the family.

Step 4: Planning the Session

- The family members can leave the room and define their roles and the problem they wish to present. The nature of the problem will be a surprise to the therapists. The family needs to define a problem or reason for coming to the family session.

- The two therapists may wish to think through their relationship briefly. One way to start the session is by an informal "joining" with the family through conversation. Other therapists prefer to start immediately. A useful way to start the process is to employ a form of circular questioning in which the therapists ask the family members if someone can answer the question "Why are you here?" This same question is then asked of each family member. Elicit each family member's perception of the problem. In this way, family therapists learn about different perspectives on the same problem. Follow cultural norms by asking who is in charge and having that person speak first.

After each member of the family has spoken, one or both of the therapists may wish to summarize the family as a whole. Many families will hold one member responsible for the problem. In many family therapy sessions, the therapist at this point often will reframe/reinterpret the individual problem as an issue of family interaction: "What is going on with Jane/John is not an individual problem but a family issue we are going to examine."

Again, the task of the two therapists is simply to draw out four different (or similar) interpretations of the problem. Using questioning, listening, and summarization skills is helpful. Avoid giving advice and making interpretations; try to see the family as it sees itself.

- The family observers have several roles: 1) They all can be participants or observers; the therapists should feel free to stop the interview in mid-session and ask the observers for help and suggestions. 2) Four observers should be assigned to various members of the family. Their task is to identify the cognitive-developmental level of one family member. Two observers may watch the therapists and assess the CDL of their questions. The rest of the group should note the CDL of the family as a whole. Use the same feedback forms for the individual practice session as in the preceding exercise.

You will find, for example, that some families present at the concrete level and others at the formal level. In addition, different members within the family may be talking about the problem from different levels.

Step 5: Conduct a 5- to 10-Minute Interviewing Session

The therapists and family will discuss the varying perceptions of the problem for 5 minutes while the observers keep track of their progress and classify the statements of each. Again, you will find it helpful to videotape and/or audiotape practice sessions.

However, family dynamics often confuse even the most effective therapists. Thus the therapists should feel free to stop for a moment in the middle of the session and ask the external observers for their reactions and suggestions. Family therapy specialists may note the similarity of this training procedure to the "reflecting team" concept in which experts view a family session through a one-way mirror and contact the therapists by telephone with specific suggestions for action.

Step 6: Provide Immediate Feedback and Complete Notes (5 Minutes)

This is a highly structured session, and there is often immediate need to personally "process" and discuss the session. In particular, it is helpful for the therapists to ask the family "What stands out for you from this practice session?" Allow some time to provide true personal reactions to the practice.

At this point, the observers should sit back and let the participants take control. Use this time to complete your classification and notes.

Step 7: Review the Practice Session and Provide Feedback (15 Minutes)

When giving feedback, allow the therapists and the family receiving the feedback to be in charge. At this point, the observers can share their observations. Again, feedback should be specific, concrete, and nonjudgmental and attention should be given to strengths of the interview.

Generalization: Taking Developmental Assessment Home

Many ideas are presented in books and in workshops designed for professional practice of counseling and therapy. Most of these books are left on the shelf, unused, to gather dust and then are forgotten. The question for you at this point is whether or not you will incorporate the concepts of developmental assessment into your daily life and into regular interview practice.

To "take developmental assessment concepts home" requires some commitment to action on your part. In effect, ideas and abstractions are presented here. Ultimately, it is your concrete practice and action that counts. Following are some activities that have been found especially useful in ensuring that these basic ideas are used.

Activity 1: Personal Observation of Individuals in Daily Life

A beginning step toward useful generalization of developmental assessment is to observe those you come into contact with in daily life. At what cognitive-developmental level are friends and family members talking to you? At what CDL are you answering? Do they talk about issues at several levels or at one level? Do they move through developmental progressions (for example, starting with concretes and then moving to formal abstractions)?

Can you notice mismatches between the cognitive-developmental levels of two or more individuals? You may find considerable misunderstanding and conflict between a concrete and a formal approach to problem solving.

Plan to observe at least one person per day during the coming week. Do not hesitate to observe yourself now and then. Summarize your observations in a format similar to the one that follows on page 49.

Activity 2: Observation of a Family, Group, or Organization

Following the same method and format as above, observe a group. You will find that there is a general "tone" of a family, group, or organization that can be assessed at one of the cognitive-developmental levels. Different members of the group will have different ideas about the interactions and CDL of the group.

Record your observations using an adaptation of the form in activity 1.

Cognitive-Developmental Level Identification

Observation Notes

Describe what the person said concretely and specifically. Use the person's main words.

_____

_____

_____

_____

_____

This individual seems to be primarily: SM CO FO D/S
Cite specific evidence.

_____

_____

_____

Individuals often present themselves simultaneously at several levels. Note other CDLs of this person, citing specific evidence justifying your observation.

___ SM _____

_____

_____

___ CO _____

_____

_____

___ FO _____

_____

_____

___ D/S _____

_____

_____

Activity 3: Taking Developmental Assessment to the Interview

Each day, listen carefully to one client in a helping interview. You will find that it is possible to make a general assessment of CDL (the overall way a client conceptually approaches a particular problem) and of the levels within that problem. The client may have an overall formal approach to thinking about the problem but, on prompting from you, may move at times to the concrete level. This type of client may have some difficulty in working at the sensorimotor level. Most clients need to develop their basic concrete skills. Many have allowed themselves to become so abstract in the formal and dialectic/systemic areas that they have lost touch with reality.

Again, provide specific evidence that you have been able to assess the cognitive-developmental level of your own clients.

Activity 4: Consider the Yakima Nation Proverb

The smooth surface of the water does
not reveal the depths.

The lesson is—see the problem from more
than one point of view.

DCT stresses the importance of helping clients see different frames of reference and experience their lives from several different perspectives. What does this proverb say to you at this time?

_____

_____

_____

_____

_____

_____

Suggested Supplementary Reading and Activities

Additional Reading

Ivey, A. 1986. *Developmental therapy: Theory into practice.* San Francisco: Jossey-Bass.

First read "The Purloined Consciousness" in Chapter 4. Pages 133 through 142 provide a philosophical and practical background for assessment of client cognitive-developmental level. Pages 162 through 169 provide additional data on ideas about assessment. Exercises around construct 1 (page 170) and construct 3 (page 175) may be especially useful.

A more theoretical discussion of the ideas in this chapter may be found in Chapter 3, "Therapy as Development: Facilitating Cognitive-Developmental Change." The exercises on pages 125 through 130 will help expand the frame of reference of this chapter.

Gilligan, C. 1982. *In a different voice.* Cambridge, Mass.: Harvard University Press.

Kegan, R. 1982. *The evolving self.* Cambridge, Mass.: Harvard University Press.

Kohlberg, L. 1981. *The philosophy of moral development.* New York: Harper & Row.

These are three critical books on developmental theory. Despite their theoretical value, they have not been used widely in clinical and counseling practice. The technology and methods of DCT could prove useful in making these books more accessible and useful for the interview process.

Specifically, for Gilligan, Kegan, and Kohlberg (or other cognitive or developmental theorists), the practical interviewing task is to learn how to recognize key constructs in the client's natural language and behavior during the interview. For example, using Gilligan's concept of relational behavior, it is useful to look for language that implies relationship. If the client says, "My relationship with my lover is critical to me," this is obviously relational behavior. However, if the client says, "My new lover will help me get ahead because of connections," this is obviously more autonomous, nonrelational language. Many individuals are simultaneously relational and autonomous (for example, "I really care about the people at my work, and I find that caring helps us produce more and suggests to me that I am an effective leader.").

In Kohlberg's framework, a medium level of moral development (authority and maintaining social order) is manifested when the client says, "I won't take a new lover because the church says I must be true." It is not necessary to go through long and complex training to learn abstract scoring systems of developmental theory. Clients let us know in the here and now of the interview or family session what their relational moral orientations are.

An important and useful clinical and research task is to translate the ideas of these key developmental theorists into practical frameworks for assessing and understanding the conceptual worlds of our clients. The technology and methods of developmental therapy and DCT are useful for this purpose.

Select one theorist above and present specific ideas for identifying that aspect in the natural language of the client in the interview. For example, following Kohlberg's moral development theory, write client statements representing each of his levels. Then randomize the statements and have colleagues rate them. In this way, it will be possible for you to develop a reliable training instrument that others can use to recognize Kohlberg's levels in the interview.

Then, as with the DCT model presented in this chapter, provide your trainees or research subjects with written statements and have them classify moral development on the basis of your training system.

Combrink-Graham, L. 1985. A developmental model for family systems. *Family Process,* 24: 139–150.

Liddle, H., ed. 1983. *Family therapy collections: Clinical implications of the family life cycle.* Vol. 7. Rockville, Md.: Aspen Systems.

These two writings provide additional data on family life cycle. The first is especially useful in extending Haley's basic model to more complex levels. The second provides useful clinical suggestions for the practice of family therapy.

Family members present themselves at varying cognitive-developmental levels. You may think about your own family. Perhaps you are a predominantly formal-operational individual and you may have had conflicts with a more concrete member of your family. Examine family interaction to see the interplay of these concepts with individuals. In addition, you will find that some families operate predominantly at one level, despite individual differences in cognitive-developmental level.

Research Suggestions

Formalize one of the suggestions above into a research project. For example, generate a list of possible client statements representing each level of Kohlberg's moral development theory. Give these statements to colleagues and see if they can rate these statements with adequate inter-rater agreement. Then, provide your raters with transcripts of actual interviews dealing with moral issues. Can they rate these interviews reliably? Does the moral developmental level of the client, as measured by their natural language in the session, change from the beginning to the end of the interview or treatment series?

Classify one of your own past interviews using the DCT classification system. Have a colleague rate the same interview and calculate your own interrater agreement. Do your clients change the level of their cognitions through their interactions with you?

Answers to Chapter Exercise

Classifying Cognitive-Developmental Level

1. SM—overwhelmed by emotions; frequent topic jumps; some concrete elements as well.
2. CO—some concrete description here.
3. FO—relatively advanced formal; able to see a variety of repeating patterns.
4. D/S—able to operate on systems and see complex relationships.
5. SM—emphasis on direct sensory experience; a certain amount of concreteness present as well.
6. CO—description with no analysis.
7. FO—words such a *pattern* or *typical of me* , which are characteristic of formal thinking.
8. D/S—multiperspective thinking; ability to operate on systems.

   (The final four are more complex and are mixtures of varying levels.)

9. CO and FO—almost any response can be classified into more than one grouping. (Children just about to enter into adolescence present with a mixture of formal and concrete thought.)
10. CO—although primarily still in SM, pieces of conversation are clearly concrete; examples of childish formal thought evident in such statements as "Daddy is always like that." (Most young children are able to see and name patterns in their parents' behavior.)
11. CO/FO—a mixture is characteristic of clients about to make critical transformations. (Our therapeutic task usually is to start at the concrete level and get things clear before we move to the pattern thinking required at the formal level.)
12. FO—particularly clear example of how formal thinking can be preoperational and a problem. (Some clients are so involved in identifying people and patterns that they are unable to see concrete change or the systemic nature of the event.)

3 Developmental Strategies

Specific Interventions to Facilitate Client Cognitive and Affective Development

The Pahmiss-Pahmiss are moved to
   learn to tend the sick or injured
In an emergency, or as a patient nurse.
Man or woman, they may be
Able to heal a burn, set a bone, or
Serve a pregnant woman at the
   time of birth.
They use, with modesty, those skills
Which it is a comfort to know
Are always there, and close at hand.

Yakima Nation Proverb

Developmental counseling and therapy can be described as an integrative, learning-based theory about human growth and change. As clients develop, they follow identifiable patterns. The preceding chapter showed how to identify the various cognitive and affective styles. Given variations in the developmental levels of our clients and the fact that a single client will often present multiple levels, we as professional helpers need to have an array of skills and theories available so that we can change in the moment with the changing needs of the client.

This chapter focuses on two central dimensions of DCT that can aid in helping clients in expanding developmental potential:

1. Specific questions and interventions can be used to facilitate client development in the interview. (These DCT interventions can themselves form the basis for treatment.)

2. Traditional therapy and counseling theory can be organized in a developmental perspective. (DCT uses a learning framework for integrating seemingly competing theories of counseling and therapy.)

As a professional counselor or therapist, you bring a significant number of skills and understandings to the interview. Helpers need to be able to work quickly in crisis situations to help those suffering trauma. We also must be able to be patient with and understand those facing life's challenges. Drawing from the Yakima proverb, we need to use, with modesty, our skills and to learn from and with our clients.

Specific Questioning Strategies for Different Developmental Levels

Basic to the developmental counseling and therapy model is the premise that the actions and thoughts of the therapist affect how the client thinks about and discusses issues in the interview. Some therapists like to think they are totally objective and never influence what their clients say. The term *therapeutic neutrality* describes this point of view.

You cannot *not* affect the client's world. The very fact that you are in an interview with a client changes the client's way of experiencing the problem. DCT talks about mutual influence issues in counseling and therapy. Data clearly indicate that clients talk about what their therapists reinforce. For example, close examination of the client Gloria in the well-known film *Three Approaches to Psychotherapy* showed that the client learned to follow the language system of three different therapists (Meara et al., 1981). In this case, Gloria talked like Carl Rogers when talking to Rogers, like Albert Ellis when talking to Ellis, and like Fritz Perls when talking to Perls.

For each of the four developmental levels, specific developmental strategies have been generated that lead clients to talk about their issues at each developmental level. Although these questions are designed to be maximally open in terms of content, they also attempt to lead the client to discuss issues from a specific developmental frame of reference.

The specific questions presented here are distilled from a wide array of possible questions that can help clients expand their cognitive and affective development. These questions are taken from the Standard Cognitive-Developmental Interview (SCDI) (see Appendix 1). This standard interview provides an extensive list of questions that can help expand client development both horizontally and vertically.

Horizontal development. Individuals and families cannot grow and progress effectively unless a solid developmental foundation has been established. DCT stresses that it is important to help clients expand their understanding at their current level. Thus, expanding sensorimotor functioning may be needed before moving to concrete and formal understandings. Similarly, it is important to help a formal-operational or dialectic/systemic client expand this type of cognition before helping them progress to expanded sensorimotor and concrete levels.

Vertical development. Vertical development involves moving "up" to more complex ways of thinking or "down" to build more solid foundations. Higher is not necessarily better. Vertical development involves helping a client expand developmental potential at other levels than where he or she started. Often, vertical development will be facilitated by a return to basic sensorimotor and concrete cognitions.

For clarity, the following DCT interventions are focused on specific questions. Questions are sometimes controversial in the helping process. Specifically, some authorities state that questions come from the interviewer and do not represent the client's perspective. Furthermore, questions can be used to control the session and disempower the client. DCT argues that the questions presented here are open and actually facilitate clients in talking about their own issues as they see, hear, and feel them. What happens with DCT systematic intervention procedures is that clients and families do talk about issues from their own personal experience and they learn how to take new perspectives on themselves, but always from their own frame of reference. For a more detailed discussion of this important issue, see the discussion of dialectics in Chapters 6 and 7 (Ivey, 1986), where the interview and therapy are conceptualized as holistic in nature. It would be possible, of course, to facilitate client discussion at each of the developmental levels through less directive means. For example, note how the transcript of Carl Rogers (presented later in this chapter) facilitates client discussion at varying cognitive-developmental levels.

Along with the specific questions, DCT strongly recommends extensive use of listening skills, such as encouragement, paraphrasing, reflection of feeling, and summarization. A high level of empathy, helper genuineness, and respect are needed or the systematic questioning procedures can be reduced to meaninglessness. *These questions, particularly at the sensorimotor level, can be quite powerful and moving to the client.* At times, new insights gained by the client can be extremely unsettling. Use these procedures with care, according to the needs of each client. Seek clinical supervision periodically when using these concepts.

Let us begin to examine these strategies using a simple and straightforward exercise. Most of us procrastinate and delay at times. For practice, take the topic of procrastination and work through the following set of questions. Imagine that a counselor is asking you the questions. Write down your answers or speak into an audiotape recorder. As a first step, you are asked to think about yourself and a developmental transition, such as an issue of separation. (This issue could be the first day of school, life at camp as a child, the loss of a loved one, leaving home for college or a major trip, or divorce.) After you have written your response, you can assess your own initial cognitive-developmental level on this issue.

1. *Initial cognitive-developmental level.* Could you tell me what occurs for you when you think of a time of leaving?

_____

_____

_____

_____

Using what you have learned about developmental assessment, at what level did you present your discussion about leaving? Circle one of the following and summarize evidence justifying your decision.

SM CO FO D/S   Cite specific evidence below.

_____

_____

2. *Sensorimotor.* Think of a specific time involving leaving. Can you get a specific image in your mind of that time of leaving? (The more specific, the better.) Most of us have a single, key visual, auditory, or kinesthetic image or recollection of important life scenes. Describe what you see. What do you hear? What do you feel—in particular, what and where do you feel this in your body? (The location of a felt body sense can be especially helpful.)

_____

_____

_____

_____

This overlapping focus on see/hear/feel can be very powerful in helping clients recreate their past experiences and these techniques should be used, with sensitivity and caution, in practice sessions and with your clients. Emotion is easily stirred by this simple exercise if an adequate foundation of trust and understanding has been previously generated.

Expanding horizontal development at the sensorimotor level can include deeper emphasis on images from the past and present, gestalt exercises, imagery techniques, and a wide array of therapeutic alternatives (which are discussed later in this chapter).

3. *Concrete-operational.* Could you give a specific example of a time you left? Describe in detail what happened. How do you feel about leaving?

_____

_____

_____

_____

Concreteness is an important counseling construct. One of the best ways to cope with overly abstract clients is to ask them for concrete, specific examples of issues. When we obtain these specifics, our understanding often changes.

Expansion of development at this level demands that the therapist be willing to encourage and listen to a number of concrete stories and examples. It is in this sometimes frustrating but nonetheless important type of work that the formal-operational counselor often becomes impatient and moves too fast.

4. *Formal-operational.* Does this relate to other situations involving leaving? Is this a pattern? Have you felt this way before? How do you feel when you look at these things in this way?

_____

_____

_____

_____

Many counselors and therapists operate at this level. We tend to like to work in the abstract world of ideas, with an emphasis on self-understanding and repeating patterns of thought and action. Expansion of thinking at this level, of course, can be highly beneficial. Instead of solving just one concrete problem, the client solves many problems by recognizing a common pattern.

5. *Dialectic/systemic.* Select one of the following three questions: (1) Looking back on your responses earlier, what stands out for you? How would you integrate what you have learned? (2) Where did this come from? How might your thoughts and feelings about leaving have originated in your family of origin? (3) From how many different perspectives could you talk about what leaving means for you?

_____

_____

_____

_____

Dialectic/systemic questions help us think about our thinking patterns. Questions at this level help us integrate past thinking into new perspectives. At this level, we begin to see how our emotions, concrete behavior, and formal thought patterns have been influenced by the systems we operate and live in.

In completing this exercise, you will have talked about the question at four different developmental levels. You may find that you simultaneously have taken four different perspectives on the same issue. Even in a brief exercise such as this, people will obtain a valuable new way of looking at an old situation. One of the major goals of many approaches to therapy and counseling is helping clients take a multiperspective point of view of their problems.

The questions above are not new. They are part of the vocabulary and skills of most effective counselors and therapists. What DCT offers that is new is the observation that these questions can be arranged in a systematic sequence similar to that of Piaget's stages of learning. This learning sequence can be applied more consciously in the interview. Rather than moving through each level by having the client answer one or two questions, it is better to help clients develop sufficient understanding at each developmental level before moving on.

Thus, the DCT questioning sequence should be familiar to you from your past courses and your own practice of counseling and therapy. Coupled with developmental assessment, this questioning strategy can help you focus your interventions more precisely and systematically. It will also help you recognize when clients are not responding. A common problem in therapy is the client who talks about emotion but does not deal with it. You can use the DCT model questions to encourage the client to explore emotions at cognitive-developmental levels other than the one he or she is seemingly most comfortable with.

The DCT questioning sequence has also been found clinically useful in work with families. By making minor changes in the DCT sequence (such as the following), helpers can encourage families to view their issues from varying cognitive-developmental perspectives. For example:

You said, your husband was insensitive. Could you give me a concrete example of that?

When he did that, could you get a specific image in your mind? What did you see/hear/feel?

Is this a pattern for the two of you?

Where did that rule come from in your family of origin?

You say you have a lot of conflict. Could the family give me a more specific example of that?

Is there a single image that the four of you could come up with that summarizes the conflict? What do you see/hear/feel?

Does that happen elsewhere in your family? Is that a pattern?

Is there a rule underlying those patterns? Where did you learn those patterns? Is there a flaw in that rule?

Those who work with children and early adolescents will find it useful to adapt these assessment and questioning techniques.   With the excited or over-stimulated child, simple, clear focusing on single elements of sensory experience ("What did you see?" "Hear?" "Feel?") will often help the child calm down. Do not expect a clear linear story from young children until you have allowed them to present the experience in their own way. Then it may be possible to draw out the concrete linear details of what happened.

With older children and adolescents, use of late concrete, causal questions can be especially effective ("*If* you get mad when you are teased, *then* what do the other kids do?") You can follow up by early formal, pattern questions ("Does that happen a lot?" "Have you gotten mad before in other situations?") If challenged sufficiently and patiently, these youngsters can be encouraged to learn formal ways of thinking about themselves and their interactions.

Note that the questioning process for moving children and adolescents to other levels of cognitive development is very similar to that of adult counseling. What is important here, however, is the helper's willingness to move more slowly and build a more solid sensorimotor and concrete foundation before attempting to encourage late concrete or formal thinking patterns.

In-classroom observations of effective teachers reveal that they use the systematic questioning and teaching styles similar to DCT, even though they have not heard of DCT. Less effective teachers tend to use random sequences of learning that fail to take into account children's and adolescents' cognitive styles. Surviving as a teacher at every level demands that one match one's teaching strategy to the cognitive abilities of the learner. We have all had the frustrating experience of listening to some teachers who are so abstract, formal-operational, and analytical that we simply cannot understand them. These teachers might have been more effective if they had been willing to provide more concrete examples.

The systematic questioning strategies of DCT are useful in work with children, adolescents, and adults, both in counseling and in the classroom. Thus far the discussion has focused on cognitive development. Where does emotion come into this picture?

Facilitating Emotional Development

No affect without cognition; no cognition without affect.

Affective development cannot really be separated from cognitive develop-ment. DCT views emotion as a special form of cognition that is always attached to experience and thought. Sensorimotor cognitions and affective cognitions are particularly difficult to separate and are often one and the same. Other forms of emotional expression and development are equally important for full adult development, but experiencing the richness associated with sensorimotor emotional experience is especially important.

Questions that bring out sensorimotor affective and cognitive experience have been reviewed in the preceding section. It is often helpful to anchor emotions in specific parts of the body. Most clients are able to recognize a specific part of their body where the emotion seems to be felt. Both negative and positive emotions can be anchored in this way.

At the later sensorimotor level, it is sometimes helpful simply to provide names for emotions that clients cannot quite describe. Posing questions such as "Do you feel X?" or reflecting feelings and naming the unspoken emotion are also skills useful at this level.

At the early concrete level, the task is to draw out the linear specifics of a problem or situation; the focus here is more on naming emotions that may be attached to various parts of the story. Again, the naming of emotions may be useful as are simple reflections of feeling (e.g., sad, glad, mad). Emotions also tend to be all good or all bad, with relatively little shading of expression.

At the late concrete level, search for causal relations: "Do you feel X because . . . " Skill-training programs all focus on reflecting feelings at this level (see Carkhuff, 1969; Egan, 1990; and Ivey, 1988). The causal reflection of feeling can be helpful in understanding the basis of emotional experience.

At the formal level, the more abstract notions of Rogers (1961) are characteristic. Whereas concrete skill-training programs focus on identifying and clarifying feelings, the formal-operational approach to emotions is to examine emotion itself. This abstract form of emotional reasoning is much used in counselor and therapist training programs. For some, such analysis of emotion makes the therapy process more cognitive than emotional. Reflecting on feelings can be a way for a client and/or therapist to avoid direct contact with the power of emotional reality.

Despite their pitfalls, formal approaches to emotions are an important part of any treatment program. Using these approaches, clients learn how to examine their emotions and discover underlying patterns of how the self relates to past emotional experience. Examples of counselor approaches to emotion for the first three levels follow:

Client: I feel very guilty about my parents. I've ignored them for years. They made me very angry early on, but perhaps now is the time to make amends.

Counselor: (using sensorimotor affect) Take that feeling of guilt. (pause) Where is it located in your body? What image comes to your mind? What do you see? Hear? Feel?

Counselor: (using concrete affect) You feel guilty because you've ignored your parents for years. You felt angry before, but now your feeling is one more of *caring* ? (The counselor here names the unsaid feeling but uses a questioning tone of voice so the client can define the feeling.)

Counselor: (using formal affect) You seem to have a pattern of feeling anger toward your parents that now seems to be changing. You're becoming aware that your feelings are changing over time. As that happens, how do you feel about yourself in this process? (focus on internal self and affective development) You have some mixed feelings about your parents, which seem to center on guilt and anger, but at the same time, I hear you striving for something more. Could you go further with that? (focus on complexity)

The dialectic/systemic approach to emotional development is the most complex. The central focus is on examining and, at times, encouraging the client to experience varying emotional reactions to the same situation. Much of the emotional work at the prior three levels is oriented toward identifying and clarifying emotions. The primary purpose of dialectic/systemic approaches to emotion is to encourage understanding of the complexity, context, and developmental history of emotional experience. As one encounters this complexity, it is easy to become lost in abstractions and intellectualization. Yet, at times it is possible at this level to integrate the other three levels in a more holistic, emotional experience in which the client both experiences and reflects on feelings.

There are multiple possibilities for exploring emotion at the dialectic/systemic level, as follows:

Approach 1: Emotions develop over time
As I hear it, your feelings about your parents have changed over time. Could we explore that change in emotion? First, let's look at how you felt as a child toward them, then at your teenage years, and then at what is occurring now in your life. What events happened at each stage leading to those changes?

Approach 2: Transference issues
When you mentioned guilt, you looked at me questioningly. Could you go back to that moment and tell me how you felt and what you were thinking just as you said that? Do you have any fantasies about what I was thinking and feeling? (Other issues between the client and the counselor could be explored in the same fashion. Here the client learns that he or she is repeating old issues in the here and now of the interview with the therapist.)

Approach 3: Family systems
Your feelings and thoughts were generated in a family context, perhaps out of some family rule or rules. What rules did your family operate under? Specifically, can you identify some things that are important in your family that showed up in repeating messages you got as a child? What was your role in the family? How did your family relate to the extended family? The neighborhood and community?

Obviously, there are many possible forms of dialectic/systemic approaches to emotional understanding. In all the above approaches, the client learns how to consider emotional experience in a broader context. This type of complex exploration of emotions can be beneficial, but clearly, complexity is not necessarily better unless accompanied by sensorimotor experience and concrete action.

Think about your own parents and your feelings toward them. Can you identify sensorimotor images and feelings, concrete emotions surrounding a specific situation, patterns of feelings, and how all these feelings might change in context?

Can you develop an image of your parents when you were younger? What do you see? Hear? Feel? Can you locate that feeling in your body?

_____

_____

Describe a specific situation that occurs to you in relation to your parents. In sequence, what happened? Name the feelings you had at that time or now. Can you write the causal statement, "I feel X because . . . " ?

_____

_____

Did those feelings occur in other situations with your parents? Was there a pattern?

_____

_____

Over time, as you view the image, the situation, and the pattern, do the meanings change? Can you see varying perspectives in which you might feel differently at different times?

_____

_____

Following is a discussion of counseling and therapy theories and how they may be used to facilitate client cognitive and affective development. You will find that the questions and concepts presented thus far in this chapter can be useful additions to your work in other theoretical orientations.

Relating Counseling and Therapy Theories to Development

The changing "seasons" of human development are summarized in the developmental sphere of Figure 3-1. The four cognitive levels are represented as circular movement through the life space. The effective therapist meets the client where he or she is, using developmentally appropriate interventions, expanding client developmental potential before attempting to move vertically (either "higher" to the next stage or deeper, returning to foundation levels).

Note especially the core of the developmental sphere and how it returns to the beginning. Having achieved so-called higher levels of consciousness is not the end of development. We always return to the beginning again as we face new challenges and new developmental tasks. There is no end to development.

Higher consciousness is not necessarily better. Recall the flower . . .

Consider the following from *Developmental Therapy* (Ivey, 1986, p. 111). Which is the "higher" consciousness?

Sensorimotor	Seeing and experiencing a flower
Concrete	Placing the flower in an arrangement
Formal	Writing a poem about the arrangement
Dialectic	Analyzing the poem about the flower (or analyzing the analysis of the poem about the flower)

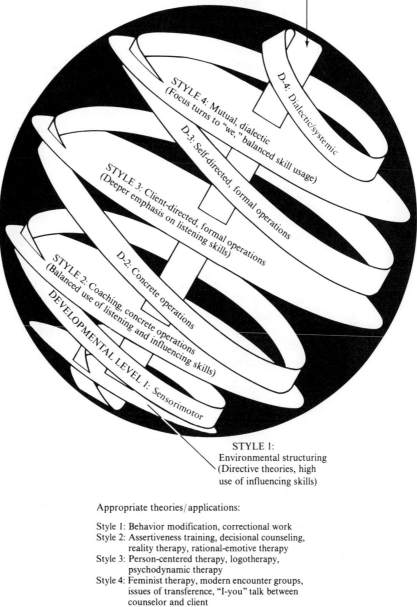

And with each problem solved, each developmental task met, you and the client must return to the beginning or to another level to work on other developmental opportunities and problems.

STYLE 4: Mutual, dialectic (Focus turns to "we," balanced skill usage)

D-4: Dialectic/systemic

D-3: Self-directed, formal operations

STYLE 3: Client-directed, formal operations (Deeper emphasis on listening skills)

D-2: Concrete operations

STYLE 2: Coaching, concrete operations (Balanced use of listening and influencing skills)

DEVELOPMENTAL LEVEL 1: Sensorimotor

STYLE 1:
Environmental structuring
(Directive theories, high use of influencing skills)

Appropriate theories/applications:

Style 1: Behavior modification, correctional work
Style 2: Assertiveness training, decisional counseling, reality therapy, rational-emotive therapy
Style 3: Person-centered therapy, logotherapy, psychodynamic therapy
Style 4: Feminist therapy, modern encounter groups, issues of transference, "I-you" talk between counselor and client

Figure 3-1. Four Therapeutic Environmental Styles and Their Relationship to Developmental Therapy. The developmental theory of psychotherapy is based on the paradox of development: to arrive where we started and to know the place for the first time. Life is simulatneously a journey, a destination, and a state of being. (This diagram was first drawn by Lois T. Grady and is used here with her permission.)

Have we arrived at the "end" only to begin again?

The sphere also gives us another way to think about the whole person. The words *fully rounded* come to mind. If a person or family is to reach developmental potential, they need a balance of sensorimotor, concrete, formal, and dialectic/systemic cognitive and affective understandings. Imagine a distorted sphere heavy at the top with abstract cognitions but spindly at the bottom, having little sensorimotor or concrete foundation. Or think about a pear-shaped sphere, heavy on the bottom but thin on the top.

The developmental sphere also shows us that different theoretical approaches seem to relate better to some client developmental levels than others. For example, if the client is very concrete, a formal Rogerian approach may be ineffective and a behavioral intervention may be needed.

The developmental sphere suggests that counseling and therapy theory can be organized into four basic types. As you review this abbreviated list, circle those theories and methods with which you personally feel skilled. Underline those you would like to add to your repertoire. Finally, since the list is incomplete, you may wish to add theories and techniques you believe are representative of this cognitive-developmental level.

Sensorimotor theories and techniques. Counselors and therapists tend to use structuring methods, such as behavioral modification, gestalt exercises, relaxation training, and environment interventions (including nutrition and physical exercise). Drug therapy and the structuring of environment (as in a psychiatric hospital) are another type of sensorimotor orientation.

List additional skills, techniques and theories.

_____

_____

_____

_____

Concrete-operational theories and techniques. The therapist operates more as a coach and may use behavioral methods such as thought stopping, assertiveness training, and life-skills training. Reality therapy, structured problem-solving methods, decisional counseling, and vocational placement exemplify methods of this level. Late concrete-operational level is represented by the logical-consequences concepts of Adler and Dreikurs, and the "A-B-C" analysis of logic used by Ellis in his rational-emotive therapy.

List additional skills, techniques, and theories.

_____

_____

_____

_____

Formal-operational theories and techniques. As client thinking patterns mature, counselors tend to use formal modes of treatment (such as Rogerian and psychodynamic approaches and logotherapy). Most counselors and therapists are formal thinkers and thus often feel most comfortable with these theories even though many of their clients may be at a more concrete level.

List additional skills, techniques, and theories.

_____

_____

_____

_____

Dialectic/systemic theories and techniques. Therapists and clients at this level often operate in a more mutual fashion. The individual begins to use data to form multiple perspectives and sees the self as operating in a world of complex systems. Feminist therapy is an example of this approach, in that women are encouraged to note how much individual "pathology" results from a sexist system. Cultural identity theories (see Chapter 7) and much of traditional family therapy are in this mode. Issues of transference and countertransference in the psychodynamic tradition are also illustrative of dialectic/systemic level.

List additional skills, techniques, and theories.

_____

_____

_____

_____

At this point, you may want to review the above list and your own additions; they represent your own evolving eclectic or metatheoretical approach to counseling and psychotherapy.

Working from the developmental sphere helps us remember that if the client wants to examine the nature of self, it does little good to offer concrete assertiveness training. In this case, Rogerian and psychodynamic concepts may be more appropriate. Similarly, if the client is at the concrete level, he or she may have real difficulty in understanding the psychoanalytic or feminist dialectician.

We need to match our therapeutic style to the developmental needs of the client. The therapist, while matching the theoretical framework to client CDL, also needs to include appropriate mismatching. For example, after a formal client has generated a good sense of self, it may be wise to add Gestalt exercises to enhance sensory experience and assertiveness training to provide concrete action skills. This type of mismatching challenges clients to expand their developmental potential at new levels of being.

We should not stereotype different theories or their advocates. Effective therapists of many different persuasions appear to follow the systematic, sequential, developmental sequences suggested here. Rogerian client-centered therapy is considered as predominantly formal-operational in nature, since it focuses on patterns of the self. However, Rogers does work at multiple levels, as this excerpt from *On Becoming a Person* (Rogers, 1961, p. 93) illustrates. (Commentary from a DCT standpoint in the second column is from Ivey's *Developmental Therapy* [1986, pp. 114–115].)

Therapy Transcript [1]

Mrs. O: I have the feeling it isn't guilt. (pause, she weeps) Of course, I mean, I can't verbalize it yet. (then with a rush of emotion) It's just being terribly hurt.

Rogers: M-hm. It isn't guilt except in the sense of being wounded somehow.

Mrs. O: (weeping) It's—you know—often I've been guilty of it myself, but in later years when I've heard parents say to their children "Stop crying," I've had a feeling, a hurt, as though, well, why should they tell them to stop crying?

They feeling [*sic*] sorry for themselves, and who can feel more adequately sorry for himself than the child. Well, that is sort of what—I mean, as thought I mean, I thought that they should let them cry. And—feel sorry for him too, maybe. In a rather objective kind of way. Well, that's—that's something of the kind of thing I've been experiencing. I mean now—just right now. And in—in—

Rogers: That catches a little more the flavor of the feeling that it's almost as if you're really weeping for yourself.

Mrs. O: Yeah, and again, you see there's conflict. Our culture is such that, I mean, one doesn't indulge in self-pity. But this isn't —I mean, I feel it doesn't quite have that connotation. It may have.

DCT Analysis

Here Mrs. Oak is her feelings. There is no separation of self from emotion, no separation of subject from object. This experience of emotion is important for working through. Some theorists would prefer to work more in depth at this level than Rogers does in this excerpt. (This exemplifies sensorimotor experience.)

Mrs. Oak's transfer of her own feelings to the children is an example of preoperational, magical feelings. Her thoughts may indeed be correct, but she is demonstrating somewhat inappropriate affect. We also see the beginnings of concrete operations when Mrs. Oak says, "I've had a feeling   . . . "

Mrs. Oak is now thinking about her feelings and exhibiting formal operations on them by thinking about them.

Rogers supports the formal-operational thinking and clarifies it with a reflection of meaning.

Here we see a highly intellectualized, formal-operational analysis of emotions that approaches the fourth level of postformal thinking. Nonetheless, the intellectual analysis remains rooted in sensorimotor experience. The client is still weeping. This is a particularly beautiful example of simultaneously working at several cognitive levels, which is possible in effective psychotherapy. Some clients have the problem that all they are able to do is think about feelings. Stuck in the epistemology of *episteme*, or knowledge, they are unable to experience *noesis* and the transformation back to sensorimotor experiencing.   [That is, being stuck in a formal way of thinking, they are unable to experience at a sensorimotor level.]

[1] From Rogers, Carl. *On Becoming a Person. Copyright © 1961, Houghton Mifflin Company.*

Depending on the specific developmental task of the client, suitable treatment interventions may vary. Our very human clients are too complex to "wrap up" with a few quick words and concepts. Objections could be made by other theorists to Rogers's work with Mrs. Oak. Fritz Perls (gestalt therapy), for example, might object to Rogers taking Mrs. Oak so quickly to intellectual generalizations. Gestalt therapists often prefer to develop a more comprehensive foundation in sensorimotor experiencing before turning to analysis and issues of meaning. The goal of both gestalt theorists and cognitive-behaviorists would be behavior change in addition to cognitive growth.

In practice, many theorists and practitioners follow a common sequencing in the therapy process. Effective helpers seem to ground their work in sensorimotor experience, examine concrete action, and then reflect on patterns of experience. This learning sequence seems to undergird many different therapies. Some less effective practitioners try to force or allow their clients to work at only one cognitive-developmental level. Then when clients do not improve or change, they label the client resistant or lacking motivation for change.

As a final step in this chapter, let us explore how to integrate DCT practice and theory using the many alternative modes of helping available in the developmental sphere.

Moving Clients Through Developmental Levels Using Varying Treatments

A client facing divorce must work through a variety of developmental tasks. Before the divorce, his or her overall cognitive-developmental level may be complex formal-operational. During the divorce, the client may be able to think effectively on the job. But when it comes to dealing with the emotional and concrete aspects of divorce, the same person may be totally nonfunctional. Sophisticated perspective taking may be lost. In many ways, the client working through divorce is preoperational.

Following is a list of some of the developmental tasks faced by a person going through divorce (or the end of any long-term relationship). Some of the tasks are primarily concrete (finding a place to live); others are sensorimotor (allowing oneself to cry and grieve); still others are formal (learning to reflect on one's self and why the relationship ended).

Circle the level(s) of each task as you see it. Use the space to make notes about your family member, yourself, or a friend or client as they faced this task. How effectively did they (or you, working through your own separation) move through these tasks?

SM CO FO D/S   Obtaining a lawyer _____

SM CO FO D/S   Finding new housing _____

SM CO FO D/S   Developing a new support network _____

SM CO FO D/S   Working effectively on the job or obtaining work _____

SM CO DO D/S   Relating with children_____

SM CO FO D/S   Planning finances and managing money _____

SM CO FO D/S   Starting new dating relationships_____

SM CO FO D/S   Acknowledging feelings and emotional experience_____

SM CO FO D/S   Maintaining suitable exercise/health program_____

SM CO FO D/S   Eating nutritional meals_____

SM CO FO D/S   Gaining a positive self-concept_____

SM CO FO D/S   Relating with family of origin_____

SM CO FO D/S   Other_____

SM CO FO D/S   Other_____

Few going through divorce handle all these issues effectively. Some of the above problems are best solved by concrete-operational methods, such as direct advice and decision making. Other problems require formal therapies and family systems approaches.

The divorcing person must also deal in sufficient depth with emotional experience. At the sensorimotor level, you may see a client overwhelmed by the facts of the situation. Crying, random behavior, and even the adult version of the two-year-old tantrum may occur. Or the purpose of sensorimotor functioning may be to deny emotions. Furthermore, a treatment plan may involve other sensorimotor modalities, such as meal planning and an exercise program. Expansion of such sensorimotor foundations is an example of horizontal development.

Moving to concrete operations, divorcing clients may be unable to act. They may need concrete advice about what they need to do next to find housing or a lawyer or to make adequate financial arrangements. At times, even the individual who has always carefully planned ahead finds that the concrete specifics of a divorce are simply too much to handle. Direct decisional counseling is often helpful at this point.

If a solid foundation of concrete and sensorimotor experience has been developed, the divorcing client may be able to move vertically and recognize repeating patterns of behavior and thought that caused the marriage breakup. Divorce can lead to massive self-examination, and here Rogerian and psychodynamic theories are most helpful. However, some divorcing clients will use formal analysis as a way to avoid critical expression of deeper feelings and taking concrete action.

At the late formal level, the client may be able to recognize that he or she is repeating with a dating partner the pattern played out in the divorcing relationship. Here the client can examine patterns of patterns, often through some type of psychodynamic formulation.

At the more complex dialectic/systemic level, the client may become more aware of context. Women may see divorce as a gender issue related to male oppression (and men may feel the same way but may view oppression from another perspective). An important goal for therapy is helping this type of client move to a more multiperspective frame, perhaps through systems formulations such as family therapy or feminist counseling.

Another type of dialectic/systemic reasoning may appear when the client notes that one of the critical issues in the divorce was perfectionism, a trait that has been "in the family" for generations. Family systems thinking integrated in the interview can be especially helpful. Or you may wish to engage in couple and/or family counseling and work with a larger group.

Finally, examination of transference and countertransference patterns in psychodynamic work requires dialectic/systemic thinking, since the nature of therapist/client relationships is explored. In the later stage of psychoanalytic treatment, clients and their therapists will use this form of reasoning as clients discover that they are repeating their past pattern of relationships in relating to the therapist. For example, clients going through divorce will often relate to their therapists as they related to their ex-spouses. The ability to reflect on oneself and one's system of relationships requires highly advanced abstract thinking. Full psychoanalytic treatment is seldom successful unless the client is highly verbal and abstract. (Chapter 6 presents DCT's practical approach to this critical issue.)

No matter how sophisticated the thinking pattern, there always seems to be something more to learn, experience, and understand. Thus, as we reach the so-called highest level of dialectic thinking, we may note that the core of our being returns us to the beginning. Once we solve our problems, no matter how complex our thinking, we find ourselves needing to return to beginning sensorimotor awareness and concrete action. You must take the sophisticated awareness of the intellectual dialectic level (the world of abstractions and ideas) back to concrete awareness and action, or no movement or growth will occur.

The outline of varying levels of treatment corresponds with the increasingly eclectic orientations to helping. However, DCT suggests that eclecticism can be informed by a broader, neo-Piagetian theory of learning. DCT is compatible with existing modes of helping and adds a rationale for much of eclectically oriented approaches to helping.

Chapter Summary

A smooth blending of both horizontal and vertical development is recommended by DCT. Thus, the specific questions and recommended DCT interventions can be adapted and integrated into the practice of many other helping theories. The specifics of the model include (1) assessing the developmental level of the client, (2) matching your theory to the specific needs of the client, (3) changing your approach as the client grows and develops, and (4) modifying and adapting your theory of choice (if working with a single theory) as your client changes.

Counseling and therapy theories can be organized according to the four developmental levels: (1) body work, experiential awareness, and environmental structuring theories are oriented toward sensorimotor growth; (2) assertiveness training and problem-solving approaches are examples of concrete-operational methods; (3) Rogerian client-centered and psychodynamic orientations are related to formal operations; 4) feminist therapy, Black consciousness raising, and family systems are examples of the dialectic/systemic level.

Each therapeutic system also operates at multiple levels. Different theories of counseling and therapy seem to be more effective and more focused on varying developmental levels. However, each theory in some way devotes some attention to all levels.

DCT offers specific questioning sequences oriented toward the four developmental levels. These interventions can be used by themselves as a treatment alternative, or they may be integrated into various types of counseling and psychotherapy practice.

Affective development cannot truly be separated from cognitive development. When one moves to a developmental model and discovers the power of sensorimotor experiencing, it is easy to forget the value of emotional experience at the concrete, formal, and dialectic/systemic levels. The latter, in particular, needs more attention in counseling and therapy, as it provides an integration of emotion missing from concrete and formal approaches to emotion currently popular in counseling and therapy.

Human experience is so complex that no theory (including this developmental model) is sufficient to describe all events. The core of the developmental sphere shows us that we constantly return to the beginning for further exploration of new developmental tasks.

CAUTION! Experience has shown that questioning, particularly on issues of imaging, and making horizontal movement at the sensorimotor level is very powerful. A sophisticated counselor commented, "I always thought I was good at feelings. Now I know that this was only at the formal level. At the sensorimotor level, I experience a deeper form of emotion that I have been trying to escape from much of my life." Many participants in DCT training have experienced real, powerful emotions when using the visualization techniques suggested here. Always work within professional ethical standards and with a suitable consultant or supervisor.

Theory into Practice

As we take the theory of developmental questioning strategies into practice, the following specific objectives will be emphasized. By the end of this section, you may be able to

1. Identify specific theoretical orientations using the perspective of the developmental sphere.
2. Develop specific goals for each of the developmental levels.
3. Ask specific questions in a role-played interview in which your "client" will respond at the predicted developmental level.

Several counseling and therapy theories and techniques are listed below. Classify each theory or technique as being primarily oriented within one or two of the four developmental levels. Use the space for your possible disagreements with that classification or notes from conversation with others in your group. If you don't know a theory or technique well, either write down your general impression or leave that item blank.

SM CO FO D/S Relaxation training

_____

_____

SM CO FO D/S Movement and dance therapy

_____

_____

SM CO FO D/S Play therapy for children

_____

_____

SM CO FO D/S Behavior modification

_____

_____

SM CO FO D/S Decisional counseling (that is, vocational choice)

_____

_____

SM CO FO D/S Assertiveness training

_____

_____

SM CO FO D/S Haley's problem-solving family approach

_____

_____

SM CO FO D/S Cognitive-behavioral (Beck, Ellis)

_____

_____

SM CO FO D/S Adolescent self-esteem group

_____

_____

_____

SM CO FO D/S Rogerian client-centered

_____

_____

SM CO FO D/S Psychodynamic therapy

_____

_____

SM CO FO D/S Family therapy (as generally practiced)

_____

_____

SM CO FO D/S Feminist therapy

_____

_____

SM CO FO D/S Encounter groups

_____

_____

SM CO FO D/S Transactional analysis

_____

_____

In the previous theoretical discussion, it was noted that most theories and techniques exemplify several developmental levels. Provide examples of how one theory or technique from the above list can be related to all four developmental levels.

Next, examine your own conception of helping. What theories and methods do you find most helpful? Sort out your conceptions of helping using the following format. What specific skills and theories have you mastered that seem to be appropriate at varying developmental levels? Do you find yourself able to work at all developmental levels, or are you stronger at some levels than at others?

Theory 1

Sensorimotor:_____

_____

Concrete:_____

_____

Formal:_____

_____

Dialectic/systemic:_____

_____

Your Own Theory and Methods

Sensorimotor:_____

_____

Concrete:_____

_____

Formal:_____

_____

Dialectic/systemic:_____

_____

Specific Questions and Goals for Each Developmental Level

Applying developmental questions can be made easier by practice with the sequence and its variations. Box 3-1, on the next page, is an abbreviated developmental strategies questioning sequence that has been found useful in early practice. A more expanded set of questions oriented to eight levels can be found in Appendixes 1 and 2.

Ask a partner to role-play a client. Sit down with this list of questions in your lap. (Don't try to memorize the questions at this point.) Go through each stage, step-by-step. After you have gone through the series, exchange roles and go through them again.

Stop after each step in the interview and discuss with your client what has just happened. Were you and your client able to achieve the goal of that particular interview segment?

In this exercise, it is particularly important to share information with your client. Tell him or her what is about to happen and what your goal is. Then, together evaluate whether or not that goal was achieved. Manthei (1988) argues that such sharing of goals and methods is a useful counseling technique or style in itself. We tend to overmystify our techniques. Many clients appreciate an openness about our purposes and may be more willing to take risks if they understand what is going to happen and what we are looking for.

Box 3-1. Developmental Strategies Questioning Sequence (abbreviated)

---

1. Opening Presentation of Issue

Could you tell me what you'd like to talk about today?
What happens for you when you focus on your family?

Goal: Obtain story of from 50 to 100 words. Assess overall functioning of client on varying cognitive-developmental levels.

Use questions, encourages, paraphrasing, and reflection of feeling to bring out data, but try to impact the client's story minimally. Get the story as he or she constructs it. Summarize key facts and feelings about what the client has said before moving on.

2. Sensorimotor/Elemental

Could you think of one visual image that occurs to you in that situation?
What are you seeing? Hearing? Feeling? It will be helpful to locate the feeling in the body.

Goal: Elicit one example and then ask what was seen/heard/felt. Aim for here-and-now experiencing. Accept randomness.

Summarize at the end of the segment. You may want to ask "What one thing stands out for you from this?"

3. Concrete/Situational

Could you give me a specific example of the situation/issue/problem?
Can you describe your feelings in the situation?

Goal: Obtain a linear description of the event. At late concrete operations, look for if/then causal reasoning.

Ask "What did he or she do? Say? What happened before? What happened next? What happened after?" Possibly pose the question "If he or she did X, then what happened?" Summarize before moving on. For affective development, ask "What did you feel?" The statement "You felt X because . . ." helps integrate cognition with affect at this level.

4. Formal/Pattern

Does this happen in other situations? (or) Is this a pattern for you?
Do you feel that way in other situations? Are those feelings a pattern for you?

Goal: Talk about repeating patterns and situations and/or talk about self.

Ask "What were you saying to yourself when that happened? Have you felt like that in other situations?" Again, reflect feelings and paraphrase as appropriate. Summarize key facts and feelings carefully before moving on.

(continues)

Box 3-1. Developmental Strategies Questioning Sequence (abbreviated) *(continued)*

---

5. Dialectic/Systemic/Integrative

Begin by summarizing all that has been said. Ask "How do you put together/organize all that you told me? What one thing stands out for you most? How many different ways could you describe your feelings and how they change?"

Goals: (1) to obtain an integrated summary of what has been said; (2) to enable the client to see how reality is co-constructed, not developed from a single view; (3) to obtain different perspectives on the same situation and be aware that each is just one perspective; (4) to note flaws in the present construction, co-construction, or perspective, and move to action.

As we move toward more complex reasoning, several options are open. Before using any of them, summarize what the client has been saying over the entire series of questions.

Integration: How do you put together/organize all that you told me? What one thing stands out for you most?

Co-construction: What rule were you (they) operating under? Where did that rule come from? How might someone else (perhaps another family member) describe the situation? (Feelings can be examined using the same questions.)

Multiple perspectives: How could we describe this from the point of view of some other person or using another theoretical framework or language system? How else might we put it together using another framework?

Deconstruction and action: Can you see some flaws in the reasoning or in the patterns of feelings above? How might you change the rules? Given these possibilities, what action might you take?

A Role-Played Practice Session for Developmental Strategies

Step 1: Divide into Practice Groups

Get acquainted with each other informally before beginning.

Step 2: Select a Group Leader

The leader's task is to ensure that the group follows the specific steps of the practice session.

Step 3: Assign Roles for the Practice Session

- Role-played client. The role-played client will be cooperative, talk freely about the topic, and not give the interviewer a difficult time.
- Interviewer. The interviewer will work through the developmental strategies, going through all levels without stopping. It is wise to have the list of questions available and to refer to them throughout the session.

- Observers 1 and 2. Both observers will fill out the same feedback form, summarizing their observations. Does the client talk about issues as predicted in the questioning sequence? Does the counselor enable the client to reach the specific criteria for discussion at each developmental level?

Step 4: Plan the Session

- The interviewer and client need first to agree on the topic. The interviewer may wish to facilitate client talk using his or her own natural style of interviewing. A useful topic for this session may be procrastination or an interpersonal conflict in the past or present.
- The client may think through how he or she wishes to talk about the agreed-on topic throughout the session.
- The two observers can examine the feedback forms and be ready to complete the form for the most valuable feedback.

Step 5: Conduct a 15-Minute Interviewing Session

The interviewer and client will go through the specific stages while the observers keep track of their progress and note the achievement of criterion levels. It is helpful to videotape and/or audiotape practice sessions.

Step 6: Provide Immediate Feedback and Complete Notes (5 Minutes)

- Again, it is helpful for the interviewer to ask the client "What stands out for you from this practice session?" Allow the client time to provide true personal reactions to the practice.
- The interviewer needs the same opportunity to reflect on what happened. The client may ask the interviewer for his or her personal reactions to the session.
- At this point, the observers should sit back and let the participants take control. Use this time to complete your classification and notes.

Step 7: Review the Practice Session and Provide Feedback
(15 to 30 Minutes)

The interviewer should be the person who asks for feedback rather than getting it without being asked. The observers can share their observations from the feedback form. As usual, feedback should be specific, and concrete and nonjudgmental. Pay attention to strengths of the interview. Just as with clients, trainees will grow and develop from getting feedback on what they do right. Pay special attention to each level and how the client responded each time.

Feedback Sheet with Criteria for Each Level

1. Opening presentation of issue. How does the client organize and describe the problem?

Check all that apply: ___ S/M   ___ CO ___ FO ___ D/S

Specific evidence for this assessment:

_____

_____

2. Sensorimotor. Were the following accomplished? Check all that apply.

___ Client was able to describe a single image of the situation/problem/issue.

___ Client described what was seen in sensory terms (ideally, in present tense).

___ Sounds were described.

___ Feelings were discussed that were closely related to or integrated with cognition.

___ Random elements of the situation were presented.

___ Client located feelings in the body.

Cite specific evidence for this assessment:

_____

_____

_____

3. Concrete. Were the following accomplished? Check all that apply.

___ Client described a specific example of the situation/problem/issue.

___ Concrete details were presented.

___ Linear sequences, with cause-and-effect thinking, were presented,

___ More than one situation was presented, but not seen as pattern.

___ Feelings such as "I felt X" or "I felt X about Y" were presented.

Cite specific evidence for this assessment:

_____

_____

_____

4. Formal. Were the following accomplished? Check all that apply.

___ Client discussed two or more situations and recognized similarities.

___ Client discussed repeating patterns of behavior, thought, or action.

(continues)

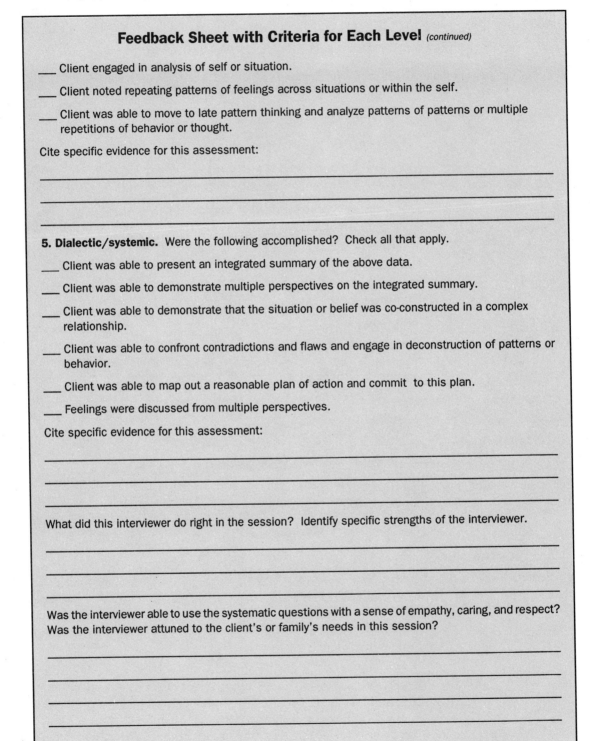

Feedback Sheet with Criteria for Each Level *(continued)*

___ Client engaged in analysis of self or situation.

___ Client noted repeating patterns of feelings across situations or within the self.

___ Client was able to move to late pattern thinking and analyze patterns of patterns or multiple repetitions of behavior or thought.

Cite specific evidence for this assessment:

_____

_____

_____

5. Dialectic/systemic. Were the following accomplished? Check all that apply.

___ Client was able to present an integrated summary of the above data.

___ Client was able to demonstrate multiple perspectives on the integrated summary.

___ Client was able to demonstrate that the situation or belief was co-constructed in a complex relationship.

___ Client was able to confront contradictions and flaws and engage in deconstruction of patterns or behavior.

___ Client was able to map out a reasonable plan of action and commit to this plan.

___ Feelings were discussed from multiple perspectives.

Cite specific evidence for this assessment:

_____

_____

_____

What did this interviewer do right in the session? Identify specific strengths of the interviewer.

_____

_____

_____

Was the interviewer able to use the systematic questions with a sense of empathy, caring, and respect? Was the interviewer attuned to the client's or family's needs in this session?

_____

_____

_____

_____

Client and Counselor Developmental Level in a Role-Played
Family Counseling Practice Session

An extension of the preceding exercise is in a role-played family counseling session. Practice groups of six work best in this situation. Given the complexity of the many personalities, video-or audiotape is especially useful. From 1 to 2 hours will be required for development and debriefing of the family session.

Step 1: Select Four to Six Participants

Two of these will be co-therapists and the remainder constitute the family. The rest of the members of the class or workshop will observe the entire process and later serve as process consultants who reflect on the session.

Step 2: Have the Workshop Leader Assume the Leadership Role

Due to the complexity of the process, the workshop leader needs to ensure that the group follows the specific steps of the practice session.

Step 3: Assign Roles for the Practice Session

- Role-played family. For this session, any family organization may be used. This could range from counseling of couples to gay-lesbian families to single-parent families. The family or couple will be cooperative and talk freely about the topic. A useful first topic is difficulty in couple communication or a teenager who is acting out.
- Therapists. Two therapists or counselors can work together for this session.
- Workshop/class observers. All remaining individuals in the session will sit in a circle around the family or couple.

Step 4: Plan the Session

- The family needs to define a problem or reason for coming to the family session. The family can leave the room and define their roles and the problem they wish to present. The nature of the problem will be a surprise to the therapists.
- The two therapists may wish to think through their relationship briefly. Their task is to use the standard set of developmental questions with the family. Direct the questions to the whole family and note which individuals respond first. This will indicate family functioning. Also ask the same questions of other family members and note different levels of cognitive and affective functioning. The first task of the co-therapists is to define the family problem, as in the family exercise in Chapter 2.

Next, it will be helpful to have the family describe one concrete example of their general family problem. The therapists should use concrete-level questioning skills, as indicated in the developmental questioning sequence. Although it may feel artificial at first, direct questions to specific family members or specific subsystems of the family so that they can work together to answer the questions. Ask other family members to assist at times of confusion and stalemate.

This procedure can be followed by questioning at the sensorimotor level, then at the formal and at the dialectic/systemic levels. The task for the therapists is to demonstrate that they can affect the way the family discusses their issues in the interview, just as in the individual examples.

■ The family observers have several roles: (1) They all can be participants/observers; the therapists should feel free to stop the interview in mid-session and ask the observers for help and suggestions. (2) Four observers should be assigned to various members of the family. Their task is to identify the cognitive-developmental level of one family member. Two observers may watch the therapists and assess the CDL of their questions. The rest of the group should note the general CDL of the family as a whole. Use the same feedback forms for the individual practice session as in the preceding exercise.

You will find, for example, that some families present at the concrete level and others at the formal level. Then, within the family, different members may be talking about the problem from different levels.

Step 5: Conduct a 30-Minute Interviewing Session

The therapists and family will discuss the varying perceptions of the problem for five minutes while the observers keep track of their progress and classify the statements of each. Again, it is helpful to videotape or audiotape practice sessions.

Families often confuse even the most effective therapists. Thus, the therapists should feel free to stop for a moment in the middle of the session and ask the external observers for their reactions and suggestions. (This training procedure is similar to the "family team" concept.)

Step 6: Provide Immediate Feedback and Complete Notes (10 Minutes)

This is a highly structured session, and there is often immediate personal need to "process" and discuss the session. In particular, it is helpful for the therapists to ask the family "What stands out for you from this practice session?" Allow yourself some time to provide true personal reactions to the practice.

At this point, the observers should sit back and let the participants take control. Use this time to complete your classification and notes.

Step 7: Review the Practice Session and Provide Feedback (15 to 30 Minutes)

It is important in giving feedback to allow the therapists and family receiving the feedback to be in charge. At this point, the observers can share their observations. As usual, feedback should be specific, concrete, and nonjudgmental. Pay attention to strengths of the interview.

Generalization: Taking Developmental Questions Home

The question now is how to take the concepts of developmental strategies for horizontal and vertical development into your daily life and into practice.

Following are some activities that can be especially useful in ensuring that these basic ideas are used practically.

Activity 1: Personal Practice with Individuals in Daily Life

A beginning step toward useful generalization of developmental assessment is to practice these skills with those you come into contact with in daily life. When friends or family talk to you about issues, what cognitive-developmental level are they using? When a friend or a family member has a specific issue, ask their permission to go through the developmental strategies questioning sequence. Share the sequence with them and discuss each level as you work through it.

You will find that your understanding and ability to communicate with children is improved when you use the DCT framework. The simple language and concepts of the sensorimotor and concrete levels are basic to communicating with children. With practice, you will find that children can engage in a type of formal pattern thinking. DCT proposes that early adolescents particularly can benefit from encouragement from adults in learning formal pattern thinking.

It is particularly important to recall in this exercise, and in the following exercise, that sensorimotor questions and imaging procedures are powerful and can easily cause tears and deep emotional experiencing. Use these skills ethically, with sensitivity and care.

Summarize your impressions of this experience and obtain specific feedback from your friends or family members about their reactions.

Activity 2: Observation and Practice with a Family, Classroom, Group, or Organization

Observe a group in interaction. Note the cognitive-developmental level and the communication style of the family members, teacher, students, and group members. What impact do leaders and key family members have on the group?

Using the same method and format as in Activity 1, obtain the consent of a classroom, group, couple, or family. Let them know before you start the purpose of your interview and show them the questions. Take them through the questioning sequence and report on (1) the cognitive-developmental level of the group and its members, and (2) what happened as you went through each of the additional four levels. (You may want to add some more extensive questions from the Standard Cognitive-Developmental Interview in Appendix 1).

Again, be particularly sensitive to and aware of ethical and professional issues surrounding sensorimotor imaging. Report on your observations and obtain feedback from the group members.

Activity 3: The Acid Test—The Interview

It will be most helpful if you can find a recent audiotape or videotape of your own interviewing style and theory. Listen to this tape and classify yourself and the client as to developmental level. Particularly note the developmental level of your questions and the level at which your client responded to them.

What has been your theoretical orientation? Is it primarily concrete, formal, sensorimotor, or dialectic? Undoubtedly, regardless of your theory of choice, you function with your clients at several developmental levels. Discuss the above issues and present specific examples from your own work illustrating how you operate at multiple levels.

Finally, carefully employ the skills presented in this chapter with one client in counseling or therapy per day. Again, you may want to inform your client what you are about before you start and why it might be beneficial to them. As you become more acquainted with the value of the conceptual and practical developmental model, you may find yourself using the concepts in your interviews.

Activity 4: Consider the Yakima Nation Proverb

> The Pahmiss-Pahmiss are moved to
>   learn to tend the sick or injured
> In an emergency, or as a patient nurse.
> Man or woman, they may be
> Able to heal a burn, set a bone, or
> Serve a pregnant woman at the
>   time of birth.
> They use, with modesty, those skills
> Which it is a comfort to know
> Are always there, and close at hand.

DCT skills and concepts are eclectically oriented. They can be useful in a crisis situation, or they can be used strategically in short-term counseling and long-term therapy. The developmental sphere offers a conceptual framework for integrating many distinct modes of helping in an overall treatment plan. But unless you personally integrate these concepts in your own unique way, they are useless. What skills and strategies from this chapter would you like to focus on in your daily practice? What does this proverb say to you?

_____

_____

_____

_____

_____

Suggested Supplemental Reading and Activities

Additional Reading

Ivey, A. 1986. *Developmental therapy: Theory into practice.* San Francisco: Jossey-Bass.

Pages 105 through 125 of Chapter 3 are particularly relevant, giving special attention to the dialectics of affect. A very useful extension of the ideas presented here is to generate a specific set of affective developmental questions to complement the more cognitive questions presented here. Special attention may be given to construct 4 (page 129) on new constructions of affect.

Material on style-shift counseling, the developmental sphere, and interview examples may be found in Chapter 4 on pages 140 through 162. The exercises of construct 2 on page 172 may also be interesting.

Breunlin, D. 1985. *The family therapy collections.* Vol. 14. *Stages: Patterns of change over time.* Rockville, Md.: Aspen Systems.

This volume presents a family therapy view of the change process. Included are strategies for each phase of family therapy. DCT maintains that families have distinct individual and total family cognitive-developmental levels. A helpful exercise is to examine the family therapy process and determine which family interventions are most effective for varying cognitive-developmental levels of individuals and families.

Ivey, A., S. Rigazio-DiGilio, and M. Ivey. 1987. Standard Cognitive-Developmental Interview. (See Appendix 1.)

Appendix 1 provides a more complex and detailed set of developmental strategies for a single interview: the Cognitive-Developmental Standard Interview. This interview provides specifics for eight levels of cognitive development. The interview was used with inpatient, depressed clients and provided the basic reliability and predictive data supporting the constructs of this book (see Rigazio-DiGilio, 1989).

It is helpful to test this standard interview in all the practice and take-home situations described in this chapter. The questions are useful in widely varying clinical and counseling situations.

Gilligan, C. 1982. *In a different voice.* Cambridge, Mass.: Harvard University Press.

Kegan, R. 1982. *The evolving self.* Cambridge, Mass.: Harvard University Press.

Kohlberg, L. 1981. *The philosophy of moral development.* New York: Harper & Row.

Use one aspect or concept from one of the above books to develop specific questioning strategies that show how to help clients talk about issues in a certain way.

For example, in defining Gilligan's "relational behavior," one would expect clients to talk differently about relational issues as compared to those clients focused on autonomy. For example, the statement "I care about my family" may be contrasted with "I have an important job to do." The former statement is relational. Questions that might lead to relational reasoning include:

> "Can you get an image of yourself in a relationship? What
>   do you see/hear/feel?"
> "Could you give me a specific example of a recent relationship?
>   What were your feelings in that relationship?"
> "Do you have a pattern of putting others before you? What
>   is the pattern of feelings that goes with that?"
> " Where did you learn your patterns of caring in your
>   family?"

These questions are but a small beginning illustration of how sensorimotor, concrete, formal, and dialectic/systemic questioning strategies might be combined with Gilligan's relational thought. This combination approach should help all expand their awareness of relationship issues.

A difficult but important exercise is to apply the beginning ideas of developmental strategies to varying developmental theories. The key contribution of this developmental model may be that it enables us to see how to translate useful developmental theory into practical interviewing.

Select one aspect or concept of one developmental theorist and present specific ideas for questioning and interviewing strategies that enable clients to understand how that concept applies to them, their lives, and their representation of the world.

Ivey, A. 1990. Practice Rating Interview . (See Appendix 3.)

With your present knowledge of and experience with DCT, you may find it helpful to examine the interview in Appendix 3. This interview is designed so that you can classify both counselor and client statements. You will find a transcript of a session that will give you practice in assessing counselor and client statements as to developmental level. This practice will help you learn to recognize client developmental levels in the here and now of the interview and will also help you start monitoring your own questions and interventions. What developmental level do you manifest most often in your interviewing interventions?

The interview in Appendix 3 also provides you with a beginning understanding of how to rate and classify interviews for research purposes at four and at eight developmental levels. The interview presented here is easier to rate than real interviews. With practice over time, you can achieve 0.90 interrater agreement for research purposes. Larger segments of interviews are easier to classify as reliable than are single counselor or client statements.

Research Suggestion

One desired outcome of successful counseling and therapy may be increased cognitive complexity. For example, a client may discuss problems in a formal-operational pattern mode of thought. Successful therapy might include interventions aimed at the sensorimotor, concrete, and dialectic/systemic levels. Specific measurement of attainment of these levels is possible. Consider an interview at the beginning and at the end. Does the client's cognitive-developmental level change on a specific topic during that session? Over a period of sessions? What specific interventions and leads on the part of the therapist contributed to that change?

You will find that it is possible to classify client cognitive-developmental level on a specific developmental task at the beginning of therapy or counseling and then to note developmental progressions throughout the interview series. Recall that developmental progression for many clients will include greater ability to experience at the concrete and sensorimotor levels. It would be an oversimplification to think of developmental progression as always moving toward formal and dialectic/systemic modes of thought. Generally speaking, we would like to see clients expanding development *both* horizontally and vertically.

In a similar fashion, it would be possible to construct training interviews for rating Gilligan, Kohlberg, Kegan, or other developmental theorists. These training interviews would be highly useful research vehicles that, in turn, could be used to measure changes in relational behavior or moral development in the interview or treatment series.

4 Confrontation and Perturbation

Creation of the New

The FLAME never repeats itself.

The lesson is—it is wise to doubt

the right course to follow.

Yakima Nation Proverb

The creation of the New[1] is a central task of therapy and counseling. Clients come to us stuck and immobilized, repeating again and again ineffective behaviors, thoughts, and feelings of the past. Creating something new may require changes at all concrete and abstract DCT levels. But sometimes change in only one level is sufficient to re-establish movement toward development.

Intentionality provides us with a goal for the creation of the New (Ivey, Ivey, & Simek-Downing, 1987, p. 10):

> The person who acts with intentionality has a sense of capability. He or she can generate new behaviors in a given situation and approach a problem from different points of view. The intentional, fully functioning individual is not bound to one course of action, but can respond in the moment to changing life situations and look forward to longer-term goals.

Intentionality involves creativity—the willingness to take new perspectives, generate new behaviors, and find new meanings in old situations. Intentionality brings purpose for the creative process, and the development of intentionality in our clients provides us with a goal as we seek to create the New in our helping interviews. Development, either horizontal or vertical, requires creativity—the generation of new possibilities.

Clients in therapy need to be perturbed and confronted with their contradictions. Out of this perturbation comes creative synthesis and growth. Creativity, whether in children or adults, is the transformation of previously existing structures into something new. Perturbation moves clients to new ways of organizing and viewing the world.

Our task as therapists is to help clients reorganize old structures of behaving and thinking and find more effective and creative ways of being in the world. This chapter focuses on how you can facilitate creative expression in the client and observe the process of client creativity in the interview.

The final portion of the chapter extends the concept of creation of the New to the complex issues of death and dying and shows how working through stages of grieving can be a natural part of the developmental process. Much of counseling and therapy focuses on issues of frustration, loss, and failure. The natural stages of consciousness associated with death and dying provide a framework for helping clients accept the inevitable.

Creativity is necessary for generating the New and learning how to cope with the difficulties we face in life.

---

[1] The theologian Paul Tillich (1964) talks about the New as containing three aspects—creation, restoration, and fulfillment. He relates the concept of the New as critical to being. In effect, being creates itself and renews itself over time, restores itself to what it was originally, returns to the beginning (see the developmental sphere), and fulfills itself by developing a new reality of being over time.

Creativity, Confrontation, and Perturbation

What do you see in Figure 4-1? Take some time and record your initial impressions below. What occurs for you when you focus on the picture?

_____

_____

_____

_____

At first glance, some people see an old hag, whereas others see a young woman. Take some time with the picture until you can see both.

Lack of intentionality can be described as "stuckness"—only seeing one way of doing things. Lack of intentionality is illustrated by the individual who only sees one person in this picture. Many people find it difficult to see both women. "Multiple seeing" requires you to let go of previous impressions and restructure old information in new ways.

Figure 4-1. A Figure to Figure. (Originally drawn by W. E. Hill and published in *Puck*, November 6, 1905. First used for psychological purposes by E. G. Boring, "A New Ambiguous Figure," *American Journal of Psychology*, 1930.)

If you look again at the picture of the two women and relax, you can perhaps see the two images alternating: first, the old hag, then the young woman. With a little more relaxed concentration, it is possible to see both at once. This is multiple seeing. Work with the drawing and attempt to see both women at once.

Why is the woman with the large nose and jutting chin generally seen as an old hag, whereas the woman with a normal-sized nose seen as young? Some of this judgment is created by cultural and sexual stereotypes. Although the old hag has some indications of age, why should her physiognomy be considered less pleasing? Beauty is defined for us by our cultural background.

Multiple seeing is another way to describe intentionality. The pieces of the picture remain the same, but as we construct ideas about the picture in our mind, we see many different things. The ability to see the same picture or client simultaneously from multiple perspectives is invaluable in counseling and psychotherapy.

The next section describes the mechanism of creativity and offers some specifics on how the counselor can provide useful environments most likely to facilitate client growth.

Chance and Deliberation in Creativity

Piaget describes the mechanism of creativity as the primary circular reaction, the active repeating of results that were first achieved by chance (Piaget, 1963; Gallagher & Reid, 1981). This description is important, as it demystifies the creative process. The following are key points of the primary circular reaction:

1. Chance variation in behavior or thought is basic to creativity. Creativity happens; the moment of discovery cannot be planned. Although we may systematically examine the picture of the two women, there is something beyond this deliberate search—an inevitable "aha" experience when we see a new perspective.

2. Human beings tire of the old and search for the New even though at times they may not know what they are searching for. We also find the New through mistakes, oversights, and surprises. We can enhance our experience of the New by placing ourselves in an environment that facilitates the creative spark.

3. Discovering new thoughts and behaviors through chance is not enough. A child learning a new skill or a client learning a new behavior needs to repeat actions actively and with conscious intent. While creativity may not be planned, planning and action are required to reinforce the new skill or learning. This conscious repetition helps us establish and maintain new behaviors and ideas. What began as chance becomes systematic and deliberate.

This primary circular reaction may be illustrated more concretely by the example of how infants learn. The infant is in a crib with a rattle suspended overhead. Small infants reach out randomly. They have not yet learned that they can affect things in their environment. With enough random reaching (and with the rattle being close enough), the child will eventually knock the rattle by chance. Often, merely touching the rattle will increase the activity level of the child (feedback from the primary circular reaction). If the rattle is again touched by chance, the child gradually becomes able to reach for and touch the rattle deliberately.

Although the environment provided by the parents (the suspended rattle) gives the child the opportunity for learning, learning only occurs within the child. We cannot teach; however, we can provide opportunities for learning. In this example, chance behavior in a facilitative learning environment is followed by the active repeating of the experience.

We can apply the same principles to therapy.

1. The client comes to us stuck, or immobilized. The client has old, assimilated structures that result in this immobility. Our task is to provide an environment that allows for development of movement.
2. The client reaches out, and almost by chance, one of our interventions is useful (providing the client accommodates to the new experience).
3. We and the client then deliberately seek to repeat the experience so that the learning will become more fixed and easily assimilated by the client. When this learning has occurred, the client has assimilated something new.[2]

As counselors, we like to think that our conscious efforts, derived from our careful theoretical study, are what change the client. But ask a client what was the most helpful aspect of a session. It rarely is your brilliant intervention. More likely clients will tell you that it was some small thing you did unintentionally that was most helpful. Often, through interaction with you, the individuals or families generate on their own the creative spark that gets them moving.

A family coming to therapy may present only their narrow perception of reality. The therapist offers a different view—a separate reality, so to speak. A family already has important structures that can be recombined in a new, more effective way. Through "mixing" with the therapist, the family can examine and reconstruct feelings, meanings, and behaviors.

Can you think of a special moment of creative insight you have had—a time when you created something new? This moment could involve the understanding of a complex concept, the learning of a new skill, or the generation of a new idea. What was the creative moment?

_____

_____

_____

---

[2]Twin processes of assimilation and accommodation provide the background for developmental change. In summary form, assimilation can be described as our past learnings. We have assimilated and integrated a representation of the world. These assimilated representations (ideas about the world) form the lens through which we look at the world. Persons who have rigidly assimilated patterns are unable to take in or accommodate to new data; they find change difficult. Accommodation is the process through which we absorb and incorporate new information from the environment. The two processes need to be balanced. Too much accommodation results in continual change and no stability, whereas too much assimilation results in stagnation. A detailed elaboration of these concepts and their implications for the practice of counseling and therapy may be found in Chapter 2 of Ivey's (1986) *Developmental Therapy*. In this chapter, information processing theory is joined with Piagetian concepts and broadly applied to developmental processes.

What in the surrounding environment may have helped spark the new learning? Creation usually does not come without some form of external stimulus or support.

_____

_____

_____

The primary circular reaction stresses the importance of deliberation and practice to "fix" the new idea or skill. How does this dimension of the creative process apply to your experience?

_____

_____

_____

New constructions, perceptions, and behaviors occur in and belong to the client. However, you as counselor or therapist can provide an environment that can facilitate growth and development and the deliberation that helps stabilize the new creation.

Perturbation and Confrontation: Environmental Motivators of Change

Discrepancy, incongruity, and paradox rule the lives of many clients. There may be discrepancies between a real self and an ideal self, a present behavior and a goal behavior, rational and irrational ideas, or between a problem and a desired solution. Clients come to us with many unresolved conflicts and contradictions.

Our task is to provide clients with an environment conducive to expansion, transformation, change, and developmental growth. We can do this by applying skills, strategies, and the multitude of theoretical approaches available to us. Any one of many approaches may "perturb" the environment and encourage change.

Perturbation is an important term in Piagetian theory. Essentially, the word means to disrupt the status quo, to break homeostasis, to produce a sense of unease. Perturbation is very similar to the counseling term *confrontation*, which means to point out discrepancies or incongruities in the client's thinking or behavior. The skill of confrontation can be used to perturb the client's equilibrium and open the way for the client to construct new knowledge, thoughts, and behaviors.

Both support and challenge are needed to facilitate change. We can usually best confront clients if we have built with them a relationship of trust and understanding. Direct confrontation is not the only challenge we can offer. Effective perturbation can result from reframing and interpretation and from good questioning and good listening skills. Once a client has been effectively perturbed, returning to a supportive counseling style may help them maintain their new learnings more effectively.

Thus far we have examined Piaget's theories as they apply to clients. It is also useful to examine Piaget's questioning style. Piaget was constantly asking children questions or setting up situations that perturbed the status quo. The questions Piaget asked are not just assessment and information-gathering techniques, they are also treatments in themselves. Questions are interventions that challenge the status quo, perturb the individual, and create an opportunity for change.

By asking questions such as the following, Piaget perturbed, or confronted, the child's conception of reality. Piaget did not give sufficient attention to the effect his questions had in the evolution of the child's thought processes. Consider the following questions asked by Piaget (1972):

When you go for a walk in the evening, does the moon stay still?

What makes the clouds move?

How does this bicycle work?

Here are several more examples (Piaget, 1965):

Is it fair to keep children waiting in shops and to serve the grown-ups first?

A father had two boys. One of them always grumbled when he was sent [to fetch] messages. The other one didn't like being sent either, but he always went without saying a word. So the father used to send the boy who didn't grumble on messages oftener than the other one. What do you think of that?

If anyone hits you, what do you do?

When a child is perturbed with a contradiction, there is a natural effort to resolve the contradiction and develop a new synthesis. Children present many interesting and amusing ways to resolve the various contradictions that are posed to them.

Art Linkletter, a radio and television personality popular during the 1950s, was able to draw out fascinating pearls of wisdom and amusing anecdotes from children. Following are some examples from his book *Kids Say the Darndest Things!* (1957). Note how his questions perturb the children and move them to creative solutions. Here again, we see how the interviewer affects the changing cognitions of the interviewee.

Where does the sun go at night?

Behind the clouds?

Then where does the moon come from?

Well, naturally, it gets too hot back of the clouds when the sun goes there, so the moon *has* to come out.

What does the saying "a wet blanket" mean?

It's the blanket baby lies on.

What does the expression "The grass is always greener in the other fellow's yard" mean to you?

That's easy. He's using better fertilizer than you are.

Both Piaget and Linkletter were effective interviewers. Their questioning techniques perturbed children and thus help us better understand children's cognitive processes. In the three examples from Linkletter, the meaning-making process of each child takes varying forms. The explanation of where the sun goes is characteristic of magical, late sensorimotor thinking, whereas the responses to the two sayings represent a charming form of concrete thought.

Can you recall similar examples of childish meaning making in your own life or perhaps with children you have known? Can you identify clients you have had who present unusual or magical modes of meaning making? If you have difficulty recalling a specific incident, remember your belief in Santa Claus or a similar figure. Children (and parents) often dream up clever ways to explain Santa's behavior.

_____

_____

_____

_____

How did you, your child, or your client change their faulty or magical thinking processes? Assuming you no longer believe in Santa, what happened when you changed your thinking about his reality?

_____

_____

_____

How can you use this example of the change process from magical meaning making to concrete reality in your own counseling and therapy process—particularly when you deal with children, adolescents, and adults who may use a form of magical thinking?

_____

_____

_____

Clients have varying forms of meaning making. They may engage in magical thinking, they may be overly concrete, or they may be overly abstract and formal. Our task is to facilitate cognitive development. We can do this through our questioning techniques (as described in earlier chapters), by using an array of theoretical techniques, and through the counseling skill of confrontation.

Confrontation and the Creation of the New

Counseling and therapy rely on perturbing clients' ways of thinking and behaving. Therapeutic theory is oriented toward understanding the client's world and then promoting change through varying forms of perturbation. A Rogerian may perturb through careful listening. The therapist, through accurate mirroring of the client's words, may be able to perturb the client and thus motivate her or him toward positive movement. The behaviorist may perturb by environmental change or assertiveness skills training. The rational-emotive counselor may perturb by challenging illogical thought patterns.

Families also need to be perturbed. The family may consider the bulimic, anorexic, or acting-out teenager to be the problem but fail to see how parental difficulties and family enmeshment contribute to the situation. Minuchin (1974) sometimes begins his interviews by asking the family to define why they have come to therapy. The family then talks about the anorexic daughter, for instance, as the problem, and the anorexic agrees with this definition. Minuchin's first intervention is simple but profound. He carefully and respectfully summarizes each family member's problem definition and then redefines it by saying that the family has the problem, not the individual. This interpretive reframe offers a new view that perturbs the family system of thinking. The reframe then becomes the focus of the remaining therapy sessions.

The questioning skills presented in Chapters 2 and 3 are oriented toward perturbing clients and encouraging them to find new meanings in their old structures. Much like Piaget and Linkletter, the skilled use of questions helps clients learn to look at themselves and the world differently.

The skill of confrontation is another way to challenge and perturb clients who are stuck and repeating patterns of thought and behavior. The counselor first observes the client's conflict and the incongruities, discrepancies, and mixed messages in the client's statements and behaviors. These observations are then fed back to the client in a clear, concise, nonjudgmental manner. The following are examples of confrontations a helper might use when working with a client having difficulties with love relationships:

On one hand, you say you love your spouse, but on the other hand, you continue with your lover. How do you put that together?

As I hear you, you seem to be saying two things. First, you say you love the tenderness yet this very tenderness seems to frighten you. What sense do you make of that?

I hear you saying that that doesn't bother you, but your fist is closed tightly right now as if in anger.

Each of these confrontations actively focuses on the client's verbal or nonverbal discrepancies. Questioning techniques tend to be confrontive and the focus is on incongruity. In using questioning approaches (such as Piaget's), the therapist controls the direction of the interview. However, the technique of confrontation focuses on the client's statements as they reflect his or her world view. By paraphrasing and summarizing these observations, the therapist can help the client generate new ideas.

There are six basic types of observations that are helpful in noting incongruities—namely, discrepancies or conflict:

1. Between two verbal statements (at any of the four DCT levels)
2. Between statements and actions outside the interview (formal/concrete or concrete/concrete)
3. Between statements and nonverbal behavior in the interview (between any of the four DCT levels and sensorimotor behavior)
4. Between two nonverbal behaviors (sensorimotor)
5. Between two or more people (any developmental level)
6. Between any of the above and the context (dialectic/systemic)

Once having observed the discrepancy, it is useful to feed back your observations to the client. Using the phrasing "On one hand . . . , but on the other hand . . . " is a very useful way to nonjudgmentally communicate observations. By adding an open question such as "What sense do you make of that?" or "How do you respond to what I observed?" or "How do you put that together?" you encourage the client to make a new synthesis. If you move your hands as if balancing the contradiction, you increase the sensorimotor impact of the question.

With families, you can use similar language. In addition, you may add such questions or suggestions as "Can you help your daughter/son figure this out?" or "How do think your mother and father will react to that?" or some other modified form of circular questioning in which you encourage family members to present their views more clearly. These questioning procedures help families bring out "hidden" secrets that are often well known to all but never discussed.

The counselor in skilled confrontation captures the essence of the client's problem, feeds it back clearly and concisely, and tries to help the client resolve discrepancies. Effective confrontation and perturbation aids problem resolution. Questioning and confrontation perturb clients and encourage them to generate new meanings and behaviors.

The primary circular reaction described earlier consists of three dimensions:

1. The client comes to us stuck or immobilized. Our task is to provide an environment that allows for client development.
2. The client reaches out, and almost by chance one of our interventions is useful.
3. The counselor and the client then deliberately seek to repeat the experience so that learning occurs.

Providing an environment that allows for development may involve the judicious use of counseling theory, skilled questioning techniques, and/or constructive confrontation. All three approaches encourage client development. The client is the primary meaning maker in the client-counselor relationship, and he or she reaches out to us. We usually try several interventions before one works, seemingly by chance. At this point, we try to repeat the chance learning experience so new learning is fixed and becomes part of the client's new way of being. Therapist and client together have created the New.

Confrontations and perturbations can be cognitive, affective, or behavioral. Behavioral change can lead to cognitive change, and thus behavioral confrontation is preferred as a first approach. Blending cognitive and behavioral confrontations can be especially helpful, for often the discrepancy is between thought and action—saying one thing but doing another.

Evaluating the Effectiveness of Our Interventions: The Confrontation Impact Scale (CIS)

When confronted, clients have a variety of responses. Ideally, they will respond actively to your confrontation, generate new ideas, and move forward. However, they may ignore or deny the fact that you have confronted them. Most often, the confrontation will be acknowledged and absorbed as part of a larger process of change.

You can assess the impact of your confrontation on your client by using the Confrontation Impact Scale (CIS). The CIS has some practical implications for the practice of counseling and therapy in that it enables the therapist to assess the impact of interventions in the here and now of the interview. In addition, this assessment helps the therapist keep the interview on track and note client growth potential. An outline of the CIS (adapted from Ivey, 1988, pp. 175–177; and Ivey, 1986, pp. 199–201) is found in Box 4-1.

The following is an exercise that will give you experience using the CIS of Box 4-1. Classify the following client responses by circling the appropriate level. (Correct responses are listed at the end of this chapter.)

Counselor statement:
"You say you are feeling OK about your father's lack of interest in you and that you've worked through your problems with him, but just as you said that, your voice tone went down, your body slumped, and you looked very discouraged." (confrontation at the formal and sensorimotor levels)

Client's response:

Level 1 2 3 4 5   "No, no such thing. I didn't do that. I didn't move at all."

Level 1 2 3 4 5   "You're right, I have worked through most of my problems. Things are moving the right way."

Level 1 2 3 4 5   "Hmmn. I did say that, but you say my body and voice changed when I talked about Dad."

Level 1 2 3 4 5   "Wow! I guess I haven't worked things through as fully with him as I thought."

Level 1 2 3 4 5   "Your feedback is helpful. I have been wondering lately if things were really as rosy as I hoped. Just hearing that from you helps me recall something that happened that week. I need to work a lot more on this."

Counselor statement:
"You've been late for work three times in the last week; the boss has talked to you about her concern and says she is about to let you go." (concrete confrontation)

Box 4-1. The Confrontation Impact Scale

You will find that virtually every helping lead you use, whether a question, reflection of feeling, or directive (whether you intend confrontation or not) leads to a client reaction that can be located on this five-point scale. Clients will sometimes deny your question or confrontation; at other times, they will recognize it. When things are going well, clients will transform their concepts into new ideas, thoughts, and plans for action.

For example, the counselor may confront a client considering divorce with this comment: "On one hand, you still seem to care for your spouse, but on the other hand, I see an underlying anger as well."

Level 1: Denial

The individual may deny that an incongruity or mixed message exists or may fail to recognize it. (For example, "I'm not angry about the divorce. It happens. I don't feel anything in particular.")

Level 2: Partial Examination

The individual may recognize a part of the discrepancy but fail to consider other dimensions. (For example, "I care, I really care. How can I make it alone?" Here the client fails to deal with issues of anger and frustration.) Alternatively, the client may move into full anger. Anger is often a level-2 response, since it covers up deeper sadness and hurt.

Level 3: Full Examination But No Change

The client may incorporate the confrontation fairly completely but make no resolution. Much of counseling operates at this level or at level 2. Until the client can examine incongruity, stuckness, and mixed messages accurately, developmental change will be difficult. (For example, "I guess I do have mixed feelings about it. I certainly do care about the marriage. We've spent years together. But I sure am angry about what has happened.") The client may also acknowledge feelings of hurt and sadness underlying the anger. An honest experience of anger as part of a complex relationship is an important level-3 goal.

Level 4: Creation of New Dimensions

At this level, the individual is able to gain a new understanding to the total picture. There is not a major restructuring but rather a gradual progression toward larger gestalts at level 5. (For example, "As I hear you, I realize that it makes sense to have mixed feelings. We had many good things. I wonder if part of my anger is about the loss of a dream that went sour and really represents my fear of loss.")

Level 5: Development of New, Larger, More Inclusive Constructs, Patterns, or Behaviors

A confrontation is most successful when the client recognizes the discrepancy, works on it, and generates new thought patterns or behaviors to cope with and perhaps resolve the incongruity. (For example, "I like the plan we've worked out. You've helped me see that mixed feelings and thoughts are part of every relationship. I've been expecting too much. I'm having dinner tonight with my spouse, and we are going to have to develop a new way of thinking about the meaning of the relationship. The divorce may still be necessary, but I need to look at it a new way. I'm sad about the idea of a breakup. It is a loss that I may not really want.")

Client response:

Level 1 2 3 4 5   "Yeah, you've got it. I'm worried that the boss has about had it with me."

Level 1 2 3 4 5   "I have so much to do, getting the kids ready. I guess I need to plan things better with them."

Level 1 2 3 4 5   "As you said that, I just realized that this is a pattern for me. I get a good job, start off well, then somehow it starts to fall apart. I think we need to work hard on that pattern."

Level 1 2 3 4 5   "Yeah, and as I think about it, the boss was pretty sympathetic with my family issues at first. I wonder if I have pushed her too far."

Level 1 2 3 4 5   "That's not what I said. The boss is out to get me."

Counselor/family interaction:

The therapist's observations of a family have been centered around the mother's overinvolvement with her physically handicapped 6-year-old son to the point where the mother is constantly watching him and helping him. The therapist asks the child to move from one chair to another, and the mother moves toward the child to help, saying, "Wait Mikey, let Mommy help." The therapist says, "Irene, how have you decided that Mike needs help?" The mother replies, "Well, the chair is high, and Mikey is nervous here in this environment." The therapist says, "Let's see if you are right. Mike, can you get down from that chair and get up into this one?" Michael looks at his mother but does what is asked. The therapist says, "Let's be sure that was not luck. Please do it again." Michael succeeds again. The therapist then says to the mother and father, "Your wife thought your son Mike needed help, but in fact, he was able to do this on his own. Could you two talk about what this all might mean?" (multiple-level confrontation— Mikey moving the chair is sensorimotor and concrete; asking parents to talk together is formal)

Level 1 2 3 4 5   (mother) "Mikey was able to get into the chair, but you forced him. He mustn't be pushed so hard."

Level 1 2 3 4 5   (father) "That's what I've been telling you, Irene. Mike can do lots of things if you'll just let him. Didn't you see what happened?"

Level 1 2 3 4 5   (mother) "Well, perhaps, but it makes me so nervous." (starts to cry)

Level 1 2 3 4 5   (father) "Could it be that both of us worry about Mike so much that we don't give him a chance to do what he actually can do?" (mother, drying eyes) "Well, maybe what the therapist is saying to us is 'Hold back a bit. Mikey can do more things on his own.' "

Level 1 2 3 4 5   (mother continues) "I guess I'm so much like my own mother. She was always hovering over me. How I hated it. Could I be doing the same thing with Mikey?" (tears)

Issues of Death and Dying as Related to Developmental Counseling and Therapy

Elisabeth Kübler-Ross expanded the world's consciousness in her classic work *On Death and Dying* (1969) in which she explores, with great sensitivity and understanding, five stages individuals work through when they face death and dying. Kübler-Ross's five stages have interesting parallels to the five levels of the Confrontation Impact Scale. Both the CIS levels and the five stages represent creative changes in understanding and consciousness. The content and objectives of the two, of course, are markedly different, but these parallels may offer some interesting ideas for helping clients deal with many complex life issues.

Kübler-Ross's five stages of death and dying can be summarized as follows:

1. Denial and isolation. When first told they are terminally ill, most people respond with immediate denial: "It can't happen to me" or "The lab tests must be mixed up." Sometimes they simply are unable to hear what the physician has just said. Some seek out faith healers and claim that the illness has been cured. Others may isolate themselves. A cancer patient, on finding she had cancer of the hip, told her family, "Don't tell anyone I am in the hospital." Kübler-Ross notes that people generally move rapidly from full denial to at least partial recognition of their condition. But some patients go to their death denying the reality of the situation, and their families may do the same.

Kübler-Ross is careful to respect all the ways individuals and families cope with death and dying. For some, avoiding the truth can be an effective and even beautiful defense. However, there are cases when both the individual and the family are aware of the nearness of death and never share their knowledge with one another, seeking to "protect" each other from worry. They thus deny themselves a chance to discuss openly what is happening.

The Confrontation Impact Scale's first two levels are "denial" and "partial examination." Clients who cope with either mild or serious difficulties use language in many ways similar to that described by Kübler-Ross.

2. Anger. Denial is soon replaced by a realization of the reality of the situation: "Why me? What have I done to deserve this?" This realization is coupled with often unreasonable anger at the situation, the family, the physician, and the hospital staff. The angry person facing death is not an easy person to be around or sympathize with. Busy nurses may avoid these people and respond to them angrily.

Underlying anger in most people is deep fear, hurt, and sadness. It is safer to be angry than to acknowledge one's fear and hurt. Anger is often a defense against pain. A young husband became immediately and irrationally angry when his bride of two weeks burned her finger on the stove. He calmed down fairly quickly and took her to the emergency room, where she received minor medical attention. Talking about the incident with his therapist the next week, he came to realize that he so loved his wife that he couldn't bear even a relatively small injury to her, since it represented potential loss and eventual death. The young husband, due to a difficult childhood, was terrified of loss and could only cope with his fear of loss through denial and anger. As he began to understand his anger, he broke into tears.

So it is with those facing dying and death. Kübler-Ross presents a lengthy interview with a dying nun, who is full of anger (pp. 73–79). The woman was resentful of the nuns who cared for her. The interview revealed that the nun's anger went back to her early childhood, when she had been expected to be a "good girl." She was furious that Hodgkin's disease was the reward she got for being good. The resentment and anger toward her family and her anticipated early death was transferred to her caregivers. Through the interview, the nun gained more peace and felt more acceptance of her condition. This interview reveals that patience and understanding are a necessary part of therapy if one is to help a client develop new understandings and meanings.

As counselor or therapist, you are not the target of your client's anger, hate, or love. People facing crisis become very much in touch with basic feelings. Responding to internal cues, they may appear angry at therapists and helpers but are really reacting to the immediate crisis or to past life history. Those who work with victims of trauma (rape, incest, child abuse, serious accidents) will often encounter manifestations of anger similar to those described by Kübler-Ross.

In terms of the Confrontation Impact Scale, anger as described here is usually a level-2 response, since it covers deeper, underlying issues. Anger may be described as a displacement of real feelings and thus a partial examination of issues. However, at the same time, the open discussion of honest and useful anger can be beneficial and represent level 3 on the CIS.

3. Bargaining. Kübler-Ross likens this stage to the child who is told "No, you cannot have the toy." The child stomps off and is angry, but may soon return, saying, "If I am very good, can I have the toy?" Adults facing death do something similar: they attempt to postpone the inevitable. This stage is relatively brief, since the fact of terminal illness does not change, and there is no one to bargain with in person. The dying person may try to bargain with God: "If I become a better person, then will you let me live?"

As mentioned above, this stage is brief and may not appear at all. In this stage, the person displays a magical way of thinking similar to what DCT terms the *preoperational problem*. Continuing the parallel with the five levels of the Confrontation Impact Scale, the bargaining stage is late level 2. The individual is trying to work on issues but has not yet confronted them directly.

4. Depression. Loss and life's difficulties make all of us sad and depressed. Whether it is poor grades, an automobile accident, or a divorce, most of us feel sad about the event but may take some time before reaching the stage of depression. We may deny ("The professor must have added the exam wrong"), become angry ("Why didn't you watch where you were going?"), or bargain ("If you'll stop beating me, I'll do a better job around the house and we won't have to get divorced."). But ultimately, reality comes to us and we must acknowledge our deep hurt, frustration, or sadness.

Facing separation and loss and the resulting natural sadness and depression is something many people cannot bear. A woman who remains with an abusive man may deny anger and spend most of her thinking time bargaining, trying to find ways she can satisfy and please her abuser.

Those facing death deal with one of life's ultimate tragedies. Thus, sadness and depression are necessary and important parts of grieving. Denying that one will die means that we are at least partially denying the joy we have had while living. When we work with depressed clients in therapy, we know that reassurance and encouragement are of little use. Similarly, it does not help much to tell the depressed patient that "it is all for the best."

Depression and sadness, then, are real parts of life, and we must allow the individual and his or her family to experience these fellings fully but not be overcome by them. To illustrate this stage, Kübler-Ross presents an interview with Mr. H (pp. 88–108). Severely depressed, Mr. H. thought he would not be able to talk for more than five minutes. He had lost hope; his father had died following a similar operation with the same surgeon. He talked about his feelings and then later explored his disappointments in his own life, particularly in his marital relationship. He was reviewing his life, searching for meaning in it, and had not been able to share his thoughts and feelings with his wife.

Mr. H's wife was described as a powerful, busy woman who felt that "life will go on the same" with or without her husband. Kübler-Ross met with her and helped her understand her husband's feelings. Her view changed, and she was able to reframe the situation and appreciate his good qualities. She was able to share herself and some of her caring with her husband for the first time in many years. His depression passed, and he went to his death peacefully.

The stage of depression described by Kübler-Ross may be viewed as a level-3 response on the CIS. Depression is often a full awareness of sadness and loss. Death is indeed something to be sad about. Unless one allows oneself to grieve and be sad, one remains enmeshed in denial, anger, or bargaining.

Depression and sadness are necessary, but if they become a focus, as happened with Mr. H, these feelings can become a serious problem. A level-3 response such as depression, when continued too long, becomes a form of level-1 denial and isolation. Kübler-Ross helped this couple transcend depression, bringing husband and wife together in a new synthesis, a more creative way of being. They could accept the situation as it was and view it from a new perspective.

5. Acceptance. The fifth stage of death and dying is acceptance—living with the inevitability of death. Some describe this as finding meaning in death and reviewing the positives in one's life; others look forward with enthusiasm to an afterlife. Whatever the person's approach, acceptance can be described as a physical sigh—a letting go, a recognition of the inevitable, a joining of oneself with the physical and spiritual environment. "Ashes to ashes, dust to dust" is not a joyful statement but it is a realistic statement of what is.

As one of Kübler-Ross's patients described it: "Acceptance should not be mistaken for a happy stage. It is almost void of feelings. It is as if the pain had gone, the struggle is over, and there comes a time for "the final rest before the long journey" (p. 113). Some people continue in denial to the end; others fight until the last; others may remain in deep depression. Thus, the period of acceptance may not be experienced at all by some. Still others, facing a slow, lingering death, may have a long period of acceptance. Each individual is unique and will work his or her way through the stages of dying differently.

Individuals who move to the stage of acceptance appear to do so most easily if they are supported and encouraged to experience the other developmental stages of the dying experience. Particularly, they need to express anger and rage, as well as their fears and sorrows and to discuss their past victories and defeats, thereby finding meaning in their lives. Again Kübler-Ross (1969) presents an excellent interview (pp. 120–137) in which she helped a couple toward an acceptance of death.

In this case, the couple had been arguing, failing to understand one another and some of the positives they had shared in their time together. Kübler-Ross helped them work through their separate needs in the death and dying process and gradually come to a more satisfactory resolution. This is particularly important as it reminds us that death and dying are not just individual issues— they are issues for the entire family.

Similarly, issues of denial and anger can be part of a family therapy process. Figley (1989) reminds us that any time there is a traumatized individual, there is usually a traumatized family as well. Not only does a family need to learn to accept death and dying, they need to recognize that a teen does have a serious alcohol or drug problem, that a father's loud talking is actually verbal abuse, or that the 97-pound daughter is indeed anorexic. One of your most important therapeutic tasks with a family is to help them move from denial of a problem to acceptance that a problem exists. With acceptance comes the possibility of transcending and coping with the problem through creative new solutions.

Acceptance of what is may be equaled to level 4 on the CIS. Nothing new can be done, but remarkably, something new—acceptance—has been added to the client's experience. The individual has transcended the very real sadness of dying by simply accepting death. Kübler-Ross describes a 76-year-old woman with terminal liver cancer. The woman offered her son and daughter-in-law ceramic figurines she had prized throughout her life. They refused the gift, saying she should continue to enjoy them, as she would be "around for a long time" and should "keep fighting." She died two months later, never having had the chance to explore the meaning of her life or to share her feelings with her loved ones. The woman was at the acceptance level; her son and daughter-in-law were still in denial. The family missed a chance to transcend the death experience and share their love and concern.

For many clients in therapy, nothing can be done about an abusive childhood, the loss of an arm in an accident, the birth of a child with severe cerebral palsy, or the loss of a job at age 55. At another level, failure in school, the breakup of a promising relationship, or being rejected by a social club are also depressing events. Clients often react to all these events by denying that they have happened, by becoming angry, or by trying to bargain their way out of them before they come to acknowledge their sadness and depression and accept the continuing hurts and problems that are part of life.

True transcendence of death is described by Kübler-Ross as hope. Love, faith, hope, and charity are difficult mystical concepts that defy real description, but they represent the moment of opportunity in which individuals and families move beyond themselves and see themselves in relationship with others and perhaps even as part of the cosmos.

The parallels between the five levels of the Confrontation Impact Scale and the Kübler-Ross stages are not perfect. Each construct was developed for a different purpose. Kübler-Ross provides a philosophical perspective. DCT and the CIS offer a more technically oriented way to relate the stages of death and dying to the general issue of loss that is so often the topic in the helping interview.

Death forces us to confront life's major incongruity. In dealing with death, we have the opportunity to confront the meaning of life and construct the New. Piaget's theory of equilibration provides a framework that helps explain the relationship between the CIS and Kübler-Ross's stages. To illustrate this concept, Piaget describes how a child develops new ways of thinking when confronted with a stimulus. The child's learning may involve denial of data, partial accommodation, a balancing of new data with the old, or what Piaget calls the "gamma solution" in which a new totality or schema is generated out of the old.[3]

Just as children must constantly construct the New when they face life's challenges, so must those facing such major issues as death and dying or trauma. Clients confronting less difficult developmental tasks also must construct the New if they are to continue growing.

Change: A Loss or an Opportunity?

Psychotherapy and counseling are about development and change. As we work through the developmental tasks of life, some changes bring about joy whereas others are painful. At times we need to work through the pain so that we can later experience joy and rebirth. As noted earlier, the theologian Paul Tillich (1964) talks about creation of the New as bringing restoration and fulfillment. But this does not deny the pain that sometimes must be endured before growth and development can be fully established.

Change does not always come easily to us or to our clients. Many clients hold on to old ineffective ways of thinking and behaving because they feel safer than dealing with the rigors of change. The major points dealing with change thus far include:

1. Change is a creative process that can occur by chance or by deliberation.
2. Piaget's primary circular reaction provides us with specific information on how change and new ideas are incorporated in the individual.

---

[3]Kübler-Ross's stages of death and dying are a reminder that some people live their entire lives in a state of denial, anger, or bargaining. This idea is explored in Ivey's *Developmental Therapy* (1986, pp. 62–69, 196–201), in which the levels of the CIS are related to the defense mechanisms of denial (level 1); displacement (level 2); rationalization (level 3); and sublimation, altruism, and humor (levels 4 and 5).

3. Perturbation and confrontation are intimately related. A task of the professional helper is to perturb or confront clients and facilitate their movement to new levels of cognition, affect, and behavior.

4. Five levels of client response to counselor interventions and perturbations may be identified through the Confrontation Impact Scale.

5. Kübler-Ross's stages of death and dying have interesting parallels to the CIS. Clients facing serious loss seem to follow her stages, and this process may extend beyond death and dying issues.

In this section we extend these five points to the exploration of the change process in general. It appears that many clients in the process of growth experience a loss before they are able to encounter the joy of the creation of the New. Recent thinking in organizational development provides some helpful linkages to consider.

Change in organizations does not come easily, and much management literature focuses on resistance to change. Bolman and Deal (1990) review this literature and conclude that change often involves feelings of loss to employees in a company or institution. An example of a change that relates to feelings of loss would be the wholesale firings and staff reductions that occurred in 1988-1990 when Wall Street investment houses laid off thousands of workers. Here, it is easy to see that management decisions can result in feelings of loss for both those given pink slips and those who remain with the company.

Organizational development consultants often seek to change procedures in a business or governmental agency. Bolman and Deal note that when a change agent moves too fast, without due consideration of the client's perspective, resistance is likely to grow. (This is also true in individual or family counseling and organizational or management consultation.) Management and cultural change in organizations represents loss for many individuals. They must give up their old "comfortable ways" of doing things. Bolman and Deal state that change agents need to recognize the employee's and client's needs to work through and mourn their losses in a supportive atmosphere. Organizations and employees may say that they wish change, but when change is actually faced, they may begin a process of grieving and loss that may build up in resistance to positive change.

We, as professional helpers, need to be aware that even though most clients say they want change, many of them resist doing something new. Resistance to change is parallel to denial as represented in the Confrontation Impact Scale or in the Kübler-Ross death and dying framework. Whether you are working with resistance or denial, your task is to help clients break through this initial phase so they can enter into new phases of growth and enjoy the more positive aspects of development.

For example, a depressed client may say he or she does not want to continue in the cycle of sadness relating to feelings of depression. However, when confronted with the possibilities of the world and the many challenges that must be faced daily, some depressed clients will return to clinical depression as safer and more comfortable than going through the agony of behavioral change.

Similarly, a child diagnosed with a conduct disorder must give up many, many things if he or she is to learn how to get along more successfully with peers, parents, and teachers. This process is especially clear in substance abusers. They may recognize the need for change, but giving up drugs or alcohol and facing the difficulties of daily life can represent a serious loss for them. It is sometimes easier to hide behind our symptoms of depression, conduct disorder, or substance abuse than face the real issues of life.

Often when you propose change to your clients via a gestalt, Rogerian, behavioral, or family systems intervention, they will behave very much like those clients described by Kübler-Ross or Bolman and Deal. Denial can be so complete that you may find that clients don't even hear what you have just said in a normal vocal tone. Alternatively, they hear you and deny your point through skillful argument ("I'm not an alcoholic. I can stop anytime I wish.") Others may move to a level-2 type of anger or bargaining in which they only work on part of what you have said. Even if a client agrees with your intervention, he or she may simply become depressed once the truth is recognized.

Often, we think of depression and sadness around our interventions as a level-3 response on the CIS. For some clients, there is a real need to mourn and feel sad about the fact that change must come. Giving up old habits is not always comfortable and many clients will sit still and still do nothing about change. They may prefer to obsess and grieve about the problem and do nothing. An obsessive client may become aware of the need to loosen up and change interaction style, but may spend most of the time grieving about the need for change and leaving old, safe, and predictable habits. It is at this awareness level (3 on the CIS and stage 4 of Kübler-Ross) that suicide becomes a real risk for seriously depressed clients, for they have allowed themselves to see more fully how very bad they feel. In addition, they may fear the changes they need to make to enable themselves to feel better.

We work through the Kübler-Ross and CIS stages by moving to acceptance and action at stage 5 and levels 4 and 5, respectively. We both think about our old behavior in new ways and implement new action oriented toward change. Here, change can be difficult and painful, but the possibilities for growth, rebirth, and development often make this part of the change process more joyful. At this point, the client or family may begin to reinterpret past pain as a useful prelude illuminating the possibility of the future.

Despite successful movement and the creativity inherent in positive change, the process for many represents loss and will be painful throughout. It is not enjoyable for an alcoholic or a borderline client to encounter a history of family abuse. Drawing from management theory, Bolman and Deal (1990) remind us that change is not always welcomed and that a supportive environment is needed for change to be fully accepted and incorporated in organizations.

Your ability to be warm and empathic and supportive is critical as you help clients and families move through the change process. Our culture tends to think of change and development as positive processes, which indeed they are. Yet, we have given insufficient attention to the need to support those who seek change. Confrontation, perturbation, and skillful interventions are not enough.

It is important that you, the change agent, be there with clients and support them throughout the process. In addition, you will want to recruit family members, co-workers, and friends at times to support clients who are working through change issues. Particularly useful in this process are support or action groups, such as Alcoholics Anonymous, a community bulimia group, or Mothers Against Drunk Driving.

For practical purposes in the individual or family session, you can use the CIS and adaptations of the Kübler-Ross framework to indicate how clients are moving in the interview. With some practice you will be able to note whether or not clients are denying your intervention, bargaining with you, or accepting what you say. Your ability to observe client response to your interventions may enable you to provide the necessary balance of support and challenging confrontation needed by the client.

The creation of the New can indeed be joyful, but many clients will see change as loss and need your support to help them move to new ways of thinking and behaving. In the long run change will be useful and joyful, but the process will be much less painful if the counselor, therapist, or change agent is fully tuned in with the needs of the individual, family, group, or organization. A useful goal may be to help the client think of change as a process of gradual illumination of possibility.

Chapter Summary

This chapter provided a brief introduction to one of the more useful aspects of the DCT framework: confrontation. With observation and practice, you will be able to see how your clients have accommodated and changed in reaction to your interventions. If you support their creative change, they have a better chance for assimilating the New and integrating it in their cognitive and behavioral repertoire.

Counseling and psychotherapy are concerned with creativity. The primary circular reaction is basic to the creation process. Clients come to us stuck and immobilized, unable to create something New in their lives. Their repetition of unsatisfactory and stuck behaviors, thoughts, and feelings is what leads most, perhaps all, clients into the helping relationship.

In therapy, clients will reach out to us through the behavior and language they use in the interview. Their behavior and language are directed by the past, but clients now interact with a new set of environmental contingencies: you and your behavior and language. The therapist's task is to provide an environment that perturbs clients' current levels of functioning, to move them toward change and renewed developmental progression. We perturb by using theoretical and practical therapeutic interventions (behavior modification, rational disputation, gestalt exercises) or through interviewing skills such as questioning, reframing, and confrontation. Those interventions that have a positive impact on clients need to be followed up if they are to become a part of clients' New way of being.

By observing discrepancies, mixed messages, conflict, and incongruity in the client's statements and behavior, we can identify instances of immobility. These inconsistencies are usually an important part of the client's problems, difficulties, and concerns. The resolution of these discrepancies is central to the helping process.

Confrontation is a therapeutic intervention that seems to cut across all theories. Confrontation, similar to the concept of Piagetian perturbation, requires clients to examine their relationship to the world. Through feeding back, summarizing, and paraphrasing discrepancies and conflict in the client's statements and behavior, you will encourage the client to look at him-or herself, to disequilibrate, or decenter, from an unsatisfactory past, and to move toward change and developmental movement.

The Confrontation Impact Scale (CIS) is a practical measure for assessing, through client language in the interview, the impact of your interventions. With practice, you will be able to classify client responses to your interventions, questions, and confrontations and you will be able to determine whether or not your intervention was heard and assimilated by the client. This feedback will help you to plan your interventions in the session to facilitate client growth.

Kübler-Ross's five stages of death and dying were presented to expand and clarify the ideas of this chapter. Her work provides a broad, rich, philosophic base that may help in transfering the ideas presented in this chapter to other settings.

Change may be viewed as either a loss or an opportunity for development. You may expect many of your clients to experience real feelings of loss as they are perturbed and move toward new ways of thinking, feeling, and behaving. Your personal support and warmth throughout the change process are particularly important.

 CAUTION! Confrontation is a powerful therapeutic and counseling skill that should be used carefully and must be based on a thorough understanding of theory and practice. Skills necessary for the effective use of confrontation include paraphrasing, reflection of feeling, and summarization. Some of the most effective confrontations use the client's language and perceptions as a base. Other confrontation skills include interpretation, reframing, and questioning. The Confrontation Impact Scale is useful for analyzing the effectiveness of interventions.

Theory into Practice

By the end of this section, you may be able to demonstrate your ability to

1. Define and describe the primary circular reaction and how it relates to your own practice of counseling and psychotherapy.
2. List the key aspects of confrontation and demonstrate your understanding by written statements.
3. Classify client statements using the Confrontation Impact Scale.

4. Generate your own ideas on how to extend the ideas and procedures in this chapter to work with those suffering loss.

5. Use the concepts of this chapter in role-played and real interviews.

The Primary Circular Reaction

The primary circular reaction is a key theoretical concept. This concept can be confusing unless you restate the main ideas of the process in your own language and apply the concept to your own practice of counseling and therapy. Briefly outline the key points of the primary circular reaction below and then, in a longer paper, describe how these central ideas may be utilized in your own helping sessions.

_____

_____

_____

_____

_____

Confrontation Practice Exercises

Six basic types of discrepancies, mixed messages, or conflicts have been identified in this chapter and are listed below. Think back on your own personal life experience or observations in counseling and therapy. Provide an example of each type of incongruity in the space provided. When have you, a friend, or a client demonstrated the several types of mixed messages, incongruity, or discrepancy?

After each example, write a confrontation statement that a counselor or therapist might use to clarify the discrepancy. The confrontation statement has two parts: (1) feeding back the essence of the discrepancy, using the client's main words, and (2) asking the client how he or she synthesizes the discrepancy (for example, "How do you put that together?" or "What sense do you make of that?")

1. Between two verbal statements (any of the four DCT levels):

_____

_____

_____

Confrontation statement:

_____

_____

_____

2. Between statements and actions outside the interview (formal/concrete or concrete/concrete):

_____

_____

Confrontation statement:

_____

_____

3. Between statements and nonverbal behavior in the interview (between any of the four DCT levels and sensorimotor behavior):

_____

_____

Confrontation statement:

_____

_____

4. Between two nonverbal behaviors (sensorimotor):

_____

_____

Confrontation statement:

_____

_____

5. Between two or more people (any developmental level):

_____

_____

Confrontation statement:

_____

_____

6. Between any of the above and the context (dialectic/systemic):

_____

_____

Confrontation statement:

_____

_____

The Confrontation Impact Scale

Imagine what a client might say at each of the five levels of the Confrontation Impact Scale to two of your confrontation statements from the preceding section. Write statements that represent each level of the CIS.

Confrontation Statement 1
Level 1: Denial

_____

_____

Level 2: Partial examination

_____

_____

Level 3: Full examination but no change

_____

_____

Level 4: Creation of new dimensions

_____

_____

Level 5: Development of new, larger, more inclusive constructs, patterns, or behaviors (the creation of the New).

_____

_____

Confrontation Statement 2
Level 1: Denial

_____

_____

Level 2: Partial examination

_____

_____

Level 3: Full examination but no change

_____

_____

Level 4: Creation of new dimensions

_____

_____

Level 5: Development of new, larger, more inclusive constructs, patterns, or behaviors (the creation of the New).

_____

_____

Coping with Issues of Loss

Kübler-Ross's five stages of death and dying were used to draw a parallel to similar stages we all work through when we face losses and defeats in life. Recall a loss or defeat you have experienced: failure in school or on the job, the breakup of a significant relationship, not making a team, or moving to a new home or school. You may wish to explore more powerful losses and sadness such as those related to the death of a loved one, having an alcoholic family member, or suffering a physical disability. Or you may want to interview a friend or family member who has experienced a loss.

See if you can identify in yourself or the other person the specific stages of loss described by Kübler-Ross. Use the space below to provide evidence supporting your assessment that the person is at this stage.

Denial

_____

_____

Anger

_____

_____

Bargaining

_____

_____

Depression

_____

_____

Acceptance

_____

_____

Practice Using the CIS in a Role-Played Session

Step 1: Divide into Practice Groups

Step 2: Select a Group Leader

Step 3: Assign Roles for the Practice Session

- Role-played client. The role-played client will talk freely about the topic but be somewhat resistant.
- Interviewer. The interviewer will attempt to identify key client discrepancies and then confront these discrepancies. Simultaneously, the interviewer will attempt to observe the level of response to confrontation of the client. Does the client deny (level 1), show partial understanding (level 2), demonstrate understanding but no change (level 3), or perhaps generate new ideas (levels 4 and 5)?
- Observer 1. The first observer will write down each interviewer statement. It is possible to reconstruct a total session using only brief notes. The observer will make a special effort to note confrontation statements.
- Observer 2. The second observer will complete the feedback sheet provided and will make a special effort to note client response on the Confrontation Impact Scale.

Step 4: Plan the Session

- The interviewer and client need first to agree on the topic. Useful topics for this session include working through the breakup of a long-term relationship (either now or in the past) or role playing a friend or family member who experienced such a breakup. The topics of procrastination or a past or present interpersonal conflict are also good.
- The client may think through how he or she wishes to talk about the agreed-on topic throughout the session.
- The two observers will examine the feedback form.

Step 5: Conduct a 15-Minute Interviewing Session

Again it is helpful to videotape or audiotape practice sessions.

Step 6: Provide Immediate Feedback and Complete Notes (5 Minutes)

Allow the client and interviewer time to provide immediate personal reactions to the practice session. At this point, the observers should let the participants take control. Use this time to complete your classification and notes.

Step 7: Review Practice Session and Provide Feedback (15 to 30 Minutes)

The interviewer should ask for feedback rather than getting it without being asked. The observers can share their observations from the feedback form and from their observations of the session. Avoid judgmental feedback.

Feedback Sheet for Observer 2

List below discrepancies, incongruities, and conflict you observed in the client.

_____

_____

_____

_____

_____

Provide specific examples of client responses at the five levels of the Confrontation Impact Scale.

Level 1: Denial

_____

_____

_____

Level 2: Partial examination

_____

_____

_____

Level 3: Full examination but no change

_____

_____

_____

Level 4: Creation of new dimensions

_____

_____

_____

Level 5: Development of new, larger, more inclusive constructs, patterns, or behaviors (the creation of the New)

_____

_____

_____

Practice with Confrontation in a Role-Played Family Session

From one to two hours are required for development and debriefing of the family session.

Step 1: Select the Participants

Participants will be a therapist, an external helper, and a group that can act as the family. The remainder of the members of the class or workshop will observe the entire process and later serve as process consultants who reflect on the session.

Step 2: Have the Workshop Leader Assume the Leadership Role

Due to the complexity of the process, the workshop leader or teacher needs to assume the leader role and ensure that the group follows the specific steps of the practice session.

Step 3: Assign Roles for the Practice Session

Role-played family. For family practice sessions, any family pattern may be used as a topic. Topics can be the typical difficulties of couple communication, an acting-out teenager, or family financial problems.

- Therapist. The therapist conducts the session.
- Helper. The helper observes the interview and, at a predetermined time, meets with the therapist to design specific confrontation interventions.
- Workshop/class observers. All remaining individuals in the session will sit in a circle around the family or couple and observe the session.

Step 4: Plan the Session

- The family members can leave the room and define their roles and the problem they wish to present. The nature of the problem will be a surprise to the therapist. The family must define a problem or reason for coming to the family session.
- The therapist may wish to think through the task of identifying incongruity and positively confronting observed discrepancies.

Again, it will be helpful to have the family describe one concrete example of general family difficulty. The therapist should use concrete-level questioning skills, as indicated in the developmental questioning sequence. Confrontations can be at the sensorimotor, concrete, formal, or dialectic/systemic level.

- The family observers have several roles: (1) They all can be participant/ observers; the therapist should feel free to stop the interview in mid-session to ask the observers for help and suggestions. (2) Four observers should be assigned to various members of the family. Their task is to identify incongruity in one family member. The rest of the group should note general conflict or discrepancy in the family as a whole. Several members of the group should use the individual feedback forms from the individual practice session.

It may be useful to use the observational feedback forms from Chapters 2 and 3 so that concepts of developmental assessment and interviewing strategies can also be considered.

Step 5: Conduct a 30-Minute Interviewing Session

The therapist and family will discuss the varying perceptions of the problem for five minutes while the observers keep track of their progress and classify the statements of each.

The therapist should stop at this point and meet with a helper to design an intervention that challenges a discrepancy, either behavioral or cognitive or both. Take ten minutes to conduct the intervention. Again, it is helpful to videotape or audiotape practice sessions.

Families often confuse even the most effective therapists. Thus, the therapist should feel free to stop for a moment in the middle of the session and ask the external helpers for their reactions and suggestions.

Step 6: Provide Immediate Feedback and Complete Notes (10 Minutes)

This is a highly structured session, and there is often immediate personal need to process and discuss the session. In particular, it is helpful for the therapist to ask the family "What stands out for you from this practice session?" Allow time to provide true personal reactions to the practice session. At this point, the observers should sit back and let the participants take control. Use this time to complete your classification and notes.

Step 7: Review Practice Session and Provide Feedback (15 to 30 Minutes)

It is important when giving feedback to allow the therapist and family receiving the feedback to be in charge. At this point, the observers can share their observations. As usual, feedback should be specific, concrete, and nonjudgmental. Pay attention to strengths of the interview.

Generalization: Taking Confrontation Concepts Home

The following activities are suggested to help you test the concepts of this chapter in the real world.

Activity 1: Practice Confrontation with Individuals in Daily Life

Look for and report incongruities you observe in yourself and others over a one-week period of time. Classify the discrepancies into the five types suggested in this chapter. What other categories beyond these five do you observe?

Gently try confrontations with those with whom you come into contact. Be nonjudgmental and use their key words as you paraphrase and summarize for them what you have observed. Use confrontation skills with sensitivity and care.

Observe how people you encounter in your day-to-day life are at different levels on the Confrontation Impact Scale. You can make this assessment in two ways: First, you can classify their reactions to comments using the scale. However, there are lifestyle issues involved as well. Some people go through life functioning at levels 1 and 2, denying all or part of the reality that surrounds them. Second, you can write down evidence of your observations of individual responses and of general lifestyle issues.

Activity 2: Observation of Families, Groups, and Organizations

Using the suggestions from activity 1, visit an open meeting of a community governance group, a PTA, or a business organization. Record your observations of discrepancies and reactions to confrontation. Look especially for positive examples of groups that enable members to achieve new discoveries representative of levels 4 and 5 of the Confrontation Impact Scale. What are these groups doing right?

With permission of the family, observe a family meal using the same suggestions from activity 1. What aspects of family life lead to growth and development? At what general level is this family functioning?

Activity 3: The Interview

Using an audiotape or videotape of one of your own interviews with an individual or family, list discrepancies and incongruities you observe. You probably confronted the client or clients at some point or you used a major intervention. At what level on the Confrontation Level Scale did the family or individual respond to your efforts? Provide specific evidence supporting your conclusion.

An even more important test is to identify the creation of the New in your clients. What specific acts of creation leading to new points of view, new behavior, or even multiperspective seeing can you document in your own work?

Apply the techniques of this chapter carefully with a client or family in counseling or therapy each day. As you learn the value of the conceptual and practical developmental model, you may find yourself using the concepts in regular interviewing practice.

Activity 4: Consider the Yakima Nation Proverb

The FLAME never repeats itself.
The lesson is—it is wise to doubt the right course to follow.

As you review this chapter, what does this proverb say to you and say about your own practice of helping others grow?

_____

_____

_____

_____

_____

_____

Suggested Supplementary Reading and Activities

Additional Reading

Ivey, A. 1986. *Developmental therapy: Theory into practice.* San Francisco: Jossey-Bass.
Chapter 5, "How Clients Move to New Developmental Levels," provides more
theoretical background for the concepts presented in this chapter. Particularly helpful
may be the discussions of Piaget's own creative process (pp. 180–181) and his concept
of creativity (pp. 183–185). A more complex version of the Confrontation Impact
Scale may be found on pages 199–201, where the five levels of the CIS are related to
such psychodynamic defense mechanisms as denial, projection, and sublimation. A
variety of clinical and research ideas based on these concepts can be used to follow
up the introduction presented in this chapter. The chapter also includes important
information on maintaining and sustaining change generated in the interview. A
variety of exercises and activities are found in the chapter.

Drum, D., and A. Lawler. 1988. *Developmental interventions: Theories, principles, and
practice.* Westerville, Ohio: Merrill.
This book provides a very helpful alternative to traditional therapeutic interventions.
Ideas for organizing and evaluating developmental interventions are presented and
complement the concepts of this chapter.

Minuchin, S., and H. Fishman. 1981. *Family therapy techniques.* Cambridge, Mass:
Harvard University Press.
Many techniques for confronting and perturbing families are used by family therapists
in an attempt to help these families toward more complete understanding. This book
offers a particularly helpful discussion of how family therapists can be more effective.

Kohlberg, L. 1981. *The philosophy of moral development.* New York: Harper & Row.
Those who have worked with Kohlberg's concepts have found that discussing moral
dilemmas is a useful way to facilitate growth over time. Those with a "higher" moral
level can confront those with "lower" levels of morality and thus help them move
"up" a stage. DCT, which combines traditional ideas about confrontation in the
interview with a developmental model, offers a systematic supplement to those
working in moral development. DCT offers specific ways to identify and measure
confrontation and its impact. Moral development training groups tend to focus, in
a general way, on discrepancies and their resolution. DCT perturbation techniques
can add precision to the confrontation approach, which is a part of moral developmental
education.

Kübler-Ross, E. 1969. *On death and dying.* New York: MacMillan.
The structure and content of this book provides important extensions for the concepts
of this chapter. The five levels of the Confrontation Impact Scale are not directly
parallel to the five stages described by Kübler-Ross, but an examination of the
similarities and differences may clarify the CIS and help provide a systematic way to
integrate ideas about death and dying into a developmental process of counseling and
psychotherapy.

Research Suggestions

1. Examine your own interviewing practice. Generate a transcript of one of
your own sessions. Classify how the client responds on the CIS to your
interventions. Have another person do the same classifications. Compute your
interrater agreement. Now, look more broadly at how the client or family
conceptualized the problem at the first part of the interview. Can you find

measurable evidence that your clients moved from denial or partial understanding of an issue to higher levels of understanding as measured by the CIS?

You may want to examine a series of interviews you have had with a client or family. Here, you can identify main themes of the therapy or counseling series and how well they moved over time. For example, perhaps they moved from partially dealing with their issues (level 2) to full examination (level 3) to development of new and larger constructs and behaviors (level 5). Which of your interventions seemed to be key in this process? In short, the larger examination of movement over time may become a useful outcome measure for your professional helping practice.

2. The specific components of the confrontation techniques and the Confrontation Impact Scale can be applied to Kohlberg-type moral dilemmas. A useful and potentially significant exercise would be to combine moral reasoning with developmental assessment and treatment strategies. Can the results of moral development perturbations, using the Kohlberg system, be reliably assessed following the methods presented in this chapter?

In addition, clients' reactions to general issues of loss and death and dying may be evaluated empirically by adapting the CIS to the work of Kübler-Ross.

Answers to Chapter Exercise

Example 1: 1, 2, 3, 4, 5
Example 2: 3, 2, 5, 4, 1
Example 3: 1, 3, 2, 4, 5

5 Development Over the Life Span

Allen E. Ivey and Sandra Rigazio-DiGilio

The child brings us immortality.
We bring the child a place to belong.

Yakima Nation Proverb

L ife-span development is more than linear growth over time. We do not just move through a series of events in our lives. Our early individual and family experiences remain with us. The manner in which we have connected with others in the past provides us with resources as we move toward autonomy and individuation.

But autonomy and individuation are not enough. We need to reattach with others throughout our lives—with friends and lovers, children, and co-workers. Balancing the twin needs of separation and attachment, connection and autonomy is one of the most important developmental tasks we all face.

The events and relationships of our lives become organized into patterns that tend to repeat again and again. Both positive and problematic aspects of the self often can be traced back to critical events in a person's life that later manifest as repeating behaviors, thoughts, and feelings.

DCT's questioning sequence provides a way to identify specific attachment and separation issues, find their origins in sensorimotor and concrete experience, and then examine life patterns.

This chapter focuses on more comprehensive life-span developmental patterns, starting with a brief review of Erikson's life-span theory and Haley's family life-cycle theory. These theories are used as a basis for three methods for integrating life-span theory into practice.

The Developmental Tasks of Individuals

Erikson's (1963) eight stages of human development each have a corresponding critical developmental issue. Erikson maintains that unless the developmental tasks of each stage have been mastered (adequate horizontal development), vertical movement to the next life stage will be impaired. For example, if a sufficient foundation of trust has not been developed, the child will have difficulty, in elementary school years, gaining a sense of competence and, in adolescence, developing a sense of identity. Erikson's life stages and developmental tasks are presented in Table 5-1. Erikson theorizes that all developmental conflicts are present throughout the life span. Certain developmental tasks are most critical at each life stage. Uncompleted developmental tasks may manifest themselves as problems later in life.

At each life stage, the conflicts that come with other life stages are still factors. That is, although the infant's major life issue may be trust versus mistrust, other developmental tasks also exist. An infant begins developing a sense of autonomy and capability as it matures physically, emotionally, and cognitively. All infants gain more impact on the world and thus achieve a sense of initiative. If this initiative is squashed by parents, a sense of guilt and inferiority may begin. The development of trust or mistrust between a child and caregiver can affect later developmental tasks. If a child generates a sense of trust, later generation of a satisfactory personal identity and intimacy with others is more easily accomplished.

On examination, the model shows that all life issues are present all the time.

Table 5-1. Erikson's Stages of Development Throughout the Life Span

Stage [a]	Developmental conflicts [b]							
Oral (sensorimotor)	**BASIC TRUST VS. MISTRUST**	Autonomy vs. shame and doubt	Initiative vs. guilt	Industry vs. inferiority	Identity vs. role confusion	Intimacy vs. isolation	Generativity vs. stagnation	Ego integrity vs. despair
Muscular-anal (mid-sensorimotor)	Basic trust vs. mistrust	**AUTONOMY VS. SHAME AND DOUBT**	Initiative vs. guilt	Industry vs. inferiority	Identity vs. role confusion	Intimacy vs. isolation	Generativity vs. stagnation	Ego integrity vs. despair
Locomotor (late sensorimotor)	Basic trust vs. mistrust	Autonomy vs. shame and doubt	**INITIATIVE VS. GUILT**	Industry vs. inferiority	Identity vs. role confusion	Intimacy vs. isolation	Generativity vs. stagnation	Ego integrity vs. despair
Latency (concrete operations)	Basic trust vs. mistrust	Autonomy vs. shame and doubt	Initiative vs. guilt	**INDUSTRY VS. INFERIORITY**	Identity vs. role confusion	Intimacy vs. isolation	Generativity vs. stagnation	Ego integrity vs. despair
Puberty and adolescence (formal operations)	Basic trust vs. mistrust	Autonomy vs. shame and doubt	Initiative vs. guilt	Industry vs. inferiority	**IDENTITY VS. ROLE CONFUSION**	Intimacy vs. isolation	Generativity vs. stagnation	Ego integrity vs. despair
Young adulthood	Basic trust vs. mistrust	Autonomy vs. shame and doubt	Initiative vs. guilt	Industry vs. inferiority	Identity vs. role confusion	**INTIMACY VS. ISOLATION**	Generativity vs. stagnation	Ego integrity vs. despair
Adulthood	Basic trust vs. mistrust	Autonomy vs. shame and doubt	Initiative vs. guilt	Industry vs. inferiority	Identity vs. role confusion	Intimacy vs. isolation	**GENERATIVITY VS. STAGNATION**	Ego integrity vs. despair
Maturity	Basic trust vs. mistrust	Autonomy vs. shame and doubt	Initiative vs. guilt	Industry vs. inferiority	Identity vs. role confusion	Intimacy vs. isolation	Generativity vs. stagnation	**EGO INTEGRITY VS. DESPAIR**

SOURCE: Adapted from *Childhood and Society*, Second Edition, by Erik H. Erikson, by permission of W.W. Norton & Company, Inc. Copyright 1950, © 1963 by W.W. Norton & Company, Inc. Copyright renewed 1978 by Erik H. Erikson.

[a] Comparable Piagetian stages are in parentheses.

[b] Central developmental conflicts are in bold caps; continuing conflicts are in regular type.

At first glance, Erikson's model seems linear, but in truth it is holistic. The developmental tasks of life repeat themselves again and again as patterns that eventually become what we call "personality." The adult struggling with the central issue of generativity versus stagnation still deals with issues of intimacy versus isolation, identity versus role confusion, and trust versus mistrust.

Different cultures resolve developmental conflicts in different ways. The predominantly White North American culture, for example, emphasizes individual autonomy. Autonomy is often less important for Hispanics and Blacks. In many cultures, autonomy is more relational and family centered. In Japanese culture, dependence on the group is the traditional goal, and totally autonomous individualism is discouraged.

Using Erikson's life-span framework without taking into account cultural differences can result in serious error. The definition of healthy trust, autonomy, initiative, and other life-stage issues varies among cultural groups. Also, men and women may differ significantly in their developmental issues at Eriksonian stages. For example, you will find in the following section that some serious criticisms are made of the Eriksonian model as it relates to women in the adolescent and later years. Even in infancy they are treated differently.

As a helping professional, you will need to address the specific life tasks of your clients. Many adult clients have never developed an adequate foundation of trust, autonomy, industry, and identity. Your therapeutic task is to help them complete and build an adequate developmental foundation. A foundation of trust is essential for full generativity in life.

Table 5-2 compares Erikson's life stages with those of Piaget, showing the individual's cognitive and affective development as he or she works through Eriksonian developmental tasks. A sense of trust is generated primarily in the sensorimotor stage. At this stage, the child is particularly vulnerable to the environment. The generation of a sense of initiative and control occurs when the child is particularly likely to engage in magical thinking (late sensorimotor). A sense of industry and competence is generated during the concrete-operational period.

Table 5-2. Piaget's Stages and Erikson's Developmental Tasks

Age (years)	Piaget	Erikson
0–2	Sensorimotor	Trust vs. mistrust
18 mo.–3 yr.		Autonomy vs. shame and doubt
2–7	Preoperational (late sensorimotor)	Initiative vs. guilt
7–12	Concrete operations	Industry vs. inferiority
12–19	Formal operations	Identity vs. role confusion

The relationship between Erikson's and Piaget's frameworks becomes particularly clear in adolescence, the period of identity development. To develop a clear identity, one must step outside oneself and think about oneself from a new perspective; this is a formal-operational task. If the adolescent does not feel good about him- or herself, owing to previous life experience (for example, the failure to develop trust or a sense of industry earlier), the generation of a positive formal-operational identity will be difficult. As this lack of positive self-identity continues over the life span, the individual will experience problems in adulthood and maturity.

Clients come to psychotherapy stuck in old, unworkable life patterns. These patterns were learned over the life span. One of the important tasks of the therapist is to find the relationship between present styles of behaving and past developmental history. Armed with this understanding, the therapist can encourage behavioral and cognitive action that will help the client overcome past developmental blocks.

DCT focuses on the basic life tasks of sensorimotor, concrete-operational, and formal-operational development. The systematic learning sequence of DCT provides an opportunity for the therapist and client to return to the beginning of development and learn about the nature of trust and mistrust (sensorimotor), industry and inferiority (concrete), and identity versus role confusion (formal). The dialectic/systemic level focuses on issues of ego integrity and the organization and meaning of experience. Failure to integrate successfully can result in despair.

Gender Issues in Development [1]

Women Follow a Developmental Path Different From Men

This statement is rapidly becoming an axiom of the helping profession since Carol Gilligan wrote her ground-breaking book, *In a Different Voice* (1982). Gilligan points out that Erikson's conception of development focuses on separateness, and Erikson's emphasis on such words as autonomy, initiation, and industry tend to focus on individuals doing or accomplishing things by themselves.

Women's developmental orientation, Gilligan maintains, is more relational in nature. She believes that women in adolescence are actually working simultaneously on issues of identity and intimacy. She talks about women as being more relational—or more attached, to use the language of Bowlby (1969, 1973). In effect, the cultural developmental task of men is to become relatively more autonomous and separate while the task of women is to become relatively more attached and relational. Extensive research has been completed on the

---

[1] Further discussions on these critical issues may be found in Chapter 7 in a section entitled "The Relational Orientation Contrasted with Individualistic Theory." Also Table 8-1 explores the implications of the interdependent approach to counseling. There are some interesting parallels between Gilligan and the Native American value system portrayed there.

complexity of women's development, which seems to bear out Gilligan's thesis (see, for example, Gilligan, Ward, & Taylor, 1988).

Gilligan (1988) proposes two separate models of the self. The first is the *separate/objective self,* which is autonomous in relation to others. This model tends to be characteristic of male development in North American culture with an emphasis on relationships between highly separated individuals, a morality based on rules and fairness, and roles based on duty or obligation.

The *connected self* is interdependent and responds to others with a sense of concern. This response is mediated through a morality of caring and connection in relationships. Gilligan (1988) notes that women's development in North American culture is more difficult then men's because the relational connected self requires more complex thought patterns.

It seems clear that developmental theory must be constantly informed by an awareness of differences between men's and women's roles in North America. Even the most cursory review reveals that values of differing cultural groups in terms of the connected self and the interdependent self must be considered in the future. For example, many Native American, Black, Hispanic, and Asian families call more attention to the connected self than does the "mainstream" White male culture.

An Interconnected Versus Linear Life-Span Development

Differences in male and female development exist throughout the life span. While it is clear that boys and girls are treated differently from infancy and experience different types of relationships and expectations from caregivers and culture, gender-oriented theory gives prime criticism to Erikson's development framework as it applies to adolescence and adult life. Neugarten (1979), for example, points out that women's development could be considered as a fan in which you can see all the pieces moving out from a central core with all the parts related to the rest. An adolescent woman, for example, may indeed be working on issues of identity, but intimacy may be a higher priority. A woman in the working world may deal with issues of generativity during her 20's, intimacy in her 30's, and perhaps rework issues around identity when she reaches 40.

Women's development may touch on some parts of Erikson's framework and in more or less detail than he suggests. Needless to say, the same variations in developmental transitions can occur with men—life is not a straight line and taking the Erikson framework too literally can cause problems.

Other Types of Transitions

Developmental transition is an important word in the Eriksonian framework and refers to our growth over the life span. This concept is considered too simplistic by Schlossberg (1989, pp. 28–29), who outlines six types of developmental transitions showing that change occurs in many ways besides aging. All of the following transitions regularly appear in counseling and therapy sessions.

Elected transitions: graduating from school, changing jobs, having a baby, retiring, moving, divorcing.

Surprise transitions: car accident, death of a child, plant closing, getting an unexpected raise or large promotion, the state cuts welfare benefits for poor mothers.

Nonevents (when the expected doesn't happen): infertility, a promotion or raise doesn't come through, child does not leave home.

Life on hold (transition "waiting to happen"): long engagement, waiting to die in a hospice, waiting for the "right person" to come along, the delay that comes while waiting for an important other person to make a key decision.

Sleeper transition (occurs almost without your awareness): becoming fat or thin, falling in love, getting bored at a job you once loved, gradually tiring of a relationship, neighborhood decays or becomes overrun with drugs.

Double whammies: retiring and losing a spouse by death; having a baby and moving back to one income; caring for ill parents at home and one of your children gets divorced and returns as well; a fire occurs, its winter, and the welfare office has lost your file. (Schlossberg notes that daily life "hassles" such as a difficult commute, a sick child, a bounced check, or a difficult boss can produce considerable stress in themselves.)

The combined implications of Gilligan, Neugarten, and Schlossberg cannot be ignored. Certainly women do move through the life span, but we need to broaden our constructs of development with special attention to issues of gender and culture.

The Family Life Cycle

Life-span developmental tasks are more complicated when family and systemic issues are considered. A teenager seeking a sense of identity may have a 35-year-old mother starting work for the first time and a 43-year-old father going through a mid-life crisis. The father faces a life issue of maintaining generativity in the face of declining physical ability. The mother, for the first time in her life, may be just beginning to gain a sense of her identity and competence in the work world. The stress of developing an identity for the teenager may be intensified by the stress in the family, as each individual attempts to resolve possibly conflicting developmental needs.

Developing an individual identity is highly related to the developmental stage and needs of each family member and the family as a whole. Each person in the family has personal developmental tasks, which may not always be in accord with those of other family members. In addition, the parents may not have worked through their own developmental tasks adequately and thus may never have established their own identity or sense of trust. All these factors deeply influence the developmental path of the child and adolescent.

Haley's life-cycle theory is represented in Figure 5-1 as an open circle. Each stage of family life has key separation and attachment tasks (see Table 1-2). For example, when children leave home, the couple faces this separation from their children as well as their own need to reattach to each other in a new way. In addition, the couple may need to begin new attachments to their children's spouses or lovers while their own parents simultaneously are becoming more dependent.

The meaning and content of Haley's life-cycle theory vary with cultural and family type differences. As noted elsewhere, the family life cycle varies for individuals of Irish, Italian, Chinese, and Jewish background, whether in North America or abroad. Also, there are fewer intact nuclear families—the family type on which Haley based his theory. Figure 5-1 thus should be modified to fit each culture and family type. Regardless of such differences, all families must in some way work through the developmental tasks associated with the family life cycle, although the tasks may be sequenced differently with varying degrees of importance, according to the culture.

The focus of much work in family therapy is on transition times and the associated separation and attachment tasks. If the family has become too enmeshed, with a resultant lack of boundary definition, children leaving home can represent a trauma and the event can trigger a severe family crisis. If the family was too separate and detached, with rigid boundaries, the couple may have problems during this time reattaching to each other and to aging parents. Again, there is a delicate balance required of individuals and families as they negotiate their way through the life cycle.

Coordinating multiple developmental tasks and needs of family members in an intact, nuclear family is complicated. Other factors, such as differing cultural and family types and the continuing impact of our complex, postindustrial society, add further complications and challenges.

Integrating Life-Span and Family Life-Cycle Theory

As this point, a useful exercise is to identify one life-span developmental stage that was or is of particular interest to you—for example, adolescent identity de-

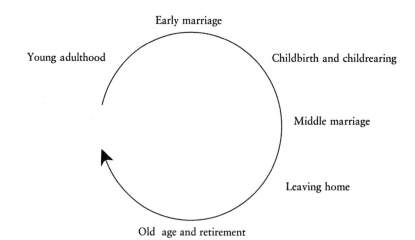

Figure 5-1. Haley's Life-Cycle Theory.

velopment. As you developed your own personal identity, other family members were struggling with their own life issues. . What happened to your parents inevitably affected your sense of self and ability to be both connected with others and autonomous. At this critical stage of development, divorce or the absence or death of one parent can be especially difficult. At times, your need to establish a separate identity may have clashed with needs of other family members working through their life issues. As you were working through your issue of identity, what Eriksonian developmental tasks were your family members facing? Did your parents achieve a sense of intimacy or of generativity?

_____

_____

_____

_____

Outline your own personal struggle with the issue of identity. How might the individual developmental needs of each family member have conflicted with your gaining a sense of identity and affected you as the person you now are?

_____

_____

_____

_____

_____

Consider those early events that affected your later life patterns of thinking, feeling, and behaving. What patterns in your present life have continued from these events?

_____

_____

_____

_____

As discussed earlier, cultural and sexual differences affect how you develop a sense of trust, autonomy, industry, and identity. How did your gender and cultural differences affect your development of these qualities?

_____

_____

_____

_____

Introspective-Developmental Counseling

Introspective developmental counseling (IDC) provides a systematic framework for examining the foundations of development.

This approach, elaborated by Tamase (1989), draws on Japanese Naikan therapy, the work of Erikson, and DCT theory and practice. Tamase argues that client personality trends and behavioral dispositions depend on life history. The goal of introspective-developmental counseling is to discover how past history repeats itself in present-day life.

Introspective-developmental counseling involves four highly structured sessions, each focusing on four foundation phases of life development: birth through preschool, elementary school, high school, and the recent past and future. These periods correspond to Eriksonian life stages and describe developmental experiences common to Western and Eastern culture.

The structured series of interviews is presented to the client as a developmental learning opportunity. The goal is to facilitate the client's understanding of personal life history in the hope that this understanding will bring about a better understanding of current life patterns. As the client works through the four interview series, he or she reviews life issues, such as family and peer relationships, life accomplishments, and problems experienced.

As clients think about their life histories, they gradually see patterns from the past that continue in their present-day lives. Clients often find that many of the issues they currently face can be better understood in the context of past life events. To put it another way, introspective-developmental counseling is oriented toward cognitive understanding of the past and the past's repetition in the present. Here again, perturbation—the questioning process itself—is a critical therapeutic intervention.

Introspective-developmental counseling can be contrasted with historical approaches to therapy such as Freudian analysis and other psychodynamic theories. Traditional approaches to therapy typically begin with an exploration of current life problems and then return to the past to search for the developmental roots of these difficulties. Tamase argues that we can review our cognitive-developmental history as a natural progression of random and concrete life events that we organize into patterns of thought and action. Through the process of introspective-developmental counseling, clients can gain new knowledge of themselves and their relations with others from a more positive, developmentally oriented frame of reference.

In developing the model, Tamase had counselors in training work through four one-hour sessions. In pairs, these counselors interviewed each other for half an hour, following seven specific questions designed to elicit information about the individual's experiences from birth through the present.[2] The IDC process proved to be a helpful growth experience for the counselor trainees, and it was found that the model could be expanded and used in counseling and therapy with clients seeking to understand themselves more fully.

---

[2] Tamase's original research questions may be obtained by writing to him at the Department of Psychology, Nara University of Education, Takabatake, Nara 630, Japan.

The first session focuses on the birth through preschool period. Tamase instructed counselors to ask seven specific questions over the course of the interview. The following list (adapted from Tamase, 1988, p. 3) presents a revised and expanded version of the original IDC questions for this period.

Introspective-Developmental Counseling Questions (birth to preschool)

1. Could you tell me about your family members (for the purpose of structuring the interview and understanding basics of the family system)? What particular important life events were they experiencing during your earliest years?
2. Is there anything about your birth that you have heard from your mother or other family member?
3. Could you tell me about your life from the earliest age you can remember?
4. What is the most impressive thing that happened prior to kindergarten?
5. What kind of behavior bothered your mother when you were a preschool child?
6. How did you feel about your parents when you were a preschool child?
7. Did you struggle with your brothers or sisters at this age?
8. Is there any particular event that made you feel either very happy or afraid at this age?
9. What single event do you recall most positively from this period of your life?
10. What patterns from this early period continue in your present life?

Tamase puts special emphasis on listening skills such as paraphrasing, reflection of feeling, and summarization. Introspective-developmental counseling does not make interpretations of the client's life history but rather helps the client make sense of his or her own life. Tamase's emphasis on listening and natural development is in marked contrast with psychodynamic orientations, which are highly interpretative and may encourage the client to adopt a particular way of viewing the world.

The questions in the list are about preschool, sensorimotor issues and as such relate to trust versus mistrust and autonomy versus shame and doubt. The first question is designed to identify the family context at this particular stage. These questions elicit random information without any particular organization. However, as the client hears data fed back and summarized by the counselor, concrete events descriptive of the period are apparent. As the session continues, clients are able to see patterns in the preschool period that later affect their development in elementary school and in later life stages.

Appendix 4 of this book contains IDC questions for the other three developmental stages. Questions for the elementary school period focus on issues of competence (industry versus inferiority). Questions for the high school period emphasize relationships with friends and family as well as academic achievement. The final session focuses on the recent past and the future. Questions are about current vocation and personal adjustment, relationships with friends and family, and current problem issues.

It is particularly important in such a systematic life review to maintain a positive orientation. There is a danger that the focus can remain solely on problems. The last question in each period, "What single event do you recall most positively from this period of your life?" is particularly important. A developmental review should not focus just on problems; it should also emphasize strengths and positives. Clients can draw on these positive events as they cope with real difficulties from the past or present. Introspective-developmental counseling can be a beneficial growth experience if the counselor is careful to pay attention to positive assets of the client throughout the life span.

Tamase (1989) has conducted a clinical evaluation of his concepts, which reveals some interesting and promising findings. A review of audiotapes of interviews in this preliminary study showed that all counselor trainees were at the formal-operational stage—that is, they were able to identify continuing patterns in their lives. The fact that all clients reported seeing new patterns and continuities in their lives raises an interesting question: Did Tamase's systematic step-by-step framework enable clients to see the patterns, or is this method only effective with formal clients? Experience has shown that the sequential, developmentally oriented questions described in Chapter 3 can help many sensorimotor or concrete clients find patterns in their lives. What seems to be most critical is that the therapist make systematic interventions and follow logical cognitive progressions. With more concrete clients, the counselor should move more slowly through the life review process and should elicit more examples from the client before attempting to help the client recognize these patterns.

Tamase also observed that sensorimotor experiences and strong feelings and images often surface during the first session (the birth through preschool period). As might be anticipated, clients tended to talk about elementary school experiences in a more concrete way, saving their formal, patterned thinking primarily for the discussion about the high school period. Finally, in the fourth session which allows for more reflection and integration of the past, clients demonstrated more dialectical/systemic thinking—that is, they were able to examine more complex patterns of their past life and see how they related to the present.

The comments of two of Tamase's clients reflect the usefulness of the process (Tamase, 1989, pp. 14–15).

> The process was very valuable to me, even though I had three previous years of therapy. It was especially useful to concentrate on one period of life at a time. This helped me to see the overall progression of my development from beginning to the present.

> One of the most predominant feelings from doing these exercises is amazement at the differences in emotions that each session brings back. The first and third seemed especially good, while the second seemed bad. Prior to introspective-developmental counseling, I was aware of a generally good childhood and past life history. I was not aware, however, of how strongly different my emotions were in regard to the different periods.

Clearly, introspective-developmental counseling is a promising, positive approach to counseling for those clients who wish to gain a better understanding of themselves and their growth process. The systematic questions and the planned review of life events offer clients the opportunity to examine themselves and to discover life patterns. Introspective-developmental counseling does not start with problems and issues of difficulty but returns to beginning life stages and enables clients, in a positive way, to review life events and their impact on the present.

A useful personal exercise is to review the questions listed on p. 129. Or you may prefer to review a later period of life using the questions in Appendix 4. Read each question silently and think about your responses. Then write down below a few key words to remind you of your responses to each of the first nine questions.

1. _____

2. _____

3. _____

4. _____

5. _____

6. _____

7. _____

8. _____

9. _____

You have now listed several seemingly unrelated events, perhaps using sensorimotor and concrete examples. If you have not included concrete examples in your responses to the questions, do so now, indicating specific experiences and events for each question on the above list.

Review your list and write down the patterns you see that have carried over to later periods of your life.

10. _____

_____

_____

_____

Now consider what you have written from a broader family perspective. How were your traits and patterns related to your own family history? Were there important crises and events that affected the family and you? Were the individual tasks your family members struggled with important in your own development?

Introspective-developmental counseling clearly shows that developmental counseling and therapy can be organized more systematically. Tamase does not see his work as therapy, although it may be therapeutic. Instead, he considers it a method for reviewing life patterns and opening the way for more extended analysis, if desired. Many clients find that answering the questions in brief individual or group sessions is helpful in making sense of their lives.

The series of four sessions outlined by Tamase could serve as part of a larger program of treatment. For example, for a client who has discovered a pattern of nonassertiveness going back to earlier periods of life, cognitive understanding may not be enough. The counselor may utilize concrete assertiveness training so that the formal-operational knowledge can become specific, concrete action. Later, rational disputation and cognitive-behavioral methods may be useful in challenging and changing the formal-operational thought patterns.

Each of Tamase's questions can be explored in more depth using the systematic questioning sequence of DCT. The four-session program can be expanded into a major program of systematic therapy if developmental crises and family events are explored in more depth. Many people who go through the IDC process will identify key developmental events that still are affecting their day-to-day lives. They may need to work through their discoveries at a more emotional level. For example, a client who reveals a traumatic event at the preschool period may be helped by carefully going through the systematic questions of DCT. The client can be asked to think of a sensorimotor image connected with the experience and the resulting emotions then may be explored in depth. The event can then be explored at the concrete, formal, and dialectic/systemic levels.

Finally, you may want to emphasize family background and family systems thinking when employing the introspective-developmental approach to counseling. The awareness of how one's life has been affected by one's family may create the desire to work through old remaining issues in family therapy.

Life-Span Therapy

Victorio Guidano (1987, 1988) has evolved a one-year systematic therapeutic program based on developmental principles. He uses this developmental approach with clients with serious psychological conditions such as depression, obsession, and agoraphobia. Guidano's assessment procedure helps the therapist trace the developmental history of the client that led to the current problem. The therapist then identifies the client's cognitive representational models of the world. These cognitive models, or ideas about the world, often cause the clients to act in a depressed, obsessed, or agoraphobic manner.

Once client and therapist understand the client's cognitive model of the world, the   client is encouraged to review this model and to see how it corresponds to actuality. At this point, the client is confronted with discrepancies between developmental understanding and events in the real world. Is it logical to be depressed, to allow oneself to be taken over by obsessions, or to fear going out into the world? Cognitive techniques such as those used by Beck (1976) are important at this stage of the therapeutic process. Behavioral techniques such as thought stopping and assertiveness training can be used to help clients apply formal-operational concepts to the concrete world.

Guidano's treatment method includes some of the confrontational techniques described in the preceding chapter. The goal is to move clients from the denial and distortions of level-1 and level-2 thinking to the construction and creation of new meanings at levels 4 and 5. Guidano, as DCT, emphasizes the separation and attachment constructs of Bowlby (1969, 1973). In the here and now of the interview, clients often repeat behavioral and cognitive patterns they learned in their families and cultures.

Guidano's approach is particularly useful in helping clients discover how their "map" of reality evolved in the family and cultural context. For example, in Western society most clients tend to be overly individualistic. They either assume too much responsibility for their problems or they blame others, particularly family members, for their difficulties. Guidano stresses the transaction between individual and family and among individual, family, and culture.

After clients achieve this level of introspection (which takes approximately a year), Guidano changes his role in the therapeutic relationship from therapist to consultant. Clients now know how to examine and challenge their cognitions and world views, and Guidano meets with clients weekly to help them to continue this process. At this stage, clients often discover how their ideas about the world evolved in a family and cultural context. The goal is not to blame the family but rather to help clients understand how cognitions develop in context so they can then take responsibility for thinking and creating new ways of being.

Life-span developmental approaches, such as Guidano's, focus on education and base remediation and treatment of developmental concepts. In life-span therapeutic models, the client is more of an equal partner with the therapist in that the client's cognitive map, rather than the therapist's theoretical map, is central to the therapeutic process. Life-span theory assumes that there is developmental logic to even the most disturbed behavior. The task of the developmentally oriented counselor is to assess and understand the client's developmental processes and then to institute treatment procedures to help the client work through developmental blocks.

DCT as a Life-Span Therapy Program

Erikson, Haley, Tamase, and Guidano provide important frameworks for life-span counseling and therapy. However, the DCT model offers even more specific guidance for helping professionals who are developmentally oriented.

The key points of a life-span approach are as follows:

The individual has specific developmental tasks at each stage of the life-span, and how these issues are resolved affects the individual throughout his or her life.

Gilligan, Neugarten, and Schlossberg remind us that gender issues in development have been given insufficient attention to date.

Individual development occurs in the context of the family and culture.

A specific questioning sequence can be used to help clients reflect on their developmental pasts. In Tamase's introspective-developmental counseling, clients begin to understand their own development in a family context.

It is possible, as Guidano's work shows, to take a positive developmental approach with a variety of clients whose problems range from "normal" to "pathological."

Thus far in this book, DCT has been primarily applied to a "normal" client population. However, specific approaches of DCT can be used in a life-span developmental framework with a variety of client populations, as Rigazio-DiGilio (1989; Rigazio-DiGilio & Ivey, in press) demonstrates in her use of systematic DCT questioning strategies with depressed inpatients.

At the beginning of the session, interviewers in the Rigazio-DiGilio study asked depressed patients a standard question: "To begin with, I would like you to respond to a statement that I hope will stimulate you in some way. I would like you to say as much as you can about what happens for you when you focus on your family." This question helps the depressed patient think about him-or herself in a more contextual, family oriented way, but does not identify a particular cognitive-developmental level.

As discussed in a previous chapter, Rigazio-DiGilio found that both interviewers and external raters were able to classify the cognitive-developmental level of depressed inpatients with 90% interrater agreement by the first 50 to 100 words spoken by the client. Most of these patients were concrete, but about 30% were formal-operational and 15% were sensorimotor.

Clients suffering from depression who function at the sensorimotor and concrete levels may have difficulty with formal-operational, cognitive approaches. It is also the case that the entrenched formal-operational depressive may resist concrete modes of therapy, particularly in the early phase of treatment. Beck (1976) has had much success with his cognitive approach to working with depressives, which is largely owing to his use of many behavioral methods. Beck often takes clients back to sensorimotor experiencing and images, concretizes events surrounding the depression, and helps patients see their self-defeating, repeating patterns.

Next, the interviewers in Rigazio-DiGilio's study took each depressed patient through the eight stages of the Standard Cognitive-Developmental Interview (see Appendix 1 and Chapter 3). Clients were asked, when they focused on a family issue, to describe one visual (sensorimotor) image that occurred for them, a concrete example of a difficulty, the formal patterns ("Does this type of thing happen a lot for you in your family?"), and dialectic/systemic issues ("What rule is your family operating under?" and "What sense do you make of all these ideas as a whole?").

Box 5-1 presents a summary of Rigazio-DiGilio's questions and examples of client responses. The systematic use of questioning strategies helps depressed patients talk about their depression from different cognitive frameworks. In addition, as they go through the interview, patients start to see patterns in their lives. At the dialectic/systemic level, they begin to discover the family and cultural roots in a manner similar to that described by Guidano's in his approach to developmental therapy.

Rigazio-DiGilio found that all depressed inpatients could move systematically from the visual image to concrete specifics of their difficulties and that all patients were able to see life patterns and how these patterns evolved in a family and cultural context. In only one interview, depressed patients, even those at the sensorimotor level, were able to discuss their depression at all four cognitive levels. In addition, all but two patients developed realistic goals for concrete behavioral change during the last segment of the interview and made a commitment to take action.

Rigazio-DiGilio does not claim that therapeutic change can be achieved in one session, but her work does illustrate that at least a beginning life-span developmental orientation and understanding can be achieved with most clients if the therapist or counselor uses DCT methods.

Rigazio-DiGilio's work with depressed patients reveals that the DCT model provides an alternative set of counseling and therapeutic strategies that can be used to expand client growth and development.

The DCT questioning sequence can be used with the life-span theories of Erikson. A more structured counseling program focusing on Erikson's conceptions but employing specific questions oriented to issues of trust, autonomy, industry, and so on is clearly possible.

Haley's (1973) family life-cycle approach can also be enhanced by developmentally oriented interventions. As already pointed out, DCT questions and strategies can be used to facilitate family development and understanding in a family therapy setting. In individual counseling, clients can benefit from a systematic review of family development over time.

The developmental counselor employs any number of traditional theories and methods that are useful. For instance, a treatment plan might include the expansion of client development at the sensorimotor level by using relaxation and Gestalt exercises, at the concrete level by using assertiveness training or decisional counseling, at the formal level by employing Rogerian or psychodynamic approaches, and at the dialectic/systemic level by using family systems or feminist therapy methods.

Other approaches to counseling and therapy such as behavioral, Rogerian, cognitive, and psychodynamic can also benefit by incorporating the sequential learning progressions of DCT questioning and intervention strategies. As noted by Ivey (1986), Rogers, Perls, and other therapists seem to employ, perhaps unconsciously, neo-Piagetian learning sequences (see Chapter 4).

Box 5-1. Inpatient Depressives' Responses to Questions in Rigazio-DiGilio's Study

Identifying Cognitive-Developmental Level:

Question: What happens for you when you focus on your family?

Response (Concrete): We get along fine, but they want me to stop taking my medication. Got two different ones I take—green and then one is orange and blue. They don't want me to take them.

Response (Formal): It all depends on what's going on. I spend too much time thinking about my family. They control me a lot.

Sensorimotor:

Question: I would like you to find one visual image that occurs for you when you focus on your family? What do you see, hear, feel?

Response: I see my parents in the messy kitchen. They are arguing. I hear shouting and I have trouble thinking. My stomach feels queasy. (My ulcer hurts; I get a headache.)

Concrete:

Question: Could you give me a specific example of how you and your family argue?

Response: Well, one time I came home late from a date. Mom met me at the door with a rolling pin. She called me a bitch. I said, "Please don't do that," and she really started yelling. I felt so scared. She said . . .

Formal:

Question: Does that happen in other situations? Is that a pattern?

Response: Oh yes, we have lots of arguments. (adds other examples) I seem to keep it all inside—seems to be a pattern with me. I think I don't usually talk because it always seems to get worse when I defend myself. It happened so often when I was a child.

Dialectic/Systemic:

Question: What is the underlying rule, and where did you learn it?

Response: I guess I learned to hold things inside. My mom was so strong that I just couldn't say anything. My grandmother was also domineering, and Mom tried very hard to please her. Poor Grandpa, he never got to say anything. No wonder I have a wall and get depressed. It is simply too much to meet all the family demands.

Question: What's wrong with that rule?

Response: Well, it certainly is part of what brought me here. I don't speak up enough for my rights. It's caused a lot of problems. I need to start speaking up for myself. (This final point became the focus for behavioral intervention and action.)

DCT and Family Perspectives

In Haley's family life cycle, family difficulties are considered within a developmental framework. Family and individual symptoms are seen as indicators of uncompleted life stages rather than as signals of pathology. Similar to DCT, Haley's view is that dysfunctional behavior and cognitions result from unfinished developmental tasks and are not just caused by interpersonal conflict or environmental stressors.

From the DCT perspective, the counseling and therapy process is similar to family development. The therapeutic process reflects the family life cycle. Working therapeutically with a family, for example, may be compared to a marriage in that trust is essential and a contract is important. For a short time, the therapist becomes as a family member. The process of understanding the presenting problem follows, and a new way of seeing and working with the problem evolves. As the family develops and grows, the therapist separates from the family. The therapeutic cycle has many parallels to the family life cycle, as is shown in the following list (adapted from DeFranck-Lynch, 1986, p. 56):

The Life Cycle of Family Therapy

1. Joining, engagement, attachment, and assessment	The therapist becomes a metaphorical family member, but one with clinical distance and defined boundaries.
2. Cognitive and behavioral interventions	The therapist participates in family life, affecting and being affected by the family.
3. Integrating, consolidating change, separation, and termination	The therapist and family separate, taking with them new views of the developmental process.

Stage 1: Joining

The counselor or therapist must accommodate to the family in the joining process. All family members need to feel that they are accepted as valuable contributors to the process. By asking open-ended questions of each individual and the family as a whole, the therapist can help each person feel comfortable and participatory. In addition, the responses to these questions enable the counselor to assess cognitive-developmental levels of the individual and of the family as a whole.

The following example (altered to disguise identifying data) shows how to assess developmental levels in a short period of time. In response to therapist inquiries, the Cachet family members introduced themselves as follows:

Ray: As you can probably tell by my accent, I'm French-Canadian. My parents came here from Montreal. I work as a cabinet maker for a living and took

> over my Dad's business because I was the oldest son. I make a good living.
> It's harder now that I'm sick, but the doctors say I will recover OK. (pre-
> dominantly concrete)

Stephanie: I'm French-Canadian, too. I have the same accent, only a little less. Let's see
... well you can see that I'm a mother. Lisa is my only child. I have lived in
Carthage almost all my life. My sister lives around the corner from me. (predominantly concrete)

Lisa: (Withdraws and whimpers. Mother spoke for her, but the child was asked
again and the mother's help was blocked.) I don't want to be here. It's
scary. Why did we have to come? I know I'm bad. I'll be good (cries again).
(predominantly sensorimotor)

The goal in this first stage of family intervention is for the helper to attach to,
or join with, the family to establish a working therapeutic system. It is important
to help the family arrive at a consensual view of the problem. This can be done
by asking the question "What do you want changed?" of the whole family and
then working out an answer with which all can agree. Again, the process of
defining the problem gives the counselor an opportunity to observe how the
family operates, and what its rules, perspectives, and organizational arrangements are.

Although family members will vary in cognitive-developmental level as they
describe the problem, the family as a whole will usually define the problem on
a single cognitive-developmental level. Some families present the problem in a
confused, illogical, sensorimotor fashion, a mode often characteristic of those in
chaos and trauma. A formal family will usually define the issue abstractly ("We
need to learn how to solve problems and talk about things more openly." or "We
always seem to be avoiding the issue.") A concrete family will usually describe
a specific event or problem needing solution ("Susie needs to start eating
properly." or "John is depressed and can't work.") As discussed in earlier
chapters, the formal family needs to work more at a concrete level, and the
concrete family needs to examine larger patterns (but only after concrete issues
are dealt with, resolved, and understood). It may not be necessary to take a
family through the full cognitive-developmental sequence.

The Cachet family described their problem to the therapist as follows:

Stephanie: I just want my daughter to behave. To stop acting or being sick. To go back
to school every day and get good grades.

Ray: That's right. I can't be bothered with these disruptions. I have to get well so I
can get back to work. You have to buck up and fly right, Lisa. That's
why we are here.

Stephanie: That's right, Lisa. Tell the therapist what's wrong. We keep getting letters
from school.

Lisa: I don't know. I don't understand. I try to be good. I just keep getting sick.
I don't know why. I don't want to be sick anymore. (whimpers and withdraws)

One can assess here that the Cachet parental authority is predominantly concrete while the daughter is operating from a sensorimotor level. The general cognitive-developmental level of the family as a whole appears to be concrete.

Many families will hold one individual—the "identified patient" (IP)—responsible for the problem. In such cases, the family frames the problem in a linear, causal way: "If only so and so would change, then everything would be fine." A key objective of family therapy is to help the family move to a dialectic/systemic frame of reference—that is, to help family members expand their view of the problem so they can see more options for change. If, with guidance and support of the therapist, the family can learn to look at itself as a system, family members will begin to understand how their interactions affect one another and how these interactions can exacerbate or alleviate the problems.

Using the following DCT questions from Box 5-2, the counselor can help the family view the problem from different perspectives. The family's responses allow the therapist to identify the family's ability to function at each cognitive-developmental level. Is the family overwhelmed by emotions? Does it see events as isolated or as connected by patterns? The questions are posed to dyads and triads within the family. The therapist's responsibility is to ensure that these dyads and triads discuss and answer the questions without assistance from other family members.

Box 5-2. DCT Questioning Strategies for Families

Sensorimotor

How do you two feel about this right now? When you see your children and husband talk this way, how do you feel? Tell your husband what you see when that happens. Did you see Jane's body react when you said that? Your wife is crying. What is happening for you now, at this moment? What, specifically, are you hearing?

Concrete

Can all of you give me an example of how (the presenting problem—bulimia, fighting, acting out) occurs? Would you two parents discuss what happens just before Jane vomits? Jane and Bob, what did your dad do afterward? What did you do? What did your mom do? How did the family deal with that afterward?

Formal

Has anything like this has ever happened before? What was done then? Was it successful or unsuccessful? Parents, please describe what else is going on in the family that has been affected by this problem. Is this a pattern for you? Looking at all of this, how do you understand what is happening?

Dialectic/systemic

Looking at all of this, how would you describe your family? Could you describe the family from another point of view? What type of rule(s) is your family operating under? Where did that rule come from? What is the flaw in that rule? What would you as a family like to do about that rule? What role does your religion or ethnicity play in the way you look at things and what you do?

By such questionings, the therapist gains an idea of the family's sense of reality at different cognitive levels and helps to foster interactions among family members.

The Cachet family then went through the Standard Cognitive Developmental Interview (see Appendix 1). This process took about an hour. Some example responses from each of the developmental levels, in abbreviated form, include:

Sensorimotor exploration, brief example:

Therapist: As the two of you (parents) see your (daughter) being so confused, how are you feeling right now?

Stephanie: I just think my daughter is out of control, and it makes me feel depressed. I'm at my wit's end. I just don't know what to do. My husband . . . (emotional tone is sad and confused)

Ray: I can't stand my wife being so sad. It bothers me to see her so upset. (emotionally flat)

Therapist: Talk to each other about how you are feeling right now.

Stephanie: You know it makes me sad and it makes me angry. (anger shows in vocal tone and flashing eyes)

Ray: I just wish you could snap out of it and take control of the situation. (angry)

Concrete exploration, brief example:

Therapist: Can you give me an example of how this sickness of Lisa's and refusal to go to school occurs?

Stephanie: Well, what happens is that Lisa starts feeling sick at night and has difficulty sleeping. I try to comfort her and calm her down, but it doesn't work. In the morning she usually feels just the same. I try to get her to go to school, but many times it won't work. I talk to her . . . I plead with her to go . . . if I take the time and trouble to force her to go, the nurse calls me and says I have to come and take her home because she's feeling ill.

Ray: I just watch it all happen. She should be more firm and take control. Pleading doesn't work. They have to straighten out their relationship. They used to be so close, I never had to worry about either of them. Things were more relaxed then.

Stephanie: I do what you suggest, but it doesn't work. She is so obstinate lately. (angry)

Ray: You really need to enforce the rules, like you used to. (angry)

Lisa: I feel sick in the morning. I just want to stay home. It starts at night. I get headaches and my tummy hurts. But I don't say nothing until morning. I don't even eat breakfast. It's hard to go to school.

The therapist moves to late concrete questions to obtain the sequence of Lisa's behavior. Stephanie describes a scene at home where Ray is working hard even though recovering from a heart attack. She tries to get Lisa to school, but Lisa stays home in bed. The sequence ends with another angry exchange.

Formal exploration, brief example:

Therapist:	Has anything like this ever happened before?
Stephanie:	When I was a girl, I never acted this way. I listened to my mother and I stayed out of my father's way.
Ray:	I took care of myself, too. I left high school to work with my father. That's the only time I saw him, in fact. He was always working, working. We never had this problem.
Therapist:	And, what's going on between the two of you now?
Ray:	Well, ever since my attack, I've been home more and I see what the two of them are doing. Stephanie says that Lisa used to do what she said, but I surely don't see it.
Stephanie:	Well, Ray, you have trouble resting and you need a lot of rest. When Lisa and I argue he has difficulty resting.
Ray:	That's right. And you seem to get depressed when you can't keep things under control. It's like when Lisa's bad you seem to get depressed. I guess there's too much happening in the family right now. We need to get on track.
Stephanie:	Yes, this can't go on—Ray sick, me depressed, and Lisa not going to school.

Ray's new presence at home appeared at the same time as Lisa's symptoms and Stephanie's depression. The family begins to understand the issue as a repeating pattern of interaction. The therapist notes that Ray is continuing his father's pattern of constant work.

Dialectic/systemic, brief example:

The family pattern is summarized by the therapist and she asks for the family rule. Again, all the exchanges in this transcript are greatly abbreviated.

Therapist:	Well, given all this, what do you imagine the rule to be that you are operating under?
Ray:	Well, practically speaking, a smooth running show is what we need. Everyone on track and getting their job done.
Stephanie:	That's the way it is supposed to be, but Lisa is not fitting in and I'm angry at her. Ray shouldn't have to hear all this turmoil.
Therapist:	So the rule seems to be a smooth running "on-track" show with everyone doing their job is best.
Ray:	Yes.
Therapist:	Can you give me some idea about where you learned this rule about everyone doing their own job and keeping on track?
Ray:	Well, we both come from French-Canadian families. Work was the way we survived. It was hard making it in Carthage in those days. Everyone had to sacrifice. Everyone always pulled their load, but we are at wit's end with Lisa.

Therapist: So dads worked, and moms always took care of the home, and the children were always good. Sounds perfect. But nothing is ever really perfect—what were some things that you may have missed working under those rules?

Stephanie: Well, I guess my mom was kind of sheltered. I guess I am, too. I mean, my husband's illness has really thrown me for a loop. I wish I could help more.

Ray: She was asking if we missed out on things as kids. I guess I missed out on being a kid. When I watch Lisa have fun I feel it in my heart. She's so pretty when she's happy. My dad worked hard and after he died, I missed out on having fun with him.

Stephanie: Me too, me too. I never got to know my dad.

Lisa: (sniffles) I don't like to see Daddy sick.

The DCT questioning sequence started with an emotional base at the sensorimotor level followed by concrete description of the interaction around the child. At the formal level, the family is beginning to see its repeating patterns; and at the dialectic/systemic level, they are beginning to see how they have recreated old intergenerational family patterns, some of which they regret.

Stage 2: Cognitive and Behavioral Interventions

The first stage of family therapy may involve from one to three interviews. The key developmental intervention in stage 2 is to help the family state the consensual family problem from a new frame of reference. This reframing (or reframe) synthesizes family data and the therapist's clinical framework into a new gestalt.

In order for the reframe to be effective, it must be accepted by all members of the family, show no judgment or blame, incorporate the developmental context of the family, and be understandable at the cognitive-developmental level of each member. Particularly important, the reframe must expand possibilities and provide opportunity for new solutions, thus engendering hope and focusing on concrete goals. An abstract dialectic/systemic reframe may be theoretically elegant but will be of little use if it is "over the family's head."

The reframe often comes near the end of the joining process and may be as simple a statement as: "This is not a problem of your daughter Jane's; rather, it is an issue of family interaction that all of us can work on. Jane is not the problem." Another approach is the positive reframe: "Jane's behavior seems to bring the family back together. Until she had her problem, you were all going separate ways. But now you are working together again." Providing a variety of perspective changes is often useful: "Another way to look at the problem is that Jane protects the family from arguments. Every time her behavior draws attention to herself, the family must put all other issues on hold."

The purpose of reframes is to help the family to look at itself as a system. The system can be examined concretely or abstractly. Interventions at this stage are most effective if matched to the cognitive-developmental level of the family. Most reframes involve formal dimensions and thus may require both interpretation and concrete behavioral enactments, or role-plays, and homework so that concrete families can understand and work through the new concepts.

DCT helps the therapist design interventions at appropriate cognitive-developmental levels to facilitate vertical or horizontal movement in the development of the family. A behavioral approach or Haley's (1976) problem-solving family theory method may be especially effective when beginning to work with a concrete family. Chaotic families may approach a sensorimotor level of functioning, in which case the therapist may need to take a stronger role in interventions.

DCT questioning techniques, the communication approach of Satir (1967), and the psychoeducational methods of Guerney (1977) are designed to help families become aware of repeating patterns. At a dialectic/systemic level, Bowen's (1978) intergenerational approach helps individuals and families understand how present behavior is derived from past rules. Carter and McGoldrick's *The Changing Family Life Cycle* (1989) provides the therapist with a wealth of detail about formal and dialectic/systemic issues of culture and family development.

More difficult to classify in terms of DCT are Minuchin's (1974) structural approach and therapies of the Milan group (for example, Palazzoli-Selvini, 1978), which can be described as multilevel interventions—the combination of specific concrete interventions with elements of formal pattern recognition.

The systematic questioning strategies of DCT can themselves be used as an intervention. The structured interview for individuals (see Appendix 1) can be used when counseling families although the sequence of questions must be modified to accommodate the multiple levels of development within the family. DCT encourages us as helping professionals to accept the various cognitive levels in the family and view these differences as resources rather than as sources of tension. Retrospective family analysis of both concrete events and patterns could involve Tamase's introspective-developmental counseling methods, although, again, with modification for multiple developmental levels. Specific questions could be derived from Haley's life-cycle approach to enable families to examine themselves and their development.

With the Cachet family, the therapist focused on the family construct of doing things well, with the following major reframe. (Note that she starts with a highly positive reframe of the family's difficult situation):

> I commend both of you for keeping the family rule of doing things well, even in the face of difficult odds with Ray's illness. I commend your strength and loyalty to each other. I commend Ray for continuing to try even though he feels so tired much of the time. I commend Stephanie for trying not to interfere and doing her best. I also commend Lisa for knowing just how to be sure that her mother's sadness and worry over Ray could be helped. Your behavior, Lisa, keeps you and your Mom fighting. And until you, Stephanie, believe it is okay to discuss your sadness with your husband, your daughter will help you stay disappointed in her.

The difficult part is that the rules about keeping on track and not showing that you are scared or angry are not working for you right now. Changing the rule to go with your present situation may be difficult. Stephanie, you say you are depressed. Ray, you say you cannot rest. Lisa, you say you are sick and unhappy. This is proof that the rules aren't working.

You both said you missed your own fathers while you were growing up and that your mothers missed much of the world. Perhaps we can look at this crisis as an opportunity rather than a burden. You may be able to use this time to rethink how you share responsibility for Lisa so that you don't have the regrets you had about your own parents—and the three of you might be able to have a little more fun.

I could help you in the next few months to try some new ways that will help your daughter know what's expected of her and allow her to feel less anxious about her mom and happier having a little time with her dad, which she's never had.

Stephanie and Ray, I'm going to ask you to try some things you've never tried before. I'm sure if you try these things then Lisa will know what she's supposed to do.

The data for this reframe obviously came from the DCT questioning sequence, and the therapist used issues of emotional importance in the past and present to motivate the family toward change. With the help of the therapist, Ray was able to recognize his withdrawal from the family in work, and Stephanie was able to find a part-time job in the community to help with the financial burden. With less attention from her mother and more from her father, Lisa's difficulties with attending school ceased. Most of the therapist's interventions were paced at the concrete level, so that the Cachet family had new alternatives for action. However, emotional thoughts about their own family history helped Ray and Stephanie change some very old patterns in their relationship. As the family interaction improved so did Ray's health, and thus the therapist was able to withdraw after ten sessions spread over four months.

Effective family developmental intervention can take many forms, but the main goal is to reframe the problem from a new perspective and help the family look at issues from a systemic context. In an individualistic society, thinking of oneself or one's family as a system is often difficult. However, the systematic approach of DCT is logical and appealing and offers much for family and individual counseling. Applying a systems approach such as DCT represents a major theoretical shift in the helping field.

Stage 3: Separation and Support for Change

As the family takes more responsibility for achieving the goals of therapy and for confronting the consequences of change, the therapist can begin the process of separation. The counselor does this by firmly reiterating the reframe, accepting and encouraging the family's new way of acting, and reinforcing the family's developmental growth patterns.

In from two to five sessions, the therapist can help the family review the therapy process and their expanded behavioral and cognitive repertoire. During this time, the family becomes more secure about their newly acquired problem-solving skills. The temptation for the formal-operational therapist may be to analyze and review, but concrete action and discussion are very important. Homework and behavioral enactment procedures help reinforce concrete achievements.

The final objective at this stage is to assist the family and its members to reorient to life without therapy. Sessions become less frequent, and the therapist may adopt more of a listener and consultant role. Respect for the various cognitive-developmental levels of family members is stressed, which helps the family learn to accept their own and others' levels of cognitive development. This acceptance and understanding of our need for support in working through life-cycle tasks is the most positive and helpful reorientation toward life problems that the family can acquire through DCT.

Chapter Summary

In the helping interview, the helping professional may focus on problems and not give enough attention to developmental processes over the life span. Clients can benefit by examining images, concrete specifics, and patterns in their lives. Life-span models, of which a number exist, can provide a useful framework for such self-examination.

This chapter further explored Erikson's eight stages of life-span development and the specific developmental tasks associated with each stage. Life-span development is complicated by family issues, and in this context Haley's six stages of the family life cycle were discussed.

The works of Gilligan, Neugarten, and Schlossberg remind us that, as we work with life-span developmental theory, we need to be constantly aware of issues of gender. The Erikson framework remains valuable, but clearly must be adapted to stand the test of viability for work with women and those of varying cultural backgrounds.

Tamase focuses on the foundation life stages of birth through preschool, elementary school, and high school and provides a highly specific, systematic program for developmental counseling over a four-interview series. Guidano's developmental model is more therapeutic in orientation and includes a method for treatment over a one-year period. A special feature of Guidano's program is that it allows for a changing therapist-client relationship. The therapist gradually becomes a consultant, helping the client direct his or her own developmental movement.

However, these and other life-span theories do not offer specific suggestions for assessment and interventions in the helping interview. The specific questioning and intervention strategies of DCT can be used in conjunction with the approaches of Erikson, Haley, Tamase, Guidano, and other life-span theorists. Clinical evidence collected from depressed inpatients shows that these specific strategies can be used with a range of clients. The concepts of DCT can themselves be used as an alternative therapeutic mode, or they can be used to supplement therapeutic skills for a wide variety of individual and family counseling approaches.

 CAUTION! Integrating counseling and therapy with developmental theory by using specific techniques in the interview represents a new process and as such, should be approached with caution and a sense of ethics. Particularly, the integration of DCT questioning strategies with Tamase's life-span analysis can bring about the deep expression of emotions, especially if sensorimotor questioning techniques are used.

Theory into Practice

By the end of this section, you may be able to demonstrate your ability to

1. Define Erikson's eight stages of individual development and Haley's six stages of the family life cycle; apply them to your own and/or a client's life history.
2. Using some of the concepts of DCT, generate your own ideas for questioning strategies to apply to Erikson's and Haley's frameworks.
3. Use the concepts of Gilligan and Schlossberg as you consider gender-related issues of development.
4. Take a client through a portion of Tamase's four developmental interviews in a role-played individual session.
5. Use a portion of Guidano's consultation approach to therapy in a role-played family session.
6. Apply DCT constructs to a family session.

Erikson's Eight Stages

Listed below are Erikson's eight life stages and the associated key developmental tasks. Identify an issue in your own life or that of a client that is associated with each stage. Then use the DCT questions for the sensorimotor, concrete, formal, and dialectic/systemic levels to generate questions that might help you or your client view that issue from varying frames of reference. (An example of responses to questions at the infancy level can be found at the end of this chapter.)

0-2 years: Trust versus mistrust.
Example of life issue:

_____

Sensorimotor question relating to issue of trust:

_____

Concrete question relating to issue of trust:

_____

Formal question relating to issue of trust:

_____

Dialectic/systemic question relating to issue of trust:

_____

On a separate sheet of paper, list examples of life issues and questions for each stage below for each level—sensorimotor, concrete, formal, dialectic/systemic.

2–4 years: Autonomy versus shame and doubt
4–7 years: Initiative versus guilt
7–12 years: Industry versus inferiority
12–19 years: Identity versus role confusion
19–30 years: Intimacy versus isolation
30–60 years: Generativity versus stagnation
60+ years: Ego integrity versus despair

Gender-Related Issues of Development

You may wish to repeat the exercise above while giving special attention to possible differences among men and women in Erikson's framework. The transitions described by Schlossberg also appear in clients who come for counseling and therapy. The woman or man who is infertile has suffered a serious loss. The man who has lost a job—just as his wife is succeeding for the first time in the workplace—will also need support. Clearly, development does not always occur in the step-by-step stages suggested by Erikson.

List examples of life issues and questions that would help clients to explore them from a DCT frame of reference. Identify an issue of importance to you— ideally one which you have experienced—and then list DCT questions that would help the client explore the issue at the four cognitive-developmental levels.

Elected transitions: graduating from school, changing jobs, having a baby, retiring, moving, divorcing.

_____

Surprise transitions: car accident, the death of a child, plant closing, getting an unexpected raise or large promotion, the state cuts welfare benefits for poor mothers.

_____

Nonevents (when the expected doesn't happen): infertility, a promotion or raise doesn't come through, or a child does not leave home.

_____

Life on hold (the transition "waiting to happen"): the long engagement, waiting to die in a hospice, waiting for the "right person" to come along, social security benefits are delayed for several months.

Sleeper transition (this occurs almost without your awareness): becoming fat or thin, falling in love, getting bored at a job you once loved, gradually tiring of a relationship, a neighborhood decays or becomes overrun with drugs.

Double whammies: retiring and losing a spouse by death; having a baby and moving back to one income; caring for ill parents at home and one of your children gets divorced and returns as well; a fire occurs, it's winter, and the welfare office has lost your file.

Haley's Life-Cycle Theory

Follow the same procedure as before for Haley's life-cycle theory. Think of several common life issues a family might encounter as they work through these life periods and write down questions for each of the stages, as before.

Young adulthood (courtship)
Example of life issue:

Sensorimotor question relating to life issue:

Concrete question relating to life issue:

Formal question relating to life issue:

Dialectic/systemic question relating to life issue:

On a separate sheet of paper list examples of life issues and questions for each of the stages below:

Early marriage
Childbirth and child rearing
Middle marriage
Children leaving home
Old age and retirement

The Haley framework, like the Erikson model, is limited. Take an alternative family style (single parent, blended family, gay family) and propose a life cycle for that family, listing the most critical developmental issues.

It was easier in the old, often sexist, totally straight, totally middle-class days. Counseling theory is more exciting nowadays, and certainly more challenging! Traditional theories simply did not allow sufficient room for us to support clients from varying backgrounds

Practice Using Introspective-Developmental Counseling Techniques in a Role-Played Session

Step 1: Divide into Practice Groups

Step 2: Select a Group Leader

Step 3: Assign Roles for the Practice Session

- Role-played client: The role-played client will talk freely about one of the four life periods outlined by Tamase.
- Interviewer: The interviewer will ask the specific questions suggested by Tamase. Have the questions available to look at from time to time. The interviewer's task is to encourage reflection. Remember to use listening skills frequently and help the client organize information through reflection of feeling and summarization.
- Observers 1 and 2: The observers will write down key words about each client response and classify the response as sensorimotor, concrete, formal, or dialectic/systemic. At the conclusion of the interview, each will note life-stage patterns that seem to recur.

Step 4: Plan the Session

The interviewer and client must first agree on the specific stage of Tamase's introspective-developmental counseling model to be reviewed. The two observers can examine the feedback form. The interview need not just follow Tamase's questioning sequence. Each individual is different, and the skilled interviewer will naturally use follow-up questions and interventions to help the client talk about his or her issues at appropriate developmental levels.

Step 5: Conduct a 30-Minute Interviewing Session

It is helpful to videotape and/or audiotape practice sessions.

Step 6: Provide Immediate Feedback and Complete Notes (5 Minutes)

Allow the client and interviewer time to provide immediate personal reactions to the practice session. At this point, the observers should turn the session over and let the participants take control. Use this time to complete your classification and notes.

Step 7: Review Practice Session and Provide Feedback (15 to 30 Minutes)

The interviewer should be the person to ask for feedback rather than getting it without being asked. The observers can share their observations from the feedback form on the next page and from their observations as the session progressed. Avoid judgmental feedback.

Practice Using Your Conceptions of Erikson's Stages in A Role-Played Session

Conduct a role-played session using the specific questions you generated as you examined the life stages of Erikson. (The general instructions for role-played practice above and the same feedback sheet may be used.) This will be a briefer family session. Use your specific questions from one family life-cycle stage and test them in a role-played situation.

Step 1: Select Three Participants

One person serves as therapist, and the two others serve as the role-played couple. The remainder of the members of the class or workshop will observe the entire process and later serve as process consultants who reflect on the session.

Step 2: Have the Workshop Leader Assume the Leadership Role

A leader is selected from outside the trio to keep track of the time and to facilitate group interaction should observers want to participate.

Step 3: Assign Roles for the Practice Session

- Role-played couple. Any family life-cycle issue may be used.
- Therapist. The therapist takes the family through the specific questions concerning one life-cycle issue. (You can also have two therapists.) The same questions may be asked of each member of the couple, or asked of only one member while the other observes and comments later. Or the two members may be asked to discuss the questions and answer them together.
- Workshop/class observers. All remaining individuals in the session will sit in a circle around the family or couple and act as observers.

Step 4: Plan the Session

- The couple leaves the room and defines their roles and the problem they wish to present. The specific nature of the problem is a surprise to the therapist.
- The therapist will at first seek to join the couple through structuring and informal discussion. At this time, the therapist can note the predominant cognitive-developmental level of each member of the couple. The first question, once the interview starts, should ideally be "What brings you here?" Note which member of the couple speaks first. Paraphrase the response and then ask the same question of the other member of the couple. Paraphrase that response and note in your summary any differences in interpretation of the problem. Work through the specific questions of the sensorimotor, concrete, formal, and dialectic/systemic levels one by one, being sure to paraphrase and

Feedback Sheet

1. Main words of client response:

_____

Classification: SM, CO, FO, D/S _____

2. Main words of client response:

_____

Classification: SM, CO, FO, D/S _____

3. Main words of client response:

_____

Classification: SM, CO, FO, D/S _____

_____

4. Main words of client response:

_____

Classification: SM, CO, FO, D/S _____

5. Main words of client response:

_____

Classification: SM, CO, FO, D/S _____

6. Main words of client response:

_____

Classification: SM, CO, FO, D/S _____

7. Main words of client response:

_____

Classification: SM, CO, FO, D/S _____

8. Main words of client response:

_____

Classification: SM, CO, FO, D/S _____

9. Main words of client response:

_____

Classification: SM, CO, FO, D/S _____

10. Main words of client response:

_____

Classification: SM, CO, FO, D/S _____

(Continue on a separate sheet of paper.)

What patterns do you observe in this client?

summarize as you go. Particularly, be sure to summarize differences of perception and belief between the two participants.

As you continue through the questions, note patterns in the couple's family system and paraphrase/and summarize these as well.

■ The family observers have several roles: (1) They all can be participant/ observers. The therapist should free feel to stop the interview in mid-session to ask the observers for help and suggestions. (2) Two observers should be assigned to the couple. Their task is to identify changing cognitive-developmental levels in each member using the feedback form. Furthermore, it may be useful for the observers to use observational feedback forms from Chapters 2, 3, and 4 so that concepts of developmental assessment and interviewing strategies are also included.

Step 5: Conduct a 30-Minute Interviewing Session

The therapist and the couple will discuss the varying perceptions of the problem for five minutes while the observers keep track of the couple's progress and classify the statements of each. Again it is helpful to videotape or audiotape practice sessions. Couples often confuse even the most effective therapist. Thus, the therapist should feel free to stop for a moment in the middle of the session and ask the observers for their reactions and suggestions.

Step 6: Provide Immediate Feedback and Complete Notes (10 Minutes)

This is a highly structured session, and there is often immediate personal need to process and discuss the session. In particular, it is helpful for the therapist to ask the family "What stands out for you from this practice session?" Allow time to provide true personal reactions to the practice. At this point, the observers should sit back and let the participants take control. Use this time to complete your classification and notes.

Step 7: Review Practice Session and Provide Feedback (15 to 30 Minutes)

It is important when giving feedback to allow the therapist and family receiving the feedback to be in charge. At this point ,the observers can share their observations. As usual, feedback should be specific, concrete, and nonjudgmental. Pay attention to strengths of the interview.

Generalization: Taking Life-Span Development Home

Activity 1: Practice with Individuals in Daily Life

As you go through this coming week, one or more of the following ideas may be used to help reinforce the ideas of this chapter.

■ Observe individuals at different stages of the life span. Can you identify specific examples of children (or adolescents or adults) working through issues of trust versus mistrust, autonomy versus shame and doubt, and so on?

- Talk with professional therapists and counselors. Is their practice developmental? Do they use developmental concepts daily in their practice? Most use the concepts for case conceptualization but not for direct intervention in the interview. How do these therapists respond to the idea of developmental counseling and therapy?

Activity 2: Observe Families, Groups, and Organizations

Observe couples and families and identify where they are in the life cycle. If possible, note the issues of individual family members, as described by Erikson, against the background of family developmental issues.

Groups and organizations also go through life stages. Think back on the groups you have encountered and the types of life-cycle issues demonstrated.

Activity 3: The Interview

Apply your knowledge of life-span developmental theory in the here and now of the interview.

- Take a client through Tamase's four interviews as a supplement to your regular practice. Inform the client of your purpose and discuss the effectiveness of each session after completing the 30- to 50-minute interview.
- Try out your own questions, using Erikson's framework, on appropriate clients. What do you observe and what do they learn? Are the clients able to identify patterns that relate to their current life style?
- Test your own individual questions, using Haley's framework, on appropriate clients. What do you observe and what do they learn? Are the the clients able to find patterns that relate to their current lifestyle?
- Read the material on Guidano's procedures carefully. Note particularly his conception of consultation with a client after the client has made progress. Find a client who is willing to test this concept and slowly change your approach from therapist to consultant to develop and a more equal relationship with the client.
- Take a client through the sequential questions listed on page 136. Is your client able to see repeating life patterns and perhaps even act on them?

Activity 4: Consider the Yakima Nation Proverb

The child brings us immortality.
We bring the child a place to belong.

As you review this chapter, what does this proverb say to you and to your own practice of helping others grow?

_____

_____

_____

_____

Suggested Supplementary Reading and Activities [3]

Additional Reading

Ivey, A. 1986. *Developmental therapy: Theory into practice.* SanFrancisco: Jossey-Bass.
"Development over the Life Span" is the title of Chapter 8 in the above work. The emphasis in this chapter is on unconscious development, whereas the life-span concepts in this current chapter focus on conscious awareness of the developmental process. Pages 304 through 317 of *Developmental Therapy* are most relevant to the material presented in the current chapter. Exercises from constructs 1 and 2 provide a follow-up of the ideas of the current chapter.

Erikson, E. 1963. *Childhood and society.* (2nd ed.) New York: Norton. (lst ed. 1950).
This book was cited previously in Chapter 1. Reading Erikson's book should enable you to generate a more complex set of structured interviews for different client issues, such as the set of interviews Tamase uses in his introspective-developmental counseling. Give special attention to Erikson's thoughts on culture. Review your questions to determine their relevancy to different cultural groups.

Haley, J. 1973. *Uncommon therapy.* New York: Norton.

Haley, J. 1980. *Leaving home: The therapy of disturbed young people.* New York: McGraw-Hill.
Haley's first book was recommended in Chapter 1. The second provides an elaboration on Haley's life-cycle theories. Haley's life-cycle theory of family development has deeply influenced family therapy theory. However, Haley tends to take a middle-class, economically advantaged view. Examine Haley's framework in more detail and outline family life cycles that might be more appropriate to less financially advantaged, single-parent homes, to various cultural groups, or to gay families. Would it be helpful to generate new, more appropriate developmental questioning strategies for these groups?

Guidano, V. 1987. *The complexity of self: A developmental approach to psychopathology and therapy.* New York: Guilford.
Pathological problems are not typically considered in a developmental framework. Guidano quite effectively shows the developmental logic of a variety of psychopathological issues. Undergirding Guidano's therapeutic approach is a commitment to the developmental logic of disturbance. Once a client understands the personal cognitive map and how that map was developmentally constructed, a more positive approach to human change is possible.
    The appendix of Guidano's book contains strategies for cognitive therapy that follow from two basic questions: (1) What kind of developmental stages brought about this individual's personal cognitive organization? and (2) In what way is that personal cognitive organization determining the form of moment-to-moment experience? Review these strategies and examine how they inform the concepts of this current chapter and how they might be used in your own counseling practice.

Belenky, M., B. Clinchy, N. Goldberger, and J. Tarule, 1986. *Women's ways of knowing: The development of self, voice, and mind.* New York: Basic Books.
An innovative, important statement on women's development in this culture. Four types of women's knowledge are discussed: received, subjective, procedural, and constructed. The discussion of the authors has been critical and formative for many women and should be read by men as well. Women working with DCT have pointed out that these four types of women's knowledge can be related to DCT levels. A possible research direction for the future may be to relate the two systems and examine possible differences in male and female cognitive styles.

---

[3] Readings by Carol Gilligan and Nancy Schlossberg were suggested earlier in this book, but would be useful again as supplementary reading.

Research Suggestion

Do clients change their cognitive-developmental level in response to changing counselor questions? Rigazio-DiGilio (1989) and Tamase (1989) have both found that clients change their way of talking about an issue when different types of questioning strategies are used. You may wish to replicate their findings using the specific types of questions they used. Alternatively, you may wish to conduct research on your own set of Erikson or Haley questions modified by gender issues that you identify. Do clients change their cognitive-developmental level in response to your questions as the theory predicts?

Sample Responses to Chapter Exercise

Examples of life issues relating to trust: jealousy, suspiciousness, feeling alone, difficulty in maintaining relationships.

SM: Taking that feeling of aloneness, get with that feeling. Can you give me a visual picture of what you see or what comes to your mind?

CO: Could you give me a specific example with details of what happened before, during, and after that picture of aloneness you gave me in your family?

FO: Is that a pattern? Does that happen in other situations?

D/S: As you think back on what we've talked about relating to trust, how do you put it all together? What sense do you make of it?

6 Using DCT with Personality Disorders

A Positive Developmental View

Time is a relationship between events,

Kept fresh in memory by selected objects on

knotted hemp.

Connection is as vital as separation.

By the time she is a grandmother,

The unity of life is wrapped

and remembered

in a Time Ball.[1]

Yakima Nation Proverb

---

[1] A Yakima woman used a hemp string to "tie her history or diary throughout her life. To do this, she would mark her first courtship with a bead or knot as well as her marriage and any other event in her life. After each year, the story was tied onto her ball of hemp." ("The Yakima Time Ball," 1984, p. 2).

Connection is as vital as separation. We have twin tasks in our developmental progression. To survive, we must be simultaneously attached to others but also separate. Relationship, connection, and attachment provide a foundation for a sense of trust and intimacy. As we move to the developmental tasks of autonomy and identity, we must define our separate boundaries from our family and others.

A client's history over the life span, as presented to the counselor, is somewhat like the Yakima Time Ball. Sometimes the client's life is ensnarled, and we need to help untie the knots, find underlying patterns of development, and free the individual for further growth.

This chapter presents ideas for generating treatment plans based on a lifespan developmental framework. These ideas are expanded in Chapter 8. Many readers, particularly those who work with "normal" populations in, for example, schools or governmental agencies may wonder why the emphasis of this chapter is on what is traditionally termed *pathology*. This chapter illustrates that DCT techniques can be effective for difficult, entrenched clients as well as less "pathological" populations.

In this chapter, DCT and other developmental theories will be applied to Axis II personality disorders and, more briefly, to Axis 1 clinical syndromes as classified by the American Psychiatric Association's (1987) *Diagnostic and Statistical Manual of Mental Disorders* (DSM-III-R).[2] Concrete suggestions for developmental assessment and treatment of these problems are presented and should be helpful in undoing the complex and sometimes tightly knotted life time balls we see in many of our clients and patients. The approaches in this chapter can help you approach difficult therapeutic problems from a more positive, developmental frame of reference.

Developmental Blocks Versus Pathology

DCT views most of what is traditionally termed *pathology* as the result of developmental blocks or impasses. Experience with the DCT model reveals that using a developmental approach is possible and effective with moderately and severely disturbed clients. Preceding chapters discussed work by Rigazio-DiGilio (1989) showing that the same DCT techniques and skills used for normal developmental issues also work effectively with depressive inpatients, thereby demonstrating that it is not necessary to rely solely on traditional remedial methods in the clinical setting.

Genetics, biochemistry, and temperament are often factors in pathology, and thus medical methods for addressing these factors are, at times, very appropriate. Mania and depression often respond best to drug therapy. Addressing a developmental block solely through counseling does little good if the real problem is a thyroid or hormone imbalance. The focus of DCT, however, is on the potential of people to address and overcome their own blocks.

---

[2] The Diagnostic and Statistical Manual is revised periodically. Please refer to the latest edition for possible changes in descriptions of personality disorders, especially the dependent personality.

Professionals in day-care centers and elementary schools see many children and families suffering severe distress, and school counselors' work is increasingly focused on preventing pathology. Given the pressures of modern society, the economic system, and the vulnerability of individuals and families, pathology and severe distress are increasingly evident. Most pathology does not start in adulthood or evolve in a vacuum. Severe problems often have their roots in the developmental history of the client. Narcissistic and borderline disorders do not begin at age 22; they are rooted in infancy and early childhood. A potential antisocial personality disorder can be recognized in elementary school or high school.

DCT takes the position that personality disorders or styles generally have their roots in the developmental past and in the family. However, severe trauma, such as that experienced by a Vietnam veteran, a survivor of the killing fields of Cambodia, or other extreme experiences certainly can bring out similar symptoms. This chapter does not explore post-traumatic stress disorder, but videotapes discussing the treatment of these issues have been developed (see, for example, Ivey and Ivey, 1990.)

Family therapy theory has been effective in addressing pathological issues. Family theorists speak of the identified patient (IP). The IP can be a daughter with anorexia or bulimia, or a son who has stolen a car, a father with depression, or a mother suffering from an anxiety disorder. Traditionally, pathology is seen as residing in the individual. Family theory takes a different view. Pathology is the result of family interactions gone awry in a difficult world. The family generates a common world view that narrows and focuses its difficulties on one or more family members.

The treatment plan ideas presented in this chapter are oriented toward DSM-III-R personality disorders but are equally applicable for premarital counseling, vocational development, and child developmental guidance. Although the chapter discusses Axis I and II disorders, the treatment plans used for these cases are applicable in many ways to "normal" developmental issues.

By the time you complete this chapter and have practiced the exercises, you may be able to

1. *Identify positive aspects of pathology.* DCT assumes that pathological behavior once had developmental utility but is currently counterproductive. Thus, DCT considers the terms *developmental personality style* and *personality disorder* to be interchangeable.

2. *Recognize in the interview how the clients are repeating their developmental past with you.* DCT proposes that what clients learn about relationships in their developmental histories is repeated with you in the session. By noting clients' behavior and your reactions to it, you can use the therapist or counselor relationship more powerfully to help clients overcome developmental blocks and move on to the next task.

3. *Anticipate clients' relationship problems with their families of origin, in their current living arrangements, and at work.* Clients not only repeat with you what they have learned in the past, they also repeat these patterns in other relationships.

4. *Generate treatment plans for developmental personality types (or personality disorders) and depression using a developmental framework.* DCT suggests specific types of counselor-client relationships based on life-span issues of separation and attachment. A comprehensive, eclectic treatment plan for these clients is presented that integrates DCT with other counseling and therapy theories.

This chapter follows a different structure from preceding chapters and is longer and probably should not be read at one sitting. It is important that you actively involve yourself with the ideas of this chapter and complete the exercises individually or in small groups. Box 6-1 summarizes DCT concepts presented in Chapters 1 through 5, should you need to refresh your recall of the basic points of DCT.

Identifying Client Developmental History in the Interview

"How clients treat you is how they were treated. . . . This is our clue for treatment" (Bowlby, 1987). This important statement provides a useful context in which to experience our clients in the helping interview. If you observe the

Box 6-1. Summary of DCT Concepts to This Point

Six Key Practical Dimensions of Developmental Counseling and Therapy

1. It is possible to assess the cognitive-developmental level of clients or families in the interview by observing their language and behavior. (see Chapter 2).

2. Individuals and families may present their preoperational problems at the sensorimotor, concrete, formal, or dialectic/systemic level or they may present at multiple levels (see Chapter 2).

3. Counselors and therapists can make interventions that match or mismatch clients' cognitive-developmental level. For example, if the client presents at the formal, abstract level, it may be helpful first to match that level to expand horizontal development. Later, it may be more advantageous to mismatch your approach to encourage the abstract, formal client to consider issues at the concrete or even the sensorimotor level (see Chapter 3).

4. A variety of questions and interventions can help families and individuals expand and transform cognitions at each level to newer, more creative ways of thinking. Confrontation and perturbation are often crucial in helping clients create the New (see Chapter 4).

5. Different theories of helping (for example, psychoanalytic, behavioral, Gestalt) seem to function more effectively at various cognitive-developmental levels (see Chapter 2).

6. Life-span developmental theory, family life-cycle theory, introspective-developmental counseling, Guidano's life-span approach, and DCT can be integrated with individual and family counseling and therapy. Unlike other theories, DCT provides specific guidelines for questioning strategies, assessment of client developmental level, and designing interventions (see Chapter 5).

client and how the client's behavior affects you, you will be able to identify, with some accuracy, key aspects of the client's developmental history.

This chapter focuses on developing systematic treatment plans using a life-span developmental framework. Bowlby's attachment theory (1969; 1973) provides us with some guidelines for assessing client attachment and separation patterns in the interview. This here-and-now assessment provides useful clues to the client's developmental history. Bowlby's concepts of developmental history, coupled with the developmental counseling and therapy model, provide a basis for developing a comprehensive treatment plan.

Clients express their current understandings and repeat their developmental history with you in the here and now of the session. Their past patterns of separation and attachment tend to repeat again and again. The way clients develop relationships with you as therapist or counselor in the session provide critical clues to their developmental past and present (see Bowlby, 1969, 1973; Ivey, 1968).

In essence, Bowlby is saying, "Listen to the client, observe the client, and note your reactions." One of the most valuable sources of data for counseling and therapy lies in your interaction with the client. When counseling a family, think about what your first instinctive reaction would be, and instead of responding, see how the family reacts. Clients will almost always bring out something they want to work on or that is troubling them. Families unconsciously try to bring you into their system, and joining the family is basic to the helping process. At the same time, awareness of what has happened to you, the family therapist, as a result of being in contact with this family is valuable data for understanding the family and for later treatment.

If the client is overattached or dependent on you, chances are that he or she learned this type of relationship in the past and is repeating an old family or personal pattern with you. If the client is distant, cool, and detached, this, too, represents a learned pattern from the past. Clients tend to react to us according to behavioral and cognitive patterns related to their developmental history. Families act similarly. As a therapist, you often represent someone or something from the family's developmental and intergenerational history. Thus, the way you develop rapport with an individual or join the family is of critical importance.

The classification system of personality disorders according to the *Diagnostic and Statistic Manual of Mental Disorders* (DSM-III-R) provides an excellent starting place for developing a practical understanding of how clients repeat their developmental past in the present (American Psychiatric Association, 1987). However, DSM-III-R is a diagnostic system and thus does not provide much information on problem development or solution. This is where DCT constructs can be helpful.

Although DSM-III-R uses the term *personality disorder,* perhaps a more appropriate term would be *developmental personality style.* A developmental personality style is the summation of the important things learned over an individual's life span. These developmental experiences tend to be repeated in the counseling and therapy interview.

Take, for example, Tom, a 24-year-old man who comes to see you in the midst of the breakup of a long-term relationship. At the start of the session, he bursts into tears and says, "I need help. I need you to help me get Donnie back to me. I need her." The client has a pleading look in his eyes; his body is slumped. He looks to you for an answer. He tells you in concrete detail how hard he tries to please Donnie. As the interview continues, he frequently asks your advice in a supplicating tone, as if he were trying to please you as well. In your own body, you note a tense feeling in your stomach, as if he is trying to take something from you. During the week before the next session, he calls you three times, asking for advice and suggestions.

Table 6-1 on pp. 164-165 presents the DSM-III-R categorizations of the American Psychiatric Association for developmental personality styles. Which of these eleven personality styles or disorders (paranoid, schizoid, schizotypal, antisocial, borderline, histrionic, narcissistic, avoidant, dependent, obsessive-compulsive, passive-aggressive) best describes our client? You are not expected to be expert in diagnosis at this point; just use your commonsense understanding of these diagnostic categories. Which classification seems to fit?

_____

Which classification does not make sense at all? That is, which of the eleven personality types would probably not initiate the type of relationship with you described above?

_____

This client represents a primarily dependent style. Borderline, histrionic, and passive-aggressive types may manifest similar behaviors, but a dependent developmental style tends to consistently exhibit dependency. The paranoid, avoidant, or antisocial personality styles would not exhibit this orientation.

List all the characteristic thoughts and behaviors you would expect with a client with a dependent personality style. Draw on your own personal experience with dependency, also considering people you have known who seem overly dependent on others. Then compare your list with the DSM-III-R list of diagnostic criteria for dependent types as shown in Box 6-2.

_____

_____

_____

_____

_____

_____

_____

_____

Box 6-2. Diagnostic Criteria for and Behaviors Expected of Dependent Personalities

---

Diagnostic Criteria for 301.60 Dependent Personality Disorder (DSM-III-R)

A pervasive pattern of dependent and submissive behavior, beginning by early adulthood and present in a variety of contexts, is indicated by at least *five* of the following:

1. Is unable to make everyday decisions without an excessive amount of advice or reassurance from others.
2. Allows others to make most of his or her important decisions (for example, where to live, what job to take).
3. Agrees with people, even when he or she believes they are wrong, because of fear of being rejected.
4. Has difficulty initiating projects or doing things on his or her own.
5. Volunteers to do things that are unpleasant or demeaning in order to get other people to like him or her.
6. Feels uncomfortable or helpless when alone, or goes to great lengths to avoid being alone.
7. Feels devastated or helpless when close relationships end.
8. Is frequently preoccupied with fears of being abandoned.
9. Is easily hurt by criticism or disapproval (American Psychiatric Association, 1987, p. 354).

Possible Behaviors Expected in a Dependent Personality Style

In the interview

The client is likely to ask you for advice and suggestions and may follow your ideas carefully, eventually placing much of the responsibility for action on you. The client may phone you frequently, show up early for appointments, and, in general, ingratiate him- or herself. If you observe yourself and your body, you may find yourself feeling trapped and closed in by this client.

On the job

The client will tend to have difficulties when he or she must act independently and make decisions. When told specifically what to do by a supporting and warm boss, the dependent client may do well. The client may feel personally devastated by negative performance evaluations. Vocational counseling may involve assertiveness training, job-skills training, and supportive efforts to help the client feel better about him- or herself.

Family history

Expect a family history in which the client was not allowed to make decisions and was told exactly what to do and when. The client was not rewarded for independent action. Probably one (or more) member of the family also models dependent behavior. In effect, the family history did not allow any true self capable of independent action to develop. There may be a history of abandonment or threats of leave taking in the family.

Table 6-1. Developmental Personality Styles

Style and positive aspect	Behavior/thoughts in session	Possible family history	Predicted current relationships	Possible treatment approach
Paranoid It is important to watch out for injustice	Suspicious, takes remarks out of context and interprets them to support own frame of reference	Probable history of persecution, active family rejection	Controlling behavior, anticipates exploitation quick to anger, may mistrust friends and family	Always be honest, never defensive; structure ahead of time; don't argue, you'll only lose
Schizoid It is useful to be a loner or independent of others at times	Relationship with therapist fragile, constricted body stance, little emotion shown, problems accepting support	Cold family; received little affection, rewarded for being alone and on own, may be identified patient in otherwise normal family	Loner; few friends, superficial relationships	Be consistent, warm supportive—no pressure; social skills training may be helpful
Schizotypal Ability to see things differently than others see them	Ideas of reference, social anxiety, odd magical beliefs, odd behavior, limited affect, distant, vague	Chaotic family style; family anxious/ambivalent with mixed messages, combination of intrusion/rejection	Loner; no close friends, perhaps an unusual or "different" peer group	Same as above; behavior may be seen as engulfing; important to maintain verbal tracking on single topic
Antisocial It is sometimes necessary to be impulsive and take care of our own needs	Acts out; cannot sustain task, involved in crime, drugs, truancy, physical fights; cruel, maltreats family; tries to "con" therapist	Probable abuse as child; avoidant family forced child to take matters into own hands; little affection in home	Abusive, exploitive relationships; fear of abandonment	Be open, honest, and set clear limits; avoid entanglement; expect client to leave treatment if you get close
Borderline Intensity in relationships is desirable at times	Pushes therapist's "buttons" skillfully; impulsive, intense anger or caring, suicidal gestures	Enmeshed family during early childhood; lack of support for individuation; probable sexual abuse	Serial, intense relationships; may have close friends, relationships may move rapidly between extreme closeness and distance	Confront engulfment and support individuation— that is, do opposite of family; group/systems approaches are useful
Histrionic All could benefit at times with open access to emotions	Seeks reassurance; seductive, concerned with appearance, too much affect; self-centered, vague conversation	Enmeshed, engulfing family, with little support for individuation; possible sexual abuse/seduction; little family expectation for accomplishment; aware of others not of self	Similar to the borderline without the externalized anger; Actions directed inward rather than outward	Encourage individuation; use assertiveness, skills training, consciousness raising; examine history of problem; use cognitive-behavioral and systems interventions

Table 6-1. Developmental Personality Styles (continued)

Style and positive aspect	Behavior/thoughts in session	Possible family history	Predicted current relationships	Possible treatment approach
Narcissistic A strong belief in ourselves is necessary for good mental health	Grandiose, self-important, sees self as very unique; sense of entitlement; lacks empathy, oriented toward success and perfection	Received perfect mirroring for accomplishments rather than for self; engulfing family; child enacts family's wishes; anxious/ambivalent caregiver	Focuses on selfish needs, tends to engulf others with needs; is charming to get wishes met, Don Juan type, may pair with borderline.	Interpret behavior; look to past; employ cognitive-behavioral, systems, sensitivity training in a group
Avoidant It is useful to deny or avoid some things	Avoids people, shy; unwilling to become involved; distant, exaggerates risk	Either engulfing family or avoidant family; enacting what the family modeled	Not many friends; easily becomes dependent on them or therapist	Use many behavioral and cognitive techniques, assertiveness training and relaxation training useful
Dependent We all need to depend on others	Dependency on therapist even outside of session; indecision, little sense of self	Engulfing, controlling family; not allowed to make decisions; rewarded for inaction, told what to do	Dependent on friends; drives people away with demands	Reward action, support efforts for self, use paradox, assertiveness techniques
Obsessive-Compulsive Maintaining order and a system is necessary for job success	Perfectionistic and inflexibile; focuses on details, making lists, devoted to work; limited affect, money oriented, indecisive	Overattached family that wanted achievement; oriented to perfection, like narcissist, but keenly aware of others with a limited sense of self	Controlling, limited affect, demands perfection from others, hard worker; cries at sad movies	Reflect and provoke feeling, orient to client's personal needs, support development of self-concept, orient to body awareness
Passive-Aggressive All of us are entitled to procrastinate at times	Procrastination; seems to agree with therapist, then undercuts; seems to accept therapist, but then challenges authority	Perhaps obsessive family; individual instead moves away from perfectionism and fights back; a more healthy defense needs to be developed	"Couch potato," skilled at getting back at and at criticizing others; defends by doing nothing; resents suggestions; not pleasant on the job	Let them learn the consequences of their behavior; do not do things for them, but confront and interpret and pay special attention to their reactions

Further Work with the Dependent Type

Returning to our example of Tom: Tom's behavior and language in the interview shows that he replicates with you the pattern of his dependency on Donnie. Careful observation of clients' behavior in the interview will reveal that they tell you much about themselves, their current relationships, and their developmental history. All you need to do is listen, observe, and be aware of your own reactions.

If the client is acting in a dependent way with you, there is an excellent chance that he or she currently acts in a similar fashion with others. We can assume that the client was quite dependent on Donnie and exhibited similar behaviors again and again, eventually driving Donnie away from the relationship. Similar to Donnie, you may have found that you avoid and reject overly dependent individuals and clients.

Generally speaking, clients continue with therapists those patterns they have learned in earlier life. Antisocial or acting-out clients may try to "con" us; initially, we may be attracted by their flattery and only later learn that we were taken in. The borderline personality client often has an attractive, magnetic energy, and you may believe the claim that you are the best and only therapist who can help them. Only later, when they become angry or jealous or too demanding, may you realize the trap you have let yourselves in for. The paranoid individual tends to be suspicious of our interventions; the narcissist seeks our approval and admiration; the passive-aggressive tempts us to retaliate.

Returning to the example of the dependent style—we can anticipate that Tom has a history of overly dependent relationships. In each new relationship, we can expect Tom to exhibit specific behaviors and language that replicate his pattern with Donnie. (Perhaps you have noted in your own personal relationships that you tend to repeat certain patterns of interaction, again and again. Many of us are attracted to relationships that enable us to repeat stuck patterns.)

How is a dependent client likely to relate to you in the interview? What behaviors and thoughts can you expect? List below the characteristics you think are associated with the dependent style. Then compare your ideas with others or to the list of behaviors in Box 6-2.

_____

_____

_____

_____

How might you feel about a dependent client after the first interview, particularly if you were not prepared to encounter this type? What is your image of a dependent person? What do you see, hear, and feel? Most important, what do you feel in your own body as you concentrate on that image? Can you locate that feeling in a specific place in your body? What thoughts do you have?

_____

_____

How do you think the dependent person would behave on the job? What behaviors might work well for the client? What might work against vocational success?

_____

_____

_____

_____

It is also possible to anticipate the client's past developmental history, particularly as manifested in the family. What do you imagine Tom's family interaction was over time? (Review Table 6-1 on developmental personality styles, the specific diagnostic criteria of DSM-III-R in Box 6-2, and your own impressions listed above.) Define some of the family dynamics you would expect from Tom's here-and-now behavior in the interview.

_____

_____

_____

_____

_____

_____

_____

_____

Much of our behavior is learned in the family and culture within which we develop. Although it is difficult to separate individual and environmental influences, the family developmental history of the dependent personality may include, among other influences, a mother or father who modeled the dependent style or as a young child or adolescent the dependent client may have been told repeatedly that he or she was not competent. The dependent client may not have been allowed to make decisions. He or she may have been rewarded for inaction and procrastination. There likely may have been an engulfing family style that led to little sense of self.

The clinical syndromes of Axis I, which include anxiety, depression, and agoraphobia, might also trouble the dependent individual. A dependent personality style is not likely to be associated with hyperactivity, conduct disorder, or manic episodes.

Some Important Cautions

As we have seen, Bowlby's statement—"How clients treat you is how they were treated"—can be useful in identifying the client's developmental history. However, Bowlby, and most theoreticians, would caution that the interaction a client has with a therapist involves other dimensions as well, as follows:

1. Clients may react to you in a manner you interpret as similar to the way they reacted to their mother and father. However, family members are not the only individuals clients continue their behaviors with. The important figure may be an uncle or a friend, or the reaction may be connected to a significant event or a specific trauma.

2. Psychodynamic theory emphasizes the importance of defense mechanisms that protect the ego from deeper issues. The client may appear to be continuing behavior from the past, but deeper examination may reveal this behavior to be reaction-formation—that the client does exactly the opposite of how he or she was treated. The behavior and thought patterns can also represent denial, projection, sublimation, or any of a number of complex defense mechanisms.

Psychodynamic personality theory often describes therapy as peeling off the layers of an onion. The first layer is the behavior we see, but underlying layers may reveal a vastly different pattern of personality and life experience. Similarly, social learning theorists, using vastly different terminology, emphasize these phenomena as well.

3. Relatively few individuals have "pure" personality disorders or developmental personality styles. Often, clients will react to you in one way in one situation and then their reactions will radically shift in another situation. Although the DSM-III-R classification system is useful, it can lead to stereotyping and labeling.

4. For many, it is more useful to consider repeating past behavior from a family systems context. All of us learn much of our behavior and ways of thinking in the family. Psychodynamic theory tends to use intrapsychic phenomena, and the task of psychodynamic therapy is to learn how the client's unconscious functions—often a lengthy and complex task. The same objective can be accomplished more easily by learning how the client's family functioned and the place the client had in the family. You will often find that clients are repeating their individual family style with you in the interview.

5. Cultural issues affect the meaning of all behavior and thought patterns. What might appear to be pathology may be natural behavior in the culture. For example, an Italian-American client may be considered by an individualistic British-American therapist to be overly enmeshed in the family, whereas close family ties are a cultural value for Italians. Cultural values, particularly those learned in the family, will always be a factor in how the client treats you.

These five points could be elaborated further. They are presented here as important guidelines for understanding our relationships with the client. Clients do repeat their developmental past in the interview, but your interpretation of their behavior must be made with caution.

Finding Positives and Survival Skills of Developmental Personality Styles

One of the key goals in DCT is to help the client approach developmental tasks in the following maxim: "Help people reach their full potential. Catch them doing something right."

Let's consider the example of the dependent personality. What is right about the dependent style? Can we reframe dependency in a positive way? Perhaps we can view dependency in this way: It is not possible to relate to others fully unless one can let go and be dependent at times. Human nature requires dependency on parents, and dependency on close friends and family, lovers, and spouses is often appropriate and necessary. We all need to be able to be dependent on others at times to achieve intimate, trusting attachments.

Think about times when you were dependent or allowed yourself to be dependent. Or, perhaps, conversely, you dealt with problems in relationships by being controlling rather than allowing yourself to recognize your own needs and weakness.

_____

_____

_____

_____

Connection and attachment are obviously important for the dependent person. Separation and autonomy are feared. With certain types of individuals, the dependent person can develop close and caring relationships. However, the dependent type matched with an antisocial type can become a victim of abuse.

Dependent behavior and thinking is often learned in the family as a survival mechanism. Dependent clients often have authoritarian parents who don't allow them to make decisions. The family reward structure may deny the child, adolescent, or spouse autonomous decision making. Thus, the only way the individual could survive in that family may have been to be dependent. The dependency that protected the individual in the past is no longer functional and remains as a harmful vestige. As helpers, we need to respect the functionality of dependency and its positive values but also help the client achieve a balance between dependent attachments and autonomy.

Other "disorders," as categorized by DSM-III-R, also have positive aspects. The energy of the borderline personality is attractive. Some paranoia is useful in some situations—as when buying a used car. A bit of healthy narcissism is necessary for mental health and a good self-concept. Most of us would prefer some obsessiveness in our bankers and accountants. Since these "disorders" have positive and necessary aspects, DCT uses the term _developmental personality style_ instead of _personality disorder_. We need a balance of several styles to maintain mental health and effective development over the life span.

Borderline and narcissistic personality styles also learned these modes as survival mechanisms that worked (for a time) in their families. The borderline personality may have learned to appear cheerful, hardworking, and energetic while simultaneously maintaining silence about sexual abuse. The narcissist may have enjoyed the adulation of parents as a child and adolescent but never had a chance to develop a healthy, independent sense of self. Clients with both personality styles tend to repeat their family histories with you in the interview.

DCT maintains that we need to do more than label clients according to personality styles. We also need to identify where these styles came from, their usefulness in the past, and the current value of some aspects of that style.

Integrating Positives and Negatives of Developmental Personality Styles

From your interaction with the client in the interview, it is possible, with some accuracy, to predict

1. Positives and survival skills of the client's personality style. These should be identified clearly and be respected and supported. The goal of therapy is to balance, not eliminate key personal qualities.
2. The client's family history—how the client was treated at home.
3. The client's personal relationships. The client is likely relating to you in some ways similar to how he or she currently relates to important others.
4. How the client will likely react in the vocational world.
5. What problems may be anticipated according to Axis I of DSM-III-R.
6. What types of treatment are most likely to be helpful. (This topic will be discussed in detail in a later section.)
7. How you will react to the personality style over time. Here it is important for you to examine your own life history and your own personal thoughts and feelings to determine whether or not you are indeed able to provide the type of relationship the client needs.

These seven areas can be predicted with each developmental personality style identified in DSM-III-R.

An important caution is necessary. Relatively few clients present themselves as just one style. Research and clinical experience reveal that personality styles tend to overlap. Clients may be dependent at one time, passive-aggressive at another, and even antisocial at still another. And these changes may all occur in the space of ten minutes in a single session. Or these overlaps may not be apparent for several sessions, and you may not realize until later that individuals cannot be categorized in a single dimension.

The borderline client is not always borderline. At times, the antisocial individual can be extremely responsible and helpful. The DSM-III-R classifications were not designed to be exclusive. When one uses diagnostic categories, there is a tendency to think of people in terms of labels. Clients and families vary; it is our task as helpers to be flexible in our approach. The use and understanding of such classification systems as DSM-III-R give us a basis of understanding.

Very few of us have only one personality style—just as it is true that a "pure" personality disorder is relatively rare. Limiting ourselves to only one way of being could indeed be pathological and create problems. Think about yourself. How do you behave with a close friend, at a party, in an encounter group, or when the police pull you over for a traffic violation? How do these behaviors differ?

_____

_____

Object relations theorists talk about "part object relations units." In object relations theory, a "whole object" may be defined as a whole person. Any individual consists of many parts, or units. Just as none of us are all good or all bad, no client is all dependent or all borderline. When clients react to us in the interview, we experience only certain parts of them at one time. Over a longer series of interviews, we can get a better idea of the whole person. For a useful and practical introduction to object relations theory see, Masterson (1981,1985).

When a client surprises us with a new behavior or thought that is uncharacteristic of their past behavior, we have likely touched a new part object relations unit (or, in other terminology, a different part of the person or a subpersonality). This is especially true of the borderline client. Things are going along smoothly, and you feel you are making progress. Then, in an instant, the client reacts angrily, you feel defensive or angry yourself, and the session seems to fall apart. In this encounter, the part object relations unit has been activated.

Families, both normal and pathological, vary in the way family members treat one another. Families do not tend to produce "pure" personality types. Depending on situations and the people we meet, most of us are dependent at times, avoidant at other points, and perhaps even antisocial or somewhat paranoid. Research and clinical experience with the personality disorders has revealed extensive overlapping and developmental complexity on Axis II.

The complexity of client style does not negate the value of Bowlby's observation and the usefulness of noting client interaction. Just expect that clients will be more complex than your first assessments. A client who acts in a dependent fashion with you is likely enacting the developmental past, but you should be prepared to see the "dependent" client shift style from time to time and interact with you in a new way—perhaps in a narcissistic style. The difficult task of the therapist or counselor is to note the change in style and to change the nature of the client-therapist relationship. For example, if there is a shift of personality from dependent to narcissistic, you might change a supportive therapeutic style to one that is more interpretive.

Given this introduction to assessing developmental personality styles, let us return to your reactions to the dependent personality and examine how your reactions may affect the interview. With these data, we can then turn to the matter of treatment alternatives.

Discovering Your Own Developmental Blind Spots

Bowlby stated that how our clients relate to us in the interview is our clue for treatment. Before developing a treatment plan, it is critical that counselors and therapists be aware of their personal developmental history. It is important to explore how your own past experiences, feelings, and thoughts about this particular client might affect the interview. If you allow yourself some experiential reflection and analysis, you will find that certain key attitudes and feelings from your own past and current relationships may strongly influence your relationship with clients and the treatment plan you generate.

The basis of developmental counseling and therapy is the co-construction of reality in which the client affects you the therapist as you affect the client. You have knowledge, skills, and experience that can be helpful to the client. You need to be aware of these strengths. At the same time, you must be aware of blind spots that can hurt the interviewing interaction. One way to get in touch with your own developmental history, past and present, is to go through key developmental sequences of awareness.

Take a moment to think of a specific dependent person you have known. Or perhaps think of a time when you felt dependent on others and needy. If you have a current client who represents the dependent style, you may want to focus on your feelings and thoughts about that client. Relax and concentrate on getting a clear visual image. Or, you may get an image of a voice or a sound. Now, try to locate, in your body, the feelings you associate with dependency. Locating feelings in specific parts of the body is particularly helpful in generating deeper understandings of present and past developmental issues.)

Can you locate a specific feeling in your body? Describe it here.

_____

_____

_____

_____

It is wise to repeat the above exercise from a positive standpoint. Did you have a positive experience of having someone dependent on you or of being dependent on someone? These positive frames are important in helping you avoid blind spots in the session.

Can you locate a specific feeling in your body?

_____

_____

_____

_____

Next, stay with one of the feelings and think back to a specific situation in your own life when you experienced that feeling. This can be a current or a past situation, perhaps in adolescence or childhood. Describe the situation in your own words. What were you thinking? What were you feeling? What happened before? What happened afterward?

_____

_____

Is that situation a recurring pattern in your life? Does it occur in other situations? Reflect on your own feelings about yourself and issues of dependency.

_____

_____

_____

_____

Where did your patterns of feelings about dependency come from? Particularly, where did they come from in your family history? What was your family attitude toward dependency? Where did your family learn that attitude and the behaviors that go with it? What are some of the strengths in your developmental history surrounding this issue? What are the weaknesses?

_____

_____

_____

_____

Now review the above exercise. Did you focus on a positive experience of dependency or on one that was less positive? Whatever the focus, think about your choice and its implications for your own work with dependent clients. Then repeat this exercise using the opposite experience. What did you learn?

_____

_____

_____

_____

Given the above information, what potential difficulties might you have with the dependent client? What strengths do you have to offer? Some people don't like dependent styles and, because of their developmental history, become impatient with such clients. Others, because of their own personal style, may take over for the dependent client and offer too much nurturance and support. In either case, it is possible to repeat with the client the client's past developmental history. You as counselor can end up acting like a parent, sibling, or other important figure from the client's past history. Another term for this is *counter-transference*—you as helper repeat your own developmental history with the client and fail to recognize the client as a unique individual.

An extension of the counter-transference concept is *projective identification* (Klein, 1975). Projective identification in its most simple terms is the drawing out in others what is within you. It is *not* seeing yourself in others, it is actually "making or producing" in the other person your own behaviors or problems. Your desire becomes the client's desire. This concept is important therapeutically because it implies that you often produce your own problems in the client. It can become the most serious counter-transference issue. Having clients enact your unconscious wishes is always a possibility, and it is here that supervision and personal awareness is especially important.

A critical first step in generating a treatment plan is self-awareness. What have you learned about yourself that might affect the way you work with clients who present a dependent developmental personality style?

_____

_____

_____

_____

_____

_____

_____

Again, the same exercise is useful for understanding all the developmental personality styles. It is critical that you learn to recognize how your own past history, beliefs, and current experience may be affecting your behavior in the here and now of the interview.

Skilled counselors and therapists learn over time to be aware of their immediate bodily reactions to the client. With care and skillful timing, they learn to use these internal physical clues as ways to understand the client and to pick the specific interventions that may be helpful. These physical clues can help tell us what part of ourselves and our family developmental history has been triggered by our clients. Needless to say, it usually takes time and considerable clinical experience and practice to gain this level of awareness.

Building the Basis for Treatment

Developing a treatment plan for dependent clients involves, first and foremost, treating them differently than they've been treated in the past. We do not want to repeat old patterns from either our own or the client's developmental history.

Using your intuition and your experience with developmental counseling and therapy, outline some treatment guidelines and goals for the dependent developmental personality style.

_____

_____

_____

_____

_____

_____

_____

_____

The following subsections contain specific cautions and developmental guidelines for generating a treatment plan for the dependent client.

Provide a Positive Base for Development

We do not grow and develop in negative or impoverished environments. Positive resources in the client, the environment, and the client-therapist relationship need to be identified.

What is right and functional about this client? What does he or she do well? What positive assets does the client have? Some time should be spent in each session identifying specific strengths on which the client can build. Sometimes it is wise to begin a session with a search for a positive asset: "Before we start, what's new and good for you this week?" More likely you will want to spend time throughout the session identifying and emphasizing positive strengths. Family therapist Salvador Minuchin emphasizes focusing on strengths of the family. Rogers also stresses positive regard and interpretive, positive reframing. Most sessions should include a summary of positives as the interview is about to end.

Where can the client find positive resources in family, friends, or community? If these resources are not immediately available, work on assertiveness and social skills training may be necessary to help generate resources. Developing a support network beyond the counselor or therapist is essential.

You as a counselor are a critical positive resource or asset for the client. Your being there when needed and demonstrating caring and understanding may be the most important aspect of a treatment plan. In this regard, it is particularly important that you be clear about your own attitudes toward the client's difficulties and that you avoid counter-transference and involvement of your own issues. Being a positive resource requires that you meet the Rogerian conditions of nonjudgmentalness, respect, and authenticity. The dependent client (and other personality styles) will test the relationship constantly. Authenticity of self is not enough; you will need to be authentic in the relationship, which is ever changing and evolving.

In addition to being respectful and authentic, you must challenge and confront at times. If you have a solid base of trust, are able to listen well, and have some sense of your own personal issues surrounding the client's concerns, it then becomes possible for you to challenge and confront more forcefully and effectively. When used judiciously in the interview, creative confrontation and perturbation can be a positive resource.

Be Aware of the Changing Nature of the Relationship in the Interview

Positive, seemingly supportive relationships may at times be ineffective. At issue is what type of relationship the dependent person really needs. The antisocial or borderline personality also needs positive relationships, but the nature of the relationship with these clients may differ dramatically from that of the dependent client. *Your relationship in the interview may have to change as you work with different types of clients* (see Table 6-1 for examples). Furthermore, regardless of developmental history, as clients grow and develop you will find yourself changing counseling style and growing with the client. You do not want to continue old styles of helping even though they were very useful to the client in your past interviews.

Defining an appropriate relationship with the dependent client can be facilitated by personal authenticity coupled with careful observation and anticipation of client developmental history. A dependent client, for example, will tend to seek reassurance and comfort and may ask for considerable support and guidance in making decisions. If you give too much support and direction, you may replicate early family and personal relationships. It is important at this point to avoid this repetition and do something different.

"Doing something different" will vary with the specific developmental history and needs of each client, regardless of you or your client's personality style. Do not label clients; people are too complex. Few people are just dependent; most of us are a mix of various personality styles. In general, however, a warm, caring relationship is essential for the dependent client, but the helper must maintain separateness and not merge with the sometimes clinging client. At times, this requires firmness and distance, but always with an underlying sense of caring. Many dependent clients seek the caring and closeness that eluded them in past relationships. They will respond positively to the Rogerian conditions and may need considerable support before they develop their own sense of self. The client is learning to attach to an important human being—you!

At the same time, the client faces developmental tasks of individuation and separation. One can only individuate from a positive relational base. The difficult task for you in your work with dependency issues is to simultaneously support both attachment and separation tasks. In particular, however, dependent clients need to learn how to be on their own and to regard their lives and achievements as worthwhile, independent contributions. The major goal, of course, is independence and autonomy. You will want to affirm separation/or individuation efforts. You will also need to establish firm boundaries in your relationship with this type of client to ensure that you do not become enmeshed.

The French psychoanalyst Jacques Lacan once said, "Love is giving the client what he (or she) does not have." Antisocial and borderline personalities tend not to have firm controls and may benefit from a therapeutic relationship that has firm boundaries and consistency. The obsessive personality may benefit more from warmth and gradual movement toward a more inconsistent and spontaneous relationship. With the first two client types, you want to reward adherence to the rules; with the obsessive, you want to reward breaking the rules.

If you are successful, your balancing of attachment and separation, individuation and relationship, embeddedness and boundaries will have to change as your client develops. You can, and perhaps even must, rely on these basic Rogerian conditions of trust and rapport, but these will manifest differently as the client grows and becomes a more mature adult, adolescent, or child.

According to DCT, dependent clients can be operating at the sensorimotor, concrete, formal, or even dialectic/systemic level. It is best to join, or attach to clients at their predominant cognitive-developmental level, but attachments are formed most firmly at the sensorimotor level. Thus, carefully changing counselor developmental style is essential. Unless a firm relationship has been established as a basis, little change may be expected from counseling or therapy.

Formulate a Developmental Treatment Plan

DCT argues that we all have many complex developmental tasks as we move through the life span. We need to experience life as it is at a sensorimotor level, and we need to be able to describe and act in concrete situations. Full development requires that we be able to see patterns in our lives and reflect on the nature of ourselves. At the dialectic/systemic level, we need to be able to reflect on systems of operations and live and work within the family, community, and culture.

Establishing a developmental treatment plan, whether for the dependent developmental personality style or for other personality styles, depends on the immediate needs and capacities of the client, the time available, the skills and knowledge of the therapist, and a multitude of environmental constraints.

There is no "correct" treatment plan. However, we do know that some treatments are more likely to be effective than others. Cummings (1977, 1985) has been a leader in generating detailed treatment plans for specific problems and disorders. With depressed clients, we now know that behavioral work, such as assertiveness training, plus work on key cognitions is useful. Again, clients need work at multiple levels of cognition and action, and concrete action must be associated with formal thought.

Research shows that taking clients through the DCT systematic questioning sequence (see Chapter 3) is highly therapeutic in itself. In the process of working through sensorimotor, concrete, formal, and dialectic/systemic aspects of dependency, the client experiences self and situations in new ways. Thus, the client makes new discoveries about him- or herself and often spontaneously generates new ideas for action. Viewing oneself through the four perspectives of DCT encourages the client to think in new ways about self and others.

DCT points out that varying theories are appropriate at varying cognitive-developmental levels (see Chapter 3). To develop their full potential, dependent clients may benefit from the following:

Sensorimotor counseling. Gestalt exercises, imagery, relaxation, and body work (nutrition and exercise) all are necessary foundations for development. Some dependent clients (particularly those who are overly intellectualized) may only need work at this level. If dependency has become extreme, behavior modification and environmental controls may be necessary as well as some medication.

Concrete therapy. Assertiveness training is an obvious treatment of choice for dependent clients. But they may also benefit from vocational and career counseling, reality therapy, and the logical A-B-C phase of rational-emotive therapy, which challenges and confronts belief systems. A variety of behavioral treatments, including thought stopping, charting, and contingency analysis, also may be employed. Social skills training may be essential. Again, any one of these approaches may be sufficient to alleviate the dependency.

Formal counseling. Many dependent individuals lack a real sense of self and personal meaning. If they are verbal, they are likely to respond to Rogerian and logotherapy methods. If they are more analytically oriented, a variety of psychodynamic therapies may be helpful. Intellectualized personality types may need to start with formal counseling before they are willing to explore sensorimotor and concrete realities—they need to think before they do.

Dialectic/systemic therapy. A family therapist might want to bring in the family of origin or the current family or living group to analyze where the pattern of dependency originated and to attack it at the system level, thus providing real support for maintenance of change. A dependent style may profit from group work or men's or women's consciousness-raising sessions. Research reveals that more women than men are diagnosed as dependent. Is the developmental block personal to the woman or is it created by society and the environment?

There are many ways to develop a broad treatment plan for the dependent developmental personality style, and similarly, there are many ways to work with any personality style. The preceding list provides alternatives for whatever type of personality style we encounter as helping professionals. Table 6-1 provides specific guidance as to which alternatives are appropriate for the eleven developmental personality styles.

Given the complexity and magnitude of alternatives, specifically the developmental counseling and therapy model adds the following:

1. It provides a comprehensive "map" of the possibilities that appear to be logical while remaining open to alternatives. DCT makes possible a systematic plan and rationale for integrating different theories in an organized treatment plan.

2. It does not argue that a single theory or therapy is best. What is "best" depends on the specific client and the specific counselor, who operate in a specific family, societal, and cultural context.

3. It may help all of us become aware that no one has the ultimate "right" answer; we must remain open to new findings of research and systematic clinical testing. Evidence now being provided by researchers, such as Cummings, clearly indicates that certain treatment programs are preferable to others. We need several alternative treatments at hand to meet varying client needs.

4. Offers a positive orientation not based on pathology and remediation but rather on developmental progression—clients do not need to consider themselves solely responsible for their problems.

5. It gives therapists an organizing framework for specific interventions in the interview (which will be discussed in the next section).

6. It includes four- and eight-level questioning and intervention strategies that can be used in themselves as a method of treating clients.

Few helping professionals have mastered all the theories and techniques discussed above. In the short term, beginning counselors should master one treatment modality at the concrete level and one at the formal level. The cognitive-behavioral approach to therapy is helpful in this regard as it integrates at least the first three levels of treatment.

The lack of a dialectic/systemic focus in most individual helping theories may explain the rapid increase of family orientations to therapy. However, all theories have something to offer clients at all developmental levels. Most professionals either learn to modify their theories to meet varying client needs or, as expertise is gained, add new theory and practical techniques.

Generating a Long-Term Treatment Plan for the Dependent Client

Develop a comprehensive treatment plan for a dependent client, using what you know about the dependent developmental personality style in combination with your own counseling and therapy knowledge and other resources available in your work setting or community. The exercise in this section asks you for two different treatment plans. The first assumes a client who is willing to spend a year or possibly more in the process. Here you can employ all the knowledge, experience, and referral sources available to you.

However, few clients have the luxury of unlimited time and resources. Thus, the second part of the exercise asks you to assume that you have only ten sessions to work with the client. Your mode of treatment should be designed to accommodate this limitation.

This exercise may also help you identify your own eclectic or general theory of helping the dependent personality. Eclecticism involves a commitment to many theoretical perspectives. DCT argues that an eclectic or general theory may not go far enough. Theories need to change with the specific requirements of the client or family. You may find that you apply one theory of helping with a dependent individual but use a very different theory when working with the antisocial client.

Read and work through this exercise using as your "client" either a case you are aware of or an individual or friend who has aspects of the dependent style.

1. *Positive assets and strengths.* How will you develop a positive base for treatment both in each interview and over the longer period? What does this client bring as internal and external assets and strengths?

_____

_____

_____

You might consider making a detailed survey of past successes of the client. Having this information at hand may be useful when difficult times occur throughout counseling. Again, it is critical that you remember the positives and the past survival value of the client's behavior.

2. *Key relationship issues.* What is your personal history and attitude toward dependency? What type of relationship with the client will you strive for? How will you change that relationship as the client develops? What balance of attachment and separation behaviors does this individual need?

_____

_____

_____

_____

_____

_____

Review your self-assessment in earlier sections of the chapter. Are you ready to work with the dependent personality style? Most professionals have their own blind spots and inadequacies, which are sometimes significant enough to indicate that the client be referred to someone else.

3. *Treatment possibilities at each developmental level.* These treatment options must be based on your own personal competence. You may want to refer to the list of suggested treatment alternatives at each developmental level presented in Table 6-1. List below only those treatments that make sense to you for this particular client. Also, recall that taking the dependent through the DCT systematic questioning sequence is a viable treatment alternative.

Plan for sensorimotor treatment. What techniques/and theories will you use?

_____

_____

_____

_____

Plan for concrete-operational treatment. Which techniques/and theories will you use?

_____

_____

_____

_____

Plan for formal-operational treatment. Which techniques/and theories will you use?

_____

_____

_____

Plan for dialectic/systemic treatment. Which techniques/and theories will you use? Will you include some family interventions?

_____

_____

_____

4. *Client/counselor contract for the treatment plan.* Should a treatment plan be shared with the client? Traditionally, professionals have kept their ideas about treatment from the client on the theory that they may be more effective. However, DCT suggests that you consider sharing your treatment plan with the client and jointly develop a plan oriented toward mutual responsibility and accountability. By sharing information, you may discover that all the client needs or wants is a good program of jogging, relaxation training, and nutrition. Assertiveness training is often considered a treatment of choice for the dependent personality style. Those clients desiring long-term therapy might want to pursue psychoanalytic work. Family systems therapy in conjunction with the individual treatment plan may be critical.

Appendix 4 presents two sample client contracts for counseling and therapy. How much would you involve your clients in decisions about the nature and length of counseling and therapy?

_____

_____

_____

5. *The ten-session treatment.* Completing all of the above treatments might take a year or more. In some case, many years of treatment are warranted. More often, your agency, health insurance company, or client constraints indicate brief therapy and counseling. In the helping field, the trend is increasingly toward treatment programs that aim to achieve specific goals in a certain length of time.

Given ten interviews, what would be your treatment plan? How would you present the plan to the client? How much will the client participate in decisions about that treatment plan?

Extending DCT to Other Developmental Personality Styles

As noted throughout this chapter, the assessment and treatment plan outlined above is not restricted to the dependent client. The same step-by-step procedures indicated on the preceding pages may be employed in work with many types of problems that clients present.

Table 6-1 lists the developmental personality styles classified by DSM-III-R with positive aspects of each style, things to look for in the interview, possible family history, predicted relationships, and possible treatment approaches.

This listing is of course, only an introduction to the many complex developmental personality styles. Again, people are almost always mixes of styles rather than "pure" types. It is very important to have formal training, supervision, and experience in classifying client styles. You might find that therapy for yourself about your own issues is helpful in overcoming your blind spots and in learning how to understand the client's world view more completely.

The Borderline Personality Style

One of the most interesting and difficult types of developmental styles is that of the borderline personality. Extensive writings on treatment programs for these individuals exist. The work of Masterson (1981,1985) is particularly compatible with the DCT approach. Masterson suggests that the key developmental period of the borderline is from 15 to 22 months of age. This is Erikson's autonomy versus shame and doubt period and Piaget's mid-sensorimotor period. Masterson argues that the relationship of caregiver and child for the borderline involves intense, confusing messages. The child is punished for attempts to individuate and become autonomous and is rewarded with engulfment by the caregiver when the child seeks to attach again.

Masterson's theoretical and clinical work helps further clarify Bowlby's statement, "How clients treat you is how they were treated. This is our clue for treatment." Borderlines often demonstrate affective instability in the interview. They may care deeply for and depend on the therapist for a period of time and then suddenly mistrust the therapist and be extremely distant or angry. These alternations may appear over several weeks or they may come out dramatically in a single session. Borderlines are often capable of establishing quick, close relationships, which they just as quickly break.

Masterson's view is that the borderline developmental personality style results from the engulfment these individuals experienced in infancy. The child desires, but fears, autonomy. If the child moves toward autonomy, the caregiver (often a borderline type) rejects the child. If the child moves toward the caregiver, engulfment usually follows. Thus, the child (later, the borderline adult) is caught in a vicious circle in which no sense of self is permitted. The child becomes an extension of the caregiver, and is used for the caregiver's ends. The individual, maturing into an adult, remains fixated at this early developmental stage and will behave with others as he or she was treated. The borderline individual is also often a victim of sexual abuse, and as an adult can be abusive, thus continuing the exploitation begun in early childhood.

Masterson suggests that the therapist establish a firm relationship with the borderline, rewarding efforts at separation and individuation while simultaneously ignoring and reflecting back the client's seductive efforts to establish an overly close relationship. It is crucial that the therapist or counselor maintain his or her own autonomy. Masterson recommends that nonjudgmental confrontation be central to the treatment plan for the borderline type.

As the client develops in the clearly defined relationship with the therapist, Masterson recommends "communicative matching," which essentially means supporting and rewarding clients' efforts to find their real selves and do what they want rather than what was suggested by their families.

A DCT treatment plan for the borderline follows the same outline as suggested for the dependent personality style. Given the complexity of the borderline type, the counselor's own self-awareness is particularly important. The therapist-client relationship provides an opportunity for the therapist to act differently than the borderline's caregiver. However, the borderline client will do everything in her or his power to repeat the same pattern that existed in childhood. Masterson suggests that relationship counseling is at the core of treatment of borderlines—and perhaps, by extension, at the core of treatment of all developmental personality disorders.

While this relationship is being established the professional can develop a DCT treatment plan at the sensorimotor, concrete, formal, and dialectic/ systemic levels. Some of the specific approaches and techniques of alternative treatment plans encourage a more mature helper-client relationship, particularly if the client is involved in developing the treatment plan.

To reinforce the concepts presented in this chapter, generate a developmental assessment and treatment plan, using procedures presented here, for a specific developmental personality disorder of interest to you. (One of the most important exercises of the "Theory into Practice" section concerns this task.)

Although time consuming, doing these exercises will give you a broad understanding of other developmental personality styles and of the DCT framework, which can be used in many other settings. Understanding each personality style is extremely useful in counseling and therapy, since clients often manifest at least part of their difficulties as a personality style issue.

In our work as professional helpers, we will encounter normal clients who manifest aspects of these styles in conjunction with other life difficulties.

Severely distressed clients with anxiety disorders, phobias, depression and other DSM-III-R Axis I classifications also manifest different personality styles.

Our task as developmental counselors is to discover the client's development blocks and help the client move beyond them. Sometimes, however, developmental difficulties and personality style have strengths and positives on which further, more effective development can be based.

Treatment Planning with DSM-III-R Axis Disorders

This section briefly outlines applications of DCT to the more severe Axis I disorders of depression and agoraphobia. You have gained experience (from previous chapters) in applying the developmental model to a variety of "normal" counseling issues. Assessment and treatment frameworks outlined for Axis I and II personality styles are also applicable to vocational, college, and premarital counseling as well as to many issues of daily life.

Depression

Previous chapters explored Rigazio-DiGilio's (1989) work with short- and long-term depressed inpatients that showed that the patients could respond to the neo-Piagetian questions of DCT. By using the expanded eight levels of questioning of the Standard Cognitive-Developmental Interview (SCDI) (see Appendix 1), depressed patients could be helped to look at themselves and their situations from the perspective of each of the four basic cognitive-developmental levels.

A beginning form of DCT treatment, termed at the time *media therapy,* was used by Ivey in 1971 with a group of depressed inpatients at a VA hospital in Northhampton, Massachusetts. Media therapy employed the then-new medium of videotape. Media therapy sessions lasted approximately one hour and occurred twice a week, usually for a period of six weeks. In each session, a patient was interviewed for from five to ten minutes; the interview was followed by immediate feedback and discussion of the tape. The therapist acted as a consultant to the patient, with the patient deciding how to use the video feedback.

In retrospect, the developmental structure of media therapy is apparent. In the early sessions of videotape feedback, depressed clients noted eye contact, body language, and appearance issues (for example, "I look at the floor all the time"). These sensorimotor issues were treated with microskills practice in attending behavior (see Ivey, 1971; Ivey and Authier, 1978), Gestalt activation exercises, and relaxation training. (All drugs were suspended during the time of the clinical study.)

Once patients had mastered foundation skills, videotape-based assertiveness training focusing on specific problems was instituted. Patients selected the inter-personal areas of importance to them and role-played themselves encountering these problem areas. These concrete skills-training sessions included such areas as learning how to talk with one's wife, walking through a large department store without anxiety, supervising employees in a fast food outlet, and dealing with issues of racism in finding housing. Individual "me kits" were developed for patients outlining their curriculum of skills and the potential pitfalls they might face in the "outside" world.

Although the focus was on sensorimotor and concrete tasks, a critical point was reached in about the fourth week of treatment. Patients spontaneously would state, "I realize I *can do* something about my depression." This "can-do" transformation represents the move to a formal-operational way of viewing the problem. Once several concrete successes were achieved, the client spontaneously connected them in a can-do pattern. The focus remained on action, but patients also moved to an early formal-operational level.

At this point, skills training was continued, but now an emphasis on patterns of problem solving became the focus of therapy. Self-oriented activities—me kits, (personal journals of competencies and feelings)—were instituted.

However, when the family was brought in for a discharge interview, the patient's behavior and thinking began to disintegrate in the family interaction. Thus, as a final step of treatment, patients' families were brought in and a plan for change in the home was instituted. This early dialectic/systemic, or family therapy, approach was essential to avoid the "rotating door" syndrome in which patients leave and reenter the hospital again and again. Even the best treatment program can be negated by family and environmental factors.

The early work in media therapy remains valid today and was replicated in clinical demonstrations with inpatients at the Prince of Wales Hospital in Sydney, Australia, in 1981. Media therapy, with its microskills base, was the precursor to the DCT treatment framework. Approximately 50% of media therapy participants were diagnosed as seriously depressed. The media therapy framework also was found useful with manic and schizophrenic patients. (One long-term patient who had been in the hospital two years was out of the hospital in six weeks of media therapy.) There were also promising results with patients manifesting conduct disorders. Critical to the success of this approach was developing an informal contract in which patients identified their own goals and modes of treatment. For example, not all patients responded to Gestalt exercises and relaxation. Jointly forming the contract for treatment and helping the patient establish goals may be as important as the DCT or media therapy approach itself.

The experience with depressed patients demonstrates that the DCT specific questioning interventions and step-by-step treatment plan (which were also used with dependent clients) can be used effectively with many, perhaps all, types of Axis I personality disorders. DCT tends to avoid drug therapy but recognizes that this type of sensorimotor treatment can be effective for some types of patients, usually those afflicted with severe developmental blockage.

Agoraphobia

Gonçalves (1988) worked with many agoraphobics, both in Portugal and the United States, using the DCT model. He first makes a careful assessment of client functioning at each of the four major developmental levels and then creates a treatment plan in consultation with the client.

Key developmental issues for agoraphobics at the sensorimotor level include an inability to recognize, discriminate, and accept bodily feelings. Complaints of anxiety manifesting at the gastric, intestinal, respiratory, cardiac, and motor areas are common for agoraphobics. The agoraphobic experiences derealization or depersonalization—fantasies of losing control, serious threats to physical well-being—and inability to deal with the external world. These characteristics are typical of late sensorimotor magical thinking.

Gonçalves finds that Gestalt relaxation and breathing exercises, and biofeedback are especially useful for the somaticized conditions. Gestalt exercises, implosion, and imagery exercises are also useful for reworking faulty thinking patterns.

A central concrete-developmental issue for agoraphobics is the inability to decenter from perceptual experience. For example, the agoraphobic tends to stay too much at the sensorimotor direct experience level, thus avoiding taking action in the world. As a result, the agoraphobic is unable to change his or her actions or affect environmental constraints; the agoraphobic then resorts to escapist and avoidant behavior. Gonçalves found that systematic desensitization and assertiveness training was useful in addressing these problems. Also critical to this phase of treatment is *in vivo* exposure, or flooding, in which the agoraphobic is exposed to frightening situations.

At the formal level, critical developmental issues include the inability to separate thought from action, extensive cognitive distortions (for example, incorrect inference, overabstraction and overgeneralization, extensive and irrelevant self-reference, and dichotomous thinking), and an inability to represent and think about the world in accurate, useful terms.

Therapeutic techniques for this stage focus on language and thought—or, in Gonçalves' terminology, cognitive-restructuring and rational disputation. Self-instruction strategies, such as journal keeping and bibliotherapy, are also included. Such specific problem-focused treatment methods are more effective than longer-term treatments such as psychodynamic approaches.

Dialectic/systemic developmental issues for the agoraphobic include an inability to step back, identify, and challenge underlying personal systems of belief—particularly personal constructs relating to the Eriksonian stages of trust and autonomy (especially control issues). The agoraphobic makes basic assumptions about the world and needs to learn to examine these assumptions and their validity. Gonçalves's work is individually focused; at the dialectic/systemic level, individuals are encouraged to examine their difficulties in a variety of contexts.

Gonçalves's experience led him to focus on self-awareness exercises, such as stream-of-consciousness and mirror-time exercises (Mahoney, 1988) in which clients talk to themselves, with limited guidance from the therapist. Drama therapy (Joyce-Muniz, 1988), Kelly's (1955) fixed-role therapy, and metaphor are also part of Gonçalves's treatment approach for this level.

Gonçalves's conceptualizations of the agoraphobic are an excellent example of how the counselor and clinician can adapt the general framework of DCT to a personal counseling style. Each of us has our own special interests in and competencies with theories and techniques. The open sharing of our expertise with the client in the contracting and goal-setting processes is critical for effective treatment planning.

Chapter Summary

DCT considers pathology to be developmental blocks or "delays." Biological differences obviously have an impact on development in that genetic background interacts with the environment. It is of little use to only provide counseling when the issue is a thyroid deficiency. Recognizing the importance of biological factors, the first task of the developmentally oriented counselor is to stop thinking of clients as "normal" and "abnormal" and to substitute a more positive, developmentally oriented terminology.

The relationship between counselor and client remains central in DCT, but it is a flexible relationship, tailored to the developmental needs of the client. The depressed, agoraphobic, dependent, or antisocial client each will work best with different types of therapeutic approaches. Some clients do best with a firm, distant relationship; others benefit from a close, warm, supportive relationship. The therapist-client relationship must also include perturbation to encourage client growth and development.

Bowlby suggests that we have twin tasks in life: we must learn how to attach to others and, simultaneously, learn how to be separate and autonomous. Each client has different needs for an attached, close relationship and for separation and autonomy. The first two Eriksonian developmental tasks are trust (versus mistrust) and autonomy (versus shame and doubt). Bowlby claims that clients enact their developmental history with the therapist based on their experiences at these fundamental life stages.

Varying cultures place differing emphases on separation and attachment. North American and much of European culture focus on individuation and separation. The more relational cultures of southern Europe, the Middle East, and Asia tend to emphasize attachment. Family therapists have documented the problems encountered by an autonomous therapist who attempts to counsel a relational client (McGoldrick, Pearce, & Giordano, 1982). These concepts are outlined in more detail in the following chapter on multicultural issues in counseling and therapy.

In generating a treatment plan, DCT suggests that you first examine yourself and your own developmental history. What does this particular client and her or his particular problem mean to you? You can explore what this client represents in your own developmental history by using the four-level developmental questioning strategies for self-examination. Of course, we will not be able to be competent in all treatment approaches. It is therefore necessary that we be aware of alternatives to our methods and share these openly with our clients.

Contracting with the client is central to the DCT process. Rather than impose your theory and interventions on the client, focus on clients' goals for therapy and organize your interventions around their needs rather than your own. A written contract focused on sensorimotor, concrete, formal, and dialectic/systemic treatment options can then be developed. In areas where you are not competent, you may wish to maintain a case management/consultant relationship with the client. (The case management function is outlined in detail in Chapter 8.)

Knowledge of DSM-III-R "disorders" is essential for all counselors and therapists. Although DSM-III-R is oriented toward a "pathological" model, it nonetheless provides a useful organization system for many types of developmental problems that manifest in the interview. Problems as varying as developmental personality styles and severe developmental blocks (such as depression, agoraphobia, and schizophrenia) are amenable to the developmental method.

The Yakima Time Ball image recalls to us the many developmental milestones we all must pass. Life is a developmental process recorded in our minds—knots and all.

 CAUTION! Labels can be dangerous. Terms such as *borderline* and *dependent* have been used in this chapter in a more positive, developmental sense. However, these words are still considered by most to be indicators of pathology—an excuse used by some to dismiss the individual as barely human. Since all in the helping profession encounter the DSM-III-R categorization system, it is important to generate counseling and clinical categories that parallel this classification framework but from a more humane, developmental perspective.

All of us are mixtures of many developmental personality styles, which are often situationally activated. Adopting a paranoid style may be useful when buying a used car, and the spontaneity of a borderline style may help us enjoy the moment to its fullest. As we work with these personality styles, we must respect the positives of each style.

Theory into Practice

Following are some key objectives you may have mastered by the time you complete the exercises in this chapter, which include the ability to

1. Recognize how your own developmental history may play itself out in the interview.
2. Generate a developmentally oriented treatment plan for a variety of clients with different developmental blocks or problems.
3. Use the systematic DCT questioning strategies in role-plays with a variety of developmental personality styles.

Identifying Your Own Developmental History

Return to the chapter section entitled "Discovering Your Own Developmental Blind Spots," which lists some specific exercises that may help you learn about some key aspects of your own developmental history that you need to take into account as you meet with clients in the helping interview (p. 171).

There are many other ways you can learn about yourself and the potential difficulties of counter-transference and projective identification. Many of the exercises in this book, particularly in Chapters 1 and 5, focus on you looking at your own developmental past and how it may affect the present. Reviewing these exercises at a deeper level can be beneficial.

Another useful self-discovery exercise is the generation of a family genogram in which you lay out your own family tree. If you give special attention to family characteristics, you will find that many of your own behaviors and beliefs can be traced back several generations, often to the original cultural setting from which your family came.

These exercises must be repeated more than once, particularly as you work with new types of clients. The first step toward effective developmentally oriented counseling is self-awareness.

Most of us have certain clients that are difficult for us. We also have favorite types of clients. List below your difficult clients and those you look forward to meeting with. If you are in counseling practice, think back on the types of people you get along well with and those that are more troublesome for you. These personal relationships may reappear in the here and now of the helping interview.

Who are the clients or people you enjoy working with?

_____

_____

_____

Who are the clients or people you find more difficult?

_____

_____

_____

Work through the four-level DCT questioning exercises for self-knowledge (What do you see/hear/feel? Can you give a concrete example? Is there a pattern? As you reflect on the total system, what do you learn?) with one individual from your list. As you work at the sensorimotor level, pay particular attention to how the images you have affect your body. As you develop increasing skills, your body awareness is often your best clue for how to take action in the interview. You may wish to have a friend or colleague whom you trust interview you and take you through this exercise.

Summarize what you have learned in a journal and refer to it from time to time.

Generate a Developmentally Oriented Treatment Plan

In reading through this chapter, you have hopefully already generated your own treatment plan for a dependent personality style. At this point, it is useful to develop a treatment plan for another personality style or for an Axis I disorder. You can do this in a small group. Members of your group probably will have slightly different treatment plans, depending on their own life histories and their counseling and therapy knowledge and competencies. Summarize your treatment plan and compare it with those of others.

Pay special attention to developing treatment contracts with the client. How do you and your group feel about this issue? Together, list specific treatment goals using each of the four developmental levels.

1. Decide on a specific developmental personality style or Axis I issue.
2. Using your intuition, work through the following six steps to define that style and then consult DSM-III-R and other sources to add to or modify your original impression.

   a. What are the positives and survival skills of the client? These should be identified clearly, respected, and supported. The goal of therapy is to balance, not eliminate, these key personality qualities.
   b. What is the anticipated family history? How was client treated at home?
   c. What is the expected nature of current personal relationships?
   d. How are the ways the client relates to others likely to manifest in interviews with you?
   e. How is the client likely to react in the vocational world?
   f. What possible Axis I or Axis II problems may be anticipated?

3. Generate a treatment plan for the developmental personality style or Axis I problem.

   a. How will you develop a positive base for treatment in current interviews and over the long term?
   b. What are the key relationship issues for you for this style? What is your personal history and attitude surrounding this issue? What type of relationship will you strive for? How will you change that relationship as the client develops? What balance of attachment and separation behaviors does this client need?
   c. How will you generate a treatment plan at the sensorimotor, concrete, formal, and dialectic/systemic levels? How would you use the specific questioning and intervention strategies of DCT with this type of client?
   d. Do you plan to generate a client-counselor contract for a treatment plan?

Practice with DCT in a Role-Played Interview

The following exercise has been especially helpful in making clear and concrete the concepts of DCT for Axis II developmental personality styles and more severe Axis I problems. In this exercise, the client adopts one of the personality styles (dependent, narcissistic, and so on) or a more severe disturbance (conduct disorder, depression, agoraphobia).

Most of us have had certain incidents or periods in our lives when we have been especially dependent or mistrustful (paranoid), have acted out (antisocial or conduct disorder), or have been overly self-focused (narcissistic). Most of us also have experienced at least mild depression, slight phobias, and some part of the total confusion of schizophrenics.

Role-play a client, and identify the part of yourself that represents a particular developmental personality style. Enlarge on that part of yourself and allow it to take over the role-play. This exercise will give you an opportunity to learn about the personality style.

Discussing your own issues can be a powerful experience. It is particularly important that you work with a group you trust and that a qualified supervisor is immediately available. During the sensorimotor questioning sequence, this exercise can become highly emotional. You may prefer to role-play a client you have had. If so, be sure to inform your interviewer that you are role-playing a client.

Step 6, "Provide immediate feedback," is used differently in this role-play. The focus is on the counselor and his or her feelings and thoughts during the role-played interview.

Step 1: Divide into Practice Groups

Step 2: Select a Group Leader

Step 3: Assign Roles for the Practice Session

- Role-played client. The role-played client will be an Axis II developmental personality style or an Axis I personality problem as discussed above.
- Interviewer. The interviewer will ask the DCT four-level questions. Alternatively, you could use the introspective-developmental counseling framework of Tamase and conduct a review of this part of the client's life. Remember to use listening skills frequently and help the client organize information through reflection of feeling and summarization.
- Observers 1 and 2. The observers will provide specific feedback on the relationship between the client and counselor at each part of the interview.

Step 4: Plan the Session

The interviewer and client first need to agree on the topic to be reviewed. This is an informal miniversion of the DCT counselor-client contract. The two observers can examine the feedback form.

Step 5: Conduct a 30-Minute Interviewing Session

Again, it is helpful to videotape and/or audiotape practice sessions.

Step 6: Provide Immediate Feedback and Complete Notes (5 to 20 Minutes)

Allow the client and interviewer time to provide immediate personal reactions to the practice session. After this has been done, the observers and the role-played client can focus on the thoughts and feelings of the counselor. Ask the counselor to generate a specific visual image of the interview and then go through the specific four-level questioning strategies with the counselor. It is important during this process to ask the counselor for his or her bodily feeling when the image of the client was called to mind. This part of the exercise is particularly helpful to the counselor's understanding how personal issues may affect the counseling process.

Feedback Form for Role-Played

Sessions with DSM-III-R Personality Types

DSM-III-R issue presented by client in this interview.

_____

Observer 1. List the specific behaviors the client presents in the interview that do or do not exemplify the problem (as categorized by DSM-III-R).

_____

_____

_____

_____

_____

How does this list compare with descriptions of the problem in DSM-III-R?

_____

_____

_____

Observer 2. Pay primary attention to the role-played interviewer. List nonverbal behavior in the interview (points at which the interviewer hesitated or took one direction when another might have been possible) as well as key words selected by the interviewer.

_____

_____

_____

_____

Use this list as a framework for helping the interviewer understand his or her behavior in the role-played session.

Step 7: Review Practice Session and Provide Feedback (15 to 30 Minutes)

The interviewer should be the one who asks for feedback rather than receiving it without being asked. The observers can share their observations from the feedback form and from their observations as the session progressed. Avoid judgmental feedback.

Practice in a Role-Played Family Session

Families are often the origin of problems described in DSM-III-R. In this role-play, select an issue of interest to the group and role-play with a four-member intact family. One member of the family will volunteer to serve as the identified patient and the family members will take roles as they imagine them to be in such a family. Depression, anoxeria or bulimia, or Axis I or Axis II issues can be used as the topic. One to two hours will be required for development and debriefing of the family session.

Step 1: Select Four to Six Participants

Two individuals can be selected as co-therapists. The other participants will be the family. The remainder of the members of the class or workshop will observe the entire process and later serve as process consultants who reflect on the session.

Step 2: Have the Workshop Leader Assume the Leadership Role

Due to the complexity of the process, the workshop leader or teacher should assume the leader role and ensure that the group follows the specific steps of the practice session.

Step 3: Assign Roles for the Practice Session

- Role-played family. Any problem described in DSM-III-R may be selected.
- Therapists. Two therapists or counselors can work together for this session.
- Workshop/class observers. All remaining individuals in the session will sit in a circle around the family.

Step 4: Plan the Session

- The family can leave the room and define their roles and the problem they wish to present. The nature of the problem will not be a surprise to the therapists. The family should realize that they must role-play the rigid viewpoint that the IP is the problem. In the role-play, the family members should demonstrate their own rigidity as it affects family members.

- The two therapists may wish to think through their relationship briefly. Begin the session by focusing on what brought the family to treatment. Then ask how they have tried to solve the problem. Pay special attention to strengths of the family and reframe their efforts positively when possible. One technique to use at this point is to ask the family, "If you had to see this problem another way, a way that makes it solvable, how would you see it?" Finally, reframe the problem from a new point of view.

- The family observers have several roles: (1) They all can be participant/observers. The therapists should feel free to stop the interview in mid-session to ask the observers for help and suggestions. (2) Four observers should be assigned to observe various members of the family. The observers' task is to identify how each member participates in and supports the developmental problem of the IP. Two observers should observe the therapists and note their personal style of relating to this family. How do the therapists repeat their own family history in this role-played interview? Several members of the group may use the individual feedback forms from the practice sessions at the end of each of the chapters in this book.

Step 5: Conduct a 30-Minute Interviewing Session

It is helpful to videotape and/or audiotape practice sessions.

Families often confuse even the most effective therapists. Thus, the therapists should feel free to stop for a moment in the middle of the session and ask the external observers for their reactions and suggestions. It may be informative to look for issues in the developmental history of the therapists that affect their relationship with the family.

Step 6: Provide Immediate Feedback and Complete Notes (10 Minutes)

This is a highly structured session, and there is often immediate personal need to process and discuss the session. In particular, it is helpful for the therapists to ask the family "What stands out for you from this practice session?" Allow time to provide true personal reactions to the practice. At this point, the observers should sit back and let the participants take control. Use this time to complete your classification and notes. It may be especially helpful if each family therapist identifies a single visual image of the family, locates where in the body that image is felt, and then explores his or her own developmental history using the systematic questions of DCT.

Step 7: Review Practice Session and Provide Feedback (15 to 30 Minutes)

It is important when giving feedback to allow the therapists and family receiving the feedback to be in charge. At this point, the observers can share their observations. As usual, feedback should be specific, concrete, and nonjudgmental. Pay attention to the strengths of the interview.

Generalization: Taking Treatment Plans Home

Activity 1: Generate a Treatment Plan for One of Your Own Clients

Select one client with whom you are currently working and, with a supervisor or colleague, work through the specific steps of a DCT treatment plan, paying special attention to how your own developmental history relates to that particular client in the interview.

As you begin (perhaps even now), focus on one visual image of your client, locate a feeling in your body, and see where that leads you.

Activity 2: Seek Supervision on a Case Problem Using the DCT Model

For all of us, there are times in interviews that don't go as well as we might have wished. Select a difficult time in an interview or an entire interview that was difficult and explore what was going on inside you. The supervisor may find the DCT questioning sequence helpful in this process.

Activity 3: Consider the Yakima Nation Proverb

>Time is a relationship between events,
>Kept fresh in memory by selected objects on knotted hemp.
>Connection is as vital as separation.
>By the time she is a grandmother,
>The unity of life is wrapped
>>and remembered
>>in a Time Ball.

What does this proverb say to you at this point?

_____

_____

_____

_____

Suggested Supplementary Reading and Activities

Additional Reading

Ivey, A. 1986. *Developmental therapy: Theory into practice.* San Francisco: Jossey-Bass.
Much of the self-analysis requested in this chapter moves beyond formal operations to the dialectic level. Pages 119-125 and 151-162 of *Developmental Therapy* can aid in the type of self-understanding recommended in this chapter. The exercises of construct 4 on pages 129-130 and construct 2 on pages 172-175 may be especially useful.

Information on separation/and attachment issues and DCT's relationship to the approaches of Bowlby and Masterson may be found on pages 97-101 and 263-284 and in the last chapter of the book. For additional help, review the exercises of construct 4 on pages 129-130, construct 3 on pages 297-299, and constructs 1 and 2 on pages 341-343.

If you wish a developmental challenge, read the description of the work of Jacques Lacan on pages 275-284. The work on Anthony Gregorc on pages 284-292 is also interesting.   Constructs 4 and 5 on pages 299-302 provide practical applications of these ideas.

American Psychiatric Association. 1987. *Diagnostic and statistic manual of mental disorders* (DSM-III-R). Washington, D. C.: American Psychiatric Association.
This controversial book has generally been seen as totally antithetical to the positive developmental frame of reference. Coming from the psychiatric frame of reference, it clearly has a medical, remedial orientation. Labels are dangerous things to attach to complex individuals such as we all are. DCT considers the DSM-III-R approach to have serious limitations but realizes that it synthesizes the diagnostic wisdom of 100 years of work with troubled individuals.   If used with care and if each developmental personality style or developmental block is reframed in terms of its positives, DSM-III-R can be a valuable source of information and a guideline for organizing our clients' thought patterns and behavior.

An awareness of how to work with key problems identified in DSM-III-R is necessary for every helping professional, if only to give the helper an idea of when to refer a client. (Use the latest available editions of DSM-III-R to keep current.)

Bowlby, J. 1969. *Attachment*. New York: Basic Books.

Bowlby, J. 1973. *Separation*. New York: Basic Books.
These two books provide a foundation for Bowlby's important work on relationships. Well written and rich in clinical detail, they offer important extensions of the basic ideas in this chapter.

Masterson, J. 1981. *The narcissistic and borderline disorders*. New York: Brunner/Mazel.

Masterson, J. 1985. *The real self: A developmental, self, and object relations approach*. New York: Brunner/Mazel.
Masterson skillfully blends theory and practice in a comprehensive review of his treatment approach with these difficult client types. Both books are compatible with the DCT frame of reference, although Masterson's orientation is toward the pathological frame. His more recent work on the real self reflects movement toward a more positive developmental approach.

Millon, T., and G. Everly. 1985. *Personality and its disorders: A biosocial learning approach*. New York: Wiley.
This book provides a balanced view of personality disorders from social and biological perspectives and is a useful supplement to this chapter.

Allen, D. 1988. *Unifying individual and family therapies*. San Francisco: Jossey-Bass.
Individual problems often have roots in family development. This book shows how to apply family concepts in the individual interview and elaborates on personality disorder and its origins.

Research Suggestion

The Standard Cognitive-Developmental Interview (Appendix 1) has been clinically effective in helping depressed clients develop new perspectives on their issues. This interview can be used with any of the developmental personality styles. A variety of process and outcome studies may be generated from the interviews.

7 Multicultural Development

Justice for the individual
Is a part of justice for the
   Community;
And exists for one, only when
   both are satisfied.
So it is that personal freedom
Must be limited by security
   for others;
And the mature person is a servant to
   the People.

Yakima Nation Proverb

Until late in the last century, the severely disturbed were despised and ill treated by society. Pioneers in the treatment of mental illness reversed the tradition of neglect and abuse, developing treatment programs that more effectively addressed the needs of the deeply troubled. The first breakthrough in mental health care was an awareness of the role of societal oppression in mental disturbance.

Eventually, mental health care focused on individual problems and less on society's responsibility for those problems. Thus, responsibility for the illness and for change was again placed on the individual. The field of social work, however, has continued to emphasize that the individual lives in a social context and that change in the environment is of equal or more importance than change in the individual. The mental health of individuals living in oppressive situations may be better addressed by making changes in society.

In some parts of world, among them some Native American nations, Africa, Asia, and the South Pacific, the severely disturbed are not despised and ill treated. Rather they are often revered and rewarded as having a closer spiritual connection. These cultures found that the alternative perspective provided by many whom we would call "mentally ill" was valuable for everyone's survival. There are those who state that the "true measure of a culture is the way it takes care of its unfortunates."

Given the individualistic tradition of Western society, counseling and therapy, in themselves, cannot accomplish the balance between autonomous individualism and communal relationship proposed by the Yakima elders in the proverb that opens this chapter. Many counseling and therapy theories, rooted as they are in individualistic Western culture, place the locus of the problem with the individual. Family systems and organizational theories are attempts to balance this view, reminding us that we live in relationship to those around us.

Despite the positive intentions of both individual and systemic therapeutic theories, it is possible that the Black identity movement, the women's movement, and gay liberation have done more for the mental health of oppressed individuals and groups than have all of the counseling and therapy theories combined. These movements have helped us all become aware of the critical role that societal and cultural factors play in individual and family development.

In the United States, Blacks spearheaded a new understanding of the impact of social oppression. Until the Black movement, Blacks often concluded that lack of success was an individual failing. Martin Luther King, Jr., symbolized a new awareness—that racism, not the failure of Black individuals, was the problem.

Following the Black movement was Betty Freidan's book *The Feminine Mystique* (1977), which named "the problem which has no name"—sexism. Women gained broader understandings and more personal power as they came to understand their role in a community and social context.

This chapter extends the developmental model to issues of multicultural counseling and development. Conceptions of minority identity development are explored first, followed by a description of the importance of cultural issues in the counseling process and specific ideas for more culturally relevant counseling and therapy.

What Is Culture?

The word *culture* in the following discussion is interpreted broadly. Culture can be associated with a racial group (Black, Asian) or an ethnic group (Polish, Cuban, Mexican) as well as with gender, religion, economic status, nationality, physical capacity or handicap, or affectional orientation. These larger categories also have subcategories. For instance, Black culture in the United States can be further subdivided into Caribbean, Mississippi, Harlem, or African Black culture.

There may be even more variability in individuals than in cultures [1] (see, for example, Pedersen, 1988). Class and economic differences, religion, and family experiences contribute to each individual's unique personal history—a distinctive personal culture. It is dangerous to use multicultural approaches to stereotype individuals. Justice must serve both the community and the individual.

Thus, culture consists two sometimes conflicting components: each group has a distinctly different culture, and each individual has a distinctive personal culture. If we become accustomed to thinking in a cultural framework, we may fail to see the unique individual before us. If we focus too much on the individual, we may fail to see how this individual is affected by cultural history.

Culture, then, is both an abstraction and a concrete particular. In its abstract form, culture cannot be seen, heard, or felt. It is a way of being—the norms and customs of a group. Culture becomes a concrete particular in the specific individual and his or her family. But no one individual or single family totally represents the culture.

The philosopher Hegel talked about the universal and the particular. The particular carries the spirit of the universal, but is less than the universal. The universal does not and cannot exist outside of the particular. Culture does not and cannot exist outside of particular individuals and families who embody part of the spirit of the culture.

For the practice of counseling and therapy, especially from a DCT perspective, we need to be aware of culture and its many and changing manifestations. The sensorimotor and concrete experience of each individual is deeply affected by abstract formal and dialectic/systemic dimensions. Each individual, family, and culture represents a different way of being.

---

[1] There are almost as many definitions of the word "culture" as there are people who seek to define it. Culture is interpreted in this chapter in a broad sense. However, there are those who would criticize the usage here and would prefer to talk about Western culture. They might prefer defining groupings, such as religion, race, gender, etc., as "subcultures." They might comment particularly that all cultures have men and women and therefore gender does not represent a culture in itself. To me, the author, this route implies a hierarchy in which some category of culture is put above some other category. Some of us *first* identify ourselves as women or men, Jewish or Moslem, Black or Mexican. *Then* we consider some other category (e.g., broad Western culture) as a subculture in which we partake to greater or lesser degree.

Most would agree when one uses the word "culture" that the particular interpretation and definition should be outlined clearly. If one takes the broad interpretation here, then most of us are indeed multicultural as we are members of more than one cultural grouping (for example, you may be Cuban, female, living in Miami, Catholic, etc.).

Life-span development and the family life cycle both exist within a cultural context. One of the important tasks we as helpers face is sorting out what are the individual and what are the cultural artifacts of the developmental process. Some argue that families are the basis of culture; some hold that the physical environment dictates the culture. Whatever the view, culture and its impact on the individual and the family must be an important consideration in counseling and therapy.

Facilitating Awareness of Multicultural Issues

How can we facilitate an understanding and awareness of the many critical multicultural issues in counseling and therapy? Specific goals for training counselors and therapists have been generated by the Division of Counseling Psychology (see Table 7-1) that serve as guidelines for the helping professional in developing such awareness.

Clearly, any one book or training program can only begin to provide a way to deal with these complex issues. It is obvious, however, that multicultural issues are important and that ethical practice requires that we address them seriously. Counseling and therapy theory is usually based on a White, middle-class Euro-American, highly individualistic, often ethnocentric ethic. In addition, instances of racism, sexism, and other forms of prejudice can and do exist in this framework.

The goals of this book and particularly of this chapter focus on the following aspects of the culturally effective counselor and therapist:

Table 7-1. The Culturally Skilled Counselor or Therapist

Beliefs and attitudes	Knowledge	Skills
Has moved from being culturally unaware to being aware and sensitive to his or her own cultural heritage and to valuing and respecting differences	Has a good understanding of the sociopolitical system's operation in the United States, with respect to the treatment of minorities	Is able to generate a wide variety of verbal and nonverbal messages
Is aware of his or her own values and biases and how they may affect minority clients	Possesses specific knowledge and information about the particular group he or she is working with	Is able to send and receive both verbal and nonverbal messages accurately and appropriately.
Is comfortable with differences that exist between the counselor and client in terms of race and beliefs	Has a clear and explicit knowledge and understanding of the generic characteristics of counseling and therapy	Is able to exercise institutional intervention skills on behalf of the client, when appropriate.
Is sensitive to circumstances (personal biases, stage of ethnic identity, sociopolitical influences, and so on) that may dictate referral of the minority client to members of his or her own race	Is aware of institutional barriers that prevent minorities from using mental health services	

SOURCE: From "Cross-cultural competencies," by D. Sue et al., 1982, *Counseling Psychologist, 10*, p. 49.

1. *Beliefs and attitudes.* Several areas of ethnic, gender, and racial identity are examined in this chapter. All of them relate to the basic concepts of the integrative minority identity development theory (Atkinson, Morten, & Sue, 1989).

2. *Knowledge.* Each theory of identity development here tells us something important about a cultural grouping. In addition you will find that DCT concepts of earlier chapters are enriched as they are related to these important constructs.

3. *Skills.* The emphasis here is on skills that can help us understand different cultural groups. Specific exercises concerning issues of multicultural consciousness are presented.

Minority identity development theory preceded developmental counseling and therapy. One of the important factors that led eventually to the DCT framework was experience with Bailey Jackson's Black identity theory (1975). His four-level theory is outlined in this chapter in some detail. You will find that the ideas here are becoming foundation material for a multiculturally aware professional practice of helping.

Thus, we often use language to supply some connections between and among the different approaches to identity development, but it should be clear that these theories have assisted DCT growth and help show how it can become culturally relevant.

Minority Identity Development Theory (MIDT)

Minority identity development theory (MIDT) considers the developmental stages of Blacks, women, and other cultural minorities. (Atkinson, Morten, & Sue, 1989). The key precepts of MIDT are summarized in Table 7-2.

As Table 7-2 on the next page shows, the first stage of Black consciousness is conformity to the status quo. The Black individual tends to see the White individual as better and deprecates both the self and the Black group. Self-hate is characteristic of this stage. While once common for Blacks, self-hate is now quite rare. Blacks at this stage tend to discriminate against members of other minorities, are less aware of racism and oppression, and may even deny that racism is the problem. The conformist stage is also experienced by other minorities—for instance, a homosexual who is afraid to "come out of the closet" or a handicapped individual who sees the physically able as superior.

Dissonance is the second consciousness stage according to MIDT. In this stage, the Black individual is perturbed by awareness of incongruity in society, which fails to provide opportunity and self-respect. Awareness of racism begins at this stage.

The critical step toward resistance and immersion occurs at the third stage. Self-respect begins to grow, but much of this self-respect is gained through opposition to dominant White culture. Anger is characteristic at this stage. The Black identity movement as a whole went through this angry period as Blacks became aware of centuries of racism and oppression. Similarly, women, gays,

Table 7-2. Minority Identity Development Theory

Stages of MIDT	Attitude toward self	Attitude toward others of same minority	Attitude toward other minority groups	Attitude toward dominant group
1. Conformity	Self-deprecating	Group-deprecating	Discriminatory	Group appreciating
2. Dissonance	Conflict between self-appreciating and self-deprecating	Conflict between group deprecating and group appreciating	Conflict between dominantly held views of minority hierarchy and feelings of shared experience	Conflict between group appreciating and group deprecating
3 Resistance and immersion	Self-appreciating	Group appreciating	Conflict between feelings of empathy for other minority experiences and feelings of culturocentrism	Group deprecating
4. Introspection	Concern with basis of self-appreciation	Concern with nature of unequivocal appreciation	Concern with ethnocentric basis for judging others	Concern with basis of group depreciation
5. Synergetic articulation and awareness	Self-appreciating	Group appreciating	Group appreciating	Selective appreciating

SOURCE: From *Counseling American Minorities*, p. 44, by D. W. Atkinson, G. Morten, and D. Sue, 1989, Dubuque, Iowa: W. C. Brown. (Reprinted by permission.)

and the handicapped have experienced anger in their own consciousness-raising process. There is a tendency, at this stage, to focus on specific wrongs of society and to work actively to address injustices. This is a stage of taking action in the world.

The fourth consciousness stage corresponds in many ways to the thoughtfulness of the formal-operational period. As Blacks develop increased awareness, they often focus on issues of Black pride and racial identity, and the opposition to White culture becomes less important than in past stages. There is a danger that analysis of racism and discrimination patterns can replace concrete action. For example, a deaf individual may seek the company of other deaf people and withdraw from contact with the majority of hearing individuals.

At stage five, synergistic articulation and awareness, the Black individual appreciates him-or herself as an individual and group member while simultaneously being more sympathetic to other minority groups. Whites are viewed selectively; their good qualities are valued, but the effects of past and present racism and discrimination are not forgotten.

Just as with the developmental personality styles of DCT, each stage has positives and survival value. For example, the stage-2 pattern of resistance is essential if one is to live in a racist society; similarly, at times it is wise to conform (stage 1). MIDT tends to favor stage 5, but always with awareness of the importance of alternative types of consciousness.

MIDT has specific implications for counseling and therapy. Only in certain situations can a White counselor or therapist work with an Asian, Black, or Hispanic client at stage 2—resistance. One could also question the wisdom of a White counselor working with minority individuals at stage 1. At stage 1, the individual may need active confrontation and perturbation to help him or her move to the stage of dissonance, which is a necessary first step in expanding self-awareness.

The skilled White counselor might likely be able to help some minority clients who are at stage 4, but it could be expected that the client would carefully analyze the behavior and motives of the counselor. Blacks at stage 5 might well be open to counseling from a White counselor and might even be able to deal with racism that might show up in the session.

In this type of work, ethical issues need to be given serious consideration. If a helping professional has a bias against clients of certain backgrounds, these helpers should avoid such therapeutic situations. Unfortunately, many people are unaware of their own biases. Referral of some cases is necessary, but the question of to whom to refer remains. The helping professions have not yet outlined useful guidelines for such dilemmas. While these difficult issues are explored, it is important that all helping professionals, beginning and experienced, receive training and supervision focused on cultural differences.

It is not just the White counselor who must learn to deal with minority individuals from a different perspective. Challenges exist in many dimensions. For instance, a woman at the conformist stage who accepts the present status quo might have difficulty counseling a woman in stage 2 or 3. A Puerto Rican client at stage 3 (resistance) might well reject the well-intentioned efforts toward introspection of a stage-4 Puerto Rican counselor. At stage 5, Hispanics from Cuba, Puerto Rico, and Mexico might communicate easily, but at earlier stages, mistrust and misunderstandings could occur.

Minority identity development theory, a useful way of conceptualizing the development of consciousness of many types of minority groups, becomes even more useful when related to the DCT framework.

Enriching DCT from the MIDT Perspective

The five stages of MIDT roughly correspond to the four levels of DCT, as shown in Table 7-3. The second stage of MIDT is similar to the late sensorimotor level; perturbation and conflict are necessary in the critical transition from an embedded mode to concrete thought. Black identity theory, as described in the table, is based on the theories of Jackson (1975), and feminist identity development and developmental challenges are a combination of Jackson's ideas with the four-level DCT concepts.

Table 7-3. DCT Levels and Group Identity Development Theory (GIDT)

Level	Black identity theory	Feminist identity development	Developmental challenges
Sensorimotor[a] (embedded consciousness)	Accepts status quo; failure to succeed considered a personal failing	Lacks awareness of sexism; "buys into" existing system.	Disability considered a personal fault/shame; may hide disability; conforms
Concrete-operational (action)	Resistance; anger and action	Aware of women's oppression; anger and action	Aware of discrimination against handicapped; anger and action
Formal-operational (self-examination)	Redefinition; Black pride; introspection	Pride in being female; separatism.	Knows self-worth and personal distinctiveness
Dialectic/systemic	Internalization; values all perspectives and uses each appropriately	Takes multiperspective; sees men selectively; thinks and acts	Sees disability in social context; understands benefits for self and others

[a]Parallel stages of MIDT (see Table 7-2).

The final level of group identity development is at times controversial. MIDT and Jackson's model focus more on relationships with other cultures and developing a synthesis with other cultural groupings. Some question synthesis as the ultimate goal and suggest that giving more attention to becoming firm in one's own cultural frame may be necessary. See, for example, Helms (1985) and Parham and Helms (1981).

There are distinctions between the DCT model and the group identity theories. DCT levels reflect processes of cognition and affect, whereas group identity stages focus on the content of what is said or done at each stage. Thus, DCT provides a theoretical framework for these theories, and group identity theories offer concrete information for each stage.

The DCT framework is helpful for identifying the consciousness stage of clients in the interview. The DCT treatment plan approach may also be useful in generating culturally relevant programs, particularly since DCT involves the client in the process of treatment planning. Perturbation and confrontation may be particularly useful in pointing out contradictions to clients at stage 1 of either the MIDT or Black identity theories. DCT's four-stage questioning sequence must be adapted to meet the needs of special groups.

Given, this brief introduction, can you identify the group identity stage of clients in the following examples? Circle the group identity stage that seems most appropriate. (Answers are provided at the end of this chapter.) As you determine the stages, realize that if you are of a different group than the speaker, you may not be able to hear what is being said and may likely miss key data.

1 2 3 4 1. (Cambodian) The United States is best. I just want to be an American like everyone else.

1 2 3 4   2. (Cambodian) I've been ripped off. America doesn't care about me. White people are just plain racist and Blacks aren't much better.

1 2 3 4   3. (Cambodian) I need to get back to my roots and think about my homeland. Its too much hassle dealing with this culture. I need time to think.

1 2 3 4   4. (Cambodian) As I look at it now, the United States does have much to offer, although I know I must fight racism. I'm glad I took time to recapture my Cambodian identity.

1 2 3 4   5. (woman) I've just come back from the picket line. The affirmative action program at the plant just isn't working. I'm going to do something about it. It really makes me angry.

1 2 3 4   6. (woman) I don't see why people are picketing the plant. I'm doing fine. Sure, I work hard as a secretary and I'd like more pay, but I sure don't want to handle lumber in the yard.

1 2 3 4   7. (woman) I'm tired of the hassle. I'm supporting the strike, but I need time to think for awhile. I just want to be with women and think it through. Men just seem irrelevant to me.

1 2 3 4   8. (woman) Well, I'm going to work on the picket line, but I also know that we've got to work with those men in the plant who understand our point of view. We've got to work together to change a lot of people's minds.

1 2 3 4   9. (blind) I've learned a lot about life by listening and touching. I know I've missed a lot in terms of seeing. I've been angry at the discrimination I've faced, but I'm excited to see all the improvements for the blind that have come in recent years. It's been worth it.

1 2 3 4   10. (Chinese) I'm fed up with this university. Everywhere I turn, I find more and more racism. The history texts distort my background; the housing office ignores the discrimination. We've got to get organized.

1 2 3 4   11. (Jewish) There's no discrimination in this country. I've got along fine. I do have to watch things a bit, but things are OK.

1 2 3 4   12. (Nigerian foreign student) Discrimination is certainly an issue for me in this country. But I've learned to sit back and live and play with other Nigerians. We have our own agenda anyway.

Needless to say, few members of minority groups will talk about their group identity issues solely at one stage. As discussed elsewhere, we are all a mix of stages. Therefore, expect these clients to present issues at multiple stages and to include academic, personal, and social problems along with issues of group identity development.

Each client you work with is unique and different. In using group identity theories, it is critical not to stereotype clients. The preceding discussion is oriented toward a group cultural framework and thus emphasizes group differences. There is always the danger that emphasis on groups will cause us to overlook the unique individual before us. And conversely, our failure to be aware of common group differences may lead us to impose our values on a culturally different individual. A balance of individual and group awareness is essential.

Fostering White Awareness: The Frontier of Multicultural Training

In U. S. society, the dominant White Euro-American cultural group is in particular need of self-awareness. Efforts at multicultural awareness will be fruitless unless Whites begin to examine and know themselves.

Ponterotto (1988) has adapted the racial identity theory of Parham and Helms (1981) using a stage model for racial consciousness raising of White counselor trainees. Ponterotto's framework can also be applied to White identity development. He identifies four stages of thinking and behavior of counselors in training when educated about multicultural issues and cultural oppression; namely (1) preexposure, (2) exposure, (3) zealotry or defensiveness, and (4) integration. These stages are roughly comparable to the four levels of DCT.

Counselors and therapists in the preexposure stage tend not to think about multicultural issues in counseling. They may say, for example, that "all clients are just people." Many, perhaps even most, professional helpers are at this stage. Counselor and therapist training still offers only a modicum of multicultural information, and the dominant theories utilized are those of White, male, middle-class individuals who are usually of the individualistic Euro-American tradition. However, changes in this situation are occurring. The American Psychological Association recently established a division of culturally oriented psychologists. Also, the Association for Multicultural Counseling and Development has been an active participant within the American Association for Counseling and Development for a considerable period of time.

To move counselors and therapists out of their preexposure stage requires information, confrontation, and perturbation. The facts of discrimination of various minorities are certain to perturb any serious student of counseling and therapy. This will enable a move to the exposure period, which is analogous to the late sensorimotor level of DCT.

Following exposure to the facts and issues of multicultural awareness, Ponterotto notes that White students tend to move in one of two directions: zealotry or defensiveness. A fairly large minority of Whites become angry about racism. They are disappointed in texts and theories they realize have not been culturally fair or relevant to minorities, the poor, and the handicapped. These students may become zealots and work actively to make their training programs more culturally relevant. Zealotry parallels stage 2 of GIDT (Table 7-3), stage 3 of MIDT (Table 7-2), and concrete operations of DCT.

A second, perhaps larger, group of counselor trainees becomes defensive. These individuals tend to take criticism of White culture, theories, and systems personally. They become passive recipients of information and "retreat back into the predictability of the White culture" (Helms, 1985, p. 156). This reaction parallels stage 3 of GIDT and the formal-operational level of DCT. A major difference is that some in this group manage to avoid truly encountering the concrete facts of racism and cultural oppression. Intellectualization and formal operational distancing are useful techniques but can be counterproductive, enabling us to be emotionally safe and keep our distance from serious problems within the culture and the helping professions (see also stage 4 of MIDT).

Other counselor trainees use this passive phase as a time to reflect on the complex issues of racism and discrimination. This process is similar to DCT dialectic/systemic mode of thinking and the final stages of both MIDT and GIDT. These individuals have a more reflective learning style. As the final stages of multicultural training are encountered, Ponterotto (1988, p. 153) finds that:

> the strong dichotomous feelings emergent in the zealot-defensiveness level subside. . . . Students become more balanced in their multicultural interest and endeavors. Likewise, those students who had withdrawn from active class participation during the zealot-defensive level have been led to process their feelings with the instructor and classmates and now become more open, acquiring a renewed interest, respect, and appreciation for cultural differences.

Following are some statements representing various stages of multicultural understanding. Indicate at which level the individuals are conceptualizing multicultural issues. (Answers are listed at the conclusion of the chapter.) When the speaker is identified as counseling student or factory worker, assume that you are the person making the comment so that you avoid stereotyping these two groups.

1 2 3 4   1. (counseling student) People are people. Why all this fuss about racism and sexism? We're all struggling.

1 2 3 4   2. (counseling student) I now see what I've been missing. It really ticks me off. The therapy theory course doesn't mention issues of racial or sexual discrimination. I'm going to see that something is done about it.

1 2 3 4   3. (counseling student) I can certainly understand why people get upset about racism, but as I think about it, there isn't a lot I can do. I need to go off and think about it some more.

1 2 3 4   4. (counseling student) Developing full multicultural understanding may take some time. My own goal is to work more on where I come from ethnically. As I understand my background, I should be better able to understand others. At the same time, I can't let that be enough. I'll take some action as well.

1 2 3 4   5. (factory worker) Job discrimination at this factory is terrible. There are no women or Mexicans in management, and the salaries for some people doing the same job are different.

1 2 3 4   6. (factory worker) We have no discrimination here. We promote strictly on merit. Everyone gets treated the same.

1 2 3 4   7. (factory worker) Our plant is full of discrimination. It's been a pattern for a long time. I'm not sure that action will change things. We need more study.

1 2 3 4   8. (factory worker) The time is now. We've done our homework and learned about patterns of systematic discrimination. We've outlined our strategies. I can understand why the manager is so difficult. He comes from a very traditional, conservative tradition. I think I can work with him. Our action plan will make a difference.

Multicultural awareness is the frontier of counseling and therapy training. Increasing White understanding of and action in dealing with issues of racism, sexism, handicapism, homophobia, ageism, religious prejudice, and other issues of discrimination is central to the future of the helping field.

Generating Increasing Understanding of Multicultural Issues Using DCT

There are many ways to facilitate personal growth and development in the multicultural area. One way is by using the systematic intervention procedures suggested by DCT. You have seen that it is possible to identify various cognitive-developmental levels as they relate to multicultural issues. The next question is how to facilitate both horizontal and vertical development.

The following paragraphs outline ways a helping professional can expand multicultural consciousness. The goal is to help the individual become aware of her or his own history of oppression and then use this self-knowledge to develop empathy with others' pain and hurt.

Let us assume that you (or an individual you know) have a low awareness of multicultural issues. You have had little contact with culturally different people and lack an understanding of cultural differences. You may display conscious or unconscious racist, sexist, and discriminatory thoughts and behavior. Very likely, your family environment encourages or nurtures these attitudes. One route toward generating multicultural awareness is for you to become aware of your own cultural history. Cultural history here is defined broadly as issues concerned with race, ethnicity, gender, religion, economic status, nationality, physical capacity or handicap, and affectional orientation.

In addition, it is helpful to become aware of your own experiences with discrimination. Most of us, whether we are in a majority or minority, have experienced discrimination of some type. This discrimination may have manifested as actual racism, jokes about your ethnic heritage, not being allowed to do something because of your sex, religious bigotry, not having enough money to do something necessary for you or your family. Or, as a White American abroad, you may have experienced prejudice against the United States, or you may have experienced the difficulty of functioning in the world with a broken leg, or you may have an older friend or family member who was fired as he or she neared retirement. If you are gay or lesbian or have close friends who are, you undoubtedly know the personal pain that comes from discrimination. Allowing yourself to examine your own personal experience of discrimination can help you become less prejudiced about the struggles of other people.

Other topics can help you get in touch with your own history of discrimination. For example, many athletes find themselves stereotyped as "dumb jocks." Good students are seen as "nerds." You're considered "out of it" if you don't wear the right clothes. Perhaps you were teased unmercifully as a child. Or you may be the child of alcoholic parents. Individuals who won't go along with the prevailing majority often suffer forms of discrimination not unlike racism and sexism. Being different is often a handicap in itself.

Review the discussion above and select a discriminatory issue that is relevant to you. The exercise will be more profitable if you can identify a specific issue you have experienced personally, but you may wish to work through the exercise focusing on a friend or family member. What area of multicultural awareness did you select, and why is it important to you personally?

_____

_____

_____

_____

As you begin this exercise, think back on your family and your family members' attitudes and behaviors, particularly those that either stereotyped individuals or groups or those that encouraged understanding of differences. How has your family history affected your present levels and stages of understanding?

_____

_____

_____

_____

Give a specific instance when you or a friend suffered from some type of discrimination? Get a visual image of that situation. What do you see/hear/feel? Can you locate a specific feeling in your body? Where in your body? Focus particularly on your emotions and kinesthetic feelings. Can you recreate the past situation in the present?

_____

_____

_____

_____

What sense did you make of that event or experience at the time? Did you blame yourself for some personal inadequacy? What did the event mean to you at that time?

_____

_____

_____

_____

Describe the concrete events surrounding the situation. What happened before? What happened afterward? Who was there? How did they act? What did they say and do? How did you feel before the event, and how did you feel afterward?

_____

_____

_____

_____

Did things similar to that event happen in other situations? Was it a pattern? How did that pattern affect you and your sense of self? How did you feel about other people, perhaps in your family, who suffered from the same pattern of discrimination?

_____

_____

_____

_____

Look back at your responses above. What sense do you make of the incident now? After you have thought through the old meaning, does that old meaning still make sense, or does a new meaning now replace it? Note particularly your responses at the sensorimotor and concrete-operational levels. At what level of multicultural identity theory were you operating? Given what you have observed, what are you going to do?

_____

_____

_____

_____

Our cultural development occurs within the family. How does your family experience apply to these issues? Are there additional images, situations, and patterns that come to mind? How do your own patterns relate to your family history?

_____

_____

_____

_____

The above exercises are designed to personalize multicultural issues and make them more relevant to you. Many of the problems we face in life result in some way from our experience of discrimination, stereotyping, and lack of understanding.

The following exercise is more difficult. Select one of the suggested areas of discrimination above with which you are less familiar. It is important to choose a topic you know is difficult for you to understand and encounter. What topic did you select? Why?

_____

_____

_____

_____

Imagine that you are an individual of that cultural group. Generate a visual image of a type of discrimination you might encounter. What would you see/ hear/ and feel? Where was the feeling located in your body?

_____

_____

_____

_____

What sense would you make out of this discriminatory situation? What would it mean to you if you experienced that event?

_____

_____

_____

_____

Imagine a series of concrete events, such as the one above, that repeat again and again. What would life be like? What would it mean to you if you experienced repeated discrimination? What would it mean to your family?

_____

_____

_____

_____

How do you integrate this brief exercise with the previous exercise in which you examined your own personal experience with discrimination? What was similar? What was different?

_____

_____

Those working through the above two exercises often find that the kinesthetic feelings are very similar for the real and the fantasized images. It hurts to be the object of discrimination. Most people first tend to blame themselves when they are discriminated against. Self-blame and self-hate is an example of MIDT's stage 1 (conformity). As you tried to make sense of your own personal experiences with discrimination, you may have experienced some aspect of stage 2 (dissonance) wherein you realized that others were not treating you fairly. If you felt angry when you thought the event concretely, you were probably experiencing something similar to stage 3 (resistance). On the other hand, if you distanced yourself from the situation, you may have been in stage 4 (introspection).

We all face discrimination and prejudice in some form throughout our lives. One way our hurt can be integrated is to blame others, which blame manifests as racism, religious prejudice, and other forms of systematic intolerance. Again, recalling Bowlby, "How clients treat you is how they were treated." The hurt in people is often so deep that it is easier for them to blame others than to see the situation for what it is—simple injustice.

Another alternative is stage-5 synergetic articulation and awareness: you accept yourself and others and work toward eliminating all types of prejudice and discrimination. What are you going to do about these issues? What is your next step?

Adapting Therapeutic Theory for Use in Other Cultures

This section explores several dimensions of how more culturally relevant therapeutic theory and practice can be developed. Much of present-day therapeutic theory is individualistic in nature; thus, the first issue to consider is the need for a more relational approach to human change. The concepts of culture-specific counseling are summarized, and feminist theory is used as a concrete example. Then recent work describing the process of generating culture-specific counseling theory and practice is presented.

Relational Versus Individualistic Theory

Generating culturally appropriate theories rests on an awareness of the importance of the relational orientation in contrast to the individualistic tradition so prominent in Western psychology. Gilligan (1982) points out that the individualistic autonomous frame is primarily male in origin. She views women's development and describes a relational orientation in which caring and relationships with others provides the basis for thought and action. If you take the relational orientation, you must think more complexly—How will others be affected by your decision? How can harmony be maintained among varying individuals and groups?

Some individuals, most often women, are more oriented toward relationships than toward individuation, separation, and autonomy. Some families stress the importance of relationship whereas others take pride in their independence from one another. As discussed earlier, many people of Italian or Jewish background focus on the family as the preeminent factor in existence, and many of those with British background emphasize boundaries and independence from others.

As with identifying DCT level, it is possible to determine from the natural language of the client whether or not the individual is operating in a relational or an autonomous framework. Gilligan's description of the relational and autonomous orientations is exemplified in the transcript below (Gilligan, 1982, pp. 35–36). Two children, both eleven years of age, are asked the same question: "When responsibility to oneself and responsibility to others conflict, how should one chose?"

Jake: You go about one-fourth to the others and three-fourths to yourself. . . . The most important thing in your decision should be yourself, don't let yourself be guided totally by other people, . . .

Amy: Well, it really depends on the situation. If you have a responsibility to somebody else, then you keep it to a certain extent, but to the extent that it is really going to hurt you or stop you from doing something that you really, really, want, then I think maybe you should put yourself first. But if it is your responsibility to somebody really close to you, you've just got to decide which is more important, yourself or that person. . . . Some people put themselves and things for themselves before they put other people, and some people really care about people.

Jake has taken an individualistic, autonomous stance. Amy's thinking is more complex, but her last sentence, "Some people really care about people," illustrates an underlying relational thinking pattern. Gilligan expands on the example, showing that women in North American culture, and perhaps all cultures, focus on the more complex concepts involved in relational thinking.

When one thinks relationally, one must take into account many more factors—perspectives of and interconnections with others—than if one thinks in the more typical linear autonomous mode. Researchers have often claimed that men are more advanced thinkers than women. Gilligan proffers "a different voice," suggesting that perhaps the female-oriented relational approach is more complex, while also recognizing that both autonomous and relational orientations are important.

Most therapy and counseling theory focuses on the individual. The goal is first self-actualization; then attention is directed to the group. The emphasis on individual responsibility and decision making in Euro-American therapeutic theories is so deeply entrenched that proposing that this idea is a cultural artifact is not popular.

Family therapy theory clearly shows that we as individuals exist in a context of relationship and interconnectedness. A healthy family encourages individuation and autonomy but does so within a context of relationship. At issue is the difficult task of balancing separation and attachment, engagement and disengagement.

Gilligan's question—"When responsibility to oneself and responsibility to others conflict, how should one choose?"—is itself culturally based in individualism. The underlying assumption is that the individual chooses. In other more relational cultures, the assumption may be that the group chooses, and the word *we* might be substituted for the word *one*—"When responsibility to oneself and responsibility to others conflict, how should we choose?" The simple change of a single word emphasizes the individual in relationship to the group.

A Japanese child of a traditional family might respond to the question differently than Jake and Amy—for example, "I must be in harmony with others or I have little value." Here the importance of the individual in relationship to the group is primary. Counseling from a "we" orientation focuses on the individual in harmony with others, whereas counseling from an "I" focus centers on how individuals can achieve their autonomous goals. The "we" orientation is apparent in the Yakima proverb—"Justice for the individual is a part of justice for the Community." Black, Asian, Hispanic, Italian, Greek, and many other groups in North America emphasize the importance of group relationships.

Tamase (1988) has used introspective-developmental counseling (IDC) techniques in both the United States and Japan. Although the generic process of IDC works well in both cultures, Japanese and U.S. students focused on different issues during the structured interviews. Japanese students tended to emphasize group and school-related academic issues more than U.S. students did. Although more research is needed, it seems apparent that the Japanese and U.S. cultures focus on different issues over the life span. If so, life-span developmental theories such as those of Erikson and Haley, should be applied to Japanese culture with great care.

Also working in Japan, Fukuhara (1984) explored developmental change and growth in a seven-session interview with an 18-year-old university client. In the first interview, the client clearly exhibited an embedded sensorimotor consciousness, but the orientation is clearly relational. Over the seven sessions, the young woman moved from sensorimotor description and confused feelings to concrete, linear description, and, finally, toward a more autonomous consciousness similar to the formal-operational level of DCT. Although the framework of DCT can be used effectively with Japanese individuals, the content of questions and conversation are culturally different. (See Ivey [1986, pp. 251–256] for a more complete description and analysis of this case.)

In the helping interview, it is useful to be able to recognize relational and autonomous thinking in the language used by the client. In general, autonomous thinkers tend to be more concrete, and relational thinkers tend to be more formal, although eager to translate thought into real-world practice.

In the interview, the way you pose questions may encourage either a relational or autonomous response. Classify each of the following counselor statements as relational or autonomous or both.

R A 1. Could you tell me about what happened for you this past week?(concrete)

R A 2. How has it been for you and Christine this week? (concrete or abstract, depending on client response)

R A 3. Right now, your hand is shaking. (sensorimotor)

R A 4. Right now, something is going on between us. (formal)

R A 5. You say you are depressed. How well are you sleeping? (concrete)

R A 6. Could you tell me what occurs for you when you focus on your family. (formal but sufficiently concrete so that client can answer at any level)

R A 7. How do you make sense of this interview? (formal)

R A 8. How do you think our relationship in this session ties in with what you told me about your parents? (late formal, almost dialectic/systemic)

R A 9. As I hear you, you seem to be saying that you want to be closer to Jon, but you also want to retain your own identity. You want to change the relationship. (dialectic/systemic)

R A 10. As I hear you, you seem to be feeling better about the way you are handling things. (formal)

When seeking to help a client become either more autonomous or relational, it is effective to make your interventions at all four DCT levels. As with separation or attachment goals, so with relational or autonomy goals—"rounded development" is critical.

Culture-Specific Counseling and Therapy

Counseling theory is just beginning to gain a more relational orientation, particularly as new culture-specific theories of helping evolve. Culture-specific counseling points out that different cultures have differing ways of helping and solving problems and thus it is necessary to generate specific theories of counseling and therapy (Minor, 1983). Most therapeutic theory to this point has been based in Euro-American culture. Minority identity developmental theory (MIDT) focuses on how individuals function in a culture in which they are dominated by others. Culture-specific counseling builds on MIDT but uses the enlightenments of newly raised consciousness to address specific needs of a particular culture.

Nwachuku and Ivey (1989, pp. 2–3) summarize Minor's orientation to the helping process as follows:

We must start our counseling theory from the point of view of the culture. In culture-specific counseling, the focus changes to "How does a particular culture view the helping relationship? How did they solve problems in the past? Can specific counseling skills be adapted from the frame of reference of the culture rather than from typical Western counseling theory?" All of this should lead eventually to counseling theories somewhat different from Rogers, Freud, and others.

The culture of the Inuit of Canada was the focus of Minor's study. To survive the rigors of the Arctic, the Inuit developed a culture that values both individualism and relationship. The individual's strength and ability are important for survival. When food was available, it was shared with the group, but when it was in short supply, the strongest were given what was left so that they could go out and hunt. When facing major challenges, small groups meet to make decisions, but special attention is paid to strong individuals in the group. Words have less value in this culture than in others, and long silences often occur in these meetings. The role of women is clearly secondary.

It is difficult to import individualistic, word-focused approaches to helping into such a culture. In addition, the opinion of a White counselor with little knowledge of the Arctic is not respected, and the questions typical of a White North American helping approach are considered rude. Taking into consideration Inuit cultural traits and natural helping style, Minor saw the need for and suggests a more culturally appropriate approach to helping. She suggests that counseling with the Inuit be more tolerant of silence, be less hurried, and less oriented to problem resolution. Special attention needs to be paid to how the individual relates to the family, the peer group, and the village culture. An individually oriented solution simply will not work. An individual change must be in harmony with others.

In essence, Minor has confronted (perturbed) the mainstream counseling and therapy approach. She throws out traditional theory and methods for the moment and begins to build the helping approach from the frame of reference of the culture. Later, Western knowledge, skills, research, and theory are considered and adapted to the specific culture.

Culture-Specific Counseling with the Igbo of Nigeria

Nwachuku (1989) put Minor's theoretical perspectives and suggestions into practice by generating a culture-specific theory of counseling and therapy for the Igbo of Nigeria. The specific steps he took are straightforward and can be adapted and replicated in other cultural situations. Nwachuku's recommendations are paraphrased below:

1. Study the culture in general without looking for issues of helping and counseling and therapy. Seek to learn how the culture views the world, learn the language and figures of speech, note important rituals and symbols, and the place food has in the total system. What impact does geography have on this culture? What is the history of this culture? In short, a general anthropological analysis needs to be conducted.

This first step can be used when devising culture-specific approaches for the diverse subgroups in North American society, namely, the aging, the physically handicapped, women and men, established Mexican-Americans (as opposed to new arrivals to the country) and so on.

2. Select key aspects of the culture that intuitively seem important and summarize them. Consult with those in the culture for agreement and disagreement and additional items that might be included.

Nwachuku selected the following key aspects of Igbo culture: (1) individualistic behavior is interwoven with group solidarity; (2) the values of the extended family and of the community are respected; (3) childrearing and early learning are responsibilities shared by members of the immediate family and the community; (4) although proud, clannish, and competitive, the Igbo are receptive to change, value the aged, and respect elders; (5) value is given to industry, aggressiveness, and intelligence; (6) proverbs, quotations, and figures of speech are important parts of the communication system.

Needless to say, not all of these key aspects of Igbo culture are compatible with Western counseling theories. Clearly, an Igbo theory of helping would require more attention to relationship and family and community issues than Western theory allows. A richer, more figurative language might be required. The Igbo's receptiveness to change, competitiveness, and some emphasis on the individual suggest that some aspects of Western counseling could be adapted and used with this culture.

3. Using this information as a base, identify how the culture has traditionally solved problems and provided help for those in need.

As might be anticipated, given the values and behaviors described, Igbo helping efforts were historically centered in the community, and there was considerable emphasis on sharing. Elders were given more status in Igbo than in Western culture. Also, key factors in individual growth over time are different for the Igbo—for example, the meaning of such words as *trust*, *autonomy*, and *identity* are very different. Thus, Erikson's framework remains helpful, but it is apparent that what is considered mentally healthy in Igbo culture is quite different from what is considered healthy in U.S. culture. Similarly, the family life cycle varies, so family intervention techniques must change.

4. Identify concrete skills and strategies that the culture has traditionally used in the helping relationship. Look for patterns within these strategies and begin the organization of a culturally relevant theory.

5. Test the theory in practice; change and adapt it as new information becomes available.

In a preliminary test of this model, Nwachuku used videotapes that presented Igbo counselors using Igbo natural helping styles. In the interviews, the counselors would focus their listening skills on the client and also on the nuclear family and the extended family of the client. Western counseling theory would tend first to focus only on the individual. The counseling approach for the Igbo had a broader, more relational perspective. Whereas a Western counselor would do more listening, Igbo counselors took a more participatory, influencing approach. Problem conceptualization of the Igbo is similar to that of the Yakima. Both look at how the individual and the community can work together effectively. When conflict between the individual and the community arises, it is the responsibility of the individual to accede to the community. The community takes precedent over even the family.

Nwachuku's work has interesting and important implications for Western counseling. North America does not have one unified culture, but counseling and therapy theory tends to consider this to be the fact. Women have different life experiences from men, as do Blacks and Native American Indians, Chinese-Americans and Cambodian-Americans, and gay men and lesbians. There is a real need to consider what a culturally relevant theory might be for each group.

Feminist Theory and Culture-Specific Therapy

The feminist approach to therapeutic theory and practice is particularly advanced (see Ballou & Gabalac, 1984) and offers some specifics that may have relevance to other cultural groups. Feminist theory developed from a history of examining the nature of women in society. Next, feminist counseling and therapy techniques were identified and refined. Now we are at the stage where feminist theory and practice are becoming part of—and thereby enriching—traditional therapeutic theory and practice.

Some specific aspects of feminist therapy theory follow, which will, of course, need adapting before they are applied in different cultural settings:

1. *Egalitarian relationships.* Feminist therapy seeks to eliminate the traditional hierarchy of helping and work on a more co-equal basis with the client.
2. *Community involvement.* Therapy does not end with the session but is extended through community action programs such as women's groups, legal aid, and other services.
3. *Active participatory style.* Most feminist therapists share their opinions and life experiences openly and work actively to help women move toward a more feminist perspective.
4. *Information giving.* Counseling does not involve just listening but also sharing with women the history of women, how women have been oppressed, and specific ways in which women can more effectively regain their rights.
5. *Personal validation.* Since many women come from oppressed situations (which may include abuse and intimidation), feminist therapy often focuses on finding what is right about the client and providing strong personal support and validation.

Feminist therapy seeks to balance issues of individual autonomy and relationship. The egalitarian therapeutic relationship is basic to this approach to helping contrast with some approaches that place the helper in a hierarchical position. The theory and the helping relationship seem to be more in accord with women's development in North American culture.

As we move toward extending culture-specific therapy and treatment to other groups and cultures, the well-articulated feminist position may serve as a useful structural model. This does not mean that feminist theory should be imported into other cultures; rather the process of developing a culturally relevant theory is what is most important. The basic question is, "How did this group develop and what is the natural helping style?" With this knowledge and awareness, perhaps we can begin the generation of several new and innovative approaches to the helping field.

 CAUTION! As stated many times in this chapter, discussion of group differences is helpful but can result in stereotyping. Each individual client is unique. Cultural descriptions such as those presented in this chapter are normative and describe a mythical "average" person. It is important in multicultural counseling to balance an appreciation of cultural influence with a focus on the individual person.

Chapter Summary

Multicultural counseling is about our responsibility to community members as well as to ourselves. As mature counselors and therapists, we should be servants of the people. Specific competencies of the culturally skilled counselor were introduced in this chapter. Five stages of minority identity theory development (MIDT) were then presented and related to DCT's four levels. It is possible to identify the multicultural stage of clients and counselors in the natural language used in the interview. It is also possible to recognize whether an individual has a predominantly autonomous or relational orientation by their conversation.

Developing White self-awareness is crucial to an understanding of racism. The counseling tradition in Western culture is oriented toward the individual; this perspective has positives as well as negatives. Anthropological and psychological studies indicate that individuals differ as much or more than cultures.

The four-level intervention questions and techniques of DCT can help clients and counselor trainees in reviewing their own personal histories of issues of discrimination. As individuals get more in touch with their own issues and past hurts related to prejudice and discrimination, they will be more open to learning about others whose cultural experiences differ from their own.

Traditional counseling and therapy theory is predominantly White, male, and Euro-American. Specific suggestions were presented for generating more culturally relevant counseling and therapy theories.

Theory into Practice

By the end of this section, you may be able to:

1. Identify commonalities of the several identity development theories and generate your own multicultural identity developmental theory for a group of interest to you.
2. Use some of the concepts of this chapter in role-played and real interviews.
3. Generate the beginning of a culture-specific counseling and therapy theory.

Organizing Identity Development Theories

Several different theories of identity development have been presented in this chapter, including minority identity development theory, Black identity development, feminist identity development, developmental challenges to identity development, and Ponterotto's four stages of multicultural awareness.

Make a chart that places these theories in relationship to one another. A possible organizational framework for these theories is the four-level framework of DCT, but other organizations can work also. Note the similarities and differences between the categories. Does making this comparison suggest some additional categories?

Outlining a New Developmental Identity Theory

The following task could be completed in brief outline form, or expanded into a major paper (or even dissertation), or even tested empirically. As a first step, determine how much time you wish to give to this complex exercise.

Using the chart you have just completed, select one theory from the array of multicultural therapy possibilities and write a specific identity theory, using from four to six levels (race, ethnicity, gender, religion, age, developmental disability, affectional orientation, nationality, and so on). Define each level briefly.

Begin this process by identifying an individual (or family) in that cultural group who is unaware and accepts the status quo. Identify that person or persons and list some specific behaviors and thoughts you might expect.

_____

_____

_____

_____

_____

_____

Based on this beginning, list other stages of identity development and define them as well.

Finally, write what the person might say at each level. Consider developing a short "test" for the levels, such as that in the chapter exercise in which you identified levels from short statements and then compared your classification with the "answers" at the end of the chapter. Give this test to a colleague.

_____

_____

_____

_____

_____

_____

_____

_____

Practice in a Role-Played Session Using Multicultural Awareness Questions

The format for this exercise is similar to that of other role-plays, the exception being that the client is asked to play his or her real self and to honestly explore how he or she has personally experienced issues of prejudice and racism. The specific questions used in the individual exercises of this chapter (pages 209-211) can serve as the framework for the practice session.

Step 1: Divide into Practice Groups

Step 2: Select a Group Leader

Step 3: Assign Roles for the Practice Session

- Role-played client. The role-played client will discuss a real past issue in which he or she experienced discrimination and/or prejudice. The client should share only what he or she feels comfortable sharing.
- Interviewer. The interviewer will ask the specific DCT four-level questions, as outlined in this chapter. The questions are adapted to meet the specific needs of this client. The interviewer will not be intrusive and will especially try to understand the client's frame of reference.
- Observers 1 and 2 . The observers will observe the session but will not take notes. They will be available after the role-play for discussion and mutual support.

Step 4: Plan the Session

The interviewer and client need first to agree on the specific topic to be reviewed.

Step 5: Conduct a 15-Minute Interviewing Session

You will find it helpful to videotape or audiotape practice sessions.

Step 6: Provide Immediate Feedback (15 to 20 Minutes)

Allow the client and interviewer time to provide immediate personal reactions to the practice session. After this has been done, the observers and the role-played client can focus on the thoughts and feelings of all members of the group. An open sharing of issues may be beneficial. Avoid judgmental feedback.

Step 7: Generate a Fantasy About Another Cultural Group (20 Minutes)

In the groups, generate a fantasy about how a member of an oppressed multicultural group might experience the same DCT four-level questions. Do this as a group rather than an individual discussion.

Practice in a Role-Played Family Session

Families also encounter discrimination and have difficulty in certain cultural settings. For this practice role-play, it is suggested that the participants acting as the family role-play a military family that is entering therapy because of discrimination experienced in a new neighborhood. The children are doing poorly in school and are having a difficult time dealing with social cliques. The father is a noncommissioned officer with 22 years of service. The wife works as a secretary. Neither went to college. The neighborhood and school are predominantly upper-middle class, with definite social groupings—cliques—originating in the local women's group and country club. Typically, families such as this will talk about school difficulties and might even be unaware of their oppression. They may feel it is their fault they don't fit in.

The example could also be a Jewish family in Catholic neighborhood, a Black family in a totally white suburb, a lesbian couple in a small town, or a Chinese family in a new housing development. From one to two hours will be required for development and debriefing of the family session.

Step 1: Select Four to Six Participants

Decide whether you wish to have the remainder of the group constitute themselves as a family. The remainder of the members of the class or workshop will observe the entire process and later serve as process consultants who reflect on the session.

Step 2: Have the Workshop Leader Assume the Leadership Role

Due to the complexity of the process, the workshop leader or teacher should assume the leadership role and ensure that the group follows the specific steps of the practice session.

Step 3: Assign Roles for the Practice session

- Role-played family. The role of the family can be as discussed above.
- Therapists. Two therapists can work together for this session.
- Workshop/class observers. All remaining individuals in the session will sit in a circle around the family and process information as described in step 4.

Step 4: Plan the Session

- The family can leave the room to define their roles and the specifics of the problem they wish to present. The nature of the problem will be a surprise to the therapists in the session.
- The two therapists may wish to think through their relationship briefly. The suggested aim of this session is to help the family become aware that the school problem is also a family and community problem. It is particularly important to help the family move away from the self-blame characteristic of stage-1 awareness. You may find that family members become angry and/or fearful as the problem expands.

- The family observers have two main roles: (1) They all can be participant/observers; the therapists should free feel to stop the interview in mid-session to ask the observers for help and suggestions. (2) They can identify the consciousness level of each individual member of the family and the specific interventions used by the therapists that seem to perturb and move the family to a broader understanding of the situation. (For record keeping and feedback, refer to pages 202 and 205 for a summary of key classifications.)

Step 5: Conduct a 30-Minute Interviewing Session

It is helpful to videotape and/or audiotape practice sessions. Families often confuse even the most effective therapist. Thus, the therapists should feel free to stop for a moment in the middle of the session and ask the external observers for their reactions and suggestions. It may be informative to look for issues in the developmental history of the therapists that affect their relationship with the family.

Step 6: Provide Immediate Feedback and Complete Notes (10 Minutes)

This is a highly structured session, and there is often immediate personal need to process and discuss the session. In particular, it is helpful for the therapists to ask the family, "What stands out for you from this practice session?" Allow time to provide true personal reactions to the practice. At this point, the observers should sit back and let the participants take control. Use this time to complete your classification and notes. It may be especially helpful if the therapists ask the family members to identify visual images, locate these in their bodies, and then explore their own developmental history using the systematic questions of DCT.

Step 7: Review Practice Session and Provide Feedback (15 to 30 Minutes)

It is important when giving feedback to allow the therapists and family receiving the feedback to be in charge. At this point, the observers can share their observations. As usual, feedback should be specific, concrete, nonjudgmental. Pay attention to strengths of the interview.

Generating Culture-Specific Counseling Theory

The five specific steps for generating a culture-specific counseling theory presented in the chapter are repeated here. Select one multicultural area or topic of special interest to you and complete as many of the following steps as you can. The specific topic can repeat and expand on any ideas presented in the chapter.

What multicultural group or project do you wish to select, and what is the reason for your choice? For this practice exercise, you need not be a member of that group, but remember that your observations are not likely to be as culturally appropriate as those of a member of that culture. Teams of two (one from the culture and one not from it) may be quite effective for this exercise.

_____

_____

The five specific steps of Nwachuku (1989) are paraphrased below for your reference.

1. Study the culture in general without looking for issues of counseling and therapy. Seek to learn how the culture views the world, family, and community structure and note its important rituals and symbols. What impact does geography have on this culture. What is the history of this culture? In short, a general anthropological analysis needs to be conducted. The possibilities are infinite. If you write a preliminary report, restrict yourself to six pages.

2. Select key aspects of the culture that intuitively seem important and summarize them. You should ideally have from five to ten key characteristics. If possible, consult with those in the culture for confirmation that these are key aspects and for additional suggestions.

3. Using this information as a base, identify how the culture has traditionally solved problems and provided help for those in need. Do this as specifically as possible, providing examples.

4. Identify concrete skills and strategies the culture has traditionally used in the helping relationship. List the concrete skills in one-half to one page. This is a beginning. Look for patterns within these strategies and begin outlining a culturally relevant theory.

5. Test your theory in practice and change and adapt it as new information becomes available. The ideal exercise at this point would be to generate videotapes exemplifying the culture, just as Nwachuku did. Another option is to write statements indicating various levels of consciousness in that culture or to write a summary of key aspects of that theory.

Generalization: Taking Multicultural Skills Home

Activity 1: Observe Individuals in Daily Life

Listen to friends and colleagues when they talk about various groups and note these individuals' levels of consciousness. You may ask close friends or family, in a nonjudgmental fashion, "How do you see or think about (the particular group)?" Note their responses and then assess their level or levels of consciousness.

Many, perhaps most, people you listen to will be at the conformist, or preexposure (sensorimotor), consciousness. You may wish to perturb or confront them gently with new or additional data. This confrontation is necessary to move them to MIDT's stage 2—dissonance (late sensorimotor). Is it possible to start the movement from the embedded consciousness of stage 1 to the beginning confusion of the dissonance period?

Similarly, you may facilitate movement and further growth for those at the dissonance stage by moving to the concretes or abstractions of stage 3—resistance and/or immersion—and stage 4—introspection. Consider asking

The stage-2 individual, "Please give me a specific example."
The stage-3 individual, "Is that a repeating pattern?"
The stage-4 individual, "How do you put it together? What are you going to do about it?"

In each case, the individual is challenged and confronted with the basic questions that relate to the next cognitive-developmental level. This type of perturbation, used skillfully, can be most effective. But until an adequate horizontal foundation has been established, it does little good to attempt to raise consciousness. Thus, the best intervention for most people at stage 2 is simply to create more and more dissonance, for those at the concrete stage 3, include more specifics; at stage 4, allow the opportunity for introspection. Individuals who have completed the developmental tasks of each stage of consciousness seem to move naturally to the next stage.

Activity 2: Develop a Plan for Expanding Multicultural Awareness

Table 7-1 lists the characteristics of a culturally skilled counselor and therapist. Use this table as a basis for generating your own long-term growth plan in multicultural counseling. Write below one thing you are going to do differently next week in terms of multicultural counseling and therapy.

_____

_____

_____

_____

Activity 3: The Interview

Counseling and therapy seek to be value free. How can the obviously value-laden approaches of this chapter be taken into clinical practice? The individual or family that presents a problem with discrimination and prejudice can be helped greatly through the theory and practice of culture-specific counseling and minority identity development theory.

The basic model to apply, either with individuals or families, is as follows: (1) Join the client's construction of the problem where the client is. How does the individual or family understand the problem? (It is useful to follow the classification systems of MIDT, which will help you understand the level of consciousness.) (2) Perturb the client's current level of thinking by using confrontation skills that focus on discrepancies between the individual and the environment. (3) Help the client struggle with that understanding and realize that anger (common in stage 3) may result from your confrontation. Understand and join the client struggling to incorporate this new perspective.

To consolidate this new level of understanding, expand awareness through sensorimotor, concrete, formal, and dialectic/systemic interventions. An angry client or family may need relaxation training to temper high emotion, or concrete skills training for specifics on coping with the environment, or a formal understanding of patterns that they can expect to repeat in the society.

Activity 4: Consider the Yakima Nation Proverb

> Justice for the individual
> Is a part of justice for the
>   Community;
> And exists for one, only when
>   both are satisfied.
> So it is that personal freedom
> Must be limited by security
>   for others;
> And the mature person is a servant to
>   the People.

The Yakima proverb may now be clearer in its relationship to the counseling and therapy process than it was at the beginning of this chapter. As you review this chapter, what does this proverb say to you and about your practice?

_____

_____

_____

_____

_____

_____

_____

Suggested Supplementary Reading and Activities

Additional Reading

Sue, D. W. 1990. *Counseling the culturally different.* 3rd ed. New York: Wiley.
    This is the best-known and most popular book on multicultural counseling currently available. This most recent edition provides a solid grounding in multicultural theory and useful and specific chapters on important U.S. minority groups.

McGoldrick, M., J. Pearce, and J. Giordano. 1982. *Ethnicity and family therapy.* New York: Guilford.
    In some ways, family therapy theory is ahead of individual therapy theory when it comes to multicultural issues. This book was ahead of its time in 1982. When it appears in updated form, it may become a classic in the field.

Pedersen, P. 1988. *A handbook for developing multicultural awareness.* Washington, D.C.: American Association for Counseling and Development.
    A highly specific treatment with many exercises, Pedersen's handbook offers a frame of reference that focuses on how each individual represents a unique human culture.

Ballou, M., and N. Gabalac. 1984. *A feminist position on mental health.* Springfield, Ill.: Thomas.

Gilligan, C. 1982. *In a different voice.* Cambridge, Mass.: Harvard University Press.
These are two important books that help explain the need for a more relational approach to counseling and therapy.

Ivey, A. 1986. *Developmental therapy: Theory into practice.* San Francisco: Jossey-Bass.
Chapter 7, particularly pages 261–275 discusses the DCT framework as it applies to relational theory and practice. Special attention is given to Gilligan's frame of reference. Constructs 1 and 2 on pages 293–296 provide relevant exercises to accompany this current chapter. Development in a cultural context is discussed on pages 317–322, and construct 3 on pages 343–344 provides additional culturally based exercises.

Research Suggestion

Several important research projects evolve from the ideas presented in this chapter, including the following:

1. A training program for classification of relational and autonomous responses in clients and counselors could be developed and tested. These ratings could include the several developmental levels of DCT. These programs then could be tested in video- or audiotaped training sessions to determine if therapists can use these concepts in the interview.

2. Training and research programs similar to those described in number 1 could be generated for any of the multicultural identity theories.

3. Answers to the following questions—"How effective are confrontations of varying types in expanding multicultural awareness? Is a sensorimotor, concrete, formal, or dialectic/systemic confrontation most effective? How well is cognitive change maintained, and does it demonstrate itself in concrete action?"—could provide a basis for research.

4. Systematic research on culture-specific counseling and therapy theories currently being generated could be undertaken.

Answers to Chapter Exercises

Answers to Chapter Exercises Group Identity Stage (pp. 204-205)

1. 1	5. 2	9. 4
2. 2	6. 1	10. 2
3. 3	7. 3	11. 1
4. 4	8. 4	12. 3

Multicultural Awareness Level (pp. 207-208)

1. 1	5. 2
2. 2	6. 1
3. 3	7. 3
4. 4	8. 4

Relational Versus Autonomous (p. 215)

1.	A	6.	A, R
2.	R	7.	A
3.	A	8.	R
4.	R	9.	A, R
5.	A	10.	A

8 Network Interventions and DCT

Allen E. Ivey and Mary Bradford Ivey[1]

Good Counsel is a mark of wisdom,

Whether in the family, or the circle of society.

Good Counsel is modest, not assertive;

Considerate of the opinion of others.

How we shall proceed together

Is as important as what we now should do.

Good Counsel will create

A consensus which unites.

Yakima Nation Proverb

---

[1] Portions of this chapter are taken from a presentation by Mary Bradford Ivey at the Virginia Technical University Conference on Exemplary Programs in Elementary Counseling, Blacksburg, Virginia, May 1988.

This chapter seeks to expand the base of individual and family change by using a broadly based network approach that focuses on developing a consensus between client and counselor and on examining their relationship with each other and with the surrounding community.

Philosophically and practically, there is much in the Yakima nation cosmology that can provide an overarching model for Good Counsel. Good Counsel, as conceived by the Yakimas focuses on interdependence and harmony of the individual within him- or herself, a relational family orientation, and congruence with the extended family and community. Good Counsel also involves a balance between person and environment—the individual and culture work together for worth and dignity.

Traditionally, the role of the therapist in individualistic Euro-American approaches to counseling and therapy has been to "act on" the client, with the therapist at the top of the hierarchy and the client in the secondary position. Some family therapy theory continues this tradition, emphasizing that the purposes of interventions be kept secret from the family. In both individual and family counseling, single units (the person or the family) are held responsible for change.

More recently, family and individual counseling theory has moved toward more client participation. Behavioral psychologists, in particular, openly share their treatment plans with clients. Family therapists have discovered that strategic and paradoxical interventions and their purposes can be shared with the client. Feminist therapy emphasizes an egalitarian relationship with the client and recognizes that societal and cultural factors influence client development. There is also an increasing awareness that family and individual theory may be better served by coordinated, mutual efforts than by competition about which is the more effective approach.

We as individuals exist in a community—a network of interactions. This chapter presents a case example illustrating how varying individual, family, and organizational interventions can be integrated.

The Network Approach

Seeking to provide Good Counsel, we often learn that our best individual or family interventions often fail because something else, beyond our or the client's control, goes wrong in the system. The best vocational intervention we can design will fail if there is inequality and discrimination in the social system and the job market. The best family therapy and community interventions seldom fully succeed if one key individual remains entrenched in the problem. Good Counsel requires individuals and the systems within which they live to work together in harmony.

The network concept is similar to the social work ecosystems approach of Germain (1973), who defines this method as "science concerned with the adaptive fit of organisms and their environments and with the means by which they achieve a dynamic equilibrium in mutuality" (p. 326). This quotation

Table 8-1. White Middle-Class Values Contrasted with Native American

Key areas	White middle-class therapy values	Traditional Native American values
Goal of therapy and problem-solving relationship	Independence, self-actualization	Interdependence of individual and group
Relations with people	Emphasis on individual autonomy	Emphasis on community determination
Formulation of goals	Goals are often decided based on the theory of therapy and tend to be individualistic	Mutual goal setting that includes individual and community
Group decisional process	Hierarchical meetings; those in power decide; one person, one vote; Family therapy example: "Hold the Hierarchy"	Consensus of all involved; (process may be time consuming)
Relationship to nature and the environment	Control the environment through individual initiative; environment and nature seen as irrelevant	Generate harmony between individual and environment

summarizes a theoretical orientation that captures the essence of Good Counsel—individuals and environments in mutual growth and development.

Counseling and therapy are based on cultural values. Table 8-1 contrasts North American White middle-class therapy values with traditional Native American values. Although there is some risk in generalizing the values of the over 350 Native American nations, there are some commonalities that provide a useful basis for a network/ecosystems framework. Traditional Native American cultural values for helping and decision making can be used as a basis for developing a counseling and therapy style more oriented toward the person and the environment.

As always, when discussing cultural norms, we must attempt to avoid stereotyping. Just as there are many very different White middle-class people, so do Native American nations and individuals differ. The Swinomish and Lummi nations of northern Washington state are very different from the Hopi and Navajo nations of the Southwest. And the Native American groups in adjoining territories are themselves distinct. Beyond differences among nations, individuals in any one group are unique and different. Effective counseling and therapy with Native American individuals, or with clients of any other group, should take into account the unique individual whose culture affects him or her differently. This same point is true for White individuals.

Carolyn Attneave, a Native American psychologist, conceptualized network therapy in 1969 (see also Attneave, 1982; Speck & Attneave, 1973). Network therapy argues that individuals and their families cannot be satisfactorily treated in one-on-one counseling or in family sessions. For significant change to occur, social support systems need to be developed in the extended family, the community, and, if possible, in the broader society.

There are many aspects of Native American culture and family life that have useful implications for a more integrated practice of counseling and therapy. La Fromboise and Low (1989, p. 121) comment on some of these aspects:

> Traditionally, Indian people live in relational networks that serve to support and nurture strong bonds of mutual assistance and affection. Many tribes still engage in a traditional system of collective interdependence, with family members responsible not only to one another but also to the clan and tribe to which they belong. The Lakota Sioux use the term *tiospaye* to describe a traditional, community way of life in which an individual's well-being remains the responsibility of the extended family. . . . When problems arise among Indian youth, they become problems of the community as well. The family, kin, and friends join together to observe the youth's behavior, draw the youth out of isolation, and integrate that person back into the activities of the group.

Traditional Western therapy too often seeks to change individuals and families in isolation. Newer, more ecologically oriented ways of helping employ case management techniques, with the full awareness that an entire community network of extended family and professional helpers may be required to bring about significant and lasting change.

For example, in working with an alcoholic woman and her family, network therapists would bring together the woman, the immediate family, the extended family (parents, grandparents, siblings, in-laws), and the woman's employer and colleagues. Beyond that, key individuals such as the owner of the local bar, the police, neighbors, social service workers, individual and family therapists, and the parish priest might be brought in for a two-hour or longer session.

The network therapist would review the family problem and essentially facilitate a community meeting about how the problem of alcoholism might be solved. As might be anticipated, the bar owner might receive community pressure to stop serving the woman, the social service agency might provide child-care services previously denied, and the extended family might be encouraged to institute stronger controls for the children. The decisional process in network therapy is not hierarchical or theory directed; rather it is generated from group consensus.

In the process of network therapy it is often found that the "problem" of alcoholism does not only reside in the family alone, but also in a community that allows and supports alcoholic behavior. Network therapy does not require the individual alone to change the behavior, as does traditional Western psychotherapy. Instead, the family and community systems make necessary changes as well. Network therapy is based in many of the Native-American values listed in Table 8-1, particularly those of relationship and harmony of the individual with the environment.

Lacan tells the story of Native American groups traveling the Great Plains (see Clément, 1983, pp. 76–78). When a group saw smoke on the horizon, they would stop to camp, immediately light a fire, and send up a smoke column, thus notifying the first group of their presence. If the original group wished to meet the visitors, they would send out an emissary. If the visitors received no greeting, they knew they were not welcome and moved on the next day.

Lacan considers "correct distance" an important concept. Using the Great Plains example above, he points out that each of us needs to maintain the correct distance from one another, from our families, and our from communities. Depending on life history and culture, correct distance for one person might depend on definite boundaries, whereas for another person, correct distance might involve a close embedded relationship. Different individuals, families, and cultures all have varying ideas how much closeness to or distance from one another is appropriate.

Ideally, correct distance is a matter to be negotiated among equals. At issue is how we can relate most effectively. Lacan speaks of interdependence as contrasted with egocentric dependence or independence. A central issue for individuals and their families is how to maintain a balance between trust versus mistrust, autonomy versus dependence, and attachment/relationship versus individuation/separation. Whether we are enmeshed or overly distant from others is a matter that can be resolved within the framework of interdependence. Some would argue that anything but interdependence is an illusion. Yet therapeutic techniques, strategies, and theories still tend to focus on individual, autonomous goals.

DCT suggests that interdependence, an everchanging balance between individual and system may be a more realistic therapeutic goal than individualism. Such an orientation does not denigrate the importance of the individual but rather provides a framework for viewing the person in relationship with the world. A focus on interdependence leads to increased consideration of the impact of the environment on families and individuals.

Alice Miller's work on child abuse and its lifetime aftereffects clearly indicates that an oppressive environment may prevent the generation of a sense of self. The family and cultural environments provide settings that either allow the true self to develop or that crush any attempt at autonomy. Miller's book, *The Drama of the Gifted Child* (1981), vividly illustrates how the bright, sensitive child registers the wishes and demands of a needy, possibly abusive caregiver, often so early that the young child becomes, in effect, the parent and loses childhood forever. The "drama" is that the child is never allowed to be a child.

Rather than blaming parents, Miller points out the need to recognize that families are products of culture. If we are to limit child abuse, she suggests, we will have to change family structures and oppressive cultural elements. The family is perhaps the primary embodiment of the culture. To help families and individuals change, we need also to invite change in the schools, the work setting, and the community.

Out of the interaction of individual with the environment evolves the true self. The task of the therapist who works with children or adults who have experienced abuse is to provide an enabling, liberating setting conducive to growth and development. The following case illustration combines the constructs of DCT with the goals of interdependent therapy and counseling.

Case Example: Child Abuse

The following case presentation is a composite of treatment interventions with a single child and his family and illustrates the application of DCT concepts using a network approach. (The names and setting have been altered to preserve confidentiality.)

Presenting Problem

George Wood was an 8-year-old third-grade student at the time of his second referral to the school guidance office by his teacher who complained of George's fighting on the playground and restlessness and daydreaming in the classroom. George's test scores showed he had average ability, but he was slightly behind classmates in achievement. He lived near the school with his single-parent mother and 13-year-old brother.

George's parents, both of fourth-generation Italian background, were divorced several years prior to this referral. His father had moved out of town, and his mother was currently working in a local department store. Her manfriend, employed as a mechanic, had moved in with the family about a year ago.

Past History of Counseling

George first came to the school counselor's attention in kindergarten. He was extremely restless, and his teacher thought he might be hyperactive (DSM-III-R attention deficit disorder). Before accepting the teacher's assessment, the counselor visited the classroom. Observations confirmed the teacher's general impressions but George did not appear to meet the criteria for diagnosis of hyperactivity. George was in and out of his seat, constantly interrupting the teacher or others in the class but at times could sustain attention well.

Before undertaking counseling or referral, the counselor asked George's mother to come in after school and discuss the situation. After a brief presentation, the young mother broke into tears and talked about going through a difficult divorce. With the mother's agreement, the counselor's interventions at that time focused on a classroom behavioral management program that included rewards and attention for appropriate behavior. George's mother was referred to a community mental health counselor for assistance in working through her issues, since there was not a family therapist in practice in the community at that time. In addition, his mother joined a parent education program. George's father would not participate in his child's treatment plan.

Individual counseling was attempted, but George was not a talkative child, and individual work proved slow and difficult. He did respond to games and some access to feelings was obtained in response to occasional questions posed while George played "exploring games" or hit a punching bag. George responded especially well to bibliotherapy, where the counselor read stories about divorce coupled with artwork. Psychoeducational classroom activities, such as developing understanding of self and others (DUSO) (Dinkmeyer, 1972) and structured problem solving, were increased, partially in an effort to assist George in his peer relations. In addition, the counselor arranged a weekly "divorce group" in which George and other children of divorce shared their experiences in a structured way. Although George didn't say much, he did pay attention to the others' comments.

The principles of Attneave's network therapy and of DCT provide a useful framework for evaluating this first treatment series. Individual counseling clearly would have been ineffective by itself. Furthermore, it is not likely that classroom and group treatment would be sufficient to produce the needed change. In this case, individual and group treatment was part of a network of treatment interventions that together were sufficient to produce change. Consultation with the teacher was critical, as was support for the mother during a difficult period in her life.

Family therapy theory, however, suggests that much of George's difficulties stemmed from the divorce and his present interaction with his mother. It would be have been desirable for George's mother and father to have met with a family therapist to help them work jointly for George's benefit. This would have enabled the therapist to observe the system of interactions within the family. Also, it might have been beneficial to have a therapist work with the mother and her two children. Again, no family therapist was available in the community at the time of the first contact, also many families will still refuse to enter this type of treatment.

From a DCT frame of reference, sensorimotor and concrete treatment techniques provided George with sufficient support. Consultation with the teacher, psychoeducational classroom interventions, and the referral of George's mother to therapy represent dialectic/systemic interventions. The "necessary and sufficient" conditions for therapeutic change of warmth, positive regard, and authenticity—the core conditions Rogers (1963) identified—are important beginning points. A combined network and DCT approach to treatment recognizes that multifaceted interventions are necessary if change is to be instituted and maintained.

This first round of treatment enabled George to negotiate the next two years of elementary school relatively effectively. He achieved at grade level and, in general, seemed an average student with a good peer support group. However, problems resurfaced in the third grade. At this time, a network/DCT approach was used in formulating a treatment plan for George.

As George entered this second treatment phase, it was clear that special attention must be given to many factors if solutions to fighting, restlessness, and academic achievement issues were to be found. Single intervention programs are likely to fail with children.

Conceptualizing a Network DCT Treatment Plan

The network/DCT frame of reference can be used in developmental case planning and was the basis for this second round of treatment with George. Generating a DCT/network treatment plan involves the following steps:

Step 1: Establishing a positive base for treatment. The counselor first considered George's strengths. She knew from experience that it would be difficult for him to talk. As she prepared for the first session, she identified George's positives: he is lively and energetic; he has a lovely, engaging smile; he has been able to sustain friendships, although his friends also are sometimes likely to get into trouble in school. George had problems earlier, during the family divorce, but was able to bounce back. His mother tends to be cooperative. George seems to respond positively to attention, but if he doesn't get it, he will use any way he can to gain what he wants.

Another important positive base for treatment was awareness of community resources that could be used to help George and his family. The personal strengths and knowledge of the counselor also can serve as a positive resource for the client. Never forget yourself as a positive client resource.

Step 2: Examining key relationship issues as that might affect the counselor or therapist. "How clients treat you [and others] is how they were treated." George's personality style is typical of many boys who are impulsive and attention demanding. This behavior contrasts with the more reflective, passive personality styles of most counselors and therapists.

The counselor knew that working with George was not going to be easy, even given the positives. She was aware of a tightening in her stomach as she thought through the case. She allowed herself to first magnify the tightness, then she "went with the feeling." She remembered a scene from her own childhood when an energetic boy who looked a little like George used to chase and throw sticks at her. She sighed and said to herself "George is not James, who made me so angry and frightened in the past. I'd better not confuse the two." Until she had looked at her own past feelings toward acting-out, impulsive boys, her counseling interventions with this type of client had not been effective. She found it easier to relate to active boys now that she had examined her own feelings. This allowed her to establish better and more consistent relationships.

Many therapists and counselors are not comfortable with the acting-out individual, be it child, adolescent, or adult. If you are one of these, it may be beneficial for you to work through your own feelings and developmental history surrounding these issues using the self-examination techniques suggested in Chapter 6 (in the section entitled, "Discovering Your Own Developmental Blind Spots"). It is important in doing so to have individual and group supervision.

Drawing on knowledge of her feelings about George's behavior, the counselor asked herself, "How does George's relating to me and to others somehow reflect what has happened to him in the past?" The logical first assumption is that George was parented aggressively and impulsively. For example, he might have been in a family that rewarded acting-out behavior, or the father (or mother) might have modeled impulsiveness. Emotional or physical abuse is not uncommon in the families of acting-out children.

There can be alternative explanations, of course. A busy single parent may not have a lot of time to be with a child. Impulsive, attention-seeking behavior may be the only way such a child can obtain parental involvement. Or the acting-out child may have come come from a highly controlled home environment. Their impulsiveness is, in this case, a reaction to rigidity. In all of the above situations, the acting-out or impulsive child has had the true self held back or crushed by the family. Lacking a sense of self, acting-out children often infringe on and violate other people's boundaries.

Working on the theory that George's behavior was most likely a natural response to the need for attention led the counselor to assume the need for a relationship that provided nonjudgmental, firm controls and clear boundaries. Such definition leads the child to individuation, autonomy, and separation. But there must be warmth and support for the child's true self to emerge. Achieving individuation and autonomy can best be done from a firm base of attachment.

In the preceding paragraph, the focus is on helping George become both more autonomous and more relational—an interdependent goal. Each culture has its own approach for balancing separation and attachment tasks, and thus the "correct distance" in the counseling relationship should adjust according to the cultural background of counselor and client.

Step 3: Identifying DCT treatment options. A child may be in tears in the early part of the interview, be happily talking about baseball five minutes later, be groaning about a teacher next, and then worrying about divorce. This random mix of sensorimotor, concrete, and formal styles is common for most children (and adults). Unless you have a map of this complex territory in your mind, you may lose your direction and lose the child.

George as a third grader would be expected to be very concrete. Although it would be desirable to help George see other frames of reference (formal operations), it is likely that a more structured, almost sensorimotor style might be required at first. Later, the counselor could shift counseling style as George showed increasing cognitive-developmental growth. Late concrete causal reasoning might be all that could be expected—for example, "George, *if* you continue that type of behavior, *then* the consequences will be . . . "

Box 8-1 presents assessment and treatment options for children based on the DCT framework. (Note that the constructs of network and systemic action begin to appear most clearly at the dialectic/systemic level.)

The counselor planned two sessions that focused solely on rapport building and getting to know George more personally. The first two sessions focused on game playing, with little emphasis on the problem. During the first two sessions, the counselor planned to point out to George his positive strengths and assets. In the third or fourth session, she planned to work through some of George's issues using DCT questioning strategies adapted for children. In the meantime, consultation with the teacher about George's classroom behavior was conducted and a behavioral contract was organized to be discussed with George's mother.

Box 8-1. Four Levels of Developmental Assessment and Counseling Strategies for Children

Clients talk about their problems and developmental concerns from four perspectives. Younger children will generally discuss their problems at the sensorimotor or concrete level. Some fifth and sixth graders may operate at the formal level. Relatively few individuals (children or adults) will talk about their issues at the post-formal dialectic/systemic level.

Many clients, both children and adults, will discuss their issues at two or more levels. The task of the counselor is to assess the child's cognitive-developmental level(s) on the particular problem being examined. Then the counselor can institute developmentally appropriate interventions that can change as the child develops.

Sensorimotor (What are the elements of experience?)

Assessment:

The child presents concerns in a random fashion, changing the topic frequently, and may exhibit magical or irrational thinking. The child's behavior will tend to follow the same pattern, namely, short attention span and frequent body movement.

Treatment:

The counselor needs to provide a firm structure for exploration but must simultaneously listen to random elements of conversation. Listening at this point will help the counselor better identify the problem. Listening skills, closed questions to provide structure, and frequent paraphrasing and summarization are useful. Direction should be provided as needed. Treatments may involve play therapy and games, use of an exercise room, relaxation training and breathing instruction, behavioral structuring of the classroom, and time-outs. Another, more controversial, treatment with children is the use of medication.

Concrete Operations (What are the situational descriptors?)

Assessment:

Most children talk in very concrete terms. They may either say very little in response to questions (early concrete), or they may talk endlessly about the little details of their experience (middle concrete). Late concrete thinking occurs when children can exhibit if/then causal thinking. The parallel between the counseling term *concreteness* and concrete operations should be apparent.

Treatment:

With the quiet child, well-placed closed questions are necessary to elicit concrete data. With the more verbal child, asking the question "Could you give me a specific example?" is the classic concrete opening. The counselor acts more as a coach, alternating between direct action and structuring and careful listening. The child needs help in organizing thought and behavioral patterns. Behavioral techniques, communication skills training, assertiveness training, and problem-solving counseling aimed at specific, single issues are particularly helpful. When dealing with problems in causal thinking, Adlerian logical consequences approach and Glasser's reality therapy may be useful. Classroom and group programs aimed at concrete concepts (DUSO, divorce groups, social skills groups) are especially helpful.

(continues)

Box 8-1. Levels of Developmental Assessment and Counseling Strategies for Children *(continued)*

Formal Operations (What patterns of thought and action may be discerned?)

Assessment:

Particularly in the fifth or sixth grade, children start to be able to discuss their concerns from a formal-operational frame of reference. They can talk about themselves and their feelings—sometimes even from the perspectives of others. ("I think it was Jane's fault, but Jane thinks it was mine."or, later, "I guess I need to think about my friend's feelings.") The child who recognizes commonalities in repeating behaviors or thoughts is moving toward formal thinking. This type of thinking can appear as early as the third grade—usually only on selected topics.

Treatment:

In helping the child describe self or situations, we may ask the question "Is that a pattern?" or "Does that happen in other situations?" If the child can see the underlying structural repetition, he or she is showing signs of formal thinking. The elementary counselor often has difficulty here since the treatment requires the counselor to operate more as a consultant, thus giving the child more power. Too many teachers and counselors stay at only the concrete level with children. If they are to develop more complex formal thinking patterns, children must be challenged and encouraged to examine themselves. Formal-operational theories of the self and the pattern mode of thinking abound, and a Rogerian or cognitive-behavioral style may be used if the child responds. A variety of self-oriented programs, such as self-esteem workshops, me-kits, friendship groups, and so on, can help facilitate the examination of self and perspective taking. Finally, decisional counseling aimed at working with broader patterns of behavior and thought may be useful.

Dialectic/Systemic (How did that develop in a system? How is all this integrated?)

Assessment:

Most children and adults do not ordinarily make sense of their worlds from this frame of reference. With children, dialectic/systemic thinking will manifest itself most clearly when, for example, a young woman (usually in the upper grades) starts talking seriously about sexism or when a minority student recognizes that personal difficulties may be caused by a racist system. Here, the child is operating on systems of knowledge and is learning how he or she is affected by the environment. The locus of awareness changes from the child or teacher to larger systemic concerns. As counselors, we must be aware that families and classrooms are two important systems affecting the child and give them more attention.

Treatment:

Case management techniques undergird the dialectic approach. Coordinating individual, group, family, school, and community interventions is key. Systems think-ing is manifested in family sessions and in classroom consultation. We also use systems orientations to help children deal individually or in groups with issues of racism, sexism, and handicapism. When we conduct a case conference with our colleagues and the family, we are utilizing our dialectic/systemic skills. Family counseling, referral of other family members for therapy, and coordination of cases with social services exemplify systemic action. In addition, community developmental activities may be essential. For example, if the community has a serious employment problem or serious problems with racism or other forms of discrimination, the task of the counselor may be to facilitate community action programs.

Step 4: Generating a client-counselor contract for the treatment plan. The counselor who works with children has a particular responsibility to share treatment plans with parents and involve them in the process. Box 8-2 lists some of the services of school counselors. This list should be available to all parents and can sometimes be used for planning and developing a specific client-counselor contract.

Increasingly, therapists and counselors are providing clients with statements as to their rights and the skills the therapist has to offer and generating written contracts with the client. Appendix 5 provides an example of a counselor statement that can be given to clients. The information in Box 8-2 can supplement information on client rights.

When George's mother was called, the issues with George were discussed with her. Her response to the problem was at the formal-operational level, which indicated that she could participate in and support the counseling process (that is, she was able to reflect on George's problem). Some families are at the concrete level and will be only able to respond to one or two specific problems. Occasionally, counselors will encounter adults in the family who are at an embedded sensorimotor level and are unable even to understand or name the problem. Clearly, the client-counselor contract must change as cognitive-developmental level changes.

George's mother was given the list of services offered by the counselor. In a mutual process, the counselor and George's mother discussed a behavioral management program in the classroom, George's participation in a self-esteem group, and his involvement in exploratory assessment and developmental counseling so that a more complete understanding of his issues could be gained. The counseling contract was brief, as follows:

> Specific goals for George's counseling during the three weeks are to (1) improve classroom and playground behavior, (2) openly explore reasons why George's behavior has changed for the worse, and (3) share these goals of counseling with George and involve him in the planning process as much as possible.
>
> Attached is a list of checked methods which the counselor will employ to reach these goals. (List is attached to contract.)

Step 5: Proceeding with individual treatment. The first two interviews went as planned and expected. George accepted the general goals of counseling. He was glad to play games and get out of the classroom but was not open to talking about himself or his issues. The counselor rewarded his standard social behavior with smiles, warmth, and approval. Rapport seemed to be developing. The third interview continued the same approach. In the interview George was quiet and noncommunicative. When asked if something was bothering him or if he wanted to talk, he asked to play a game. The counselor suggested a board game dealing with feelings. George played listlessly. When the counselor asked him what he liked best about school this year, like most children he said, "Recess," but he seemed sad.

Box 8-2. Counseling Services Offered by School Counselors

The following activities are offered by the school guidance office and are presented to parents so that they are informed as to the process of counseling and its possible goals. The school counselor, Jane Smith, offers the following services. In consultation with Ms. Smith, parents are encouraged to select counseling programs they believe will meet their child's needs.

As you begin, you may first want to list in this space the goals you have for your child and the specific things you might want the school to do. Also, what do you think your child wants?

_____

_____

_____

_____

Following are some services offered in this school. You may wish to check those of special interest to you for your child.

___1. Behavioral classroom consultation. Many children benefit from a more structured approach to the educational process. In consultation with the teacher and through observation of your child, it is possible to set up reward systems in the classroom. These programs are most effective if they are coordinated with parents in the home and if the specific program is negotiated with each parent.

___2. Skills training. Counseling is an educational process, and it is possible to teach your child, individually or in groups, certain basic skills such as:

___ Relaxation skills   ___ Friendship skills

___ Communication skills   ___ Social skills

___ Problem-solving skills   ___ Stress management skills

___ Other specific skills: _____

_____

___3. Group counseling. Younger children often benefit from sharing ideas and experiences with one another. Specific topic groups are offered, which include:

___ Friendship groups

___ Groups for children experiencing divorce or family change

___ Moving groups (for children about to move to another geographical area)

___ Self-esteem groups (to help children learn to appreciate themselves)

___ Other special topic groups:_____

_____

(continues)

Box 8-2. Counseling Services Offered by School Counselors *(continued)*

___4. Individual counseling. Individual one-on-one counseling is a less specific activity but may involve one or more of the following, with the resulting specific goals:

___ Problem assessment. Often a child's issues are a mystery to the parents and the school. Exploring current situations may often uncover easy solutions or lead to referral to someone else. The interviews are nonstructured.

___ Developmental counseling. Over a period of several interviews, specific questions are asked that encourage the child to look at an issue from a variety of perspectives. For example, if a child has a problem on the playground, the counselor may seek to explore the actual happenings on the playground, how the child describes the situations, whether or not there are an identifiable patterns in the child's behavior and thinking, and how that behavior might have developed. Specific questions are asked and may be reviewed by the parent before counseling begins.

___ Exploration of self. This is usually for the verbal child. The counselor listens to the child's conceptions of self and others. The aim is to develop a better sense of self and to encourage individual decision making.

___Play and activities counseling. Games are played with children in most individual counseling sessions. These range from checkers and similar games to counseling games oriented to feelings and problem solving. Interspersed in the counseling process may be questions and counseling techniques oriented to more fully understanding the child's thinking process and the problem. At times, play and activities counseling may be the only approach used.

___ Supportive counseling. A child may have experienced a crisis at home, such as divorce or death, or be in a transition stage. During such times, checking in with the counselor weekly or biweekly can be helpful.

___ 5. Consultation, referral, and parent involvement.

___Parent consultation. The school guidance office is often the place to start if you sense your child is having difficulty in school or is not achieving at his or her full potential. We believe it is essential that you be kept informed and that we obtain your input for the benefit of your child.

___ Parent education and counseling. Individual or group sessions are offered in parenting skills and child management. At times, family meetings are held, with all family members present to explore ways we can work together to facilitate your child's social and academic development.

___ Community referral. The counselor maintains a complete file of available financial, employment, medical, social work, and psychiatric support services for the child and for family members who may be interested in assistance for themselves.

___ Referral to individual educational planning (IEP) team. The counselor is often the first step in referral of a child with academic and social difficulties to the IEP. The IEP can arrange special services for your child, including special teacher support, therapeutic teaching, medical and psychiatric support, and other services.

___ Other services: _____

During the next week, George got into trouble several times for fighting on the playground and was especially rebellious in the classroom. After one particular fight, the teacher sent him to the counselor.

The counselor took a nonjudgmental approach and asked George to tell her what had happened that day on the playground. George at first talked in the random, angry fashion typical in such situations: "It wasn't my fault. He hit me first." Listening and paraphrasing eventually elicited a more linear concrete picture of the fight. With encouragement, George slowly presented a detailed concrete-operational description of his last fight.

Important in this process was the counselor's willingness to listen to a child whose primary mode of functioning is detailed concrete-operational. As is true of most concrete children, George often wandered to other topics, mostly using concrete description but also adding elements of sensorimotor and random meaning making. Throughout this discussion, it was important that the counselor maintain a focus on the primary topic of fighting but also be willing to help the child develop an adequate foundation of trust. Skilled paraphrasing, reflection of feeling, and summarization are critical interviewing skills for building a sensorimotor and concrete base of understanding.

As the counselor listened, the value of the base of trust established in the first three sessions was apparent. The counselor focused the interview on sensorimotor functioning but with a new framework—the DCT systematic questioning process. The key five minutes of that session are summarized in brief form below:

Counselor: What did you see just before you hit him? Can you see him now?

George: I see his red ugly face. He is panting and shouting.

Counselor: What are you feeling right now in your body?

George: My stomach feels queasy, like I want to throw up.

Counselor: Where have you had the same feeling before?

George: When Don (manfriend living with mother) came in drunk last week and threw the dog against the wall and then he hit me.

This questioning sequence that led to the discovery of abuse contained the following elements: (1) accepting and listening to the random events leading to the argument and fight on the playground; (2) organizing these events in a concrete linear sequence; (3) returning to the sensorimotor level, with an emphasis on what is seen, heard, and felt coupled with a free-association exercise based on the expectation that the same feeling occurred in some other situation. Here the counselor expects a pattern but introduces conditions so that the child can bring out the information. Basing counseling on a solid sensorimotor and concrete foundation is particularly important as we seek to understand the complexities of childhood cognitions. (Exactly the same sequence of counselor actions is also extremely effective with adolescents and adults in helping them discover developmental roots of present disturbance.)

Many children who are acting out or impulsive are reacting to a current problem or stage in their developmental history. Children like George cannot express fear, frustration, or anger at absent parents or to their abusers. Their tendency is to strike out at others. Similarly, abusive individuals themselves usually have a developmental history of significant trauma and, through their abusive behavior, enact their own problematic developmental history.

After uncovering the basis of George's problem, the therapeutic task is to draw out more of the sensorimotor feelings and linear concretes of the situation and then search for formal patterns of repeating events—both the repetition of the trauma in the home and the repetition of the anger not expressed to the manfriend redirected to others on the playground. This type of work takes time and is not ordinarily completed by school counselors; referral to others is required, and the counselor's role with the child becomes that of developmental case manager (coordinating various treatment services) while continuing to provide supportive counseling, group work, and classroom consultation.

Step 6: Expanding individual treatment through network involvement. On discovering the abuse, the counselor immediately contacted the mother. She came in wearing makeup over what appeared to be a black eye. She appeared to be slow moving and depressed but was able to focus on her son. The counselor reviewed her sessions with George and the discovery of abuse. The mother broke into tears, saying, "He hit me too, but now he's gone." In some sense, this case is easier than many abusive situations. In this case, the family did not hide the abuse but was willing and able to examine it. In some situations, the mother may have defended her manfriend and withdrawn George from counseling, forcing the school to take stronger action.

In cases of abuse, systems and network interventions are critical. Individual counseling for George may be beneficial, but unless the situation changes at home and support is provided in the classroom, the chances that George will resume normal development are greatly impaired. In this case, youth services were called in, and a child therapist was found for George. George's mother was referred for individual counseling at a community mental health center. Unless key family members are able to manage their lives, work with the child is likely to be fruitless. Discussion with George's brother revealed that he, too, had experienced abuse from the manfriend. Individual counseling for him was also discussed.

At this point, a family meeting was arranged. When working with a multiproblem family or an individual from a multiproblem family, there is always the possibility that treatments for different members can conflict. Thus, a family network meeting can be helpful in coordinating treatment and ensuring that all involved are aware of individual and family goals. "No secrets" is one motto of such meetings. Rather than hide problems and issues, open discussion of difficulties with key parties is important. Out of such meetings come commitments on the part of all. All family members, including children, are part of the planning process.

At this family meeting, the school counselor, a consulting family-oriented psychiatrist, and a representative from youth services met with George, his mother, and his brother. If it had been possible, George's father also would have been there, but distance was too great. More information came out in this session, and it was agreed that individual work for all three was desired, plus a series of family sessions. The mother asked that special attention be given to George's academic difficulties and his present lack of friends.

Consultation with George's teacher was important in this case. The teacher needed guidance in dealing with George at this difficult time, particularly since the teacher herself was facing divorce. The school counselor had to counsel the teacher in addition to developing class management programs. A "big brother" from the high school peer counseling program volunteered to meet with George twice weekly after school.

A family therapy team was called in to work with the family. The manfriend attended the first session, but immediately dropped out, denying his abuse. He had attended because he had again been "sleeping over" at the house. Fortunately, George's mother continued the family sessions, which included concrete interventions and specific homework assignments, and her parenting skills improved. Structural family interventions focused on child management and the fact that the mother had given up too much authority to the children. With the therapist's guidance, the mother not only began to understand how the family system was affecting the children but also to see her pattern of selecting men who might eventually abuse her. With this discovery, she was able to break the relationship with the abusive male. Later, in individual therapy, she was able to trace back her pattern of interactions with men to examples from her own family of origin.

As sometimes happens, George did not relate well with the therapist at the community mental health center and soon refused to return. Since the mother's relationship with the abusive manfriend had terminated, the school counselor took George as a longer-term client. The treatment consisted of weekly counseling and involving George in a self-esteem group. Needless to say, an 8-year-old boy is not expected to put together how the patterns of neglect and abuse result in his acting-out behavior. But the concept of repeating patterns is useful to the counselor in conceptualizing events and planning counseling interventions.

Through further individual therapy, George's mother became more assertive and supported the counseling interventions in the home. She came to four group psychoeducational programs on parenting skills taught by the counselor. With support from the counselor, the teacher became more able to plan for this sometimes-difficult child in the classroom.

Counseling and therapy are too often defined as individual or family centered. In complex cases such as the foregoing, individual change is virtually impossible unless the full network of services is utilized effectively. The school counselor in this case can be considered a developmental case manager who orchestrated the many parts of the network necessary for a satisfactory result that will last over time.

Not every community provides the rounded services discussed in this case. Few people are trained to think in terms of networks. There are few guidance counselors in elementary schools throughout the country and fewer family therapists. Schools generally do not want to provide "therapy," despite the fact that the school setting could be organized to provide a more therapeutic and supportive atmosphere. At present, the tendency remains to blame the individual (or family) for problems. However, as suggested by this case, a network approach to human development is and will continue to be cost-effective, both in financial and emotional terms.

Applying the DCT and Network Models with Adolescents and Adults

With children, the network model proposed here seems fitting: one cannot expect children to change unless their environment changes as well. For adolescents and adults, the network model, with its emphasis on balancing individual and environmental interventions, might seem to some less appropriate. This sense of "lack of fit" most likely results from the individualistic emphasis of North American culture in which the responsibility for change is placed on the individual adolescent or adult. However, the network/DCT model is equally useful for adolescents and adults.

LaFromboise and Low (1989, p. 131) describe how they used their systemic network approach with a drug-abusing Native American adolescent.

> Mark, a 16-year-old Indian male of average intelligence, has been "acting out" for more than a year. Often truant, Mark has fallen behind in his academic work. He uses drugs and alcohol, has had several violent encounters with fellow students, and has been in minor trouble with local authorities. Mark has lived with his maternal aunt and uncle on the reservation for the last ten years. His mother is a chronic alcoholic, and Mark rarely sees her. The identity of Mark's father is unknown. Recently, Mark's uncle lost his job and began to disappear for days on end. Mark has been referred by a school counselor, who has become increasingly concerned about his apparent depression.

> Getting Mark to therapy first required the support of his family to ensure that he would come. Mark's therapist emphasized the development of rapport and of defining the problem as Mark saw it. A critical cultural and individual issue in this case was negative stereotypes about Native Americans' problems with drinking. Early intervention strategies focused on challenging irrational beliefs, behavior change, and social validation. The school problem was approached through consultation with Mark's teachers, who were asked to use more small group work as opposed to the traditional lecture format. Mark was encouraged to participate in social gatherings, such as basketball tournaments, rodeos, powwows, and feasts, to help him reaffirm his Native American identity.

LaFromboise and Low suggest engaging key family members in therapy, which may require the participation of community leaders in a network meeting at the first stage. Particularly important in this session is the Native American belief that any individual's behavior reflects on the total community. Interventions with clients such as Mark and his family need to focus on cooperation, connectedness, and interdependence. The goal of such therapy is not individualistic self-actualization but the interdependent actualization of the individual in a family and community context.

Interdependence provides a goal for more ecologically oriented counseling and psychotherapy. The network model can be described as a case management approach. Counseling and therapy theory and training often focus on the myth of a skilled therapist sitting in his or her office, stimulating change in clients by brilliant conversation. Although this may be the case for a few lucky therapists, most professional helpers soon realize that their efforts are likely to be ineffective unless coupled with family, school, work, and community interventions. Furthermore, it usually takes more than one counselor or therapist when dealing with serious problems. Treatment teams and community networks of helping professionals are becoming more the norm.

Can the network model be used to generate treatment plans for adults? This section presents a case illustration that provides a structure for examining this question. Although this case is oriented toward individual counseling and therapy, an exercise in the "Theory into Practice" section in this chapter focuses on families and broader interventions.

Style-Shift Counseling and Therapy

This is the term Anderson (1983; 1987a) employs in his developmental approach to the interviewing and treatment processes. The tenets of style-shift counseling and therapy parallel those of DCT and involve a five-step process, as follows:

1. Assess the general developmental level of the client.

2. Choose a helping style that matches that level.

3. Identify developmental tasks of the client and intervene.

   (Clients may be at multiple developmental levels on varying developmental tasks.)

4. Evaluate and plan alternative actions.

5. Shift style if needed and as client develops.

Anderson's (1987b) Style-Shift Indicator is a learning instrument developed to provide an introduction to developmental assessment and treatment planning. Eight cases are presented in the instrument, and the tasks are to (1) identify the developmental level of the client and (2) rank order four treatment alternatives in order of preference. From rankings of clients, it is possible to obtain counselor and therapist scores on preferred helping styles and effectiveness of style matching.

A case from the Style-Shift Indicator follows (Anderson, 1987b, p. 8):

Case 3: Jack, age 25, out of work

Jack has been a good, steady worker with a local construction company since he failed grade 10 and quit school. Due to lack of work, he was laid off from his job. Jack was quite persistent at first in looking for another job. However, as the weeks went by he began to spend more and more time at home. Lately, his drinking has increased, and he spends a lot of late nights out, then coming home to watch the late shows.

You are a career counselor at a local community agency, and Jack comes to you seeking help because he knows he is not going anywhere with his life and says he wants to go to work soon. Jack is getting discouraged with his prospects and realizes that his life is going nowhere fast. He has no real plan for the future, is tired of construction work, and can't seem to think clearly about the future. He seems to value a "macho" approach to life, keeping emotional distance between himself and others.

Given this description, at what cognitive-developmental level is Jack? Rank order your responses by writing 1 (for first), 2, 3, and 4 next to the levels.

___ Sensorimotor   ___ Formal
___ Concrete   ___ Dialectic/systemic

From the data provided, Jack is primarily concrete. A major question, of course, is the alcohol issue. If it is a serious problem that interferes with his functioning and if he is denying that fact, Jack would be considered to be at the sensorimotor level. Distinctions between the formal and dialectic/systemic levels are more difficult. In the dialectic/systemic form of therapy, there is often a mutuality between the client and counselor. Jack might be more likely to think at this level than at the formal level. He does not appear to be reflective or interested in looking at himself and his life patterns (although he may be formal on some of life developmental tasks). The Style-Shift Indicator suggests a 2-1-4-3 ranking of Jack. (Using rankings for several cases, it is possible to determine a counselor trainee's assessment capacities and preferred treatment style.)

The Style-Shift Indicator provides four treatment options for Jack, as follows (Anderson, 1987b, p.8). Which treatment would you use first? Second? Third? Fourth?

A. Respond to Jack's feelings of poor self-worth and assist him to focus on how these feelings arose from deeper problems, and help him see how they affect his ability to do career planning or to find a job now. Help Jack clarify some of his values and priorities in life and encourage him to set his own goals so he can reach his desired position. Help him to look at self-defeating, repeating patterns in his lifestyle.

B. Call a friend of yours who has a construction company and needs casual labor. This friend has a reputation for taking on somewhat immature young men and helping them develop into responsible, skilled workers. Your friend has training sessions in the evenings to facilitate personal and work development. Follow up to ensure that Jack engages effectively in this plan.

C. After developing a relationship with him to earn his trust, tentatively confront him with his unproductive and self-destructive (drinking) behavior in a respectful way and see how much of this he wants to share with you. Assist him in evaluating his own behavior and work toward a specific job search. Include role-playing so that he knows how to present himself favorably in a job interview.

D. Discuss openly his strengths and weaknesses. Explore options available to him that will make use of his strong points. Try to keep a mutual relationship with him, providing information and sharing your experience with him. Be creative in generating ideas mutually to deal with the future, rather than trying to influence or help him directly.

Which of the above four treatments would you select as your preferred mode of action? Which would be your second choice? Third choice? What would be your least preferred treatment? List your choices in the spaces provided below.

First _____   Second _____

Third _____   Fourth _____

The style-shift evaluation of the case is as follows (Anderson, 1987a, p. 36):

> Having identified Jack as primarily concrete in his thinking, the Style-Shift Indicator suggests that the coaching, concrete-operational approach is the place to start. Jack has several developmental tasks; the most obvious of these is the matter of jobs, and the most important may be the drinking issue. He may have other family problems, interpersonal skill deficits, and so on. The DCT and style-shift models suggest joining the client's concrete frame of reference (option C above) and using coaching techniques to assist him in becoming more rational, conscious, and consequential in his thinking. Concrete behavioral treatment alternatives could be used to help him try on new behavioral patterns.
>
> A second choice might be the environmental structuring approach that a sensorimotor diagnosis would suggest (option B). Here you take greater responsibility for the client. It also assumes that alcohol is the central issue. If, for example, you could respectfully influence Jack to enter an alcohol treatment center and receive career and life planning, then you, as part of his environment, could be catalytic in "bumping" him into a new environment where he will more likely receive a concentrated and controlled therapeutic impact to counteract his quite well-established, self-defeating behavior patterns. At the sensorimotor level, counselors provide more direct influence in their client's lives.
>
> A third choice could be the mutual, creative dialogue of option D. This might work out to an extent if Jack perceived you as "cool," somehow like him, and a fellow struggler who has made it in a number of ways. However, Jack's creative powers have not been realized yet; he is stressed, and needs to "dry-out" from a possibly debilitating dependence on alcohol, and begin to have a dream for his future before he can do a lot of "brainstorming" and mutual problem solving.

The least preferred choice might be the formal-operational approach (option A) of attempting to help Jack examine, explore, and understand himself and the alternatives he has. This sounds ideal, but the information we have about Jack indicates that he is not only developmentally unready for the depth of this level, but perhaps unwilling to engage in the emotional intensity of it as well.

If we counsel Jack in a concrete coaching style and things go well, we can shift our style to a more formal-operational self-examination approach as his developmental maturity increases. If his drinking becomes worse, we may want to shift our style to a more influential sensorimotor approach. Furthermore, on the many developmental tasks of the young adult, we can anticipate that Jack may operate at different cognitive levels on each task. Flexibility and adaptability are watchwords of Anderson's style-shift theory. Undergirding the entire framework is a mutual, systemic approach in which client and counselor work together, looking at the family and environment as well as just the individual.

The case of Jack provides you with a framework for generating a network treatment plan. Although the entry point for counseling probably should be at Jack's concrete level; full treatment will require action at multiple cognitive-developmental levels. It may be helpful at this point to generate your own approach to a client such as Jack, using the steps of the DCT treatment plan framework.

1. *Establish a positive base for treatment.* What strengths can you identify in Jack that may be helpful in designing a successful treatment plan? Given the brevity of the case presentation, you will have to improvise on positives you might expect. You may find it helpful to think of a person you have known that is somewhat similar to Jack and use that person's qualities to "flesh out" your description.

_____

_____

_____

What positive strengths and resources can you identify in the environment and in important support systems such as family, friends, work, and community?

_____

_____

_____

2. *Examine key relationship issues that might affect you as the counselor or therapist.* First, what are you own general feelings about a client such as Jack? What has your personal experience been with such individuals? What feelings do you experience in your body? What images come to mind from your own developmental history? How would these events and patterns affect the here and now of your relationship with a person such as Jack?

_____

_____

_____

Given this knowledge, what type of relationship do you think you could offer Jack? What balance of attachment and separation, autonomy and relationship do you think is most appropriate?

_____

_____

_____

3. *Identify treatment options you would consider.* What key developmental tasks do you believe Jack faces? You may also find it helpful to review Erikson's life-stage and Haley's family life-cycle theories. List at least three key developmental tasks and the treatment options you might consider. Include the possibility of varying types of network interventions.

Developmental task 1:

_____

_____

_____

Developmental task 2:

_____

_____

_____

Developmental task 3:

_____

_____

_____

Develop an ideal network treatment program that includes not only individual counseling and therapy but also family therapy and involvement of the employer, community and self help groups, and other key individuals or groups. How would you coordinate these interventions?

_____

_____

_____

What cultural, ethnic, racial, or religious group did you think Jack was a member of? Identify that group and then examine your treatment plan to see if it coordinates with Jack's cultural heritage. Then imagine that Jack comes from another racial background. What impact does this change have on your treatment plan?

———————————————————————————————————

———————————————————————————————————

———————————————————————————————————

4. *Generate a client-counselor contract for a treatment plan.* On a separate piece of paper, write your own statement for a therapist-client contract in which you outline your knowledge, skills, and competencies. (See Appendix 5 for an illustration.)

In addition, imagine you have worked with Jack for from one to two sessions. List below specific goals for counseling and clear statements of what successful treatment would consist of. (Use language Jack would understand.)

———————————————————————————————————

———————————————————————————————————

———————————————————————————————————

Treatment plans, of necessity, must relate to your own knowledge and competencies. One of the values of the above exercise is that the counselor gains a sense of humility by acknowledging the very human limitations we all share. We must first identify what we can do and then contrast it with a more ideal treatment plan. Then, rather than just depending on our own inevitably limited skills, we can refer the client for assistance on some issues, working with other helpers and community members in a mutual way. Using a network framework, for therapy requires willingness to examine oneself, admit frailties, and work with colleagues in a mutual, nonhierarchical manner. Also required is the ability to reflect on one's own skills, beliefs, and attitudes—something that not all therapists, even those who have had lengthy training, are capable of.

Chapter Summary

The case studies provided here are designed to emphasize four key points:

1. A network of interventions may be required to facilitate individual development and growth. Individual counseling and therapy are often inadequate to produce change that lasts and works in the environment.

2. Children can benefit from a DCT/network approach to human change. With only slight adaptations, young children can respond to the DCT questioning and intervention strategies.

3. Individual therapy may not be the treatment of choice for individuals from some cultures. In such cases, the network of interventions selected must be changed to meet the unique needs of the many distinct and different individuals, families, and systems we encounter.

4. Network interventions need not always start with individuals. An exercise in family network interventions may be found in the following Theory into Practice section.

CAUTION!   Although there appears to be much to commend a more broadly based network approach, at times the client may feel he or she is confronting a small army of professionals. In such situations, the individual or the family may be overwhelmed by numbers and may not feel comfortable participating actively in the therapy process. Awed by professionals, clients quietly do what they are told or quickly leave therapy. In some cultures, this might appear to be culturally appropriate. (For example, the Nigerian Igbo, discussed in Chapter 7, sometimes believe the extended family to be the locus of decision making and individual control.) However, regardless of culture, a reasonable balance of individual initiative and environmental constraint needs to be achieved. DCT would argue that the concept of interdependence of individuals and their environments might serve as a useful basis for achieving this balance.

Theory into Practice

By the end of this section, you may be able to demonstrate your ability to

1. Generate a network treatment plan that takes into account the fact that other individuals might develop distinctively different plans that could also be useful to the client(s).
2. Generate examples of statements of the goals of counseling and therapy that might be used in your work with clients.
3. Examine cultural differences and how they might affect DCT and network treatment plans and contracts.

Generating Network Treatment Plans

In a small group, share treatment plans for a client such as Jack. Note similarities and differences of your plans. How do the skills, knowledge, cultural background, and beliefs of each individual in the group, including yourself, affect the treatment plan? In answering this last question, you may each want to share your responses to question 2 on page 250 in which you talked about your own developmental history and attitudes toward individuals such as Jack. How does your own life developmental history affect the approach to the interview and to treatment planning?

_____

_____

_____

_____

Generating Specific Goals in Client-Therapist Contracts

Again, in a small group, have one person role-play Jack. In consultation with him, generate a written contract for methods and goals of counseling. It is useful in this exercise if Jack first does the exercise as a formal-operational 26-year-old; second, as a more concrete individual. How does the language change in the two situations?

_____

_____

_____

_____

Considering Cultural Differences

Jack could be of a different racial, religious, ethnic, gender, age, or affectional orientation than you. He could have a physical or intellectual handicap. Furthermore, he might be at any of the five levels of minority identity development. Each situation changes the nature of the network you must consider. How would the counseling approach change with any of the above factors? What impact would these factors have on the contracting process?

_____

_____

_____

_____

Planning a Network Intervention with a Family

Imagine you are a family therapist working with a family who has a seriously alcoholic parent. You may likely have known a family who has had this difficulty and have observed the impact the problem has on everyone in the family. In thinking through this case, extend the concept of family to a network that includes relatives, employers, ministers, and anyone else who might have a significant impact on the family. Those who conduct full network interventions may work with as many as 50 to 100 people. However, limit your imagined plan to a lesser number of individuals.

1. _Establish a positive base for treatment._ What strengths can you identify in the family that may aid successful treatment?

_____

_____

_____

_____

What positive strengths and resources can you identify in the environment and important systems, including extended family, friends, work, and community resources (AA, church, mental health centers, school personnel)?

_____

_____

_____

2. *Examine key relationship issues that might affect you as the counselor or therapist.* First, what are you own general feelings about families with alcoholic issues? What has your personal experience been with such individuals and families? What feelings do you experience? Where are they located in your own body? What images come to mind from your own developmental history? How would these events and patterns affect your relationship with this type of family?

_____

_____

_____

Given this knowledge, what type of relationship, do you think you could have with this family? What balance of attachment and separation, autonomy and relationship do you think is most appropriate?

_____

_____

_____

3. *Identify treatment options you would consider.* What key developmental tasks do you believe this family faces? It may be helpful to review Erikson's lifestage and Haley's family life-cycle theories. List at least three key developmental tasks and the treatment options you might consider. To complete this task, it will help to think of a specific family and specific stages. Is the family at middle marriage, leaving home, or some other stage? How do these issues affect the total family and each family member?

Developmental task 1:

_____

_____

_____

Developmental task 2:

_____

_____

_____

Developmental task 3:

_____

_____

_____

Develop an ideal network treatment program that includes not only individual counseling and therapy but also family therapy, involvement of the employer, and community groups. How would you coordinate these interventions?

_____

_____

_____

What do you think was the cultural, ethnic, racial, or religious group of the family? Identify that group and then examine your treatment plan to see if it coordinates with cultural heritage. Then imagine that Jack comes from another racial background. What impact does this have on your treatment plan?

_____

_____

_____

4. *Generate a client-counselor contract for a treatment plan.* On a separate piece of paper, write your own statement for a therapist-client contract in which you outline your knowledge, skills, and competencies. (See Appendix 5 for an illustration.)

In addition, imagine that after the network intervention, you continue to work with the family for from one to two sessions. List below specific goals for counseling and include clear statements of what successful treatment would be (in language they could understand).

_____

_____

_____

Generalization: Taking Network Skills Home

Activity 1: Develop a Personal Statement as the Basis for Contracting with Clients

Increasingly, counselors and therapists are openly sharing legal, professional, and personal aspects of the counseling relationship. Although legal considerations dictate some of this openness, the helping profession, in general, is moving toward more mutuality with clients. Using the models of this chapter and those in Appendix 5, generate a statement you could share with your clients.

How these statements should be shared with clients is also an important and complex issue. When working with formal-operational adults, contracts can facilitate generation of trust. The sensorimotor or concrete-operational client requires a different approach. Sometimes two (or more) statements of client rights and your skills must be made. It is important to have the child client participate in the goal-setting process and not just rely on a contract between the parents and the therapist.

Activity 2: The Interview

For a single client or family, go through the specific steps of the treatment plan in consultation with a colleague or supervisor. What did you learn about yourself and your relationship with that client? How did you respond to the network concept of treatment? What specific agencies or people can you count on as resources for helping clients?

Test your statement on counseling with the client and involve the client in determining specific goals for counseling and therapy. How do you use (or not use) network concepts of treatment?

Activity 3: Consider the Yakima Nation Proverb

Good Counsel is a mark of wisdom,
Whether in the family, or the circle of society.
Good Counsel is modest, not assertive;
Considerate of the opinion of others.
How we shall proceed together
Is as important as what we now should do.
Good Counsel will create
A consensus which unites.

What does this proverb say to you at this point?

_____

_____

_____

_____

_____

_____

_____

_____

_____

_____

Suggested Supplemental Reading and Activities

Additional Reading

Ivey, A. 1986. *Developmental therapy: Theory into practice*. San Francisco: Jossey-Bass.
The practice of developmental therapy is examined and case examples are included in Chapter 6. The theoretical background of dialectics is explored in some detail. The exercises on pages 256–259 are useful extensions of the concepts of this current chapter.

Network Interventions

Attneave, C. 1969. Therapy in tribal settings and urban network interventions. *Family Process* 8: 192–210.

Attneave, C. 1982. American Indian and Alaska native families: Emigrants in their own homeland. In *Ethnicity and family therapy,* eds., M. McGoldrick, J. Pearce, and J. Giordano. New York: Guilford.

Speck, R., and C. Attneave. 1973. *Family process*. New York: Pantheon.
Individual behavior is rooted in group and social processes. Network therapy, as explored in these three references, helps us understand how individual and family treatment can be integrated with larger group constructs.

LaFromboise, T., and K. Lowe. 1989. Psychological interventions with American Indian adolescents. In *Children of color,* eds., J. Gibbs and L. Hwang. San Francisco: Jossey-Bass.
This chapter presents research and theory on interventions with Native American youth and includes a more complete description of the case of Mark described in this chapter. The book by Gibbs and Hwang is a useful compendium of interventions that can be used with children and adolescents from varied backgrounds.

Ho, Man Keung. 1987. *Family therapy with ethnic minorities*. Newbury Park, Calif.: Sage.
This book has an excellent chapter on Native American Indian and Alaskan natives (Inuits) and elaborates on the importance of network conceptions of helping.

DeLoria, V. 1969. *Custer died for your sins*. New York: Avon.
This best-selling book offers an eloquent discussion of Native American Indian nations and their history.

Abuse and Its Aftermath

Brassard, M., R. Germain, and S. Hart. 1987. *Psychological maltreatment of children and youth*. New York: Pergamon.
This book provides a comprehensive, research-based summary of child abuse in our society. In addition to the expected topics of childhood sexual and emotional abuse, challenging material is included on psychological abuse resulting from prejudice and cultural bias, racism as psychological maltreatment, and social systems abuse.

Miller, A. 1981. *The drama of the gifted child*. New York: Basic Books.

Miller, A. 1986. *Thou shalt not be aware*. New York: Meriden
These are perhaps the two most useful and stimulating books on issues of abuse. Abuse is presented as an intergenerational and cultural phenomenon, and blame is minimized.

Style-Shift Theory

Anderson, T. 1987a. *Style-shift counseling and developmental therapy with the style-shift indicator.* North Amherst, Mass.: Microtraining Associates, Inc.

Anderson, T. 1987b. *Style-shift indicator.* North Amherst, Mass.: Microtraining.
Eight cases are presented briefly and, as in the case of Jack described in this chapter, you select the helping style you believe is most appropriate. The Style-Shift Indicator provides scores on style matching and predicted treatment effectiveness. You may find it stimulating to evaluate your style of helping using this learning instrument.

Research Suggestion

Given the complexity of the network approach, traditional empirical research methods are not easily identified. However, an individual case study plan can be used in which measures of certain key data are made before, during, and after therapy. The case study approach is especially useful when specific goals for behavior and attitudinal change are contracted for early in the process. The measures can then be adjusted to fit the individual or family.

For example, for Mark, the Native American Indian adolescent discussed in this chapter, measures might be made of number of days absent from school, time between violent incidents, number of conflicts with the law, self-concept, and cultural identity. Mark should be actively involved in decisions about criteria for evaluation of interventions. For Mark's family, the return of his uncle to work and informal observations of community members could be the data measured.

Action research data such as these examples can become part of the treatment process, serving as objective indicators of client progress. Some treatment clinics require some form of action research as part of the treatment process. Clients can share in the process and be made constantly aware of their progress toward goals. The action research plan can be part of the treatment contract, thus making counselors and therapists more accountable.

Psychologists, social workers, and counselors in private practice or working in community agencies and schools have a responsibility to be accountable for their work. Integrating some way to systematically assess our interventions with individuals, family, or communities is a professional responsibility too many of us neglect.

Paraphrasing Kurt Lewin, we should have no therapeutic or counseling action without some form of research, and research should not exist independent of action in the real world. "No action without research, no research without action."

9 Developing and Supervising Helping Professionals

Extending the Concepts of DCT

Our Indian people receive a great deal of teaching from Nature, which surrounds us all. We learn from the tiniest insect and from the largest animal, from the rivers and the forests. We receive teaching from the sky and the changes of the wind. To our people, all of Nature has strong meaning.

The elders pass on the wisdom of Nature to the young. In Legends, in the recounting of personal experiences, and from the events in one's own life, the wisdom embodied in Nature and its creatures is brought home to us.

The Oak Tree endures the elements and grows slowly.

The lesson is—great age comes to those who have adjusted to their natural surroundings.

The Smooth Surface of the water does not itself reveal the depths.

The lesson is—see the problem from more than one point of view.

The Chipmunk looks us over and has an opinion about what he sees.

The lesson is—all nature is full of spirit.

Yakima Nation Proverbs

Many of the goals of developmental counseling and therapy are summarized in the Yakima proverbs. Developmental maturity, like the growth of the Oak Tree, takes time and considerable patience. We seek to help our clients gain new perspectives of themselves and the world. As helping professionals, we also need to view our field from a multiple-perspective framework.

All nature is full of spirit. Each of God's creations affects us here and now. We are interdependent. The development of a strong sense of self and autonomy is, of course, important, particularly in White North American culture. But equally vital are our connections and attachments with others. The spirit is there in all of us, yet none of us is the spirit. The spirit is something larger; it provides a unifying theme as we consider persons and situations from our multiple perspectives.

Growth requires developmental movement. If something doesn't work, don't do more of the same. Shift your style and try something new. But don't change perspectives and actions randomly; try generating new points of view in relationship to your physical and human environment.

This closing chapter presents one more perspective of the developmental framework. How can one apply DCT constructs in the developmental education of helping professionals? All in the helping field participate in case conferences or are asked to consult with a colleague on a difficult problem. And most of us must supervise another person's induction into the helping field. Training and supervising community volunteers and paraprofessionals are increasingly routine parts of the helping professional's role.

Education as Development

The goal of counseling and therapy is development. The goal of educating helpers is also development. Just as with our counseling clients, we must build an adequate foundation for future growth with counselor trainees. DCT has potentially useful implications, not only for therapist education and training but also in other settings. This section presents examples of how the DCT framework has been applied in the schools.

Many of us work or will work in the schools. The rest of us will work with individuals and families who have children in school. School-related difficulties are a common theme in therapy. DCT offers a partial explanation of some of the problems our clients face. As consultants to teachers and school administrators, we may be able to help explain why some children and adolescents aren't responding to the educational process.

One of the first educational applications of DCT was made by Brodhead (1988), who audiotaped a high school social studies classroom discussion. The teacher stated that her goal was to teach a basic principle: how to analyze a specific proverb ("Birds of a feather flock together.") and its implications for daily life. This task requires a combination of concrete and formal-operational thought. Following are selections from a typical classroom interaction during the one-hour taping done by Brodhead (1988, p. 25):

Teacher: What does that proverb mean to you, John? (This question, oriented as it is toward meaning, seems basically formal, but in our culture this type of question is quite open, and we can expect responses at almost any cognitive-developmental level.)

John: Sparrows should live with sparrows, I guess. (later concrete)

Teacher: Anything else?

John: I hang around with a lot of people that are nothing like me. (concrete)

Teacher: And what does that tell us about you? (formal question, oriented toward self)

John: Nothing. (concrete)

Teacher: So, you're saying the proverb isn't true? (formal)

John: Well, I hang around with lots of different people, but all it says is that I can find people like me if I want because . . . (teacher interrupts just as the student starts to move toward formal operations).

Teacher: Well, let's try Sue.

Sue: I think John is trying to tell us there are exceptions to any rule. Yes, birds of a feather do flock together, but there are exceptions. I think he's talking about exceptions to the rule. (Advanced formal thinking or dialectic/systemic in that she is working on the principle as a rule but simultaneously noting exceptions to the rule. She is also demonstrating an ability to take John's perspective.) For example, President Nixon selected cabinet members who in many ways were like him. They were all Republicans, were all conservative. Some of them even got into trouble like him, but not all of them. There are problems with every generalization.

Teacher: What do you think of that bird Nixon, John? (laughter) (concrete)

John: I didn't like him much. (concrete)

Teacher: John, if birds of a feather flock together, what kind of flock did Nixon gather around himself? (late concrete)

John: I suppose he liked to have people like him around him. I like people like me, but I don't like everyone the same. (John starts a firmer move toward formal thought.)

The above transcript demonstrates that the DCT classification system used in the helping interview can be readily adapted to investigating classroom and instructional processes. Similar observations of elementary classroom interaction were made by Ivey and Ivey (1987, 1990) that showed that effective teachers systematically move children through sensorimotor activities, concrete examples, and formal principles. This finding was true of observations made in kindergarten through the sixth grade classrooms. In the school setting, it is clearly possible to assess student cognitive-developmental level and then to provide teaching interventions that either expand horizontal development or perturb and lead to more complex forms of thinking. Sadly, this does not always happen.

Unfortunately, the teaching process is all too often random or narrowly focused. Formal-operational instructors working with concrete students may expect them to understand complex principles despite the fact that the teachers have not provided specific examples. Worse yet, the formal instructor may, in frustration, change from formal to concrete questions without a systematic plan, thus confusing the student. In contrast, the primarily concrete-operational instructor may be good at providing examples and specifics but may bore students who conceptualize at a level higher than the teacher.

Nagel (1987) applied DCT concepts to the teaching of writing to high school students. She found that familiar writing concepts can be classified according to the neo-Piagetian scheme. Observational writing, in which one employs sensory impressions and allows random flow of thoughts and ideas, is similar to sensorimotor experiencing. Objective description of the facts of a situation corresponds to concrete-level reasoning. Analysis requires formal thought. Postformal, or dialectic/systemic, thought requires analysis of the analysis and multiperspective thinking.

Nagel found that the quality of high school student writing improved when students went through the systematic process of DCT. Students were encouraged to start their papers by first allowing themselves to visualize scenes related to the assignment. They then wrote concrete, linear descriptions describing what they had seen, heard, and felt. Students' writing moved from late concrete description toward linear casual reasoning, with a focus on if/then thought. At the formal level, students began to analyze patterns in themselves and their writing assignments. Finally, at the postformal dialectic level, students viewed their writing topic from a multiperspective frame of reference.

These examples from the instructional process remind us that the basis of counseling is a systematic learning process. As a helper, you engage in a form of education with your clients. This does not mean you "input" information into the client. Rather, the client is the person who creates information—new thoughts and ideas and new behaviors and feelings. Your task is to provide an environment that encourages and allows the client to develop horizontally or vertically at his or her own pace.

Consultation with school personnel is an important part of daily life for many social workers, psychologists, and counselors. In these exchanges we usually focus on solving personal-emotional and vocational issues. Student-teacher interaction also contributes to student difficulties. In the preceding chapter, the school consultation model was discussed briefly as an important part of change efforts with children and adolescents. It is hoped that this example will inspire efforts to include this model in teacher education programs so that teachers will learn to assess and work with students in a more developmentally appropriate fashion. You will also find that teacher consultation profits from DCT methods.

We are all learners and constantly face new developmental tasks. As either a beginning or advanced professional, you will always face new challenges and developmental tasks. These learning opportunities, whether they take the form of a new and "difficult" client or a complex theory or technique of helping, are what keep counseling and therapy alive and exciting.

Supervision and Case Consultation: A Key Professional Role

Supervision is the process of helping both beginning and experienced therapists examine their own clinical and counseling work. Supervision is also a teaching process that is critical to the development of counselors and therapists. Through consultation with a supervisor or our peers, we all can learn about what we are doing right in our work with clients, our developmental blind spots, and our options for further growth and development.

If you are just starting as a therapist or counselor, you will benefit from supervision by professionals in your practice setting and in your university or college practicum. If you are advanced in the profession, you can benefit from peer consultation and supervision from a master therapist or from someone with a different perspective. All of us can learn more about the complex process of helping. The most proficient and forward-looking counseling centers, clinics, and agencies incorporate supervision and feedback on clinical interviewing as a matter of course. Those counselors or institutions not actively seeking such growth experiences inevitably limit their range as helpers.

Beginning therapists and counselors are motivated to seek out consultation with peers, often forming peer supervision groups on their own. One of the most important benefits of a training program is such "peer learning." After training, counselors in the work setting often find themselves supervising the work of colleagues and training community volunteers and new students.

The following sections explore the learning implications of DCT and how it extends to cognitive-developmental supervision (Carey, 1988, 1989a, 1989b) of counselors and therapists. Counselor education and supervision is becoming an increasingly standard part of a professional training curriculum.

Assessing the Cognitive-Developmental Level of Helping Professionals

Counselor trainees come to educational programs at varying levels of cognitive-development. It is also the case that different therapists in practice will discuss cases at varying cognitive levels. Similarly, paraprofessionals and community volunteers approach their work from varying cognitive-developmental levels.

A good question to ask colleagues or trainees is "Could you tell me how you conceptualize your last interview with this client or family?" or "How do you think about this particular client or family problem?" Following are examples of answers of beginning and advanced helping professionals responding to these questions. How would you classify each response using the four levels of DCT? Circle the level you select. (Answers may be found at the end of this chapter.)

SM CO FO D/S 1. I don't know. A lot happened. It was confusing. I sensed some anger. She talked a lot, but it didn't make much sense. I just listened.

SM CO FO D/S 2. Well, she came in wearing a nice blue dress and gloves. She said that she was anxious to see me. I said, "I'm glad to see you, too." Then she talked about her first date in the last two years. I maintained good eye contact and asked an open-ended question "Could you tell me what you'd like to talk about today?"

SM CO FO D/S 3. This woman is most likely obsessive. She has a pattern of doing everything in a neat way. Her mother did the same thing.

SM CO FO D/S 4. There are several perspectives I could take. First, you could define the problem as obsessive personality style, but from another frame of reference, she could be defined as just careful and organized. Her husband sees here as quite ill; she seems to agree with his frame of of reference. I tend to see it as an old family pattern that she seems to repeat in her marriage.

SM CO FO D/S 5. The family is blended and has only been together for six months. The father is an accountant, and the mother works as a school teacher. They each have two children. He has Jane, who is 12, and Sam, who's 10. She has two girls, Wilda, 14, and Harriet, 12.

SM CO FO D/S 6. They confuse me. They came in the room and I couldn't even get the kids to sit down. I find my stomach gets upset almost immediately when I'm with them. Just talking about them right now makes me tense.

SM CO FO D/S 7. Most, virtually all, blended families are having difficulty at this stage. The father comes from a strict, relatively traditional Greek home and likes to have clear-cut direction and organization. The mother is third generation Swedish-American and has less traditional ideas of male/female roles. Part of what we're facing here is cultural conflict, but there are several other ways to look at it.

SM CO FO D/S 8. The kids have a pattern of constant argument, particularly over clothes. But it seems that almost anything can set them off.

The above examples show that case conceptualization can occur at varying cognitive-developmental levels. Clearly, all levels of description are useful, but the ability to conceptualize at all levels requires the skill of multiperspective thinking.

The Value of Varying Cognitive-Developmental Levels

Although it is a worthy goal to help counselor trainees achieve a multiperspective level, the emphasis on so-called higher levels of cognitive-developmental thinking can be excessive. It is assumed that multiperspective counselors and therapists are able to function at all four levels, but in truth they may have only a theoretical understanding of all the levels. A counselor may, for instance, be so intellectualized (formal and dialectic/systemic thinking) that he or she is unable to recognize personal feelings about a client or to suggest a concrete action that might benefit the client. To be effective, counseling and therapy training and case conferences need to present the multiperspective approach and also stress the necessity of skill at all cognitive-developmental levels, according to client needs. "Higher is not better," but *more* options for interviewing are helpful.

For example, at the sensorimotor level, it is particularly helpful to note how you feel in the here-and-now relationship to the client. What do you see? What do you hear the client saying? What general feeling does that client bring out in you? Where does that feeling occur in your body? Think of a client you have had either in your own practice or in a role-play session. Chapter 7 on treatment plans emphasizes the importance of this sensorimotor skill in discovering your own blindspots and avoiding countertransference problems. This type of exercise can be part of a supervision session, a case conference, or can be used in the immediacy of the interview to help you understand and clarify the feelings that are your own and those that are the clients'.

At the concrete level, action is ultimately as important as sophisticated formal or dialectic case conception. There are many highly trained professionals who can "talk a good story" about therapy but who simply cannot execute their ideas in practice. While change in formal thought (for example, gaining a better self-concept) is sometimes a goal in therapy, most clients need to change behavioral as well as thinking patterns.

In counselor training, therapists need to know concrete interviewing skills— how to ask open questions, reflect feelings—how to structure an effective session and treatment plan, and how to carry out strategies and interventions from different therapeutic schools.

Therapist training is often too focused at the formal, theoretical level. Learning, psychoanalytic, existential, and other theories are all important. But in addition to being able to reflect on cases and generate theoretically sound case plans, counselors must be able to enact these ideas. A particular danger for the formal-operational counselor is to rigidly apply one particular theoretical frame of reference and refuse to consider alternative perspectives.

Therapeutic theory is becoming increasingly systemic, focusing on how individuals and environments affect one another. As this approach to helping has become more prevalent, there also has been a tendency to fall into the formal-operational trap of rigidity ("Family systems thinking is the only way").

More cognitively advanced counselors and therapists are able to reflect on and examine systems and systems of systems. A particular advantage of this level of cognition is to examine one's own theoretical assumptions and the ability to challenge the assumptions of major theories of helping. Again, this theoretical relativism has many advantages, but there is also the danger of becoming so focused on theory that sensorimotor impressions and concrete action are ignored. Again, higher is not necessarily better.

Thus, DCT adopts a multiperspective frame of reference, arguing for the value of all levels of counselor perception and action. The essence of this approach to counselor and therapist understanding and meaning making (in the domain of relationship dynamics) is captured by Carey, as shown in Table 9-1.

Carey (1989b), suggests that admission to counselor training programs should involve assessment of the cognitive-developmental level of candidates. Carey extends this argument for the job screening process. It is true that case management and case planning are primarily formal-operational tasks and that a counselor unable to reflect on him- or herself also may be unable to reflect on a client's needs and wishes. Given the ideas of the DCT and network treatment approaches, there is an implicit requirement that the helper be able to function at a multiperspective, dialectic/systemic frame of reference. What is the optimum level of cognitive development for helpers? The question of what cognitive-developmental skills are desirable in helpers is difficult and complex.

Table 9-1. Counselor Capabilities in Understanding Client-Counselor Dynamics Across Cognitive-Developmental Levels

Cognitive-developmental level	Counselor capabilities	
	Perspective taking	Process orientation
Sensorimotor/elemental	Enmeshed	Action
Concrete-operational/situational	Limited perspective	Technique
Formal-operational/pattern	Third-person perspective	Principle
Postformal/transformational	Multiple perspectives	Systems of principles

SOURCE: Carey, 1988, p. 3.

While Carey's point is critical, the present position of DCT is that many entry-level and professional helpers can work effectively if they are primarily concrete in their orientation. A concrete operational professional can often be more patient, empathic, and successful than the more intellectualized, formal, and dialectic/systemic thinkers. For example, professional work with children, service in group homes for the developmentally disadvantaged, or assisting the homeless requires considerable patience as well as the ability to work with the concrete issues of daily life. Many so-called higher level thinkers simply do not have the patience for this important work. DCT holds its position that higher is not necessarily better—Which is the more important and effective helper? A concrete and practical nun working with Mother Theresa in Calcutta or an intellectualized psychoanalyst working with a Wall Street broker in New York?

In your own therapy practice, you will work with other professionals of varying cognitive-developmental levels, including your supervisors, colleagues, and beginning counselor trainees and paraprofessionals you may supervise as well as physicians, nurses, lawyers, and governmental officials. The ability to understand and work with those whose thinking processes are different from your own is an extremely valuable aid in clarifying communication and is sometimes necessary for your survival as a professional.

Life-Span Cognitive-Developmental Supervision

According to Carey (1989a, p. 1),

> A quiet revolution is occurring within the helping professions. The anthem of this revolution is "development." . . . At the heart of this revolution is a recognition that the natural foundation of the helping professions is in the science of life-span human development.

Theories and concepts of applied adult development (Rodgers, 1984; Schlossberg, 1977, 1984) are basic to counselor and therapist education and supervision and are also important in the management of human service professionals in schools, community agencies, and hospitals. Although much valuable work relating developmental concepts to supervision has been conducted (see Stoltenberg and Delworth, 1987), little work has been done on how developmental theory can be used in the immediacy of mental health supervisory processes.

Carey's life-span cognitive-developmental supervision (CDS) integrates adult developmental theory, the concepts of DCT, and other key theories of human learning and meaning making. CDS focuses on the key relationships that occur between a counselor and his or her supervisor, consultant, or peers.

As a helping professional, you will experience a lifetime of counselor education and development—the need to learn about new theories, new practices, and new clients never ends. At times you may be enmeshed and unaware that a new learning task exists. Carey's life-span CDS model provides an integrating framework for the clinical supervision and personal growth process of therapist education and development.

Life-span CDS uses a phase, level, and style framework as the basis for theory. In counselor development, there are time- and sequence-related phases in which beginners (and more experienced professionals) move from lack of knowledge to more complete understanding and competence. Levels relate to changes in knowledge systems. CDS levels are somewhat similar to the four levels of DCT but are informed by a variety of developmental theories. Style refers to the fact that different people have different learning styles. Some therapists learn best cognitively; others, through affective recognition; others, through experience.

Life-span CDS offers an organized and innovative framework for enriching relationships between counselor trainers and supervisees. It also offers a system for communication among therapist colleagues and for understanding the complex relational issues of case conferences or staff planning sessions.

This chapter focuses on the stage concepts of life-span CDS, which closely resemble, but expand, the constructs of developmental counseling and therapy. The term *level* will be used here rather than Carey's term *stage* to avoid confusion.

Life-span CDS suggests that there are three key learning domains in counselor trainee-supervisor interaction (which also apply to staff conferences, peer supervision, and agency planning): modality, target, and cognitive-developmental level. These key dimensions are summarized below (as adapted from Carey, 1989b, p 2). A supervisor or trainee statement can reflect any one of these levels or include all three.

Modality refers to the learning domain on which the supervisor's statement is focused. Statements are classified as representing one of three constructs: affect, behavior, or cognition. Affect modality statements are focused on emotions or feelings; behavior modality statement on overt observable behavior; cognition modality statements, on thoughts.

    Examples: What are you feeling? *(Affective)*
                   What are you doing? *(Behavior)*
                   What are you thinking? *(Cognitive)*

Target refers to the person or relationship on which the supervisor's statement is focused. Statements are classified as being focused on one of three targets:

client, counselor-client interaction, or counselor. Essentially, the subject of the supervisor, colleague, or peer supervisor statement indicates the target.

Examples: What is the client's problem? (client)
What were you feeling in the interview?(counselor)
What is the nature of your relationship with the client? (counselor-client interaction)

Cognitive-developmental level (CDL) refers to the level of the supervisee's understanding of the case and the client. The four levels are the sensorimotor/ elemental; concrete-operational/situational; formal-operational/pattern; and dialectic/systemic/postformal/transformational. (For examples, see the earlier section entitled "Assessing the Cognitive-Developmental Level of Helping Professionals" on page 265.)

At more advanced levels of supervision training, Carey adds a fourth dimension to the target modality—counselor-supervisor interaction—in which the focus is on how both supervisee and supervisor repeat old life patterns in the supervision session. Often, counselors repeat patterns of behavior and thought that occurred with their clients as they meet with their supervisors. And, as might be anticipated, supervisors repeat, often without their awareness, their own developmental history with their supervisees in the interview, much to the detriment of the supervision and consultation process. The recognition of these unconscious processes that occur between client and trainee and trainee and supervisor may be critical in helping counseling and therapy become more effective. Figure 9-1 provides a visual summary of the CDS framework. (The three main dimensions of the target modality are included here.)

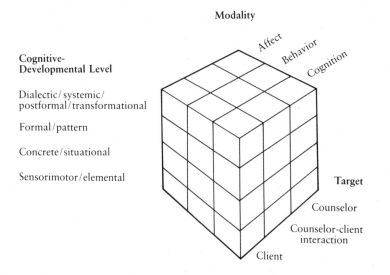

Figure 9-1. Three Dimensions of Life-Span Developmental Supervision (Carey 1989a, p. 11)

Life-span CDS emphasizes the value of using all three classifications and their subcategories in the supervisory process. Too often, supervision focuses only on theoretical conceptions of the client. For example, the bulk of a case conference may include statements such as

This client seems to be an obsessive-compulsive.

Theoretically, the problem seems to go back to early childrearing.

I disagree; there is a passive-aggressive component that needs to be considered.

The modality of all three statements is cognitive, the target is the client, and the level is formal-operational/pattern. No attention is paid to affect or behavior (or the client's thoughts, for that matter), the counselor-client interaction, or the counselor. The firm adherence to formal operations often means that case conference participants never explore the concrete behavior of the client or therapist action and fail to examine their own perspectives (dialectic/transformational), thus limiting their assessment options.

Effective supervision, counselor trainee development, and management of mental health services require supervisor flexibility and ability to work with staff at multiple levels. An intellectualizing counselor trainee needs to learn more about affect and behavior and the importance of concrete action in the interview. An over emotionalized beginning counselor may be so overwhelmed by affect and the need for concretes that calm, reflective analysis is lost. The supervisor's role is to help each type of trainee consider other aspects of the case.

Applying Life-Span Cognitive-Developmental Supervision in Your Own Work

The concepts of life-span CDS can be useful when supervising a colleague, for assessing possible counselor-client issues, and also may be adopted for family therapy supervision, group counseling supervision, and supervision of organizational consultation.

Carey provides a list of specific questions for individual supervision. Audiotaping or videotaping a session allows you to observe how you balance the several important dimensions of supervision. Carey (1989a, pp. 3–4) offers the following questions, which can be used to classify your own supervisory style and ensure that you have helped your supervisee to look at the interview from several perspectives. (These questions can be classified in multiple dimensions, but for simplicity, only one dimension is mentioned in the following examples.)

1. Modality questions: affective, behavior, and cognitive

How are you feeling right now? *(Affective)*
How are you feeling about your client? *(Affective)*
What is your client feeling? *(Affective)*

What are you doing at this point in the tape? *(Behavior)*
How did your client's nonverbal behavior change after your question? *(Behavior)*
How are the client's words and actions incongruent? *(Behavior)*

What are your goals for this client?   *(Cognitive)*
Why do you think you responded that way to your client?   *(Cognitive)*
How does the client conceptualize his/or her problem?   *(Cognitive)*

2. Target questions: counselor, counselor/client, and client

How do you feel about confrontation?   *(Counselor)*
What skills do you feel you used well?   *(Counselor)*
What thoughts run through your mind?   *(Counselor)*

Is the interpersonal distance here significant?   *(Counselor/Client)*
How do your goals differ from your client goals?   *(Counselor/Client)*
How are your mutual feelings toward one another affecting the interview?

How does the client express anger?   *(Client)*
What does this client think the problem is?   *(Client)*
What does the client rocking back in the chair at that moment mean?

3. Cognitive-developmental-level questions: sensorimotor/elemental; concrete-operational/situational; formal-operational/pattern, and dialectic/transformational

Can you describe your client's voice?
What is your client feeling when he or she uses that tone?
What are your body sensations in relation to the client?
How would you describe the nonverbal interactions?

Could you give me an example of what the client said?
What happened before? Next?
What did you do after the client appeared to be angry with you?

What interventions seem most appropriate with this client?
How do you conceptualize this client?
Do you see any pattern of repeated actions in this session?
What is the theme of the interview?

How are your mutual feelings affecting the process?
How would a Rogerian, a behaviorist, or a systems theorist describe your work?
What assumptions are you making about the client? Can you criticize those assumptions?
When you recognize this repeating pattern in yourself as a therapist, what can you do to help yourself behave differently?

Again, you do not use just one dimension at a time. For example, for the last question the modality is behavioral and the target is the therapist. Spend part of your supervision time exploring affect, behavior, and thinking. Too many supervisors target only the client and forget that the counselor and his or her feelings and behavior are equally important in the session.

You can use more than a questioning approach in the supervision process. Reflective listening skills, reframing techniques, and supervisory feedback are other ways to broaden your base of understanding. Some examples of these approaches follow:

You seem to feel anxious right now as you listen to this tape. (reflecting feeling modality, targeting the counselor at the concrete level)

Let me reframe the last few minutes. Another way to look at this client is simply to think of his problem as a reflection of a very common Irish family intergenerational pattern. (cognitive modality, targeting the client, dialectic/transformational)

You've shown a keen ability to observe nonverbal interaction between you and the client in this session. (behavioral modality, counselor and counselor-client interaction, and formal-operational/pattern)

Life-span CDS suggests that in each supervision session, you maintain some balance of modality, target, and cognitive-developmental level.

The Centrality of Emotion and Affect

No cognition without emotion, no emotion without cognition.

This statement embodies the DCT philosophy that therapy be a blend of affective and cognitive-developmental approaches. However, some theories of helping all too often relegate emotion to a role secondary to cognition. This book tries to rectify this imbalance by paying additional attention to emotional and affective development. A review of Carey's cognitive-developmental supervision reveals the key role that emotion plays not only in the interview but also in the supervision and consultation processes.

In examining yourself and your own relationships with clients, it is helpful to consider your affective development as well as your cognitive and skill development. In so doing, you need to consider the four levels of emotion in relationship to your own work.

For example, think of a client you are working with now or a role-play you have engaged in that stands out in your mind. Complete the following exercises to develop your self-awareness:

Sensorimotor. What image comes to your mind? What do you see/hear/feel? Where is that feeling located in your body?

_____

_____

_____

Concrete. Label and name the feelings you have toward that client. Can you identify a sequence of emotions? *If* that client engages in a certain type of behavior or thought pattern, *then* what do you feel?

_____

_____

_____

Formal. Do those feelings occur in your relationships with other clients? Is that a pattern? Does that pattern remind you of issues in your own life history? How might that pattern of emotion manifest itself with this particular client?

Dialectic/systemic. How did that emotion manifest in the family system while you were growing up? Is there a family rule about behavior or emotional expression that might relate to the interaction you have with a client? Are similar emotions or rules coming into play in the interview process? Given these observations, are there any flaws in the rule or anything you might want to change in your behavior in regard to this client?

These exercises in self-analysis can be used in your work as a supervisor of beginning counselors or with your colleagues. However, such self-examination requires that there be trust in the supervisor-supervisee relationship, which is not always the case. If you have developed an open, trusting relationship with a supervisor or a peer supervision group, the above questions can be rewarding and growth producing. Unfortunately, too few of us are willing to share vulnerabilities and explore how past developmental history has an impact on the here and now of the session.

There are those who argue that psychotherapy and counseling are more reflective of the counselor's developmental history than representative of exploration with the client. We all have patterns of selective listening and interpretation. Some say that what happens in therapy is the unconscious desire of the therapist.

In Chapter 6 on personality style/disorder, we discussed how DCT concepts can be used to facilitate your understanding of how your own developmental past may repeat itself in the clinician-client relationship. Similarly, the supervision process often brings out our personal history and characteristics. Supervision can be selective, and the supervisor consciously or unconsciously uses the power of supervision to enact his or her own developmental past on the supervisee. Needless to say, the supervisee may be expected to do the same thing. Breaking out of the complexity of personal history entwined in the supervision process can be a difficult, but very helpful process.

Supervisors have the same issues as their supervisees. Anyone who observes a supervision session will note that supervisors have their own agendas and goals for the supervisee. Carey (1989a) explores these supervisor issues. Research on counselor supervision too often focuses on the counselor alone. At advanced levels of supervision, the target of supervision is, in fact, the supervisee-supervisor relationship. This fourth dimension of supervision can be as valuable or more valuable than focusing on the client, the counselor, or the client-counselor relationship.

Clients bring their developmental history to the interview. Counselors bring their developmental history to their selection of theory and actions in the session. Supervisors likewise bring their own agendas and developmental history to the supervisory session. All can benefit from self-examination using ideas from the frameworks of DCT, introspective-developmental counseling, and life-span cognitive-developmental supervision. The affective dimensions of counseling and supervision may ultimately be the most valuable aspect for all participants in the process.

Chapter Summary

Educational applications of DCT show promise. You will find that it is possible to adapt all the constructs presented here for the elementary, secondary, and college classroom. Much of professional helping focuses on school-related problems, and thus DCT can be used as a base for consultation and improving classroom educational programs.

Carey's life-span cognitive-developmental supervision has been presented in this chapter. Not only can the DCT framework be used with clients, but it can also be adapted to the important relationship between a supervisor and a helper-in-training or for understanding what is going on in a case conference.

Helping professionals can be classified in much the same way DCT classifies its clients—confused or aware sensorimotor, concrete descriptive, formal pattern, and postformal/dialectic. A useful tool for discovering how helping professionals conceptualize their work is to ask, "How do you conceptualize this case?" Once you have this understanding, you can match your supervision process to the cognitive-developmental level of the client.

Carey's framework presented a cube model in which the four cognitive-developmental levels are summarized and related to *modality* (cognitive, behavior, and affect) and *target* (client, counselor-client interaction, or counselor). Carey suggests that effective supervision needs to consider all aspects of the cube. Too many supervisory and case-management sessions focus on only a few dimensions, thus missing much of what is actually occurring in the case and the supervisory process.

One's own developmental history is very likely to repeat itself in the supervision session. The supervisor may unconsciously impose a frame of reference or the supervisee may act out old patterns of authority. The life-span supervision process and the DCT questioning procedures provide a way to understand and deal with these concepts.

You will find trainees and working helping professionals who are not fully formal operational, and many more who are unable to question their own assumptions and have real difficulty in taking a multiperspective view of themselves, their cases, and the supervisory process. Carey suggests that we need to consider not admitting less complex thinkers from the admissions process in our graduate programs. The DCT position is that Carey's point should be examined carefully, but that different roles in the helping field require individuals who may be more skilled at some levels than others. Again, many concrete individuals can be far more patient and helpful than some multiperspective intellectuals. Undoubtedly this debate will continue for some time. What is your position?

Conclusion: Life-Span Counselor and Therapist Development

Whether you are just beginning or well established in your career as a helping professional, you face a lifetime of personal growth and development. New theories, new techniques and interventions, and, most of all, new clients provide a constant challenge for us to generate new ideas—to grow and develop with our clients.

DCT, introspective-developmental counseling, and life-span cognitive-developmental supervision are just the beginning of new approaches to counseling and therapy. A quiet revolution is taking place in the helping field, sparked by the realization that life-span human development is the foundation for future growth of ourselves and our clients. As the field moves beyond the previous pathological, remedial model of helping, all of us will face personal developmental tasks as we orient to this new, positive model of human development and reframe past models of helping.

Our clients come to us seeking the resolution of a problem, be it vocational choice, academic difficulty, clinical depression, or a difficult interpersonal life passage, such as leaving home, marriage, separation and divorce, retirement, or dying and death. Remediation is oriented toward a specific end—a "cure." However, there are no "cures" in counseling. Life constantly presents us with new developmental challenges—there is no endpoint to the process.

The task of counseling and therapy is not to solve problems or to effect a cure. Rather we should consider our problems as developmental opportunities for growth. There is an inevitable developmental logic to even the most serious and difficult issues clients present. For example, with the person seeking vocational direction, we want to expand career potential and improve life planning. Vocational choice must occur in a context. Successful vocational choice is a process in which the client encounters and effectively handles new problems and issues throughout his or her career. Retirement from the workplace is the only "cure" for vocational problems. Our developmental problems keep us alive.

Academic counseling often starts with helping the student "fix" the problem of choice of major or poor study habits. But this is only the beginning of the process in which the client discovers that procrastination is a behavioral pattern rooted in developmental history and that this pattern will continue in school, the workplace, and interpersonal interactions unless dealt with in the here and now. Effective academic counseling helps the client see how academic pursuits are part of life-span developmental processes.

Similarly, clinical depression and other DSM-III-R-classified "disorders" are generated from a developmental history that includes the individual's environmental and biological history and his or her development in family and social systems. Depression can be "cured" with drugs and psychotherapy, but a truly developmental approach moves beyond such a "cure" and enables the client to begin to act in the environment.

Each life problem or passage brings opportunities for development. Just as soon as an individual resolves the mid-40s crisis of meaningful existence, he or she, faces the crisis of the 50s—the decline of physical capacity. As therapists, we can focus on these crises and help our clients resolve "problems," or we can use a positive developmental focus and enable our clients to welcome change as a natural progression through the joys and challenges of life.

Some therapists feel they completed their professional developmental tasks when they completed their degree work. But after the degree, there is the state licensing examination. And after that exam, there is a bewildering array of "super-certification" programs in hypnosis, family therapy, professional psychology, social work, and medicine. Although each certification step, from degree to supercertification program, involves more work and study, it is also true that each stage provides you with the opportunity to hone your own developmental skills and thus to better serve your clients.

Counselor and therapist burnout are likely to occur when the work setting provides little or no opportunity for growth and development. Case conferences and staff meetings that strive to maintain the status quo and leave key decisions only to senior staff members lead to burned-out professionals who wish to leave the helping profession. We need more work settings in which supervisors and experienced professionals are open to development, willing to make and admit mistakes, and able to incorporate the energy and excitement of young new staff members.

The focus of a developmentally oriented helping profession is on change and growth—the exploration of the New. However, the rigid perspectives of the past inevitably reassert themselves: what was once New often becomes the old orthodoxy. Thus, the new models of DCT, introspective-developmental counseling, and life-span cognitive-developmental supervision must themselves be reevaluated and adapted as new information becomes available. In the process of constant evaluation, change and reevaluation, what is good and helpful from the past will remain as part of an everchanging, holistic approach to helping.

 CAUTION! A life-span developmentally oriented approach to helping is promising, but also poses some difficulties. Although it is desirable that the counselor function in all dimensions, some very effective helpers may not be able to do so. A concrete counselor may have difficulty with more abstract clients, or a competent theoretician may have difficulty when examining sensorimotor or concrete levels.

Such issues pose a developmental challenge to counselors and educators and to those supervising and working with colleagues of varying competencies. Although no specific suggestions are offered to address these difficulties, it is important that each of us entering the helping profession be aware of our personal strengths and limitations. Supervision and consultation with colleagues is especially important if we are to facilitate client growth and our own development as mature professionals.

Theory into Practice

This set of exercises has two objectives: to provide closure for this book and to introduce new developmental questions for the future. By the end of this concluding section, you may be able to

1. Identify and classify the modality, target, and cognitive-developmental level of written supervision statements.

2. Use DCT constructs in evaluating of yourself as a helper, the supervisory process, and case conferences.

Identifying and Classifying Modality, Target, and Cognitive-Developmental Level of Supervisors' Statements

Carey (1989b, pp. 1–2) provides the following exercise for classifying supervisors' statements:

Listed below are a series of supervisor questions and statements. Classify each statement on all three dimensions of modality, target, and cognitive-developmental level.

Modality	*Target*	*Cognitive-developmental level*
A = affect	Cl = client	SM = sensorimotor/elemental
B = behavior	I = client-therapist	CO = concrete-operational/situational
C = cognition	T = therapist	FO = formal-operational/pattern
		D/S = dialectic/systemic/transformational

Examples:

a. Do you remember where in your body you felt that?

A, T, SM. The statement focuses on the *feelings* of the *counselor* at an *elemental* level.

b. Did the client remind you of anyone else in your life?

C, T, FO. The statement focuses on *cognitive* analysis of the counselor in an attempt to detect a *formal-operational pattern*.

c. Does your client understand how his symptoms help maintain the status quo in the family system?

C, Cl, D/S. The statement focuses on the cognitive understanding of the client at a level requiring *dialectic/systemic* analysis.

d. What happened after you confronted the client?

B, I, CO. The statement focuses on *behavior* related to the *counselor-client interaction* and probes for a *concrete-operational* temporal sequence.

Quiz

All of the following are individual supervisory questions. A later segment focuses on writing responses for family supervision. (Some of the following questions are adapted from Kagan's Interpersonal Process Recall, 1980, and are used with his permission.)

_____ 1. Can you describe the climate of your relationship with the client?

_____ 2. What did you do?

_____ 3. Did you have any images?

_____ 4. Can you describe the nonverbal interaction between you and the client?

_____ 5. What basic beliefs do you seem to share with your client?

_____ 6. What is your client feeling here?

_____ 7. What is your client doing right now on the videotape?

_____ 8. What might your client be saying to herself here?

_____ 9. What did you feel after that happened?

_____ 10. What did you do next?

_____ 11. What thoughts followed that event?

_____ 12. How did you feel after your client said that?

_____ 13. What did the client do after you confronted her?

_____ 14. What did you expect from each other at the time?

_____ 15. How did the client feel after that?

_____ 16. What did your client say to his wife?

_____ 17. What did she say to herself after the incident?

_____ 18. Is this feeling you're having in this interview similar to the feelings you have had at other times in your life?

_____ 19. What would happen if you confronted her rather than using immediacy?

_____ 20. How do you conceptualize the problem in terms of your personal theory?

_____ 21. Why is your relationship so tense?

_____ 22. How would your client react if you stopped imposing so much structure?

_____ 23. How are your goals similar to and different from your client's?

_____24. Does your client identify any commonalities among people who make him angry?

_____25. How does the client typically repeat herself, which causes her trouble?

_____26. What are the client's dominant irrational beliefs?

_____27. When you feel your anxiety building in sessions, what can you do differently?

_____28. If you had it to do over, what would you do differently?

_____29. What was your role in determining the goals for counseling?

_____30. How are your feelings about each other affecting the counseling process?

_____31. What are you doing that helps prevent your client from changing?

_____32. How is your conceptualization of the problem limiting the client's growth?

_____33. How does client's anger help to maintain the marital relationship?

_____34. Can your client recognize the value of his nonassertive behavior?

_____35. What can your client learn from these conflicting aspects of his self-concept?

Suggested Responses

1. A, I, SM	13. B, I, CO	25. B, Cl, FO
2. B, I, SM	14. C, I, CO	26. C, Cl, FO
3. C, T, SM	15. A, Cl, CO	27. A, T, D/S
4. B, I, SM	16. B, Cl, CO	28. B, I, D/S
5. C, I, SM	17. C, Cl, CO	29. C, T, D/S
6. A, Cl, SM	18. A, CO, FO	30. A, I, D/S
7. B, Cl, SM	19. B, T, FO	31. B, I, D/S
8. C, Cl, SM	20. C, T, FO	32. C, I, D/S
9. A, T, CO	21. A, I, FO	33. A, Cl, D/S
10. B, T, CO	22. B, I, FO	34. B, Cl, D/S
11. C, T, CO	23. C, I, FO	35. C, Cl, D/S
12. A, I, CO	24. A, Cl, FO	

Writing Response Interventions for Supervisees Working with Families

The following supervisee has been working with a family for two sessions. The supervisor asked the formal-operational question "How do you conceptualize and make sense of this family?" The supervisee responded as follows:

Well, the mother seems to have a pattern of keeping the stepfather away from the children. When he steps in and makes a comment, she tends to invalidate his contribution, particularly if he tries to discipline them. The children, in turn, tend to taunt the stepfather as if to tempt him to intervene. He seems kind of helpless to me, and I wonder if he isn't enacting his own family developmental history with the family.

Using the life-span cognitive-developmental supervision framework, how is this supervisee talking about the family? Categorize the supervisee's statement before reading further.

This supervisee is clearly operating at the formal-operational/pattern level. The modality is cognitive, and the target is the client, specifically the family.

Using this information, write down on a separate piece of paper those interventions that will help this supervisee view the case from other frames of reference, perhaps even from a multiperspective view. (Some possible responses may be found at the conclusion of this chapter.)

1. What could you say that might enable the supervisee to talk about the family in an affective modality in a concrete way?

_____

_____

2. What intervention might you employ to enable the supervisee to target him- or herself for consideration in an affective way at the sensorimotor level?

_____

_____

3. What might you say or do to enable the supervisee to look at behavioral interaction between self and family at the concrete-operational level?

_____

_____

4. How might you encourage the supervisee to examine cognition and counselor-client interaction at the dialectic/systemic level?

_____

_____

Using DCT Constructs to Evaluate Yourself as a Helper, the Supervisory Process, and Case Conferences

Self-supervision is an alternative you can use in the interview when you do not have a supervisor to help you explore your thoughts and feelings about clients. Self-supervision is actually the most common type of supervision. Although the critical importance of formal supervision and case conferences cannot be denied, most of your work in counseling and therapy will be done alone.

The cases that predominate in supervision and case conferences are not always the ones for which supervision is most needed. Sometimes a case that is "going well" or "isn't worth talking about" is exactly the one that should be explored. Cases we know we have difficulty with force us to be somewhat objective. Those cases we think are going well may suggest more an embedded personality style of our own and may be more in need of supervision than the cases we choose to discuss with our supervisors or present at case conference sessions.

The following exploration follows the processes of DCT and life-span cognitive-developmental supervision models. The target of the examination is primarily yourself and your interaction with key clients.

1. Think of your typical case. Then think of a specific incident or set of incidents that occurs to you. Record them here.

_____

_____

Although most individuals will recall a specific case, some may describe a pattern of cases. For example, one individual working in a vocational counseling center recalled the boredom he felt about the constant repetition of cases. Rather than focusing on a specific case, he instead thought of his cases as a general blur to the extent that many clients' names escaped him (a sure sign of burnout).

In the here and now of the interview, take time periodically to note events that seem to represent much of what is going on between you and the client. These representative interactions may later give you new ideas to improve your work.

2. Give an example of how you work with your typical case. What are you doing? What goes well? What goes less well? Be as specific as you can. Can you name the feelings you have as you work with these typical cases?

_____

_____

_____

_____

In response to this question, for example, a college counselor talked about a typical middle-class client who wasn't interested in college but simply wanted to get by. The counselor's approach was a two-session series of vocational counseling, including data gathering, testing, and then a follow-up interview to discuss test results. The counselor's predominant feeling was boredom coupled with a more subtle feeling of being trapped.

During the interview, it is important to be aware of your feelings and behavior and simultaneously observe how your client is responding. It is easy to fall into routine interviewing habits and to fail to see the unique person before us.

3. Given that this is your typical case, what patterns do you observe that you

repeat again and again? What are these patterns doing for you and the client?

_____

_____

_____

_____

The college counselor discussed in question 2 felt he had already identified a pattern in his concrete work. His immediate association to question 3 was that his counseling work allowed him to continue to do "more of the same," to "go along with the flow" rather than being serious about his work. He had begun counseling with enthusiasm but over time had allowed himself to become stuck and bored.

In the here and now of the interview, note repeating patterns, particularly those that repeat from client to client. Is there something in you that brings about this consistency of behavior?

_____

_____

_____

There are helpers whose clients only talk about sex, whereas other helpers' clients never talk about sex. Is the difference in the counselors or in their clients? How are you affecting how your clients talk to you in the session?

_____

_____

_____

4. What stands out for you from this exercise? What can you do about it?

_____

_____

_____

_____

"Don't do more of the same" is the aim of this brief exercise. Look for your strengths but be aware of how, through habit, your original strengths can turn into weaknesses over time. When the above-mentioned college counselor initially developed his two-interview program, he was involved and excited; over time, what once worked well became repetitive and dull.

We all need to create the New in our helping intervention programs. While we may be very effective behavioral or Rogerian counselors, over time we may lose that effectiveness. At this stage, it can be beneficial to consider family systems theory or psychodynamic formulations. We do not have to give up our behavioral or client-centered orientations; rather, we can enter into a systemic form of training to enrich our basic skills. Contact with new ideas inevitably revitalizes our interest and allows us to develop old ideas in new ways.

What are some specific interventions, training programs, workshops, new programs, and new theories you might want to study and work on over time? Again, your creation of the New will help you enable clients to create something new and richer in their lives.

_____

_____

_____

_____

As a final step in this exercise, you may want to generate a long-term developmental plan for yourself that includes improvement of your skills at the four levels of DCT with the theories related to each of the levels described in Chapter 3.

Generalization: Taking Life-Span Cognitive-Developmental Supervision Home

The concepts of developmental counseling and therapy have been presented in some detail in this book. Many books offer valuable concepts, but unless we incorporate some specifics from these books into our daily lives and interviewing practices, our time spent acquiring the concepts—whether by reading a book, taking a course, or participating in a workshop—is wasted. Following are some final suggestions for using the concepts of this chapter to find new levels of understanding.

Activity 1: Observe Developmental Supervision in the Practicum, Supervisory Sessions, and Case Conferences

As a first step in taking home the ideas of this chapter, observe your practicum or work setting, particularly during a case conference. Note the degree of emphasis on cognition, affect, and behavior as a case is discussed. Is the target of study always the client, or are conferees able to examine the counselor and the counselor-client interaction as well? At what cognitive-developmental level is the language used in these discussions?

_____

_____

_____

_____

Activity 2: Generate Questions and Test Your Developmental Supervision Skills in the Practicum, Peer Consultation Sessions, and Case Conferences

Using as examples the questions provided throughout this chapter, generate a specific list of questions and interventions you might use to help yourself and supervisees understand their cases more fully. Develop a list of specific interventions oriented toward different cognitive-developmental levels, modalities, and targets. Videotape or audiotape your supervisory sessions and obtain feedback from peers and your supervisee.

As you become more confident in applying developmental supervision concepts, add the fourth category of target—supervisee-supervisor interaction. With experience and practice, you will find that your supervisees tend to repeat many of the behaviors you observed in their client sessions with you in the supervision session. But don't stop there. Have others supervise your supervision style. Is your own developmental history stimulating certain types of behaviors and feelings in your supervisees?

_____

_____

_____

Activity 3: Consider the Yakima Nation Proverbs

This Yakima statement and three key proverbs were selected as the final activity and statement of this book.

Our Indian people receive a great deal of teaching from Nature, which surrounds us all. We learn from the tiniest insect and from the largest animal, from the rivers and the forests. We receive teaching from the sky and the changes of the wind. To our people, all of Nature has strong meaning.

The elders pass on the wisdom of Nature to the young. In Legends, in the recounting of personal experiences, and from the events in one's own life, the wisdom embodied in Nature and its creatures is brought home to us.

The Oak Tree endures the elements and grows slowly.

The lesson is—great age comes to those who have adjusted to their natural surroundings.

The Smooth Surface of the water does not itself reveal the depths.

The lesson is—see the problem from more than one point of view.

The Chipmunk looks us over and has an opinion about what he sees.

The lesson is—all nature is full of spirit.

What have these and other Yakima proverbs meant to you and for your developmental process of counseling and therapy? Reflecting on them in totality, what stands out for you? How might you integrate the ideas of one or more in your own life and practice?

_____

_____

_____

_____

_____

_____

_____

Suggested Supplemental Reading and Activities

Additional Reading

Ivey, A. 1986. *Developmental therapy: Theory into practice.* San Francisco: Jossey-Bass. Chapter 8, "Development over the Life Span," provides a background for this final chapter. Particularly important is the material on unconscious mental development (pages 322–341). Although the word *unconscious* has been deliberately avoided in this book, many of the developmental constructs and ideas concerning developmental history relate to the idea of behavior that is beyond our immediate conscious awareness. Examination and study in this complex area would be valuable in following up the presentation of DCT here. The exercises at the conclusion of Chapter 8 may be especially useful in extending the concepts of this book and addressing personal implications and philosophy of development.

The Epilogue of *Developmental Therapy* includes Plato's Allegory of the Cave, with a commentary. The Allegory of the Cave is described as a metaphor for development—an exploration without end.

Schlossberg, N. 1984. *Counseling adults in transition.* New York: Springer.
Supervision has been described as a form of adult development. This book provides an excellent overview of an important new area of theoretical understanding.

Kagan, N. 1980. *Interpersonal process recall: A method of influencing human interaction.* Houston, Tex.: Mason Media.
This book presents a set of videotaped training materials and typescripts that are highly effective in the supervision process. These materials can help counselors and therapists examine themselves and their interactions with clients.

Kell, W., and W. Mueller. 1966. *Impact and change.* East Norwalk, Conn.: Appleton-Century-Crofts.
One of the classics of the field of supervision, this book uses a psychodynamic interpersonally oriented model of supervision that is highly compatible with the self-oriented interactional modes of supervision stressed in this chapter.

Stoltenberg, C., and U. Delworth. 1987. *Supervising counselors and therapists.* San Francisco: Jossey-Bass.

This is one of the first books to present a developmental orientation to counselor and therapist supervision. Included in the book are a comprehensive developmental model of clinical supervision and the definitive history of developmental models in the field.

Liddle, H., D. Breunlin, and R. Schnartz, eds. 1988. *Handbook of family therapy training and supervision.* New York: Guilford.

Family therapy training and supervision are examined here in six divisions: overview, models of family therapy training, pragmatics of supervision, contexts for training, special issues (cultural, research), and the future of family therapy.

Research Suggestions

Virtually all the research suggestions of the preceding chapters could be used to examine the supervision process in counselor and therapist training and education. A beginning research exercise would be to audiotape or videotape one of your own supervision sessions in which you are either supervisee or supervisor. Classify your responses according to the three dimensions suggested by Carey. Then have a colleague rate your classifications independently to check interrater reliability. Note the proportion of supervision time spent in each category. Then, in your next supervision session, see if the proportion of time spent on various aspects of the model can be changed deliberately so that all dimensions of modality, target, and cognitive-developmental level are covered.

Some other interesting questions to pursue include:

Do male and female supervisors (and supervisees) differ in their emphasis on different areas of the developmental model? Do less experienced supervisors stress different dimensions than those who are more experienced?

Do different theoretical orientations have varying balances of emphasis? (For example, one might anticipate psychodynamically oriented supervisors to pay more attention to formal operations, affect, and interaction, whereas behaviorally oriented supervisors might emphasize behavior, concrete dimensions, and the client.)

Do supervisors, over time, learn to include more dimensions?

Does the developmental supervision process affect the supervisee when he or she returns to the interview? (For example, one might anticipate that a behaviorally oriented supervisor might place more emphasis on behavior in the interview, and thus the supervisee over time becomes more behavioral.)

Answers to Chapter Exercise

1. SM	5. C
2. C	6. SM
3. F	7. D/S
4. D/S	8. F

Responses to Written Statements on Family Therapy Interventions (p. 281)

1. Could you give me an example of how this family expresses emotion?

2. As I watched you through the one-way mirror, I got the sense that you were angry at times in the session, particularly when the mother disagreed with you. Would you allow yourself to go back to that moment and reexperience those feelings?

3. The interaction between you and the other members seemed important in this session. Can you think back and give me a specific example of an interaction sequence between you and the others that stands out for you? What were you doing? Then what did they do?

4. There seems to be a repeating type of interaction between you and the family that I've seen you develop with other families as well. You've had conflicts several times with strong mothers and have identified fathers as weak. How do you react to this? Does it make any sense to you?

Appendix 1

The Standard Cognitive-Developmental Interview

Allen E. Ivey, Sandra A. Rigazio-DiGilio, and Mary Bradford Ivey

General Guidelines

In order to ensure standardization, the interviewer must adhere to the format (for example, sequence and content of questions) below. However, adaptations of this formal structure have proven useful with a wide variety of children, clients, and patients. Our clinical experience is that going through the systematic 1 to 2 hour framework is therapeutic in itself. This is because clients learn new ways to think about themselves and their issues and therefore see more alternatives for change. Use this session as a basis for exploration.

While the interview here is highly structured, the concepts could form the basis of a series of interviews or be integrated as part of the assessment or treatment of clients experiencing differing types of problems. We have found that the questions can be adapted successfully to family counseling.

The interview here attempts to focus on client cognitions, with the interviewer providing stimuli that move the client to different levels. The only techniques in the standard interview that can be used at the discretion of the interviewer are those drawn from the specific questions outlined below or from Ivey's Basic Listening Sequence (Ivey, 1971, 1988). These techniques include attending, encouraging, paraphrasing, reflecting feelings and meanings, and summarizing, and the intent of these techniques is to elicit further data and ensure clarity while minimally affecting the content of client conceptualizations. The way in which the client thinks about these conceptualizations often changes during the interview.

We have found it helpful to have the standard interview on the desk or held in the lap so that the interviewer can feel free to refer to the questions from time to time for new ideas or to recall the sequence and goals of a questioning level. Each segment of the interview has specific aims, which are summarized first in the goals of each segment and then identified specifically in terms of criteria for fulfillment of each cognitive-developmental level. With concrete clients, it is helpful to have them repeat several specific examples, which can assist them first to learn late concrete causal issues in their lives and then to identify patterns. Formal-operational clients may move so rapidly that you may need to slow them down so that they really experience their issues at the sensorimotor and concrete levels. When this is done successfully, it can help the client move from an illogical (partial) formal response to a more comprehensive and accurate response.

Do not continue to the next level of the interview until the client is able to meet the specific criteria of the previous level. With some clients, the recommended specific questions below will be most effective, and stage criteria can be easily met. With others, you will find it necessary to improvise new questions suitable for that particular client.

Again, when using this interview or its adaptations for the first few times, it is important to have the set of questions on your desk or on your lap. If this is not a research situation, you may wish to share the questions with some clients. Our experience is that if clients know what type of focus you are looking for, they participate with interest and enthusiasm. The sharing of goals can be beneficial to the process, the interviewer, and the client.

The initial question selected for the Standard Cognitive-Developmental Interview is one that allows the client to focus both on self and family. It is possible to focus solely on the individual, a specific topic, or the family. However, the dual focus of this question was preferred, since it seems to help clients in one-on-one counseling and therapy learn how their issues arise in a family context. We find that questions of this type—those integrating both individual and family content—tend to be particularly effective in helping clients look at themselves in new ways. Armed with new insights, clients are often more interested in and prepared for concrete behavioral change.

Introduction to Client

Interview Goal

To join the client and ensure comfort and cooperation.

Interviewer Task

To clarify parameters of interview and to begin the interview.

Interviewer Statements

The standard interview may be used for clinical research purposes. When used for research, the specific guidelines are adhered to rigorously. When used as a therapeutic or counseling process, the interview can be more flexible and adapted to the special needs of the client or family. We find that the standard interview may be extended over more than one session with profit.

When using the interview for research purposes say:

This interview will take approximately 45 to 90 minutes to complete. Although I will be audiotaping it, this interview will be typed out and all names deleted before anyone from the research team reviews it; therefore, confidentiality is ensured.

Opening Presentation of Family Issue

Interview Goals

To obtain a broad picture of a family issue and the key facts and feelings, as organized by the client, with minimal interference from the interviewer.

To assess the predominant cognitive-developmental level used by each client.

Interviewer Tasks

To obtain three to five sentences, or approximately 50 to 100 words, in response to the interviewer statement below.

To listen for the client's presentation of a family issue and to use this as the foundation for the next phase.

Interviewer Statements

To begin with, I would like you to respond to a statement that I hope will stimulate you in some way. I would like you to say as much as you can about what happens for you when you focus on your family.

When the client has provided from 50 to 100 words, summarize what has been said to ensure clarity.

Early Sensorimotor/Elemental Issues (Key Words: See, Hear, Feel)

Interview Goals

To obtain an understanding of how the client organizes her or his visual, auditory, and kinesthetic representations of a family issue.

To ensure the client knows you understand.

Interviewer Tasks

After making the *introductory statement* below, to use at least one question from each *sensory category* below to facilitate the client's punctuation of her/ or his sensory reality of the chosen issue, *accepting the client's randomness of presentation.*

To *not* move the client beyond the specific elements as these elements are remembered.

To focus on the client's self-perceptual frame of reference.

To aim for *here-and-now experiencing*, not understanding or interpreting.

Level Criterion

The client should talk about the situation, self, or issue in a relatively random way that concretizes the problem. The interviewer may receive fragments and pieces of sensory-based data as the client talks about what is seen, heard, and felt. Locating feelings in the body specifically is an important criterion.

Interviewer Statements

Introductory Statements

You mentioned (family issue presented). During this interview, I'm going to ask you some questions about this, and I would like you to respond as best as you can. It will be important for you to try to directly respond to the questions I ask you. To begin with, I would like you to find one visual image that occurs for you when you focus on (family issue).

Sensory Statements

(Change *are* statements to *do/did* statements if *are* seems too powerful.)

1. Visual perceptions
   a. *What are you seeing?*
   b. *Describe in detail the scene where it happened.*
2. Auditory perceptions
   a. *What are you hearing?*
   b. *How are people sounding?*
   c. *Describe the sounds in detail.*
3. Kinesthetic perceptions
   a. *What are you feeling in your body at this moment?*
   b. *How are you feeling?*
   c. *What are you feeling as this is going on?*

Summarization Statements

Summarize key perceptions of the client's, using her/or his important words and phrases.

Late Sensorimotor/Elemental Issues (Key Word: Belief)

Interview Goal

To obtain an understanding of how the client makes sense of the elemental issues: her or his interpretation of the elemental data discussed or the frame of reference that she or he brings to the interview.

Interviewer Tasks

To encourage client to discuss her or his interpretation of the example by asking any of the *interpretation questions* below.
To discourage any further experiencing statements or any discussion of facts.
To not challenge client's interpretation.
Look for irrationality in meaning making.

Level Criterion

Client should provide a frame of reference or view of reality that, to her or him, makes meaning and sense out of the sensory-based data. At this stage, the interpretation may be incomplete or irrational. In addition, it may be quite sophisticated in some cases.

Interviewer Statements

Paraphrase client's statements if necessary.

Restate key words and phrases to assist client to access her or his unique construction of the example.

Interpretation Questions

1. *How do you make sense of all of this?*
2. *What do you think about all of this?*
3. *How do you explain all of this?*
4. *How do you put all of this together?*
5. *What meaning does all of this have for you?*
6. *What one thing stands out for you from all of this?*

Summarize client's response to ensure clarity.

Early Concrete-Operational/Situational Issues (Key Word: Do)

Interview Goal

To obtain concrete and specific facts pertaining to the client's issue. (The major emphasis is on description and facts, with a limited emphasis on feelings and with no emphasis on evaluation or analysis.)

Interviewer Tasks

After obtaining a good idea of how the client experiences and interprets the situation, to summarize and assist her/or him to discuss the *concrete details of the situation in linear, sequential form,* with major emphasis on facts.

To assist the client by using any or all of the *behavioral tracking questions* listed below.

To encourage discussion of specific things that happened in as concrete a form as possible.

To discourage any further interpretation or subjective/evaluative verbalizations.

Level Criterion

The client should describe events in a linear, relatively organized sequence, with a few basic feelings. It may be that the client offers a single perspective on the problem at this stage.

Interviewer Statements

Introductory Statements

I think I have an idea about how you think and feel about . . . (family issue— paraphrase or summarize data from previous two segments). *It would now be helpful for me to get an idea of an example where these images, thoughts, and feelings occur for you. Tell me all the facts.* (In some clinical situations— nonresearch situations—it may be preferable to ask for a new example.)

Behavioral Tracking Questions

1. *Can you tell me specifically what happened?* (Use if an example has already been presented.)
2. *Could you give me a specific example?* (Use if an example has not been presented.)

The following three questions may need to be recycled frequently to get very specific details. With very concrete clients, the repetition of the same situation several times plus repetitions of parallel situations is essential if you wish to help them examine the cause-and-effect thinking of late concrete operations or discover repeating patterns underlying the concrete events at an early formal level. Unless a careful concrete foundation is built, later, more abstract thinking becomes difficult. Furthermore, very abstract, dialectic/systemic and formal clients may benefit from this careful detailing of concrete events. They often find, after this type of review, that their abstractions and interpretations of concrete events were more limited than they thought.

3. *What did you say (do) then?*
4. *And then what happened?*
5. *What did the other person say (do)?*
6. *Could you give me another specific example?*

This last question is not really early concrete, but it helps some individuals begin to see similarities. It is a question that seems to help integration over the long term.

Late Concrete-Operational/Situational Issues (Key Words: If/Then)

Interview Goals

To arrive at a mutually satisfactory system explaining the situation under discussion, usually with an if/then dimension that may lead to issues of causation.

To draw out what happens before and after the occurrence of the example or situation provided by the client.

Interviewer Tasks

To search for *antecedent and consequent* conditions while still discouraging interpretation. (The emphasis remains on description, not on evaluation or analysis. The questions below are meant to assist the client to review what happened before and after the situation.)

Level Criterion

The client may be able to organize previous segments into linear if/then statements, may be able to control and describe action, and may be able to think in terms of antecedents and consequences. Logic and reversibility may be evident, and the client may be able to think about actions and the impact of actions.

Interviewer Statements

Antecedent/Consequent Questions

1. *What happened just before all this occurred?*
2. *What happened afterward?*
3. *What was the result?*
4. *So if you do _____, then what happens?*
5. *Given all the facts as you describe them* (paraphrase or summarize previous statements), *what do you think causes or triggers what?*
6. *Could you give me another example?* (Note that this is a developmental building block that may help clients begin to see repeating patterns.)

Early Formal-Operational/Pattern Issues (Key Words: Pattern, Self)

Interview Goals

To move from description to examination and/or analysis of the facts of the situation and/or of the self.

To facilitate the client's identification and examination of repetitive behavior, thoughts, and affect related to situations perceived to be similar to the primary example and related self.

Interviewer Task

To move the client away from sensory experiences and toward *abstract thinking* by asking some of the questions below until the client demonstrates an ability to *identify and think about repeating patterns of behaviors, thoughts, and affect* that occur in situations similar to the primary example.

Level Criterion

The client will be able to offer an isomorphic situation(s) in which the same sensorimotor elements and concrete-operational issues occur. The client will be able to analyze both situation and self in this isomorphic example.

Interviewer Statements

Paraphrase and summarize the linear, sequential format described previously using the client's main constructs, key words, and phrases.

Move toward an examination of the situation by asking some of the questions below until the client provides an isomorphic example.

1. *Are there other situations that you find yourself in when you are with your family, where this same set of events and feelings occur for you?*
2. *Does this kind of thing happen a lot for you in your family?*
3. *Does this kind of thing happen a lot?*
4. *Could you give me another specific example?*

Again, this last question seems to help those who find difficulty in seeing patterns. The objective of the interviewer is to move back to very concrete situations, examine two, three, or four concrete situations in detail, and then work on the cause and effect of late concrete operations. Even very concrete clients, including children, are often able to see repeating patterns.

Move toward an examination of self by asking some of the questions below until the client shows an ability to interpret her or his repeating patterns of behavior, thought, and affect.

1. *What are you saying to yourself when that happens?*
2. *How do you think about (see) yourself in that family situation?*
3. *Have you felt (thought, acted) that way in other family situations?*
4. *You seem to have a tendency to repeat that particular behavior (thought, interpretation). For example (paraphrase).*
   a. *What do you think about this tendency of yours?*
   b. *What does this pattern of behavior (thought) mean to you?*
   c. *What function does this pattern of behavior (thought) serve for you?*

Late Formal-Operational/Pattern Issues (Key Words: Patterns of Patterns)

Interview Goals

To assist the client to identify and examine larger, consistently repeating patterns in her or his life.

To analyze these patterns from the vantage point of the self and the contextual fields within which the client interacts.

Interviewer Task

To assist the client to identify and examine similar situations and repetitive patterns of thoughts, behaviors, and actions in the self and in others from *a multitude of perspectives that account for similarities and differences.* This will be accomplished by asking some of the questions below until the client demonstrates an ability to recognize similarities, differences, and complexities.

Level Criterion

At this stage, the client may be able to examine patterns of patterns. Situationally, she or he will be able to compare and contrast different situations and coordinate this into a gestalt, and will manifest a beginning ability to gain multiple perspectives and a fundamental unity for situations. In relation to the self, the client will be able to examine patterns in the self and be able to recognize mixed and complex feelings.

Interviewer Statements

1. *You have just shared with me two or more ways where you (and others) behave (think, feel) the same way (paraphrase or summarize). You have also shared with me what you think this all means for (about) you (paraphrase or summarize).*
   a. *Do you see any way these patterns are connected?*
   b. *Putting the two issues together, how would you synthesize them?*

2. *I see the pattern of behavior and thought that you had (that can occur) with* _____ *and the pattern of behavior and thought that you had (that can occur) with* _____.
   a. *How do you think these patterns relate?*
   b. *Do these examples speak to even a larger pattern?*
   c. *What is the feeling you have connected with these examples?*
   d. *What do you think these examples speak to?*
   e. *What is similar about them?*
   f. *How do you think your way of reacting in each situation is similar?*

Dialectic/Systemic/Integrative Issues (Key Words: Integrate, Put Together)

Interview Goals

To assist the client in moving to an awareness that personal constructions of reality are co-generated via a network of relationships. (This section of the interview is limited mainly to the network of family relationships.)

To obtain a basic organizational summary of how the client integrates what has been shared.

To assist the client to perceive this integration from several perspectives.

Interviewer Task

To ask questions from the list below that assist the client to see the *impact of this network of relationships* and to *integrate the knowledge* that has been shared throughout the first half of the interview.

Level Criterion

The client should be able to generate an integrative picture of what has been shared and view this from several perspectives, some which encompass the idea of reality as co-constructed.

Interviewer Statements

Summarize information gained at the early and late formal levels and follow with a question related to (1) integration and (2) co-construction.

1. Integration
   a. *Given what you have said about your family, yourself, and your situation* (summarize using key words and phrases), *how might you make sense of all these ideas as a whole?*
   b. *What meaning do you get here?*
   c. *What stands out for you from this session?*
   d. *How would you synthesize this experience?*

2. Co-construction
   a. *It seems we have been able to determine a pattern of thinking, feeling, and behaving that repeats itself for you when you are with your family. How do you think this pattern developed in your family—either in your family*

of origin, previous family environments, or your current living arrangement?

b. *Are there other situations in your family that also contribute to the way you think and behave?*

c. *What other situations help to form the way you think and behave?*

d. *How did people learn these ways of thinking and acting in your family?*

e. *What rule are you operating under?*

f. *How do you suppose this way of thinking and acting came about for you?*

g. *How do you suppose this way of thinking or acting came about in your family?*

Dialectic/Systemic/Deconstruction/Transformational Issues[1] (Key Words: Challenge the Integration, Action)

Interview Goals

To assist the client to develop an awareness that all assumptions and rules can be challenged and found to have flaws and/or that there are a multitude of vantage points from which to perceive any assumption or rule.

To challenge the client's perceptions.

To assist the client to move toward action based on the development of alternative perspectives.

Interviewer Tasks

To assist the client to view her or his integration from several vantage points.

To discover and challenge the parameters and flaws of the client's view. (This can be done by asking a few questions from the first set of *challenging statements.*)

To assist the client to rethink her or his integration and to discover new and alternative perspectives. (This can be done by asking a few questions from the set of *alternative statements.*)

To assist the client to move toward action based on her or his situational, self, or belief system examination. This can be done by asking a few questions from the set of *action statements.*)

Level Criterion

The client will be able to criticize and challenge her or his own integrated system and discover alternative perspectives. The client will be able to move toward action based on these alternative perspectives.

---

[1] The concept of deconstruction has not been emphasized in this book. It is seen as a late postformal or dialectic/systemic form of reasoning. In essence, the concept points out that virtually all patterns of reasoning and logic have internal flaws. Deconstruction is the act of identifying flaws in constructions or verbal representations of the world, thus the word *deconstruction.* For elaboration of these concepts, see Ivey (1986, pp. 110–111, 146, 326–330, 345–346.)

Interviewer Statement

Introductory Statement

Paraphrase or summarize knowledge obtained from the previous segment.

We've seen that your original example (paraphrase and summarize) *is a typical pattern and that this pattern and your thoughts about it have developed for you within your family of origin (previous family, current family) into rules of behavior and thoughts.*

Challenging Statements

1. *I wonder if it is possible to identify any flaws in these rules—any ways that these rules for thinking and acting are not valid or reasonable? Or, how do you not get you what you need?*
2. *Can you see any flaws in what everyone has learned?*
3. *Can you see some flaws in your reasoning in the statements above? If you were to criticize your integration, what might the major issue be?*

Alternative Statements

1. *Are there other ways to look at these rules you have learned or these situations?*
2. *If you could add to or change these rules, how would you do so?*
3. *What could another point of view be on this?*
4. *How might another family member describe your situation?*

Action Statements

1. *When you are feeling that way, do you (could you) do anything about it?*
2. *Given the complexity of all these possibilities, what commitment might you follow despite all this?*
3. *Will you do anything about it?*
4. *What action will you take based on this new awareness?*
5. *What one thing stands out for you, and what will you do about it?*

Summary Statement for Interview

I hope this way of discussing you and your family offered some new thoughts for you. I appreciate your willingness to participate. Now that the interview is over, do you have any questions you might want to ask me about our session?

The Standard Cognitive-Developmental Classification System

Allen E. Ivey and Sandra A. Rigazio-DiGilio

General Guidelines

This classification system is designed to rate the Standard Cognitive-Developmental Interview. Scorers will independently classify the predominant cognitive-developmental level as revealed by the client's verbal behavior during different sections of the interview using the criteria that follow. Although most clients will operate at different levels at different times, or at multiple levels, the classification should be according to the level that predominates.

In addition, the criteria suggested here may be adapted and used to classify an interview portion or a client or counselor statement. Generally, using larger segments of verbal behavior to make a classification is most effective, but it is possible to use single client statements with some degree of reliability. It is also possible to use adaptations of these criteria to classify the verbal behavior of the interviewer, therapist, or counselor.

The rating system here is based on a typescript. However, with practice, it is possible to rate from an audiotape or videotape of the interview, or even from an observation of an actual session through a one-way mirror or videotape.

Initial Presenting Assessment

Basic Objective

To use the client's first 50 to 100 words to classify the client as being at one of the four cognitive-developmental levels.

Method

Each scorer will receive a typescript of the dialogue that occurred between the interviewer and client during the assessment phase of the interview. The task for the rater is to determine the level of cognitive development predominantly represented by the client's conceptualization of a family issue. Ratings will be made on a four-point classification scale that identifies the four basic dimensions of cognitive development: sensorimotor/elemental, concrete-operational/situational, formal-operational/pattern, and dialectic/systemic/transformational.

Although the client may operate at more than one level, the task of the scorer is to determine which of the four levels is predominantly used as a frame of reference during the assessment phase. Two methods of rating will be used as follows:

1. The raters will classify each client statement using the criteria defined on the following pages. The predominant cognitive-developmental level will be computed by percentages of client responses in each of the four cognitive-developmental categories.
2. The raters will classify the entire client statement or series of statements into one of the four categories.

Classifying the Interview Segments

Basic Objective

The rater will classify eight interview segments, presented randomly, into eight categories—the subdivisions of the basic four categories. The portions of the interview will be presented with the counselor statements deleted. (This can be considered a training procedure and as essential for research purposes. In rating ongoing interviews, it is helpful to classify both counselor and client statements.)

Method

Each scorer will receive eight intervention sections that occur during the treatment phase of the interview, divided to reflect the eight cognitive-developmental subdivisions defined below. The group of typescripts will be randomized and will include only the client statements. The task of the scorer is to holistically review each section and determine the cognitive-developmental subdivision predominantly revealed in the client statements.

Ratings will be made on an eight-point classification system that subdivides each of the four basic dimensions of developmental cognition by early and late indicators: early and late sensorimotor/elemental, early and late concrete-operational/situational, early and late formal-operational/pattern, and early and late dialectic/systemic/transformational. Again, although more than one subdivision may be identified in each section, the task of the scorer is to determine which of the eight is predominantly used by the client within each section. Raters will use only the holistic method of classification for these eight sections.

Cognitive-Developmental Dimensions: Criteria for Rating

Sensorimotor/Elemental Dimension

Early Sensorimotor/Elemental Subdivision (Key Words: See, Hear, Feel)

The client randomly focuses on fragments and pieces of sensory-based data as she or he talks about the visual, auditory, and/or kinesthetic elements of a situation or issue.

Affect

■ The client shows very minimal distinction between sensory input and emotions.

■ The client is dominated by sensory stimuli and affect.

Cognition

■ The client shows minimal ability to coordinate the elements of sensory-based data into an organized gestalt.

Late Sensorimotor/Elemental Subdivision (Key Word: Belief)

The client provides a view of reality that makes sense of the sensory-based data reflective of the situation or issue in a somewhat incomplete or irrational manner.

The late sensorimotor period, according to DCT, is a time of naming and of issues. In work with clinical populations, virtually all clients answered the meaning-oriented questions of this stage with clearly faulty reasoning. Many clients, however, respond to late sensorimotor questions with logical concrete and/or formal statements. It may require careful questioning to uncover the mistaken logic of these clients, which is not always possible. If this is the case, the client *will not* demonstrate the illogical or magical patterns expected as they discuss key issues; thus, their statements should be categorized in one of the other seven categories.

Affect

■ The client's emotions remain sensory-based and reactive.

■ The client is unable to act on her or his emotions.

Cognitive

■ The client offers interpretations that, no matter how sophisticated, are illusory and irrational and are stated in a way that reveals that the client cannot take effective actions based on the beliefs.

Concrete-Operational/Situational Dimension

Early Concrete-Operational/Situational Subdivision (Key Word: Do)

The client describes the situation or issue from a single self-perspective in a linear, relatively organized sequence of concrete specifics. Her or his explanation has a major emphasis on the facts with some focus on a few of the basic feelings.

Affect

■ The client describes general emotions simply, from one perspective and with a lack of differentiation.

■ The client expresses emotions outwardly.

Cognition

- The client focuses predominantly on a factual description of the concrete details of a situation or issue from her or his own perspective. There is minimal emphasis on evaluation or analysis.

Late Concrete-Operational/Situational Subdivision (Key Words: If/Then)

The client organizes the elements or facts of the situation or issue into linear if/then statements that may lead to issues of causation. She or he may be able to control and describe actions, and may be able to think in terms of antecedents and consequences. The focus is on facts and actions as opposed to analyzing, evaluating, or showing awareness of patterns. Logic and reversibility may be evident.

Affect

- The client is able to control and describe broad-based, undifferentiated, outwardly focused affect. He or she may say, "I feel _____ when _____ happens." Otherwise feelings are relatively undifferentiated. Awareness of mixed or ambivalent feelings is rare, for example.

Cognition

- The client demonstrates linear if/then thinking, emphasizing causality and predictability from a single perspective.
- The client is able to control and describe actions and the impact of actions.
- The client is able to apply logic and reversibility to concrete situations or issues.
- The client is able to separate thoughts and actions.

Formal-Operational/Pattern Dimension

Early Formal-Operational/Pattern Subdivision (Key Words: Pattern, Self)

The client moves away from description of sensory experience toward examining and/or analyzing the facts of a situation or issue or toward examining and analyzing the self. She or he is able to identify repetitive behavior, thoughts, and affect related to various similar situations and issues.

Affect

- The client demonstrates an awareness of the complexity of feelings and is able to separate self from feelings and reflect on them.

Cognition

- The client describes repeating patterns of thought, behavior, and affect in the self that occur across situations.
- The client engages in analysis of self and situation.

Late Formal-Operational/Pattern Subdivision
(Key Words: Patterns of Patterns)

The client is able to analyze patterns of patterns and beginning multiple perspectives of behavior, thought, and feeling from the vantage points of the self and the contextual fields within which she or he interacts. The client is able to see larger, consistently repeating patterns of behavior, thought, and feeling in her or his life and to examine how she or he thinks and feels about the evolving theme or view of reality.

Affect
- The client demonstrates an ability to analyze her or his patterns of feelings.
- The client demonstrates an ability to identify others' feelings and be empathic.
- The client demonstrates an awareness that feelings can be validly expressed in multiple ways.

Cognition
- The client demonstrates an ability to examine the patterns of self and situation.
- The client demonstrates an ability to organize and analyze different situations or issues abstractly.
- The client may coordinate and discover new patterns, compare and contrast different situations, and form this into a gestalt.

Dialectic/Systemic Dimension

Early Dialectic/Systemic/Transformational/Integrative Subdivision
(Key Words: Integrate, Put Together)

The client demonstrates an ability to generate an integrative picture that combines thought and action and shows an awareness that personal constructions of reality are co-generated via the family network.

The client is able to reflect on systems of operations and how "things go together" in an interdependent sense. Becoming increasingly multiperspective, the client is able to see a situation from several frames of reference and keep them in mind simultaneously. Underlying assumptions of perspectives may be identified.

Affect
- The client offers a wide range of emotions and recognizes that emotions can change contextually. For example, "I am sad that my wife died, but when I think about the pain she was experiencing, I feel glad that she no longer has to suffer. I feel anger when I think about the injustice of it all."
- The client recognizes that she or he can change and adapt to new situations.

Cognition

- The client demonstrates an ability to coordinate concepts and put together a holistic integrated picture.
- The client demonstrates an awareness that the evolving integration was co-constructed in a dialectical or dialogic relationship with family, history, culture, and so on.

Late Dialectic/Systemic/Deconstruction/Transformational Subdivision (Key Words: Challenge the Integration, Action)

The client demonstrates an ability to criticize and challenge her or his own integrated system and discover alternative perspectives. The client is able to think about moving toward action based on these alternative perspectives. Challenging and criticizing assumptions is important here. Ideally, action plans should follow from this analysis.

Affect

- The client is able to look at her or his entire realm of emotions and then still move beyond into an infinite reflection on reflections.

Cognition

- The client intellectualizes and challenges her or his assumptions and integrations.
- The client can identify the flaws in the reasoning and logic of her or his integration from various relational perspectives.
- The client demonstrates an ability to think about action in relation to her or his new perspectives.

Practice Rating Interview

Although single statement ratings have proved the most difficult for us to obtain interrater agreement on, we still endorse this task as a good training method. After you have become skilled with single statements, you are better prepared to deal objectively with the impressionistic ratings of groups of statements of clients, patients, counselors, or therapists. A 75 percent agreement on ratings for your first try is typical. With practice, you should be able to achieve 90 percent agreement and better with longer statements or segments of an interview.

Interview

Rate the counselor and client statements as

1 = sensorimotor/elemental
2 = concrete-operational/situational
3 = formal-operational/pattern
4 = dialectic/systemic/transformational/integrative

After you have done this, rate the statements again using the eight-point scale below. This will increase the potential for higher interrater agreement. Most clients talk primarily at concrete and formal levels, and thus when there are only two categories that can jeopardize interrater agreement.

1 = early sensorimotor
2 = late sensorimotor
3 = early concrete
4 = late concrete
5 = early formal
6 = late formal
7 = early dialectic/systemic
8 = late dialectic/systemic

The following is a hypothetical interview written for practice purposes. However, the interview is very characteristic of what happens when we use the formal structured interview strategies discussed above. Although condensed, the interview is very typical in that the client moves to more complex thinking and then onward to taking action on the problem. (Co = counselor; Cl = client)

___ 1. Co: What did you do then?

___ 2. Cl: Well, I shouted back at the teacher.

___ 3. Co: How did you feel?

___ 4. Cl: I felt awful.

___ 5. Co: Stop for a moment. Could you get a clear image of the teacher in your mind? (pause) What do you see when she said that?

___ 6. Cl: I see her red face. She's really ugly.

___ 7. Co: What are you feeling in your body right at this moment?

___ 8. Cl: Angry, furious.

___ 9. Co: Do you feel that way in any other situations?

___10. Cl: Another place I feel like that is when my mother yells at me.

___11. Co: Uh-huh, when your mom yells at you, you also feel angry.

___12. Cl: Yeah, if she gets after me, I really get mad.

___13. Co: Do you and your Mom have that type of interaction often?

___14. Cl: Yeah, all the time. We don't get along at all.

___15. Co: What is similar about the interaction between you and your teacher and you and your mom?

___16. Cl: Well, both get after me unfairly. They always tell me what to do. I hate anyone who tells me what to do.

___17. Co: What about you in those situations? What are your patterns of responding?

___18. Cl: What I tend to do is try to pull back. I know that I tend to overreact when pushed. I feel bad about myself when I do that.

___19. Co: You feel bad about yourself when you do that?

___20. Cl: Yeah, it's a pattern for me. I tend to see red and get angry first, but then I feel guilty, kind of sad, and even confused.

___21. Co: Confused?

___22. Cl: Confused in that it just isn't the way I want to be. I've been trying to change that way of being for quite awhile.

___23. Co: Tell me more.

___24. Cl: Well, in my family, the way to resolve conflict is to yell. I never have liked that, and I always backed away. The family rule is to shut up and take it. Small wonder I feel guilty so much.

___25. Co: You're wondering if your feeling so guilty is really needed.

___26. Cl: Yeah, it doesn't make sense to feel that way. I can see lots of reasons that I needn't feel guilty. I think I've been thinking wrong.

___27. Co: So you want to challenge that rule. What flaws do you see in the rule?

___28. Cl: The rule is full of holes. It hurts people and it hurts me. I need to find a new, more flexible rule. In my family and culture, that rule of authority once had validity. Now it doesn't.

___29. Co: So now that you know, what are you going to do about it?

___30. Cl: I want to work on it. I think first I should talk to my teacher.

___31. Co: Let's do a role-play. I'll be the teacher. Let's test it.

Scoring Key and Discussion

The first number listed is the four-category scoring system, the second is the eight-category system.

2,3   1. Co: What did you do then?

2,3   2. Cl: Well, I shouted back at the teacher.

2,3   3. Co: How did you feel?

2,3   4. Cl: I felt awful. (It is tempting to rate this as late sensorimotor.)

1,1   5. Co: Stop for a moment. Could you get a clear image of the teacher in your mind? (pause) What do you see when she said that? (This is a concrete lead in that it focuses on action, but the intent is to move the client to SM discussion.)

1,1   6. Cl: I see her red face. She's really ugly.

1,1   7. Co: What are you feeling in your body right at this moment?

1,1   8. Cl: Angry, furious. (Presents a single, relatively pervasive emotion.)

3,5   9. Co: Do you feel that way in any other situations? (This is FO because client is asked for pattern thinking.)

3,5   10. Cl: Another place I feel like that is when my mother yells at me. (This is hard to score, but client is able to name a pattern. It is not really clear since only another situation is identified. We would not argue much if you wanted to call it 2,4.)

2,4   11. Co: Uh-huh, when your mom yells at you, you also feel angry. (This client seems to be responding at the situational level, but we are seeking if/then reasoning.)

2,4   12. Cl: Yeah, if she gets after me, I really get mad. (This is a clear, if/then statement.)

3,5   13. Co: Do you and your mom have that type of interaction often? (The use of *often* could indicate late CO, but the abstract word *interaction* makes it FO. The emphasis here is clearly on patterns.)

3,5   14. Cl: Yeah, all the time. We don't get along at all. (This is an overgeneralization, but at the pattern level. It could be an example of a FO preoperational statement.)

3,6   15. Co: What is similar about the interaction between you and your teacher and you and your mom?

2,4   16. Cl: Well, both get after me unfairly. They always tell me what to do. I hate anyone who tells me what to do. (The last part of this statement is really more CO, when we put this together with the overgeneralization, the level is lower. In mixed statements, categorize at the lower possibility. This is a good example of some difficulties with the scoring. The client is responding fairly well in terms of ability to analyze. This statement begs for an eight-point classification system. The way you frame your thinking may determine how you rate this one. The first sentence, for example, is 2 [late sensorimotor—there is clearly overgeneralization], the second, third, and fourth are all early concrete.)

3,5   17. Co: What about you in those situations? What are your patterns of responding?

3,6   18. Cl: What I tend to do is try to pull back. I know that I tend to overreact when pushed. I feel bad about myself when I do that. (The client is now analyzing self. The word *bad* presents some problems, since it really is more concrete, but the word *overreact* is more formal. The client is clearly analyzing patterns of self and not just analyzing self.)

3,5   19. Co: You feel bad about yourself when you do that?

3,6   20. Cl: Yeah, its a pattern for me. I tend to see red and get angry first, but then I feel guilty, kind of sad, and even confused.

3,6   21. Co: Confused? (Score encouraging statements and restatements of client words at the previous client level or do not score them at all.)

3,6   22. Cl: Confused in that it just isn't the way I want to be. I've been trying to change that way of being for quite a while.

3,6   23. Co: Tell me more. (Same comment as for number 21.)

4,7   24. Cl: Well, in my family the way to resolve conflict is to yell. I never have liked that, and I always back away. The family rule is to shut up and take it. Small wonder I feel guilty so much. (The search for explanation and rules is an attempt at integration. The discussion of context is very dialectic.)

4,7   25. Co: You're wondering if your feeling so guilty is really needed. (This statement focuses more on self-analysis, but we are seeing systems of operations—here the client is looking at herself looking at the system of feelings surrounding guilt.)

4,7   26. Cl: Yeah, it doesn't make sense to feel that way. I can see lots of reasons that I needn't feel guilty. I think I've been thinking wrong. (Here the client is clearly challenging personal past assumptions and operating on systems of operations.)

4,8   27. Co: So you want to challenge that rule. What flaws do you see in the rule? (Counselor challenges the client to present integration; this is considered dialectic. This means that many cognitive-behavioral logic challenges will be rated here even though the client may be at a different level.)

4,8   28. Cl: The rule is full of holes. It hurts people and it hurts me. I need to find a new, more flexible rule. In my family and culture, that rule of authority once had validity. Now it doesn't. (Note the complex language. This individual is challenging the way things have been examined in the past, which is highly characteristic of deconstruction—challenging the flaws in one's own system of reasoning and starting to do something about it.)

2,3   29. Co: So now that you know, what are you going to do about it? (Given the context, this could be a D/S statement, but the language is classic for concrete operations. Usually after a successful challenge at the dialectic level, one returns to address new issues.)

2,4   30. Cl: I want to work on it. I think first I should talk to my teacher.

2,4   31. Co: Let's do a role-play. I'll be the teacher. Let's test it.

Appendix 4

Tamase's Introspective-Developmental Counseling Questions [1]

Tamase's introspective-developmental counseling (IDC) focuses on four major developmental periods (birth through preschool, elementary school, high school, and one's present life stage). Tamase recommends that those training to become professional helpers look at their own developmental history. He divides trainees into pairs and each interviews the other for four half-hour interviews. Out of this experience, participants often learn that their developmental history has some basic patterns that repeat themselves in their current situations and in adult life.

In addition, you will find that some of your clients may enjoy and benefit from the systematic questioning of developmental history proposed by IDC. Experience has revealed that combining DCT four-level questions with IDC questions leads to more awareness and a session that goes into more depth. The IDC questions, particularly, if combined with DCT, should be employed with sensitivity and care, for many individuals find the experience emotionally powerful.

Sharing the questions with your client before you begin may be helpful. If the individual has difficulty with a particular question, rephrase it to meet his or her interests and needs. The goal of each question is to have the client explore the general area. At times, changing the language of the question is beneficial. Frequent use of the basic listening sequence, including encouraging, paraphrasing, reflecting feelings and meanings, and summarizing, is helpful in the process.

Session 1: Birth Through Preschool Period

1. Could you tell me about your family members (for the purpose of structuring the interview and understanding basics of the family system). What particular important life events were they experiencing during your earliest years?

---

[1] The IDC questions presented here are adaptions of the original Tamase questions made jointly by Koji Tamase and Allen Ivey. The original research questions are available from Dr. Koji Tamase at the Department of Psychology, Nara University of Education, Takabatake, Nara 630, Japan.

2. Is there anything about your birth that you have heard from your mother or other family members?
3. Could you tell me about your life from the earliest age that you can remember?
4. What is the most impressive thing that happened prior to kindergarten?
5. What kind of behavior bothered your mother when you were a preschool child?
6. How did you feel about your parents when you were a preschool child?
7. Did you struggle with your brothers or sisters at this age?
8. Is there any particular event that made you feel either very unhappy or afraid at this age?
9. What single event do you recall most positively from this period of your life?
10. What patterns from this early period continue in your present life?

Session 2: Elementary School Period

1. What particular events in your family were important as a context for this period?
2. What teacher do you recall? What kind of person was this teacher?
3. Could you give me a concrete example of something that happened in the first grade?
4. What happened in the third and fourth grade? The fifth and sixth?
5. What kind of friends did you have?
6. What is the most impressive thing you can remember from your elementary school years?
7. Did you ever mistreat anyone, or were you mistreated by others in these years?
8. What was your experience with academic achievement?
9. How did things go with your brothers and sisters at this time? If you have no brothers or sisters, how was it with a person who might substitute for them?
10. What single event do you recall most positively from this period of your life?
11. What patterns from this period of your life might appear in your present-day life?

Session 3: Junior Through Senior High School Period

1. What particular events in your family were important as a context for this period?
2. Could you tell me about your friendships in high school?
3. How did things go with the opposite sex?
4. How was the relationship with your parents? How were things in your family?
5. How did things go with your brothers and sisters? If you have no brothers or sisters, how was it with a person who might substitute for them?

   6. Did you rebel against your parents?
   7. How was your academic and work life?
   8. What is the most impressive thing you can remember from your junior and senior high years?
   9. Who were the influential people in your life?
  10. How did you like to spend your time?
  11. What single event do you recall most positively from this period of your life?
  12. What patterns might continue from this period to your present-day life?

Session 4: Recent Past and Current Life Situation Session

   1. What have been important family and personal contextual issues which happened since high school that have affected you particularly?
   2. How do you think about your career now?
   3. How have you related to your family since high school?
   4. What are your current significant relationships (loved ones, spouse, own family)? How are they going?
   5. Are there any current interpersonal difficulties?
   6. What significant events have affected your life since high school?
   7. Of all the events since high school, what one event stands out for you?
   8. What job difficulties do you experience?
   9. What do you do that makes you feel good?
  10. Complete this sentence: "I am most discouraged in my life about _____."
  11. What single event do you recall most positively from this period of your life?
  12. What overall patterns do you observe from your life review, both in this session and others?

Appendix 5
Sample Information and Consent Letters

In recent years the helping profession has become more attuned to client rights and the need for the professional helper to be held accountable for his or her actions. Each state has differing sets of laws, and you should become familiar with the unique demands of your own setting and remain aware of constant changes and interpretations in the law. Boxes A5-1 and A5-2 provide model statements a professional may wish to use to acquaint clients with key issues of the interview.

Note that these statements assume a verbal, formal-operational client who is able to understand complex language. It is not yet clear how one can present these principles in simple terms that are clear to clients at all levels. Also, the use of such statements is still in its infancy and it is hoped that specific guidelines for such statements will soon appear in the literature.

As you develop your own statement, you need to take into account your own state laws and your own competencies. It is important to specify your competencies in detail, and cultural differences should also be taken into account. One of the statements below mentions gifts given to the counselor. Ethically, counselors should not accept gifts. However, there are cultural groups (for example, some Native American groups) for which gift giving is a cultural trait. It is difficult to anticipate all possibilities in any single statement, so you will want to review and rewrite your own statement over time.

Finally, you and your client may want to consider writing specific goals for the therapy or counseling and time lines on which progress toward these goals may be reviewed. This type of contract will enable you to include action research and evaluation in the interview for your and your client's benefit.

Professional Practice Statement for Psychologists

The following statement was written by Lawrence Brammer, Ph.D., A.B.B.P., Professor-Emeritus of the University of Washington, Seattle. Dr. Brammer is a well-known author, is past president of the Division of Counseling Psychology of the American Psychological Association, and is engaged in part-time practice.

Box A5-1. Professional Disclosure and Agreements

The following material is designed to facilitate understanding between us to accomplish therapeutic goals effectively and ethically. This information and these agreements conform to the letter and spirit of state laws, consumer protection principles, and professional ethics guidelines.

Confidentiality

Personal information that you share with me is confidential and will not be shared with others without your consent. If requests are made, from physicians treating you, for example, a statement of consent signed by you should be given to me. The only information that will be given to other referring professionals is confirmation that you made an appointment with me. You should understand that applying for health insurance reimbursement automatically gives me permission to supply minimal information to process the claim. Where feasible, we will discuss the request, and you will examine any reports or treatment plans before submission to the approved parties. At that time, we can discuss effects of such information, including possible harm. Even though you authorized release of the agreed-on information, you may withdraw your consent at any time by written notice to me. The main point here is our mutual concern to protect our trust as well as your rights and welfare.

Several important exceptions pertain to release of information given in confidence:

1. Threats to harm others or yourself that appear, in my judgment, to be serious, such as when someone's life or property appears to be in danger. These threats will be revealed to appropriate authorities for the protection of yourself and the other parties and to meet legal requirements.
2. If you give indications that you are abusing or neglecting others, especially children, the law requires immediate reporting to authorities to protect the children from harm.
3. Your involvement in litigation, or referral from a court where mental health is an issue, may require a waiver of confidentiality rights. Before you discuss such matters with me, it would be well to discuss the issue with your attorney.

Fees and Insurance

Fees are $____ for office time, telephone time, preparation of reports, and individual testing. Fees are payable at the end of each session, which will last approximately 50 minutes. Check your health insurance coverage for psychological services. If covered, you will file your own reimbursement claims.

Appointments

Appointments are made for consultation in my office for a mutually agreed-on time. During the first session, we will discuss the estimated number of sessions recommended to reach your goals. This agreement can be altered as the sessions progress. If an agreed on time turns out to be inconvenient, a call to cancel and rearrange appointments should be made as soon as possible. Missed appointments may be charged at the hourly rate agreed on. You are, of course, free to terminate the counseling relationship at any time.

Box A5-1. Professional Disclosure and Agreements *(continued)*

Disclosure

I expect, for your welfare, a frank disclosure of all information relevant to our work together. This includes all information pertaining to drug and alcohol usage, psychological or medical conditions, and current treatment by other professionals bearing on our counseling relationship and affecting the welfare of yourself and others.

It is necessary for our mutual protection that you provide names, addresses, and phone numbers of primary care physicians, nearest responsible relative or guardian, and place of employment.

_____

_____

My address and phone number are _____

_____

_____

You are free to raise any questions about the terms of this agreement or the nature of the counseling we will undertake. You should understand also that you can appeal our decisions or raise questions with the State Psychology Board in Olympia, the Professional Practices Committee of the Washington State Psychological Association, or the Washington Consumer Protection Agency.

The following covers my main qualifications to do psychological counseling:

Licensed psychologist in states of Washington and California
Diplomate in Counseling Psychology, American Board of Professional Psychology
Registry of Health Service Providers
Ph.D. in counseling psychology, Stanford University
Over 40 years of counseling experience in public agencies and private practice and extensive publishing on the practice of psychology.

The focus of my practice is working with adults on problems centering on life transitional changes, managing stress, making personal decisions, and adjustments to loss. In our first interview, we will discuss how I can or cannot help you reach your therapeutic goals with my background and competencies.

Agreement

I understand the statements and conditions cited above, and I agree to abide by these conditions.

Signed_____ Date_____

Counseling Practice Statement

The following statement was written by Joe Wittmer, Ph.D., N.B.C.C., and Theodore P. Remley, J.D., Ph.D., of Mississippi State University. Dr. Wittmer was central in the licensing of counselors in the state of Florida and is chairperson of counseling at the University of Florida, Gainesville. Dr. Remley holds a law degree and is chairperson of counselor education at Mississippi State University.

Box A5-2. Counseling Practice Statement

---

*(Counselor's name,
business address, and
business telephone number)*

I am pleased that you have selected me as your counselor. This document is designed to inform you about my background and to ensure that you understand our professional relationship.

I am licensed by (state) as a professional counselor. In addition, I am certified by the National Board for Certified Counselors, a private national counselor certifying agency. My counseling practice is limited to (list types of clients) and my specific counseling and therapy knowledge and competencies include:

_____

_____

I hold a _____ degree from (institution) _____

I have been a professional counselor since (year). I only accept clients in my private practice who I believe have the capacity to resolve their own problems with my assistance. I believe that as people become more accepting of themselves, they are more capable of finding happiness and contentment in their lives. However, self-awareness and self-acceptance are goals that sometimes take a long time to achieve. Some clients need only a few counseling sessions to achieve these goals, whereas others may require months or even years of counseling. As a client, you are in complete control and may end our counseling relationship at any point. I will be supportive of that decision. If counseling is successful, you should feel that you are able to face life's challenges in the future without my support or intervention.

Although our session may be very intimate psychologically, it is important for you to realize that we have a *professional* relationship rather than a personal one. Our contact is limited to the paid sessions you have with me. Please do not invite me to social gatherings, offer gifts, or ask me to relate to you in any way other than in the professional context of our counseling sessions. You will be best served if our relationship stays strictly professional and if our sessions concentrate exclusively on your concerns. You will learn a great deal about me as we work together during your counseling experience. However, it is important for you to remember that you are experiencing me only in my professional role.

Box A5-2. Counseling Practice Statement *(continued)*

I will keep confidential anything you say to me, with the following exceptions: (1) you direct me to tell someone else, (2) I determine that you are a danger to yourself or others, or (3) I am ordered by a court to disclose information.

If at any time for any reason you are dissatisfied with my services, please let me know. If I am not able to resolve your concerns, you may report your complaints to the Board for Professional Counselors in (state) at (phone number) or the National Board for Certified Counselors in (city, state) at (phone number).

In return for a fee of $_____ per session, I agree to provide counseling services for you. Sessions are ____ minutes in duration. The fee for each session will be due and must be paid at the conclusion of each session. Cash or personal checks are acceptable for payment. I will provide you with a monthly receipt for all fees paid. In the event you will not be able to keep an appointment, you must notify me 24 hours in advance. If I do not receive such advance notice, you will be responsible for paying for the session you missed.

I assure you that my services will be rendered in a professional manner consistent with accepted ethical standards. Please note that it is impossible to guarantee any specific results regarding your counseling goals. However, together we will work to achieve the best possible results for you.

If you wish to seek reimbursement for my services from your health insurance company, I will be happy to complete any forms related to your reimbursement provided by you or the insurance company. Because you will be paying me each session for my services, any later reimbursement from the insurance company should be sent directly to you. Please do not assign any payments to me.

Some health insurance companies will reimburse clients for my counseling services, and some will not. Those that do reimburse usually require that a standard amount be paid by you before reimbursement is allowed, and then usually only a percentage of my fee is reimbursable. You should contact a company representative to determine whether your insurance company will reimburse you and about what schedule of reimbursement is used.

Health insurance companies often require that I diagnose your mental conditions and indicate that you have an "illness" before they will agree to reimburse you. In the event a diagnosis is required, I will inform you of the diagnosis I plan to render before I submit it to the health insurance company. Any diagnosis made will become a part of your permanent insurance records.

If you have any questions, feel free to ask. Please sign and date both copies of this form.

_____   _____
Counselor's signature   Client's signature

_____   _____
Date   Date

References

American Psychiatric Association. 1987. *Diagnostic and statistic manual of mental disorders* (DSM-III-R). Washington, D.C.: American Psychiatric Association.

Anderson, T. 1983. *Style-shift counseling.* Ottawa: Staff Training and Development Branch. Correctional Service of Canada.

Anderson, T. 1987a. *Style-shift counseling and developmental therapy with the style-shift indicator.* North Amherst, Mass.: Microtraining Associates.

Anderson, T. 1987b *Style-shift indicator.* North Amherst, Mass.: Microtraining Associates.

Attneave, C. 1969. *Therapy in tribal settings and urban network interventions.* Family Process 8: 192–210.

Attneave, C. 1982. "American Indian and Alaska native families: Emigrants in their own homeland." In M. McGoldrick, J. Pearce, and J. Giordano, eds., *Ethnicity and family therapy,* New York: Guilford.

Atkinson, D. W., G. Morten, and D. Sue. 1989. *Counseling American minorities.* Dubuque, Iowa: Brown.

Ballou, M., and N. Gabalac. 1984. *A feminist position on mental health.* Springfield, Ill.: Thomas.

Beck, A. 1976. *Cognitive therapy and the emotional disorders.* New York: International Universities Press.

Blanchard, K., and S. Johnson. 1981 *The one-minute manager.* La Jolla, Calif.: Blanchard-Johnson.

Bolman, L. and T. Deal. 1990. *Artistry, choice, and leadership.* San Francisco: Jossey-Bass.

Bowlby, J. 1969. *Attachment.* New York: Basic Books.

Bowlby, J. 1973. *Separation.* New York: Basic Books.

Bowlby, J. 1987. Personal communication to the author. London: Tavistock Clinic, January.

Brassard, M., R. Germain, and S. Hart. 1987. *Psychological maltreatment of children and youth*. New York: Pergamon.

Brodhead, M. 1988. The development of the interpersonal skills of the teacher: A merger of microteaching, microcounseling, and developmental assessment. Unpublished comprehensive paper, University of Massachusetts, Amherst.

Carey, J. 1988. A cognitive-developmental model of supervision. Presentation at the American Psychological Association, Atlanta, August.

Carey, J. 1989a. Developmental supervision. Unpublished manuscript, University of Massacusetts, Amherst.

Carey, J. 1989b. Life-span developmental supervision. Presentation at the annual convention of the American Association for Counseling and Development, Boston, March.

Carkhuff, R. 1969. *Helping and human relations*. Vols. 1 and 2. New York: Holt, Rinehart & Winston.

Carter, B., and M. McGoldrick. 1989. *The changing family life cycle: A framework for family therapy*. 2nd ed. Needham Heights, Mass.: Allyn and Bacon.

Clément, C. 1983. *The lives and legends of Jacques Lacan*. New York: Columbia University Press.

Cummings, N. 1977. Prolonged (ideal) versus short-term (realistic) psychotherapy. Professional Psychology 8: 491–501.

Cummings, N. 1985. Personal communication, Kaiser-Permanente, San Francisco, February.

DeFranck-Lynch, B. 1986. *Therapié familiale structurale*. Paris: Les Editions ESF.

Dinkmeyer, D. 1972. *Developing understanding of self and others*. Circle Pines, Minn.: American Guidance Service.

Egan, G. 1990. *The skilled helper*. 4th ed. Pacific Grove, Calif.: Brooks/Cole.

Ellis, A. 1971. *Growth through reason*. Palo Alto, Calif.: Science and Behavior Books.

Erikson, E. 1963. *Childhood and society*. 2nd ed. New York: Norton. (lst ed. 1950)

Figley, C. 1989. *Helping traumatized families*. San Francisco: Jossey-Bass.

Fleming, P. 1986. The family life-cycle model in relation to issues of separation and attachment. Unpublished paper, University of Massachusetts, Amherst.

Frankl, V. 1959. *Man's search for meaning*. New York: Kangaroo.

Friedan, B. 1977. *The feminine mystique*. New York: Dell. (1st ed. 1963.)

Fukuhara, M. 1984. Is love enough?—From the viewpoint of counseling adolescents. Paper presented at the forty-second annual conference of the International Association of Psychologists, Mexico City.

Gallagher, J. and D. Reid. 1981. *The learning theory of Piaget and Inhelder*. Pacific Grove, Calif.: Brooks/Cole.

Gilligan, C. 1982. *In a different voice.* Cambridge, Mass.: Harvard University Press.

Germaine, C. 1973. An ecological perspective in casework practice. Social Casework 54: 323–330.

Gilligan, C. 1988. Remapping the moral domain. In C. Gilligan, J. Ward, and J. McLean Taylor, *eds, Mapping the Moral Domain.* Cambridge, Mass.: Harvard University Graduate School of Education, pp. 3–45.

Gilligan, C., J. Ward, and J. McLean Taylor, eds. 1988. *Mapping the Moral Domain.* Cambridge, Mass.: Harvard University Graduate School of Education.

Gonçalves, O. 1988. The treatment of agoraphobia conceptualized through developmental therapy. Presentation at the 1988 Conference on Counseling Psychology, University of Southern California, Los Angeles, December.

Gonçalves, O. 1989. Cognitive representation of self-narratives and self-knowledge development of agoraphobic clients. Presentation to the World Congress of Cognitive Therapy, Oxford, England.

Guerney, B. 1977. *Relationship enhancement.* San Francisco: Jossey-Bass.

Guidano, V. 1987. *The complexity of self: A developmental approach to psychopathology and therapy.* New York: Guilford.

Guidano, V. 1988. The structural approach to cognitive therapy. Presentation at the first European Summer School of Cognitive Therapy, Lisbon, Portugal, June 27–July 8.

Haley, J. 1973. *Uncommon therapy.* New York: Norton.

Haley, J. 1976. *Problem-solving therapy.* San Francisco: Jossey-Bass.

Helms, J. 1985. Toward a theoretical explanation of the effects of race on counseling: A Black and White model. Counseling Psychologist 12: 153–165.

Ho, Man Keung. 1987. *Family therapy with ethnic minorities.* Newbury Park, Calif.: Sage.

Ivey, A. 1971. *Microcounseling: Innovations in interviewing training,* Springfield, Ill.: Thomas.

Ivey, A. 1973. Media therapy: Educational change planning for psychiatric patients. *Journal of Counseling Psychology* 20: 338–343.

Ivey, A. 1986. *Developmental therapy: Theory into practice.* San Francisco: Jossey-Bass.

Ivey, A. 1988. *Intentional interviewing and counseling: Facilitating client development.* Pacific Grove, Calif.: Brooks/Cole.

Ivey, A., and J. Authier. 1978. *Microcounseling* 2nd ed. Springfield, Ill.: Thomas.

Ivey, A. and N. Gluckstern. 1982. *Basic attending skills.* North Amherst, Mass.: Microtraining Associates.

Ivey, A., and O. Gonçalves. Developmental therapy: The joining of counseling and development. *Journal of Counseling and Development* 2: 406-413.

Ivey, M., and A. Ivey. 1987. Observations of elementary teachers using the developmental therapy assessment system. Unpublished manuscript, Fort River School, Amherst, Mass.

Ivey, A. and M. Ivey. 1990. Assessing and facilitating children's cognitive development: Developmental counseling and therapy in a case of child abuse. *Journal of Counseling and Development,* 68: 299–305.

Ivey, A. and M. Ivey. 1990. *Developmental counseling and therapy.* Videotapes. North Amherst, Mass.: Microtraining.

Ivey, A., M. Ivey and L. Simek-Downing. 1987. *Counseling and psychotherapy: Integrating skills, theory, and practice.* Englewood Cliffs, N.J.: Prentice-Hall.

Jackson, B. 1975. Black identity development. *Journal of Educational Diversity and Innovation* 2: 19–25.

Joyce-Muniz, L. 1988. The implications of drama therapy for constructivism. Presentation at the first European Summer School of Cognitive Therapy, Lisbon, Portugal, June 27–July 8.

Kagan, N. 1980. *Interpersonal process recall: A method of influencing human interaction.* Houston: Mason Media.

Katz, J., and A. Ivey. 1977. White awareness: The frontier of racism awareness training. *Personnel and Guidance Journal 55*: 485–489.

Kegan, R. 1982. *The evolving self.* Cambridge, Mass.: Harvard University Press.

Kelly, G. 1955. *Psychology of personal constructs.* Vols. 1 and 2. New York: Norton.

Klein, M. 1975. *Envy and Gratitude.* London: Hogarth.

Kohlberg, L. 1981. *The philosophy of moral development.* San Francisco: Harper & Row.

Kübler-Ross, E. 1969. *On death and dying.* New York: MacMillan.

Lacan, J. 1977. *Écrits.* New York: Norton.

LaFromboise, T., and K. Low. 1989. American Indian adolescents. In J. Gibbs and L. Hwang, eds., *Children of color.* San Francisco: Jossey-Bass.

Lankton, S. 1980. *Practical magic.* Cupertino, Calif.: Meta.

Linkletter, A. 1957. *Kids say the darndest things!* Englewood Cliffs, N.J.: Prentice-Hall.

McGoldrick, M., J. Pearce, and J. Giordano. 1982. *Ethnicity and family therapy.* New York: Guilford.

Mahoney, M. 1988. Mirror time: A cognitive-constructivist view. Presentation at the first European Summer School of Cognitive Therapy, Lisbon, Portugal, June 27–July 8.

Manthei, R. 1988. Personal communciation. Christ Church University, Christ Church, New Zealand, September.

Masterson, J. 1981. *The narcissistic and borderline disorders*. New York: Brunner/Mazel.

Masterson, J. 1985. *The real self: A developmental, self, and object relations approach*. New York: Brunner/Mazel.

Meara, N., H. Pepinsky, J. Shannon and W. Murray. 1981. Comparisons of stylistic complexity of the language of counselor and client across three theoretical orientations. *Journal of Counseling Psychology* 26: 181–189.

Miller, A. 1981. *The drama of the gifted child*. New York: Basic Books.

Miller, A. 1986. *Thou shalt not be aware*. New York: Meriden.

Millon, T., and G. Everly. 1985. *Personality and its disorders: A biosocial learning approach*. New York: Wiley.

Minor, K. 1983. A review of counseling among cultures with emphasis upon culture-specific counseling within the Inuit society: A method training program. Unpublished dissertation, University of Massachusetts, Amherst.

Minuchin, S. 1974. *Families and family therapy*. Cambridge, Mass.: Harvard University Press.

Nagel, J. 1987. Using developmental therapy constructs to teach vocational high school students writing skills. Unpublished paper, University of Massachusetts, Amherst.

Neugarten, B. 1979. Time, age, and the life cycle, *American Journal of Psychiatry,* 136: 887–894.

Nwachuku, U. 1989. Culture-specific counseling: The Igbo case. Unpublished dissertation, University of Massachusetts, Amherst.

Nwachuku, U., and A. Ivey. 1989. Teaching culture-specific counseling using microtraining technology. Unpublished manuscript, University of Massachusetts, Amherst.

Palazzoli-Selvini, M. 1978. *Self-starvation: From individual to family therapy*. New York: Aronson.

Parham, T., and J. Helms. 1981. The influence of Black students' racial attitudes on preferences for counselors' race. *Journal of Counseling Psychology* 28: 250–257.

Pedersen, P. 1988. *A handbook for developing multicultural awareness*. Washington, D.C.: American Association for Counseling and Development.

Ponterotto, J. 1988. Racial consciousness development among White counselor trainees: A stage model. *Journal of Multicultural Counseling and Development* 16: 146–155.

Piaget, J. 1963. *The origins of intelligence in children*. New York: Norton. (originally published in 1926)

Piaget, J. 1965. *The moral judgement of the child.* New York: Free Press.

Piaget, J. 1972. *The child's conception of physical causality.* Totowa, N.J.: Littlefield, Adams. (originally published in 1960)

Rigazio-DiGilio, S. 1989. Developmental theory and therapy: A preliminary investigation of reliability and predictive validity using an inpatient depressive population. Unpublished dissertation, University of Massachusetts, Amherst.

Rigazio-DiGilio, S., and A. Ivey. In press. Developmental therapy and depressive disorders: Measuring cognitive levels through patient natural language. *Professional Psychology: Research and Practice.*

Rodgers, R. 1984. Theories of adult development: Research status and counseling implications. In *Handbook of Counseling Psychology,* eds., S. Brown and R. Lent. New York: Wiley.

Rogers, C. 1951. *On becoming a person.* Boston: Houghton-Mifflin.

Rogers, C. 1951. *Client-centered therapy.* Boston: Houghton-Mifflin.

Satir, V. 1967. *Conjoint family therapy.* Palo Alto, Calif.: Science and Behavior Books.

Schlossberg, N. 1977. *Counseling adults.* Pacific Grove, Calif.: Brooks/Cole.

Schlossberg, N. 1984. *Counseling adults in transition.* New York: Springer.

Schlossberg, N. 1989. *Overwhelmed: Coping with life's ups and downs.* Lexington, Mass.: Lexington.

Speck, R. and C. Attneave. 1973. *Family Process.* New York: Pantheon.

Stoltenberg, C., and U. Delworth. 1987. *Supervising counselors and therapists.* San Francisco: Jossey-Bass.

Sue, D.W. 1977. *Counseling the culturally different.* New York: Wiley.

Sue, D.W. 1981. *Counseling the culturally different.* 2nd ed. New York: Wiley.

Tamase, K. 1988. Introspective-developmental counseling. Unpublished manuscript, Nara University of Education, Japan, and the University of Massachetts, Amherst.

Tamase, K. 1989. Introspective-developmental counseling: A clinical test and evaluation. Unpublished manuscript, Nara University of Education, Japan, and the University of Massachetts, Amherst.

Tillich, P. 1964. "The importance of *New* being for Christian theology." In J. Campbell, ed., *Man and transformation.* Princeton, N.J.: Princeton University Press.

Tyler, L. 1961. *The work of the counselor.* East Norwalk, Conn.: Appleton-Century-Crofts.

Weinstein, G., and A. Alschuler. 1985. Education and counseling for self-knowledge development. *Journal of Counseling and Development* 64: 19–25.

Vaillant, G. 1977. *Adaptation to life.* Boston: Little, Brown.

Yakima Nation Museum. 1984. The Yakima Time Ball. Publication of the Yakima Nation Museum Program: Toppenish, Washington.

Name Index

Subject Index

Credits

This page constitutes an extension of the copyright page.

CHAPTER 3 **Page 66:** Text in first column from Carl Rogers, *On Becoming a Person.* Copyright © 1961 by Houghton Mifflin Company. Used with permission.

CHAPTER 5 **Page121:** Table 5-1 adapted from Erik H. Erikson, *Childhood and Society,* Second Edition, by permission of W. W. Norton & Company, Inc. Copyright © 1963 by W. W. Norton & Company, Inc. Copyright renewed 1978 by Erik H. Erikson. Permission also kindly granted by Hogarth Press, London, England.

CHAPTER 6 **Page163:** Box 6-2 from the American Psychiatric Association: *Diagnostic and Statistical Manual of Mental Disorders,* Third Edition, Revised. Washington, D. C. American Psychiatric Association, 1987. Used with permission.

CHAPTER 7 **Page 200:** Table 7-1 from D. Sue et al. *Counseling Psychologist, 10,* p. 49. Copyright 1982 by *Counseling Psychologist.* Reprinted by permission of Sage Publications, Inc. **Page 202:** Table 7-2 from Donald R. Atkinson, George Morton, and Derald Wing Sue, *Counseling American Minorities: A Cross Cultural Perspective,* Third Edition. Copyright © 1989 Wm. C. Brown Publishers, Dubuque, Iowa. All rights reserved. Reprinted by permission. **Page 213:** Passage from Gilligan, 1982. Reprinted by permission from *In a Different Voice* by Carol Gilligan. Cambridge, Mass.: Harvard University Press. Copyright © 1982 by Carol Gilligan.

CHAPTER 8 **Page 232:** Extract from T. LaFromboise and K. Low, *Children of Color,* 1989. Reprinted by permission. San Francisco: Jossey-Bass Publishers. **Pages 246-252:** Style-Shift Inventory material quoted from Terry Anderson (©1987), North Amherst, Mass.: Microtraining. By permission.

CHAPTER 9 **Pages 268, 270, 271-273:** Table 9-1, Figure 9-1, and miscellaneous material. Reprinted by permission of the author, John C. Carey.